THE CURTAIN AND THE WALL

A MODERN JOURNEY ALONG EUROPE'S COLD WAR BORDER

TIMOTHY PHILLIPS

GRANTA

Granta Publications, 12 Addison Avenue, London W11 4QR

First published in Great Britain by Granta Books, 2022
This paperback edition published by Granta Books, 2023

Text copyright © Timothy Phillips 2022

The illustration credits on p. 433 constitute an extension of this copyright page.

The quotations from Haruki Murakami on pages vii and 393 are
copyright © 2009 by Harukimurakami Archival Labyrinth.
Reprinted by permission of ICM Partners.

A CIP catalogue record for this book is available from the British Library.

3 5 7 9 10 8 6 4 2

ISBN 978 1 78378 578 0
eISBN 978 1 78378 577 3

Maps by John Gilkes
Typeset by Avon DataSet Ltd, Alcester, Warwickshire
Printed and bound by CPI Group (UK) Ltd, Croydon CR0 4YY

www.granta.com

MIX
Paper | Supporting
responsible forestry
FSC® C171272

THE CURTAIN AND THE WALL

TIMOTHY PHILLIPS is the author of *The Secret Twenties: British Intelligence, the Russians, and the Jazz Age* (Granta, 2017) and *Beslan: The Tragedy of School No. 1* (Granta, 2008). He grew up in Northern Ireland and now lives in London. He holds a doctorate in Russian from Oxford University and has written and spoken widely on British and Russian history.

'A brilliant book, not only based on an inspired idea, but also written with a keen eye for human hopes, fears and tragedies. The journey from the Arctic to the Black Sea is full of surprises. Some of the places Timothy Phillips has visited are little known, but now we are unlikely to forget them. We can enjoy meeting the resilient characters along the way, reflect on the desperation of those who tried to escape the Iron Curtain, and learn once again the priceless value of freedom' William Hague

'As borders reappear all over Europe, and as war once again begins to smudge the continent's atlas, Timothy Phillips's book arrives just when it is needed . . . Phillips travels from the North Cape to the Caucasus equipped with a mass of fascinating prior research, but also with a gift for instant befriending which brings stories and secrets from everyone he encounters' Neal Ascherson

'At a time when we seem to be entering a new Cold War, here's a book on the hangover from the original one' Michael Kerr, *Deskbound Traveller*

Also by Timothy Phillips

Beslan: The Tragedy of School No. 1

The Secret Twenties:
British Intelligence, the Russians and the Jazz Age

For Ant and Benny, one better travelled than
I and one who is always at home.

'Each of us is, more or less, an egg. Each of us is a unique, irreplaceable soul enclosed in a fragile shell. This is true of me, as it is true of each of you. And each of us, to a greater or lesser degree, is confronting a high, solid wall.'

Haruki Murakami, 'The Novelist in Wartime',
speech on accepting the Jerusalem Prize, 2009.

'The other side was so close, and yet you knew nothing about it, how things looked on the other side of the water . . . It was closed off in every way imaginable . . . That's what's so odd, the fact that we went swimming in the same water.'

Recollection by an anonymous resident of Gotland,
shared with *At the Water's Edge*, an exhibition of life
in the Baltic during the Cold War organized by the
Estonian Institute of Historical Memory in 2018.

Contents

Maps

Overview and route of author's journey

N
W E
S

—— Iron Curtain
········ Author's journey

Arctic Ocean

Grense Jakobselv

Kirkenes

Norwegian Sea

SWEDEN

FINLAND

NORWAY

Oslo

Porkkala

Vyborg

Helsinki

ESTONIA

Baltic Sea

Gotland

RUSSIA

North Sea

DENMARK

LATVIA

Liepāja

Riga

Moscow

UNITED KINGDOM

Bornholm

Rügen

LITHUANIA

To Russia

Mullafarry

IRELAND

Priwall

Schlagsdorf

BELARUS

London

Helmstedt

Berlin

Potsdam

POLAND

Atlantic Ocean

GERMANY

NETHERLANDS

BELGIUM

Aš

Prague

UKRAINE

Selb

CZECHIA

SLOVAKIA

FRANCE

SWITZ.

Vienna

Bratislava

MOLDOVA

Bay of Biscay

Gorizia/Nova Gorica

AUSTRIA

Sopron

HUNGARY

ROMANIA

SLOVENIA

Trieste

CROATIA

ITALY

BOSNIA

SERBIA

Black Sea

KOSOVO

NORTH MACEDONIA

MONTENEGRO

Tirana

BULGARIA

Gevgelija

Istanbul

ALBANIA

Thessaloniki

PORTUGAL

SPAIN

Sarandë

Corfu

GREECE

TURKEY

To Nakhchivan

SYRIA

LEBANON

MOROCCO

TUNISIA

Mediterranean Sea

ISRAEL

JORDAN

ALGERIA

LIBYA

EGYPT

Author's Note

Across Europe, the morning of 24 February 2022 was one of those moments when the course of history suddenly seemed to change. Hundreds of millions of people woke to the news that Russia's president, Vladimir Putin, had instigated a full-scale war against his country's neighbour Ukraine. Millions inside Ukraine were wrenched from their sleep by the literal impact of the first missiles; they have not slept easily since. Countless more beyond the country's borders felt the geopolitical shockwaves those detonations caused. As I write, we all continue to wonder what Putin's war will mean for the future peace of the world.

The book you are about to read is an account of my journey along the entire route of the old Iron Curtain. As I travelled, back in 2019, I found people frequently wanting to talk about the conflicts Russia had already caused in eastern Ukraine and about its illegal annexation of Crimea. Contrary to some recent reports, many experts and ordinary people knew then, before the massive escalation in hostilities, that Putin was a leader dangerously obsessed with power, with few if any limits on his behaviour, that he was a man fundamentally out of control. The debate about whether his particular acts of violence in 2022 were foreseeable will rage for decades. But what is already clear is that these events have special resonance for anyone who ever lived near the Iron Curtain.

On my recent travels, I thought often about my own first trip to the former USSR, to the Ukrainian cities of Kyiv, Zhytomyr and Uzhhorod back in 1995. I was still a schoolboy and it was an intense, magical experience. But the Ukraine I was visiting, like much of Eastern Europe, was a place of chaos and distress. Ukrainians have come so far in the intervening decades. And now those in the Kremlin with an addiction to the past are trying to destroy their gains, as well as Russians' own progress, as they pursue a nostalgic misreading of what Russia really deserves. It is an abhorrent state of affairs.

The pages that follow are not a blueprint for how to respond to naked aggression of this sort or to the very real prospect of a new Iron Curtain, a new border of borders, being driven through our continent. But they do show in new detail how Europeans survived and eventually triumphed over the last great divide to sever them. I have been fortunate enough to become the custodian of many precious stories: stories of hatred, fear and distrust, but also of courage, connection and activism. It is a privilege to share them with you.

The Cold War had more than its fair share of moments of truth. Some of you will remember them at first hand, and will recall how sometimes humanity failed to rise to the challenge: in Hungary in 1956, in Prague in 1968, and elsewhere. Fortunately, we can also recall times when people did find a way through, most notably in 1989, that year of dismantled concrete and torn-down fences. I have no doubt we are living through another moment of truth, a moment when we all must find ways to rise to the challenge, for Ukraine's sake and also for our own.

Timothy Phillips
London, July 2022

THE
CURTAIN
AND THE
WALL

Preface

Mullafarry, Republic of Ireland

If you live long enough, the borders change. Borders seem so immutable, so fixed. They really want us to believe that they are. But history tells a radically different story, especially the history of the last hundred years.

Broken, breached, overrun, and then reimposed, only to be erased once more, borders are as solid as cast iron but as brittle as rust. They govern our lives. Often they ruin lives. In many ways they are the ultimate proof of a state's power, but they are also the work of transient men and women, and as such are transient themselves.

I first realized something of the meaning of borders when I was six years old. I grew up in Northern Ireland in the Troubles, and for my parents, as for just about every other adult, the rhythm of daily life was punctuated by news of bomb attacks, incendiary devices, kidnappings, kneecappings and murders, all motivated in one way or another by a border. There were plenty of children whose lives were blighted by these events, but I was fortunate to have no direct experience of them, or of the border, until one day when I ended up in a car heading south with my little brother, my parents and my maternal grandparents.

We often went for drives as a family, but I remember it was clear from the start that this particular excursion was different. There were constant mumblings among the adults about how long the journey would take and which route it would be best to use. I also recall some out-of-character nervous hilarity about the things that might go wrong. In those years, the mid-1980s, Protestants like us tended not to cross the border much, and so, as I now understand, the very fact of the trip was causing heightened anxiety. My grandfather had purchased a new roadmap for the occasion and I demanded to be map reader. I had never really looked at a map of the whole island of Ireland before and I had not, at least not in memory, visited the Republic. Both on paper and in reality, this was to be my first encounter with a border.

We set off from home near Belfast in a really crowded car and drove for about an hour through the North. I remember a growing sense of anticipation as we approached the borderline. I can hear my mum telling me and my brother to sit quietly as we entered a slow-moving queue of vehicles that ran up to a checkpoint. My granny supported her, saying that our daddy needed to be able to concentrate now. Some kind of chicane was operating. At the checkpoint itself the driver of each vehicle was required to wind down their window and answer the questions of a member of the British security forces. 'Where are you going today, sir?' 'Is it your own vehicle, sir?' 'Would you have some identification on you, sir?' I would realize in later years that the patter was pretty unchanging, and usually delivered with the same thin veneer of politeness. Even on this first day I sensed how the adults in the car bristled as my dad gave his staccato replies. As so often at a border, the power of a state had revealed itself and all of us had been made to bend a knee.

Soon we were on our way again, on a tentative new odyssey in an unfamiliar land. I remember my instant fascination with never-before-seen road signs, the different feel and sound of new road surfaces and the unusual makes of car we saw, as well as new adverts with new fonts and even a new language. I remember how the adults began and then continued for the rest of the day to make comparisons. Was this or that thing better or worse than in Northern Ireland? (Mainly worse, it seemed.) Was this or that thing better or worse than the last time they had been down here, many years before? (Mainly unchanged.) And there were other conversations too, about politics and terrorism and the sympathies and notorious hardline views of the people in this border area.

My brother and I took note of each strange place name, only some of which our elders could tell us how to pronounce. The Gaelic words for the South, the North, Galway, Dublin and Derry all appeared frequently on signs, written up in an odd italic script, and we clumsily tried to say them aloud. I was struck by how each settlement we passed moved us further from the border I could see marked on my map. I had the feeling of going deeper and deeper into foreign territory.

Granny told us we would know we were nearing our destination when we reached a place called Ballysadare, so we watched hawkishly for the distance markers featuring this name. We invented – if that is not too strong a word for it – a song which we sang endlessly in the back of the car. *Are we near to Ballysadare? I want to go to Ballysadare. When will we get to Ballysadare?* Granny had picked the place because it featured prominently on the new map. So all of us, adults and children alike, laughed a lot when we finally arrived at the settlement and it flashed past in seconds, the tiniest of villages. This gave our song a concluding line – *Blink and you'll miss it, Ballysadare!*

What was this trip for? To my young mind that was the most perplexing thing of all. We were heading to a place where apparently my granny's family had lived and died many decades before. I simply did not understand how this could be. Why had they ended up in this foreign country? What had driven them here? How had they got on with the locals? How had they provided for themselves in this land where everything – roads, fields, mountains, houses; even little things like postboxes – was alien?

The adults explained that the border had not always existed and that Ireland had actually been one country in the past. Granny's great-grandfather – my great-great-great-grandfather,

Ben Ireland (and yes, that was his surname) – had started out in life as a gamekeeper on an estate in County Antrim, inside what was now Northern Ireland. At some point in the 1890s or early 1900s, he had moved his family to County Mayo where he had found better-paying work on another estate. For Ben the move did not entail crossing a border – indeed, nobody at that time could have imagined a border existing. Ben's new employer, a Mr Orme, was a good one, and although some of Ben's children later moved (including granny's grandfather, who came back north), Ben himself and his wife and unmarried children remained in Mayo for the rest of their lives. They lived long enough to witness a new country's difficult, violent birth; long enough to see Ireland divided and their part of the United Kingdom turn into the Irish Free State and later the Irish Republic.

On our day out the ultimate destination was the Presbyterian churchyard at Mullafarry where all these Irelands had been buried. It was a deserted place when we saw it, the church itself still functioning but only barely. The gravestone was easily located and bore the names of the people we had talked about in the car. My mum and grandfather took photographs while the rest of us walked around. Somehow we managed to get into the church – perhaps doors were just left unlocked in that part of the world back then or perhaps someone went to a neighbouring house for a key. There is a photograph of me standing in the pulpit, head barely visible behind the lectern, pretending to preach.

Afterwards, the journey acquired a kind of fairytale quality for me. Whenever it came to mind, I would see our drive to Mayo from above, as if out of a helicopter or in a film: the old brown Mazda making its way down ever-narrower country roads. And simultaneously I would see Ben Ireland and his family, good people in old-time clothing, moving round the same countryside, living in their farmhouses, helping each other in the fields, walking to church on Sundays, gathered by firesides to play music.

Ben Ireland and his wife Ellen, pictured at Glenarm, County Antrim, some years before their move to County Mayo.

But these simple idyllic scenes were always undercut in my imagination by the dramatic tension of the border, because it was the border that had struck me most forcefully that day. As with any six-year-old, what I had taken from the trip were really just snippets and fragments but they were no less vivid for that. The border as a place of control and interrogation. The border that had made the adults in my life worried and momentarily vulnerable. The people living on the other side of that line: a kind of parallel universe or a different civilization, perhaps even a dangerous one. The mix of relief and regret on getting back to our own side that evening, back to the familiar. And, although I had learned that this border was not at all old, I had also taken away a strong impression that it would exist permanently into the future.

This book is not about the Irish border. It is about a different, much bigger system of frontiers that marked and caused division throughout the whole of Europe for most of the second half of the twentieth century. Mullafarry is where I choose to begin because that early encounter with the border near home was the starting point for my understanding of borders everywhere and consequently for this journey along the Iron Curtain.

The day trip to Mayo had a powerful and lasting effect on the child that was me, and I can now see that many of the sensations I experienced back then are typical of children's responses to frontiers and contested spaces more generally. On my recent travels for this book, I have met people who also recalled being shocked by the sudden humbling of their parents at tense crossing points, who felt bewildered by the cultural differences of countries lying just a few kilometres from their front door, and who were amazed to learn that they had relatives living in those countries.

If you live long enough, the borders change. They changed for the island of Ireland in the late 1990s. The frontier there had looked set to go on causing bloodshed indefinitely but instead softened and for some even started to fade from view. For the lands of the Iron Curtain, that border had once seemed as permanent and rigidly unbreakable as any that ever existed. During the mid-1980s even the most knowledgeable experts did not foresee its obliteration just a short time later, yet that was exactly what happened between 1989 and 1991, sensationally and wonderfully.

During most of the years following, the continent's story was one of borders getting evermore open, evermore intangible, and ever-less meaningful. But we can now see that we have slipped into a new period right across the continent, when borders are once again becoming more definite, more contested and more dangerous. COVID-19 left most of us temporarily unable to leave our own countries, and even our own towns and homes. But it is abundantly clear that the pandemic cannot be blamed for what is really a much broader return of division. Already for several years before 2020, some politicians and many ordinary people had been rediscovering their love of national boundaries and nationalism, and hankering after the secure feeling that borders can bring. Some have long harboured the view that their countries had the wrong borders; now a few are willing to contemplate naked aggression to fix the error. The rhetoric and not a little of the reality of the Cold War have resurfaced in Europe. First, checkpoints, chicanes and fences went up again, and not just in the landscape but in hearts and minds as well. Then, tragically, troops and heavy artillery were threatening to redraw Europe's borders by force.

My journey along the route of the Iron Curtain took me from the meeting point of Norway and Russia high in the Arctic Circle to the border of Turkey and Azerbaijan, almost 5,000 kilometres to the south.

Let me pause for just a moment before we set off together because I realize that both my use of the term 'Iron Curtain' and the parameters and itinerary of my journey immediately raise questions. Allow me to say a few things straightaway to clarify my approach in the rest of this book and the definitions I have worked with.

The Iron Curtain must be a strong contender for the most successful metaphor ever coined. A phrase first employed to describe the burgeoning East–West division of Europe in the 1940s, it has stuck with us ever since, entering into common parlance all across the world. The Iron Curtain or *Eiserner Vorhang*, *Zheleznyi zanaves* or *Rideau de fer*, was already a settled term by the late 1940s, remaining so until the late 1980s – a perfect descriptor for a fact on the ground about which seemingly little could be done, and indeed one that served as the basic organizing principle for most global politics, military strategy and much of economic and cultural life. The phrase stayed with us into the twenty-first century because we continue to live with the consequences of the Cold War, but also because it is such convenient shorthand for any intensifying standoff between neighbouring states.

My mental image of the Iron Curtain, perhaps like yours, has its origins in Winston Churchill's famous usage in his March 1946 speech at Fulton, Missouri. Churchill talked of an Iron Curtain having 'descended across the continent', locking 'all the capitals of the ancient states of Central and Eastern Europe' into a 'Soviet sphere'. He said that curtain extended 'from Stettin in the Baltic to Trieste in the Adriatic'.

I remember learning that quotation off by heart for my A-levels and, like many history students, deploying it in every essay and exam I could. I thought Churchill had coined the metaphor, and it was only recently that I discovered he was not the first person to make the comparison between Soviet policy and a theatrical iron curtain – the safety screen that descends to separate audiences from a stage during play intervals. Others including Nazi propaganda chief Joseph Goebbels had got there before him.[1] But Churchill's speech would always be the decisive reference.

I first had the idea of travelling the route of the Iron Curtain in order to see what remained of it back in the late 1990s. My interest in Europe's East–West divide developed steadily from the age of twelve, at school and then university. I happened to go to one of the only schools in Northern Ireland that taught Russian and had my first Russian lesson at the start of September 1990, less than a year after the Berlin Wall fell and when the Soviet Union still existed. All our Russian textbooks dated from the Soviet period and referred constantly to the USSR's friendly relations with other socialist countries and the achievements and benefits of the Soviet system. Each week, we watched excerpts from a 1980 BBC television series, *Russian – Language and People*. In my Russian lessons, it was as if the Iron Curtain had never gone away.

A little later, when I went to Eastern Europe on holiday and for research, I witnessed the great changes that had happened since the Cold War's end, but, even so, always felt that the old divisions were more alive and more relevant than most people wanted to admit. The communist system had been dismantled in the early 1990s, but lots of citizens spent the first decade without it just trying to keep their heads above water. Understandably, many ended up questioning whether life really was better in this new world. Vestiges of socialism were everywhere along with old elites struggling to reinvent themselves. Years after the borders opened, there were always plenty of places where one could feel instantly catapulted back into the Eastern Bloc.

For a long time I did nothing with my idea of making a trip along the Iron Curtain. I was busy with other projects and, besides, from the early 2000s on, the Iron Curtain itself really did seem a bit less important as a way to understand Europe's present. Eastern European countries were joining NATO and the EU *en masse*, apparently consigning old divisions to history, and a new ideological conflict, the War on Terror, was dominating global politics.

Then, after the UK's Brexit referendum and Donald Trump's election as US president – with Vladimir Putin becoming evermore daring in his foreign policy, and Pegida and Alternative für Deutschland flourishing in Germany – I found myself thinking of the trip again. Some old wounds from the Cold War seemed to be opening up once more and many of the lessons the world learned during the conflict looked like they were being forgotten. The trip I now imagined still involved searching for the Iron Curtain's physical remains but it also included getting to know and spending time with the ordinary people who lived in these borderlands, hearing their memories of the Cold War and about their lives since, and their views of Europe today.

Already by 2016 this seemed like a worthwhile idea, but it has only come to feel more relevant as the years have passed. Those living closest to the Iron Curtain had a unique experience of the ideological hostility that marked, and marred, the second half of the twentieth century. In some cases they now find themselves back on that front line. I sensed that the old frontier zone would be a good place to take the temperature of Europe today in a context that explicitly connected the present with the past.

So why is this not a book about a journey from Stettin to Trieste, as Churchill's famous quote might suggest? It is true that there never was an officially agreed northern or southern limit to the Iron Curtain. Yet even in 1946 Stettin and Trieste were somewhat idiosyncratic start and end points for Churchill to choose. He himself knew that the continent's ideological division extended far to the north and south of each place, while the newly Polish city of Stettin, or Szczecin as it became known, was a particularly odd call. One could only claim it was on the Iron Curtain if one ignored the Soviet occupation of the eastern part of Germany. But in reality the USSR had no intention of giving up its German territory which went on to become the GDR (the German Democratic Republic or Deutsche Demokratische Republik (DDR)). (Churchill, no doubt, would not have wanted to admit publicly in 1946 that East Germany's fate already looked sealed.)

In order to include all the places on the continent that experienced the East–West divide as a physical reality, I decided to base my route on the European boundaries of NATO and the Warsaw Pact, the two great military alliances that dominated Cold War hostilities. Although NATO was not formed until 1949, and the Warsaw Pact only in 1955, these coordinates give a better guide to the full extent of the Iron Curtain and have allowed me to include important places that Churchill left out. The northernmost point on 'my' Iron Curtain is a spot called Grense Jakobselv, on the freezing Barents Sea, while the southernmost point, Sadarak, was the last meeting place of Turkey and the USSR, and is now the only border crossing between Turkey and Azerbaijan. Significantly, this route takes the traveller to the former USSR itself and also to the Danish island of Bornholm, which was actually still occupied by Red Army troops at the time of Churchill's speech, as well as communist Albania and capitalist Greece. Instead of Szczecin, my Iron Curtain reference point on the German Baltic coast was just to the east of Lübeck.[2]

To write this book, I travelled from Grense Jakobselv to Sadarak using every conventional mode of public transport, as well as cars, bicycles and my own feet. I completed over 1,500 kilometres of the trip on foot. I made multiple trips to some locations after discovering new information about them, or in order to speak to new people; in addition to visits I had already paid to some places, like Bratislava and Budapest, earlier in life. But the principal reason for undertaking the project was always to get a sense of the Iron Curtain in its totality, and so the centrepiece of the research is a single journey that I made along the entire route during several months in 2019, from Grense Jakobselv at −5°C all the way to Sadarak at 41°C. It is this trip that gives the book its structure, my attempt to convey Europe's great divide in all its vastness and variety.

The stories that follow are not told in chronological order, though I have attempted to be clear throughout about when specific events took place and also about how local incidents connect with wider international events. In the course of my travels, I realized with new clarity how the human mind works to keep track of different eras and stories, and indeed how natural it is for us to do this: making sense of a palimpsest of memories and impressions is a hallmark of both our individual and our collective experience. Anyone with a love of history and culture knows well the feeling of walking through a city on holiday, learning of its Gothic cathedral one minute and its Roman amphitheatre the next, before seeing its collection of Impressionist art. The reader will, I think, encounter something similar here − except that all the discrete fragments relate in some way to the Cold War or its aftermath.

What follows, then, is the story of how the continent of Europe gained and lost an Iron Curtain, and of how it learned but then seemingly forgot important lessons about openness and liberty. It is the story of my journey along that infamous Curtain's route, including, of course, the Berlin Wall, and of my conversations with the people who live beside it and whose lives have been dominated by it. When the fact of new divisions leaves us speechless, we should use the silence to listen to the past.

PART I

Nordic and Baltic countries and Russia

Arctic Ocean

N
W E
S

Porsanger
Kirkenes
Svanvik
Grense Jakobselv
Nikel
Murmansk

Barents Sea

Kola Peninsula

Arctic Circle

Norwegian Sea

SWEDEN

White Sea

FINLAND

Medvezhegorsk

SOVIET
PORKKALA

Petrozavodsk

NORWAY

Vainikkala
Turku
Helsinki
Degerby

Vyborg

St Petersburg

RUSSIA

Oslo

Stockholm

Tallinn
ESTONIA

Iron Curtain

North Sea

Gotland

Gulf of Bothnia

Baltic Sea

LATVIA
Ziemupe
Riga
Liepāja
Karosta

DENMARK

Copenhagen

LITHUANIA
Vilnius

Moscow

1

Oslo, Norway

My first destination after leaving home in London was Oslo, where I arrived on a piercingly bright April day to find Norwegians having their lunch in parks and walking round in shirtsleeves and sunglasses. Oslo, it must be said, played no special role in the Cold War, certainly no more so than a dozen other capitals around Europe. But I had to spend a single day and night there as the quickest way to get to the part of the Arctic that was once the top of the old Iron Curtain. Oslo also makes it into the book because of a couple of experiences during my twenty-four hours in the city, each of which added unexpected perspective to the journey ahead.

Norway's capital is a place famed for its style and understated wealth. Walking through its streets one is constantly aware of both: everywhere there are people wearing the latest headphones or holding the newest phone or riding an eccentrically fashionable bike. Here is a kindergarten built by a world-leading architect; over there, some social housing from the 1960s or 1970s that might be a slum elsewhere but in Norway looks as good as new.

A particularly distinctive symbol of the city's approach to opulence is the modernist rådhus, the city hall designed between the 1930s and the 1950s. I found myself in front of it while still weighed down by luggage because I had not been able to check into my hotel. The scale of its exterior with two enormous skyscraper-style towers encourages the viewer to stand and gape, especially when the backdrop is a perfect blue sky. But this brick self-confidence is also tempered by Nordic playfulness in the form of statues, murals, tapestries and mosaics.

It was only when I got inside that I found out this was the location of the annual Nobel Peace Prize ceremony. Suddenly my thoughts went to what I remembered of the old East–West struggles over Nobel prizes through the years. Here was one of the many thousands of contexts in which the continent's ideological rifts had played out – contexts which were never likely to lead to all-out war in themselves but which were vital for demonstrating and perpetuating the fundamental divide between the world's two camps.

As a rule, international recognition was something the communist system craved, especially external validation that its policies and institutions were capable of producing excellence. Hence, the maniacal focus on Olympic medals and the enduring delight as first Sputnik, then Laika, and then Yuri Gagarin beat the Americans into space. The Nobel prizes were another such currency of global success, but they were riskier. The Nobel committee have a habit of recognizing independent spirits, especially those who criticize authoritarian regimes, and so the accolade, desirable in one way, frequently created problems for both Eastern Bloc winners and their governments. Perhaps most famous in this regard was Boris Pasternak, who was awarded the literature prize in 1958. At first he sent a message to the Nobel committee saying he was 'immensely grateful, touched, proud, astonished, abashed' at the honour, but then, following orders from above, he quickly sent another declining the award. The Soviet authorities had told him that if he went to collect it he would never be allowed back in the country.[1] In 1975 Soviet nuclear physicist turned civil rights advocate Andrei Sakharov similarly was banned from attending and his wife had to go to Oslo instead and read out a speech on his behalf.

The Oslo Rådhus did not become the setting for the peace prize ceremony until December 1990, but in that year the winner was none other than Mikhail Gorbachev. His citation stated that he was being recognized for his contribution to the 'dramatic changes [that] have taken place in the relationship between East and West' and the 'new possibilities' that have opened up 'for the world community to solve its pressing problems across ideological, religious, historical and cultural dividing lines'.[2] Ironically Gorbachev was also initially unable to collect his award. In his case, domestic political trouble prevented him from leaving the USSR for the December ceremony, but he did turn up in the rådhus six months later to deliver the Nobel lecture.

I sat beside Oslo harbour later in the day with the rådhus at my back and read what Gorbachev had said there thirty years before. 'The Cold War is over,' he declared. 'The risk of a global nuclear war has practically disappeared. The Iron Curtain is gone. Germany has united, which is a momentous milestone in the history of Europe. There is not a single country on our continent which would not regard itself as fully sovereign and independent.' This was the good news – the great news – of the age.

But as well as summing up the impact of the reforms he had personally spearheaded since the mid-1980s, Gorbachev was also startlingly perceptive about the long-term opportunities and risks that lay ahead: 'Progress towards the civilization of the twenty-first century will certainly not be simple or easy . . . One cannot get rid overnight of the heavy legacy of the past or the dangers created in the post-war years. With less East–West confrontation, or even none at all, old contradictions resurface, which seemed of secondary importance compared to the threat of nuclear war. The melting ice of the Cold War reveals old conflicts and claims, and entirely new problems accumulate rapidly.' When he expressed his fears for the Soviet Union specifically – a geopolitical behemoth that would shortly fall to pieces – he used words that ring out through the decades. 'The people are tired and easily swayed by populism.'[3]

*

I really should have gone to bed early that night because I needed to be at the airport no later than 7.30 the next morning. But as I was closing the curtains in my hotel room I saw a small group of people hanging up red flags, banners and placards in the courtyard next door. One of the flags had a white hammer stitched in its top left corner and I realized that this must be some sort of left-wing political gathering. I was intrigued but also in two minds about whether to investigate. Ordinarily I would not have, but I knew that the next few months were to be full of moments like this, when I would have to decide whether to bother people or leave them alone. I said to myself that temporarily it was my duty – for the good of the journey – to bother them.

I walked back onto the street and immediately through the next archway. Four of the group of five were in their twenties or thirties, while one man with an impressive white beard looked around fifty. Having finished hanging up their flags, they were now sitting down to enjoy a box of red wine. After I explained in somewhat garbled fashion why they had piqued my interest, they invited me to join them.

They turned out to be activists of the Norwegian Labour Party, meeting to prepare for May Day in a few days' time: dusting off and patching up old banners and making new ones, and getting ready to host a big party after the main demonstration. Norwegian Labour was polling well in Oslo, they said, with fresh elections just around the corner. Party members and trade unionists would be marching with a spring in their step.

An engaged and engaging bunch, the five were internationally aware, alive to the problems of modern life, but also still hopeful about the future – hopeful without being naïve. It was a reminder of another way in which Europe is still very much connected to its Cold War past. The tradition of grassroots activism, the belief that ordinary people can make the world a better place: these were as key a feature of the Europe of the Iron Curtain as the

*Members of the Norwegian Labour Party prepare for May Day
in a courtyard in central Oslo.*

tanks, barbed wire and propaganda, and they are still an essential feature of Europe today.

When I told them that I would be flying up to Kirkenes in Finnmark county the next morning, they each had something to say about what I could expect to find. Only two had visited for themselves: Lars, on a road trip between school and university, and the older man when he served in the Norwegian navy in the 1980s. He said he had been stationed on a mine-laying vessel which regularly engaged in 'cat-and-mouse' chases with Soviet submarines – all pretty good-natured by that point in hostilities, he added, because everyone had long since worked out it was just a game. 'I think I may even have got my foot under the Iron Curtain and into Soviet waters once or twice,' he joked.

The group told me that Norway had always had a special relationship with the Soviet Union, something which continued to be the case with Russia today. There was NATO, the country's vital source of defence. But there was also a daily requirement to be careful and courteous where the Russians were concerned. This need for caution, they thought, would no doubt feel at its most acute in far-off, sparsely populated Finnmark, as far from Oslo as Oslo is from Rome but so much closer to Russia.

As the last of the wine was coaxed from the box, they chatted to me about a story that had been making headlines around the world that very day. Norwegian sailors in Finnmark had caught what journalists were calling a Russian 'spy-whale' in the domestic waters of one of Norway's islands.[4] Some believed the animal, which had been intercepted wearing a GoPro camera holder and a harness originating in St Petersburg, had been trained to place tracking devices onto Norwegian and other foreign ships. Others, including, of course, the Kremlin, said such claims were nonsense, just the latest example of collective hysteria and Russophobia from America and its NATO Allies.

Even after a few drinks, we all felt it was hard to take the 'spy-whale' theory at face value and we agreed that it would most likely be impossible to establish the truth. Then again, where Putin's regime was concerned, you could never be sure, the older man said. Another member of the group expressed his frustration at the fact that the news media could still get so excited by Cold War stories like these. It would be better if they focused more on genuinely big problems, the problems of inequality, xenophobia and climate change.

I was on my feet by this point, aware that it was almost midnight.

'That's why we joined the Labour Party in the first place: to address the big problems,' the man continued.

'Enough about big problems,' one of his friends said, standing up too and shaking my hand. 'This traveller needs to go to his bed. He has a date with a Soviet whale in just a few hours' time.'

2

Kirkenes and Grense Jakobselv, Norway

My flight to Kirkenes was full. About half the passengers were military conscripts, a mixture of young men and women in their late teens and early twenties heading north either for training or for longer stints at the border. Some chatted to each other, but most just plugged in headphones and looked – as I probably did – like they would rather be in bed.

Seen from a plane window, eastern Finnmark county is a picture of emptiness. Even before manmade borders are taken into account, the landscape leaves visitors in no doubt that this is fundamentally a frontier, a territory right up against the edge of the habitable earth. Here is blue-black sea and dramatic black rock, much of it still covered with snow even at the end of April. Here are sporadic clumps of wind-buffeted forest, but little else, including hardly any evidence of human settlement. This is wilderness. The coldest temperature ever recorded here was −42°C, as recently as 1999, and the average even in the hottest month, July, is just 10°C.

Across Finnmark, which is bigger than the Netherlands, just 75,000 people live. The handful of small settlements, of which Kirkenes is the easternmost, are hubs for commerce, administration and social contact. They have a functional appearance quite unlike highly designed Oslo and other places further south. For the majority of the year people here shuttle between heated buildings and heated cars, staying outside only for short periods. Despite the reliance on cars, one of the more memorable proofs of eastern Finnmark's utter isolation is that it gets by

The view from my plane as I descended into Kirkenes.

without any traffic lights. The nearest set is over 200 kilometres away in the Russian city of Murmansk.

Kirkenes sits in its own bay with stunning views of the Barents Sea. Mountains on both sides roll symmetrically to the coast, and each morning the Hurtigruten ferry sounds a dramatic horn as it sails between these peaks into the harbour. Away from the few places where people live, eastern Finnmark can be hauntingly beautiful. The landscape's sparse ingredients resolve into breathtaking scenes which, more often than not, one glimpses as isolated moments: a frozen fjord lit blazing bright by the sun; a bird of prey soaring high.

Despite the emptiness, Kirkenes and its surrounding territory have actually been greatly affected by humans, largely thanks to the international border. When I visited the Kirkenes Grenselandmuseet, or Borderland Museum, its registrar, Camilla Carlsen, told me about the territory's formal division back in 1826 when Sweden, which then ruled Norway, agreed to demarcate an exact borderline with Russia, replacing roughly defined marches that had sufficed since medieval times.

The indigenous Sámi people were the first to suffer for this, which like so many subsequent frontier decisions was worked out in distant capitals. The Sámi had always lived across the two jurisdictions and moved freely with the seasons, but from then on they were supposed to choose a single country for taxation and legal purposes. The edict was widely ignored, but as time went by the regime became stricter. Camilla told me that when Norway won its independence in 1905 the Oslo government immediately intensified the border regime, burning hay that 'Russian' Sámi collected in Norway to punish them for their illegal exploitation of 'Norwegian' resources. It was a foretaste of worse to come.

In the Second World War Kirkenes and the surrounding land were the site of terrible fighting between the Third Reich and the Soviet Union. In the summer of 1941 the Nazis made Kirkenes a key base for their invasion of the USSR, billeting around 100,000 troops there. They hoped to conquer Murmansk and move on quickly but got stuck and ended up staying in Kirkenes right through to 1944. The town sustained 300 separate Soviet air raids as a result, becoming the second most bombed place in Europe after the Maltese capital Valletta. Kirkenes's historic wooden core was destroyed and, postwar, the town had to be rebuilt from scratch.

It was as Kirkenes lay in ruins that the Iron Curtain slammed down emphatically on its outskirts. Surprised to be in the thick of things in the Second World War, it was now destined to remain there for the rest of the century and beyond. If there has been little in the way of overt hostility since 1945 – with one notable and chilling exception – tension has still underpinned everyday life and the region has acquired the frightening distinction of being the most atomic in the world.

This happened when Soviet military planners placed large nuclear submarine bases on the nearby Kola peninsula, leading other countries to send their subs to skulk in the international waters off the coast. The area around Kirkenes and the neighbouring part of the USSR had hardly any people in it, and looked deserted, but hosted the highest concentration of nuclear reactors anywhere. It has remained so. Thomas Nilsen, editor of the Kirkenes-based *Independent Barents Observer*, has calculated that no fewer than 18 per cent of all existing nuclear reactors can be found within a couple of hundred kilometres of Kirkenes, some of them just lying abandoned at the bottom of the sea.

This unassuming, practically unknown place has the capacity to destroy the entire planet many times over.

I stayed in Kirkenes just long enough to pick up my hire car, deposit my luggage at a wooden house I had rented, and buy some snacks at a petrol station. Now that I was actually on my journey along the Iron Curtain I was determined to get right to the very top of it as soon as possible: to the outpost of Grense Jakobselv.

The drive looked easy on paper, a mere 50 kilometres or so. But I suspected that this deep in the Arctic Circle nothing about transportation could be taken for granted, and indeed it turned out to be fairly gruelling. The road I went on had been closed until just five days earlier, gated and padlocked a few kilometres outside Kirkenes after the first heavy snow the previous December and opened again only when the Norwegian highways agency determined the thaw had definitively taken hold. On the day of my trip the definitiveness of the thaw seemed in doubt. The temperature was again −5°C, and snow and ice covered the tarmac, with fresh snow still falling. More than once as I drove I considered turning back but I worried that on subsequent days the conditions might be even worse. Instead I took to halting regularly to check I still had enough phone reception to make an emergency call if need be.

The road took me over mountains and across valleys, past lakes that are frozen solid for most of every year, and around many skiddy hairpin bends. The driving surface became steadily more pitted and potholed the further I went. After about 40 kilometres I reached the final stretch where the road hugged the Norwegian–Russian border all the way to the coast. Here, as along much of this 198-kilometre frontier, the actual dividing line runs somewhere along the bed of the River Jakobselva, famous for its salmon fishing. The border zone is clearly demarcated. A lay-by at the point where the road first draws close to the river includes boards with detailed information about the unique rules that apply in this area. Then at regular intervals bright yellow border posts stand at the roadside to mark the proximity of the limits of Norwegian sovereignty. The corresponding Russian ones, in red and green, are often visible on the Jakobselva's opposite bank. Where the river is very narrow, and Russia really just a big jump away, additional Norwegian signage is posted and CCTV cameras on long metal poles keep watch.

With just a couple of kilometres to go, the forest opened out to scrubland and dunes. Here at the edge of Norway were perhaps a dozen or so wooden houses spread along the road, vestiges of the old Grense Jakobselv fishing community, and now, one assumes, summer homes that lie unused and inaccessible for half the year. Emptier still was the scene across the border, where the only evidence of human settlement was a couple of watchtowers and some bolted-together shipping containers that reminded me of polar research stations I had seen in photographs.

The difference is significant. As I learned from people back in Kirkenes, right through the Cold War the road to Grense Jakobselv remained open to ordinary Norwegians whenever the elements allowed. By contrast there was no question of ordinary Soviet citizens getting close to the border. As elsewhere on the Iron Curtain's east side, roadblock checkpoints were located many kilometres inside the USSR to prevent anyone without official clearance approaching. In addition, all resident farmers and fishermen were forcibly ejected by Soviet authorities at an early stage.

I drove until there was no more road to drive on and parked up beside a beach where the sea lapped the sand with unexpected gentleness. The snow had stopped minutes before and with the sun splitting the clouds I got out to explore. For the next hour or so I felt perfectly alone at the top of Europe – even though I could assume that the employees of two states were actually

Warning signs on the Norwegian bank of the River Jakobselva, near Grense Jakobselv, with the Russian bank visible a few metres away.

well aware of my presence and monitoring my movements from somewhere nearby.

The principal landmark in Grense Jakobselv is King Oscar II's Chapel, a stone church built on a raised promontory in 1869 as a place for villagers to worship but also as a mark of the reach of Lutheran Christianity. There used to be a chapel on the Russian side too, indicating the start of Orthodox territory, but this has disappeared. I climbed the Norwegian chapel's steps to find the door unsurprisingly locked. Turning to descend, I halted to enjoy the view down over the coastline, from the long Norwegian promontory to my left across to the first headland of Russia on my right.

The mouth of the Jakobselva carved the picture in two. It ran just 300 metres to the east of the chapel. I now walked over to it across snowy tufts of marram grass and down onto the beach, straying beyond the yellow border posts for the first time and continuing until I reached the place where river and sea, Norway and Russia, converged. The sea and the river actually touch but, of course, the two countries remain a river's width apart at all times.

I allowed myself to linger, letting different aspects of my surroundings move in and out of focus. Local Finnmark residents later told me that they would never deliberately go beyond the yellow posts, as I had just done, not in Cold War times and not now. They said they try not even to look at the Russian frontier for too long, for fear of provoking the invisible border guards on the other side.

I looked back to the chapel and saw directly above it, on the very top of the mountain, a Norwegian base, the country's northernmost and easternmost watchtower. I observed the birds flying, crisscrossing the border carelessly as they do at manmade frontiers all across the world. I wondered how close to this point the spy-whale had swum, if indeed he was a spy-whale, on his journey from his Russian base to nose around Norwegian ships. My eye eventually fell on something I had missed before despite being just five metres away from it: a barbed wire fence that began right down at the sea on the Jakobselva's Russian bank and ran inland as far as my eye could see. Apparently, an identical fence ran here in Soviet times. It is so much lower and less solid than many of the surviving Iron Curtain barriers I would see but arguably it does its job just as well. Here, it does not need to stop people. Who is there to stop? It just needs to make a point

The Russian, previously Soviet, barbed wire fence on the River Jakobselva at Grense Jakobselv.

about exclusion and exclusivity. Spotting it was the first thing to make me feel anxious. I couldn't help wondering what would happen if I swam across the river and tried to climb through.

The Norwegian–Russian land border was the site of open belligerence just once in the Cold War, a sinister episode that few have heard of outside the immediate vicinity and specialist Norwegian military historians. On the night of 6 June 1968 Norwegian border guards at the frontier near Kirkenes heard unusually heavy traffic noise on the normally deserted Soviet roads nearby. They were unable to establish what the traffic was until the next morning when a very frightening picture confronted them. Facing each of seven Norwegian watchtowers were lines of Soviet tanks, all aiming guns into Norway.

It looked as if the tanks were just waiting for the order to advance. For the watching Norwegians it was a terrifying prospect. They lacked any tanks of their own close at hand. Their sole method of defence was standard-issue guns, which would have been useless against the superpower's heavy artillery. It was a woeful situation that suggested a staggering lack of preparedness. As would subsequently emerge, even the written instructions these poor men had about what to do in such circumstances dated back to 1949. 'Of course we were afraid,' one veteran told Norwegian public radio a few years ago. 'Finally we agreed that if they crossed the border we would just have to run as fast as we could.'[1]

The whole world would have been afraid, if it had known. Some hours later the situation got still worse when a number of the tanks opened fire. For a few awful minutes the Norwegians in the watchtowers thought they were about to become the first casualties of the Third World War. It was some small consolation when they established that the tanks were only firing blanks, at least for the time being.

In far-off Oslo Norway's generals were terrified too. The show of force was completely unexpected. They assumed it must have been motivated by Moscow's anger at a major NATO exercise, Polar Express, that was under way elsewhere in the country – but even in this context the reaction was far in excess of anything the Soviets had done before. The soldiers up in Kirkenes did not know the full extent of the Soviet mobilization. With access to other intelligence sources Oslo strategists could see, behind the 290 visible tanks, more than 4,000 other vehicles and items of heavy artillery, fighter jets in a heightened state of readiness, and an estimated 30,000 to 60,000 troops in battle positions.

Norway's high command had no detailed plan to counter such aggression. After twenty-four hours of prevarication, they finally despatched supply troops to the Finnmark watchtowers to give the men inside extra bullets for their useless guns, and issued a fresh set of instructions about what to do if an invasion started: basically to retreat, but slowly.

The 1968 standoff lasted for several days. Norwegian soldiers stationed in the picturesque village of Svanvik later recalled how Soviet tank cannons tracked their every move during the episode, even when they descended from the watchtower to go to the nearby toilet block. The Norwegian government did nothing to publicize what was happening – an act of secrecy that would surely have been impossible in a more populated part of Europe or, now, in the internet age – while the USSR issued no statement about its actions either. It came as a huge relief to everyone on the Western side when, on 12 June, the Soviets began a withdrawal.

In hindsight, we can be pretty confident that the episode really was a demonstration of the USSR's ire at Norway's active participation in NATO, as well as being an attempt to show the smaller country how little security the Western Alliance actually provided. But there may also have been a personal dimension. During a particularly difficult visit to Moscow in 1967 the Norwegian defence minister, Otto Grieg Tidemand, had quarrelled with his Soviet opposite number, Andrei Grechko.

At the end of the visit, when Tidemand was at the airport, Grechko let him know that he should get ready for a surprise. Some analysts now believe that June 1968 was that surprise.

It was an unbelievably high-stakes game for the USSR to play. As the Norwegian historian Tor Gisle Lorentzen has pointed out, 'We are talking here about young Norwegian soldiers who were facing major Soviet army forces and who for over a day did not receive any guidance from management about what was going on. From a historical perspective, few have experienced anything like it. Had shots been fired from the Norwegian side, it could have been very serious.' Moreover, we also know from Soviet veterans that the ranks of the Soviet army were deliberately misled about the reasons for the mobilization – misled in ways that could have predisposed them to be trigger happy. Army generals told them that there were large concentrations of US forces across the border and also that 'German soldiers were again marching in the streets of Norway', a lie loosely grounded on the fact that some 15 West German army medics were participating in Polar Express.[2]

The incident understandably made a deep impression on all who learned of it, but that circle was kept deliberately small right to the end of the Cold War. In the wake of the mobilization, Norway and NATO strengthened their military installations in Finnmark. By the early 1970s a battalion's worth of stores was permanently stockpiled at the garrison of Porsanger, and the nearby air station at Banak was also bolstered. Meanwhile, in and around Kirkenes, ordinary people knew well enough the gist of what had gone on, both from the evidence of their own eyes and by word of mouth. They had to contend with the fact that they would have been among the first to be wiped out or taken prisoner if the Soviets had crossed the frontier. Since the start of the Cold War this had been a theoretical threat, but now it seemed much more plausible.

*

Back in Kirkenes I woke with the dawn at around 3 a.m. the next day. Early May is the start of the white nights season, so already it was only dark for a brief time each night. In just a couple of weeks there would be no darkness at all. I allowed myself to drift in and out of sleep for a while, but it was still just 7 a.m. when I got up and began to wander about the town.

There is no ignoring Russia's proximity in Kirkenes not least because one keeps encountering Russians. Down at the port, I came across a group boarding a coach back across the border after a stay at a harbour-front hotel. I heard another couple speaking the language as they sheltered in a shop doorway lighting cigarettes on their way to work. And I soon spotted the town's substantial Russian consulate, right in the centre, and, not far off, Kirkenes's public library with its bilingual signage advertising a substantial Russian-language section.

In 1991, when the Soviet Union collapsed, large numbers of Russians started to enter eastern Finnmark for the first time since 1945. Attitudes towards them were initially very mixed. Many Norwegians liked the cheap vodka and cigarettes the Russians sold from collapsible tables at the back of their Lada cars. Others saw them as a source of cheap labour, while a more niche clientele also enjoyed the Russian prostitutes who flooded in, a phenomenon little seen in Finnmark up to that point. But with the new influx there initially came much xenophobia and stereotyping. Russians struggled to find people willing to rent accommodation to them and were frequently labelled untrustworthy, while also being subject to exploitation. Gradually more positive relations won through and over the last quarter of a century people on either side of the border have come to think of one another favourably.

Those who live this close to the frontier are now entitled to special passes allowing them unlimited entry to the other country. Many Kirkenes residents end up going to Russia weekly, filling up with discount Russian petrol and enjoying budget car maintenance, haircuts and optician visits. Norway is an expensive country but for their part the inhabitants of Nikel, the nearest Russian city to the border, tend to buy most of their hi-tech equipment at the out-of-town superstores that cluster near the Kirkenes border crossing. Even though TVs and surround-sound systems cost more in Norway, the Russians have greater confidence they are buying genuine articles and not fakes.

For most people in the border area, relations are mainly transactional, a series of commercial exchanges that are completed with smiles, a few pleasantries and, where necessary, the assistance of Google Translate. But deeper, more substantial ties have developed. Formal co-operation projects flourished between many museums and other local institutions during the 1990s and early 2000s, with professionals travelling regularly to meet one another. The Samovar Theatre in Kirkenes runs bilingual projects with Russian theatres and has often toured the Russian cities of Petrozavodsk and Murmansk. And many Russians have settled in Kirkenes, marrying locals and educating their children in the Norwegian school system.

Initially, as I learned about all this contact, I thought of it in relation to a grim zero point that I imagined persisting through the Cold War until the late 1980s. But several local people wanted to put me right in that regard. Yes, the Iron Curtain had reduced cross-border contact but seldom to zero, and many in the two communities had retained respect and even fondness for those on the other side throughout the period of official hostility.

Kirkenes's largest statue is instructive in this regard. It depicts a Soviet army soldier, an *Alyosha*. The USSR often placed such monuments in places it liberated, even when local people didn't want them. I might have assumed that was true of this one, especially after I learned of the 300 wartime air raids. But actually this *Alyosha*, erected shortly after the Nazi defeat, bears witness to a genuine and enduring bond.

I was lucky enough to spend a few hours with Ernst, a local

guide now in his eighties who is still sturdy and full of vigour. He had been a boy in Kirkenes during the German occupation. Yes, the Soviets had done huge damage as they liberated Kirkenes, Ernst said, but the locals had been grateful. The Wehrmacht soldiers were unbelievably brutal to one another and to Norwegians, he recalled. One young soldier, maybe only seventeen years of age, had dropped to his knees in the middle of the road one day and cried out that he was too weak to go on. A senior officer just walked over and shot him in the head while Ernst and others watched. Ernst showed me Soviet newsreel footage of him and his mother in a large group emerging from a mineshaft. 'We had been hiding inside that mineshaft for months,' Ernst said. 'We only dared to emerge when we knew the Germans had fled.

'Russia has been a good neighbour to the people of this part of Norway,' he went on – most importantly, when the war was over the Russians departed rather than becoming occupiers. It was the opposite of what Moscow did across most of the territory it conquered in wartime Europe. Many in Kirkenes and eastern Finnmark are still deeply thankful for that decision. As we parted, Ernst said that he had always been more frightened of Americans than Russians. 'It is American presidents who start wars not Russian ones,' he told me, wagging a finger in my face. 'Could anyone honestly say that Mr Putin was more frightening than Mr Trump?'

In Cold War times the warmth Kirkenes people like Ernst felt towards the Soviets had relatively few tangible outlets. The border was absolutely closed most of the time and very heavily militarized, and cultural exchange was severely limited. But there were annual Soviet army trips to the *Alyosha* statue to mark the anniversary of liberation every 25 October and also very occasional exchanges for soccer matches and musical concerts. During the Khrushchev Thaw in the late 1950s and early 1960s, the two governments briefly co-operated on the construction

The 1944 Soviet Army memorial in Kirkenes. Initially the soldier trampled a German eagle under foot. At some point the eagle was removed, apparently to avoid offending fellow NATO member West Germany.

of a number of hydroelectric power stations straddling their territory. This led to Norwegian workers crossing daily at temporary frontier openings, and even, for a brief window of fifty-nine days in 1960, unrestricted access for all Kirkenes residents to a special segment of USSR territory where a bar and duty-free shop operated (there was no equivalent right for Soviet citizens to come to Kirkenes).[3] Khrushchev himself was photographed with Norwegian workers at one of the power stations during a visit in July 1962. Thereafter relations cooled again, culminating in the 1968 military altercation.[4] But from the late 1970s Soviet outreach intensified once more, with local Finnmark children being invited on coach holidays to Pioneer camps on the Black Sea. Each time one of these parties formed up, the border crossing outside Kirkenes had to be opened specially.

By the time I met Thomas Nilsen, editor of the *Independent Barents Observer*, in his office in the old mining company headquarters in the centre of town, I was struggling to make sense of the different local ways of seeing Russia and the border. On the one hand, there was lasting gratitude for the 1940s liberation and much present-day enjoyment of the favourable trading conditions and other links that have developed. But on the other, everyone clearly knew they lived on a fragile geopolitical fault line. Once in the Cold War the tanks had come knocking at Kirkenes's back door and still today the adjacent part of Russia remains packed with nuclear and other weapons. The same people who regularly pop into Russia for haircuts told me that they avoid looking at the border for too long and would never venture beyond Norway's yellow border posts. What did it all mean?

Thomas, bright and energetic in his early fifties, originally came from farther south in Norway but has lived in Finnmark for more than half his adult life. He has walked step by step with Kirkenes through its changing relationship with the collapsing USSR and the new Russia. He says the townsfolk here are very susceptible to a condition that was first identified elsewhere in Scandinavia. 'It's called Stockholm Syndrome,' he says. 'Yes, this is a society that could do with some vaccination against Stockholm Syndrome.' He is not joking.

In Thomas's long experience the reality is that when you have such a big neighbour with a reputation as a bully, it always feels rational not to do anything to upset them. If that neighbour shows you even a little kindness, or something that can be interpreted as kindness, you are tempted to latch onto it, even to exaggerate it, as a source of hope. It isn't that the people of eastern Finnmark are insincere when they express goodwill towards Russia and her people. On the contrary, they really mean it. It is just that their goodwill is fundamentally founded on fear.

In military strategic terms, eastern Finnmark is at least as vulnerable now as it ever was in Cold War times. The nuclear weapons systems that the USSR developed in and around the Barents Sea were not dismantled at the end of the East–West conflict in 1991, and since 2015 they have been augmented by a new generation of weapons systems and capabilities known as 'Bastion Defence'. Just as earlier Soviet plans for the Third World War involved tanks rolling across eastern Finnmark, so the new Bastion capabilities foresee all of northern Norway being occupied very early in any future Europe-wide or global war. This is necessary as far as Russian military planners are concerned to pre-empt a successful NATO blockade of the Barents Sea that would trap Russia's nuclear-armed submarines inside and render them useless. If Russia felt sufficiently threatened or bellicose at some future point, Kirkenes would almost certainly be one of the first pieces of NATO territory it would occupy.

Thomas tells me that it had long been the habit of locals to label this and many other difficulties as '*storpolitikk*'. This literally means 'great politics', and indicates something of concern to the leaders of Oslo and Moscow that lies beyond the control of locals and therefore ought be irrelevant when considering how local relations develop. According to this mindset, *storpolitikk*, if allowed to dictate local affairs, could destabilize cross-border relations unnecessarily, harming both lives and livelihoods. Oslo's participation in international sanctions against Russia was often dismissed as *storpolitikk* too, he says, even when those sanctions arose because of great crimes Russia committed such as the illegal annexation of Crimea or the poisoning of the Skripals in the UK. Local shopkeepers were happier to focus on serving the increasing number of middle-class Russians who would drive for three hours from Murmansk to stock up on French brie, Greek yoghurt and other foodstuffs that were banned from Russian shelves.

But the idea that Kirkenes could defy the odds every time and find a win–win accommodation with Russia was self-evidently false, Thomas thinks, and always required more than a little self-delusion. A few years ago, for reasons unknown but perhaps as dry runs for parts of Bastion Defence, the Russian military started to block the GPS signal across eastern Finnmark for hours or even days at a time. This was achieved by wheeling huge jammers into place near the border. When we met, it had happened at least five times in the preceding two years, and there have been further reports since. The effect is instant and comes without warning, making electronic navigation impossible not just for the military but also for civilian aircraft landing at Kirkenes Airport, for vital emergency services such as coastguard search-and-rescue vessels, and for ordinary Norwegian citizens. It is only too easy to see how this sort of misbehaviour could lead to loss of local life. Thomas says that since time immemorial bilateral functions between Russia and Norway have typically included a toast 'for a peaceful border'. But is this really what a peaceful border looks like?

Thomas's own career has shown the limits of the *storpolitikk* opt-out in a big way. The news website he edits was founded in 2003 as a bilingual (English and Russian) source of impartial online news about the Arctic region. Ever since, it has chronicled events and issues in northern Norway, Finland and Russia, including the many business ties that have grown up between the three areas and a broad range of other social and cultural stories. It has always included coverage of opposition politics inside Russia, and analysis of resistance to the Kremlin, and of Putin's more controversial policies, as well as Russian state corruption. It is for these aspects of its work, and its popularity inside Russia, that it has latterly ended up in the Kremlin's crosshairs. The paper is Kirkenes born and bred, and Putin's government has chosen to concentrate on this fact in attacking it.

Thomas freely admits that over the last decade the balance of news he published about Russia changed. 'Negative things started happening in Russia, so we couldn't only write about positive things,' he tells me over a second cup of coffee. This angered the Russian authorities greatly. Their officials started to demand corrections to lots of articles. There were increasing accusations of deliberate troublemaking by the website and of systematic anti-Russian bias.

The Kirkenes-based Russian consul-general had already weighed in publicly on the subject before Thomas wrote an editorial in 2014 about Russia's annexation of the Crimea and the impact it might have on international co-operation in the

Arctic. After that the top Russian diplomat in northern Norway responded with open rage. Did Nilsen not know that the Crimea had been 'reunified' with Russia rather than 'annexed'? There could be no talk of 'annexation' because what had happened was the will of the Crimean people.

A full-scale campaign against the *Observer* ensued for the rest of 2014 and into 2015, with Russian politicians and officials putting direct pressure on Norwegian politicians to defund the website. Russia petitioned both national and local administrators, threatening grave consequences for bilateral co-operation if they did not act decisively. For years, the website had received significant funding in the form of grants from the national foreign ministry, which were allocated by the local Barents Secretariat, a regional body composed of representatives of the three counties of northern Norway, including Finnmark. The Barents Secretariat was also Thomas's and the other journalists' formal employer.

While the foreign ministry declined to curtail the website, the Barents Secretariat quickly caved in. 'They were afraid that our journalism would harm people-to-people co-operation,' Thomas tells me. Consequently, they rescinded the website's press accreditation – a legal necessity for all news organizations in Norway – and sacked Thomas himself. Instantly the rest of his team resigned. It was a major scandal across Norway and made many who lived far from Finnmark aware of the border tensions for the first time.

The website's future was profoundly uncertain after the Secretariat removed accreditation. Some in Russia must have hoped at that point for a complete victory. But Thomas and his journalists agreed it was vital to continue. They found a new office, their current one, and started surviving on donations and subscriptions while keeping the website freely accessible to all. They have got by like this ever since. 'We don't have cash, but we have our freedom, and that is the most important thing,'

Thomas says. It was during this relaunch that he added the word 'independent' to the publication's title both to emphasize its values and as a mark of the scars it had acquired in trying to defend them.

Working life was to remain difficult. As the whole world has been forced to realize of late, when the Russian government decides you are a threat, it is relentless in pursuit. In March 2017 Thomas was stopped by Russian border guards at the Kirkenes crossing and handed a letter naming him a danger to national security and banning him from further entry to Russia. He then found himself placed on a so-called 'Stop List' of people sanctioned by Moscow as retaliation for EU travel bans. The *Independent Barents Observer*'s servers have also been subjected to numerous 'DoS' ('denial-of-service') attacks. Finally, in February 2019, the entire website was blocked inside Russia on an ongoing basis. The pretext for this was an article about growing up gay in the indigenous Sámi community. The Russian communications regulator alleged, erroneously, that the story incited readers to commit suicide.[5]

Nilsen reflects wryly that the block means he and Russia have come full circle since 1991. Back then, when he first arrived in eastern Finnmark, he worked at a radio station in the village of Svanvik. The station had a large listenership in nearby Soviet

Thomas Nilsen, editor of the Independent Barents Observer, *pictured beside a border post on the Russian side of the frontier.*

Nikel. It played mostly pop music but while the USSR was collapsing at the start of 1991 it temporarily switched to broadcast news, providing a rolling Russian translation of the BBC World Service. Because this revealed that the Soviet army and KGB were committing acts of violence against peaceful protesters elsewhere in the USSR, the Soviet government quickly moved to block the station's signal. At that time, there was little Thomas could do. But, he says, thousands of Russians nowadays have continued to find their way to the *Observer* through VPNs. This is still the case at the time of writing in spite of the ratchet of state control in Russia being turned ever tighter.

The story of Thomas and his website offers a window onto the profound changes that Russia has undergone over the course of President Putin's long rule – and is also revelatory about the mindsets of people in eastern Finnmark and the north of Norway more generally. Thomas confirms that he has always had strong supporters in the Kirkenes community. But there are also locals who see him as a thorn in the town's side. Controversial though it was, the decision of the Barents Secretariat has stood. 'For a couple of decades, for a generation, we learned that Russia was good, we were doing business and everything was coming out right,' Thomas concludes. 'But then we suddenly start to see, "Oh shit, it's not going right." But instead of criticizing the FSB and Moscow, some up here first took the position that something or somebody in Norway must be to blame.'

A case that tested the loyalties of Kirkenes residents even more than Russia's campaign against the *Independent Barents Observer* was that of Frode Berg. It was still rumbling on at the time of my visit but has since reached a conclusion.

A man in his sixties, Berg was a Norwegian border guard who lived in the town and worked right up against the frontier until his retirement. In 2017, when already a pensioner, he was arrested on holiday in Moscow and charged with spying. The Russian authorities said he had been caught redhanded couriering envelopes of cash and instructions to Norwegian agents inside Russia. After holding him on remand for more than a year, a Russian court then convicted Berg of espionage in a hasty, largely in-camera trial and sentenced him to fourteen years' detention in a strict-regime labour camp. Most commentators agreed that, for a man of Berg's age, this represented a virtual death sentence.

I saw a banner about Frode on my first walk through Kirkenes. Strung across the front of the public library, it read 'Help Frode home!' But who should help Frode? I wondered. Ernst, with his gratitude towards the Soviet liberators of the Second World War, was clear that the answer now rested with Moscow. He, for one, was hopeful. 'Mr Putin will do something for us,' he said. Thomas Nilsen confirmed this was by no means an isolated view. 'People in Kirkenes sometimes behave like people in Murmansk when there is something difficult,' he said. '"Putin, come and save us!" they cry.' It sounded like the old myth of a benevolent Tsar intervening to correct the evil his minions have done.

Hand in hand with this outlook, locals also expressed a lot of anger towards their own government. Many in eastern Finnmark saw Oslo as primarily at fault for Berg's situation. A consensus had emerged that he probably *was* working as a spy for the Norwegians, but that he was only a low-level courier and not himself an agent runner.[6] People were convinced that the pensioner had not been made aware of the true dangers. Thomas Nilsen told me, 'There are many who blame Norway for his arrest. "Forcing this civilian to do this kind of thing," they say, as if he didn't have his own will.' People I spoke to spontaneously namechecked the case as a perfect example of Norway's *storpolitikk* making trouble by meddling in local affairs to disastrous effect. The Norwegian intelligence agencies have a particularly bad reputation in eastern Finnmark. Throughout the Cold War the population suspected that Norway's own spies were monitoring them *en masse*, as collectively unreliable. When the Iron Curtain fell, the Norwegian king apparently visited the town and apologized personally for this decades-long slur.

I continued following Frode Berg's case after I left Kirkenes. I must say I had no confidence that President Putin would lift a finger to help the old man. On that basis, I wondered if his ongoing plight might serve as a small corrective to local belief in a friendly Russia. On the other hand, I doubted how much difference it would make if the population of eastern Finnmark suddenly did become more honest about their fears of Russia or voiced more loudly their disapproval of its actions.

Thomas Nilsen pointed out that Norway was in a weak position when it came to Berg's incarceration because it lacked a high-profile Russian prisoner to trade for its man – that being the traditional way for East–West spy stories to resolve themselves. The St Petersburg 'spy-whale' that local fishermen had recently caught, Thomas felt, was unlikely to be a sufficient prize to secure Berg's release.

But then in late 2019 I heard on a BBC news bulletin that Frode Berg had indeed been freed. He was one of five spies who were swapped in a three-way deal that saw two Lithuanians and Berg exchanged for two Russians who had been in prison in Lithuania.[7] I knew that many in Kirkenes would think Putin really had smiled on them, especially since Norway itself did not free anyone. Apparently, the Russian Foreign Minister, Sergei Lavrov, had personally visited the town just a month before and told locals he was hopeful that a solution could soon be reached.

What could the people of Kirkenes do if Russia decided to march across their border? Or permanently to jam their GPS signal? Or arrest more of their townsfolk when they crossed into Russia using their permits? Or a host of other hostile acts? Assuming that locals are, relatively speaking, powerless in these and other scenarios, many are likely to continue to determine that it is better to try to keep on Russia's good side (however implausible that now sounds), to tread carefully at the door to the bear's lair for fear of attracting its attention. What the release of Frode Berg suggested, even as Russia pitilessly stirred up trouble elsewhere, was that the bear was happy, at least for the time being, to continue colluding in this fiction.

3

Porkkala, Finland

I woke with a jolt and sat upright in bed, lucky not to whack my head against the top bunk as I did so. My sleep had been interrupted by a sudden attack of unfamiliar noise and light: a prolonged roar just a few metres from the foot of the bed and a strong strobing beam filling the entire room, similar to a cinema projector's once the film has completely run through.

It took me a few seconds to remember where I was – which country as well as which building – and then another moment to realize that the cause of the disturbance was the railway tracks outside. Despite my host describing them a few hours earlier as 'basically unused now', they were, in fact, being used by a huge freight train. It was 2 a.m. I felt irrationally cross as one tends to when disturbed in the middle of the night, but then relieved that the racket was nothing more sinister. I slid out of bed and stumbled to the window just in time to see the last wagons thunder into the darkness.

I was in Mustio, a tiny Finnish village also known by the Swedish name Svartå. It lies 60 kilometres west of Helsinki and over 300 kilometres away from the Russian border, and I was staying in its former railway station on a line that really did last see passenger traffic in 1983. The station is owned by a couple who live in one half and rent out the other to holidaymakers; a self-contained apartment including a beautiful historic ticket office and waiting room. As the bunk beds indicated, it was a place intended for multiple occupancy (up to eight at a time), but I was alone. I had already found the set-up somewhat eerie as I sat reading in the living room earlier in the evening with a large collection of wooden and papier-mâché puppets as my only company. Maybe it was a bit less strange than it sounds because the station's owners were professional puppeteers. Nonetheless, when I ventured back into the living area to get a glass of water after the train had passed, I got a fresh shock from the dead-eyed marionettes staring back at me in the moonlight.

In its way, my unusual, unsettling accommodation was a fitting preparation for the weekend ahead. I had come to Finland to see Porkkala, an unusual and once very unsettled part of the country that became Soviet in the 1940s despite being very far from the Soviet border. It is a place that has retained unexpected traces from that time, both in its landscape and in the minds of a few now elderly locals. But outside Finland almost no one has heard anything about Soviet Porkkala.

Porkkala is farming country. Its fields are planted with crops. Amid the gently rolling hills, woodlands are dotted with cottages. It is pretty but not excessively so. Traversed by the great King's Road that linked the main cities and towns of the Swedish Empire – from Bergen in the west via Stockholm, Turku and Helsinki to Vyborg in the east – it was a location that many important people passed through down the centuries but where few stopped for more than a change of horses and a night's rest.

During the first half of the twentieth century, Porkkala unexpectedly became a site of great strategic importance thanks to its long peninsulas jutting into the Baltic Sea. These combine with the Estonian coastline to form the narrowest point in the mouth of the Gulf of Finland, a key feature that navies of different countries began to want to exploit either to threaten or protect the city of St Petersburg (later Petrograd, later still Leningrad) at the gulf's eastern end. During the interwar period, newly independent Finland and Estonia drew up plans to mine the channel, just 40 kilometres wide and unusually shallow, in the hope of preventing Soviet warships from playing a full role in future conflicts.[1] In the Second World War, the Germans worked with the Finns to put the same plan into action and added an extra dimension: a double net stretched across the gulf from Porkkala to the Estonian island of Naissaar to block in Soviet submarines too.

The genesis of Soviet Porkkala was this barrier's effectiveness. Even though the USSR would ultimately fight through it, Soviet admirals wanted to ensure that such a block on their freedom of movement could never be repeated. In 1944 Moscow decided that the only way to guarantee this was to seize the land on both sides of the narrows. Estonia was now entirely within the Soviet Union. In Finland, the USSR decided it would be enough to occupy just Porkkala.

The determination about how much land to take was a perfect illustration of the Soviet Union's unrivalled position more generally at the end of the Second World War, and particularly of the personal supremacy of Joseph Stalin. It was Stalin who set the size and shape of the exclave that Finland would lease to the Soviets for fifty years, and he did so by simply taking his pen and drawing the borders he desired on a map. The act, which was subsequently ratified in official agreements, was in the worst traditions of European imperialism. It is unusual to see the approach used on the territory of Europe itself: straight lines and crisp angles put down without reference to physical

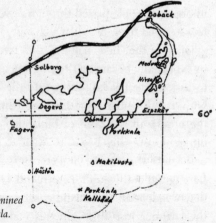

Joseph Stalin's own pen determined the shape of Soviet Porkkala.

geography, pre-existing boundaries or population settlements; a miniature version of the arbitrary frontiers drawn for Africa in the 1885 Berlin Conference or for the Middle East in the Sykes–Picot Agreement of 1916.

The Finns tried to resist, of course. The Porkkala territory was less than 25 kilometres from the centre of Helsinki. They offered an alternative site that would have put the Soviet armed forces further from the capital, but they had no leverage over Moscow. Before the end of 1944 the Finnish residents of Porkkala had had to gather their belongings and leave, supplanted by a new community of Red Fleet sailors and submariners, Soviet army soldiers, Soviet civilians and thousands of German prisoners of war.[2] In just a few months the population of Porkkala swelled fivefold to 50,000. For administrative purposes the territory was re-zoned, becoming the new westernmost and disconnected part of Leningrad Province.

I crossed into the former Soviet territory just a few minutes' drive from my railway station. It was impossible to say exactly where the frontier had run because, like the exclave's history more generally, it is not marked. The one institution that has made the Soviet occupation a focus is a tiny museum that feels like a time capsule of the 1940s and 1950s. The Degerby Igor Museum opened in 1997 in an old wooden outhouse in the village of Degerby. It once lay right at the centre of Soviet territory. The museum has since spread to occupy an adjacent former municipal hall. I was meeting one of its curators, Berndt Gottberg, a sturdy, ruddy-faced man in his seventies who had promised to lead me through the collection and then take me in his van to see other traces of Soviet rule in Porkkala.

Berndt has dedicated decades to studying the Soviet presence. As I started to look over the exhibits, he explained to me that the main reason the territory had changed hands was because the USSR was insistent it would never be invaded again. The

Bolshevik state had existed for almost thirty years by the time it took Porkkala. Through all that period, the country had either felt an attack was imminent or actually been under attack. Most devastatingly, the war against the Nazis eventually killed 27 million Soviet citizens and left large swathes of the country in ruins.

By occupying Porkkala the Kremlin was trying to neutralize a specific threat to its ships and submarines. But, Berndt said, it was also, just as in its occupation of East Germany, Czechoslovakia, Hungary and Poland, trying to ensure that future aggressors would have to engage its military long before they got near Soviet soil. The new outposts together constituted a buffer zone, intended to keep the USSR well out of harm's way. Stalin's wartime allies, Churchill and Roosevelt, had agreed in principle to this zone but both they and their successors would watch with growing horror as the reality of it – and of the Iron Curtain that was its boundary – took shape.

Berndt talked me through the upgrades the Soviets had made at Porkkala: massively expanding the pre-existing submarine base, installing a fresh chain of gun batteries along the coast, and digging out an enormous new headquarters 100 metres underground where they planned to run complex, perhaps even international, operations. He later showed me a large expanse of flat land they had ringed with hidden pillboxes. Soviet soldiers were supposed to lie in wait in these if enemy forces entered the plain. Once the enemies were all inside, they would be wiped out by the encircling Soviet troops with no chance to escape.

Berndt had some admiration for these developments but said much of the craftsmanship ought really to be attributed to the German POWs who had been forced to do the work. More generally, the main lesson he felt I should take from Soviet Porkkala – both from its physical remains and the stories he had been able to collect – related to the occupiers' wild, rough ways and their barbaric treatment of the area's nature and pre-existing culture. Berndt pointed out a display of photographs of ruined forests where only stumps and dislodged roots survived. This, he told me, was the part of Porkkala where the Soviets had practised shelling with live ammunition. The after-effects were still being felt. Elsewhere, he said, the ending of normal forest management had allowed venomous vipers to return and, in just a matter of a few years, to become endemic. Several good farmhouses had become no-good bars. If I dug in the ground anywhere near them, he said, I was guaranteed to hit a thick layer of vodka bottles. At least two other buildings were repurposed as brothels, most likely one for officers and another for other ranks.

Out in Berndt's van, our first stop was the imposing Sjundby Slot, a fortified manor dating back some 450 years. This was a headquarters for Soviet border guards. As we arrived, wet snow began falling and Berndt, who had already secured a key from the owner, ushered me quickly through the heavy main doors into a dark stone vestibule. We climbed to the first floor, a grand *piano nobile*. Back in the 1940s this had been the control room for patrols. Soviet officers had sat here at desks, receiving reports and issuing orders. Typewriters had clacked; signals equipment bleeped and crackled. I tried to imagine the thrum of it all taking place beneath the ornate woodwork and frescoes, like a continuation of scenes in hundreds of commandeered *schlosses* and manors across wartime Europe. But Berndt informed me that during the occupation almost all the original decoration had been destroyed. What I was looking at was a reproduction. The occupiers had also lifted the floorboards in one corner upstairs so that the resulting hole could be used as a toilet. For whatever reason, they had chosen to ignore the existing lavatories on the ground floor. Berndt smiled. Finns, after they were allowed back into Porkkala, found many similar 'ecological bombs' scattered across the territory.

Over the road, the manor's dairy was as pretty as a picture in the snow. Three walls still bore vestiges of painted Russian slogans, frescoes too in their way and a testimony, Berndt thought, to the fact that the land alongside had served as a kind of parade ground. On two walls were warnings about the need for troops to show discipline and self-sacrifice, while on a third – the dairy's lovely broad gable – a wider range of symbols clustered, including a red star and a May Day greeting.

We drove on a couple of kilometres and Berndt was soon pointing out yet another crime against heritage: a little house where the first novel in Finnish had been written by the author Aleksis Kivi. Berndt said that, when it handed over the territory, the Finnish government had specifically asked the USSR to look after this building. But 'of course', he continued, it ended up ruined like so much else. Today's structure is a replica.

It wasn't hard to discern that Berndt held the Soviets in low regard. During our time together he didn't exactly exhibit

The walls of the dairy at Sjundby Slot retain traces of Soviet slogans.

malice towards them. In fact, he seemed to extend more of a patronizing sympathy. But he clearly felt these occupiers had fallen well short of the kind of stewardship that any group of humans ought to show any piece of land. They had led lives dominated by terrible iron discipline, he told me, and their principal response was to drink as much alcohol as they could. I was perfectly prepared to believe that this was indeed a common response to the pressures of Stalinism. But for me the destruction Berndt described was not as unique as it seemed to him. In fact, it sounded pretty typical of occupying forces anywhere. A military's priorities are never those of local civilians. I had read of armed forces leaving historic buildings in ruins all over the world. The Soviet army and navy in Porkkala had done the same.

And there are artefacts surviving in the territory that suggest a more sophisticated side to the occupation as well. There is the church in the little town of Kirkkonummi which was deconsecrated but used as a culture hall for plays, lectures and musical performances. On at least one occasion Tchaikovsky's ballet *Swan Lake* was staged there ('Stalin's favourite ballet,' Berndt told me as we stood beside his van looking at the building). Not far away, a coloured metal archway lingers in a wood. It used to be the entrance to a stadium where sports competitions took place. There are also photographs that Berndt has collected, documenting the ordinary lives of Porkkala's military and civilian personnel, showing their simple friendships, country outings and other pastimes. In one, an open-air performance of Chekhov's *Uncle Vanya* is under way. In another, two friends pose in a motorcycle and sidecar. Others bear witness to the presence of women and children and the existence of family life.

In advance of my visit, I had told Berndt that I would like to understand more about the 10,000 Finnish citizens who had fled Porkkala in 1944. Their fate seemed the opposite of what had

Friends pose in a motorcycle and sidecar in Soviet-occupied Porkkala.

happened to the Norwegians in eastern Finnmark, where the Soviet liberation had stopped short of permanent occupation and locals had been able to continue with their lives.

Back once more in the museum, Berndt introduced me to Bengt Ull, who had experienced the evacuation as a small child and was now a little older than Berndt at seventy-eight. Over tea and cake Bengt recalled riding in a Red Cross truck away from the family farm. 'We were given pancakes when we arrived on the other side of the new frontier,' he said, as a welcome gift. Apparently the Swedish Red Cross had co-ordinated most moves out of the territory, not just the human residents but also around 8,000 farm animals. Bengt's father had then taken several months to find fresh farmland for the family to live on and several more years to fix up the new farm's dilapidated farmhouse, which was initially infested with insects.

Bengt's parents hadn't talked much about the life they lost. 'It's a Finnish tradition not to talk much,' Bengt reminded me with a smile. But he knew that they harboured little hope of returning home anytime soon. Under the terms of the original deal, Finland was to forego Porkkala until 1994, a date which seemed impossibly distant. Sometimes Finnish politicians on the radio or in the press would talk of wanting to alter the settlement but most people didn't believe a word of it.

The loss of Porkkala affected people much further afield as well. Stalin's hand-drawn frontier had cut a swathe through the main railway line from Helsinki to Turku, postwar Finland's two principal cities. From 1944 to 1947 no Finnish trains were allowed to run through, meaning that what had for decades been a routine trip became an awkward journey involving replacement bus services and lengthy detours by road. In 1947 a Finnish government minister had gone to Moscow, very much cap in hand, and asked the Soviets for a concession. A deal was struck so passenger services could resume. It seems the USSR partly agreed because the Finns would now pay a transit fee, in precious hard currency, for every train that went through.

But the humiliation of occupation became even more visible after services resumed. Because the Soviets deemed Porkkala a sensitive military zone, no passenger could be permitted to see into the area. Every Finnish train was obliged to lower its blinds while it crossed. The blinds typically stayed down for about forty minutes and, further to discourage anyone from sneaking a look or, worse still, attempting to leave the train, guards with sub-machine-guns were positioned in each carriage.[3] Some dubbed this bizarre state of affairs 'the longest train tunnel in the world'. In its quiet, rural way, it was a prefiguration of the more famous Cold War situation a few years later in Berlin, where trains also ran without stopping through foreign territory and also crisscrossed the Iron Curtain.

Berndt, Bengt and I had started talking about the train line because we were sitting beneath an original Finnish railways sign that is one of the Degerby museum's most precious acquisitions. It warns passengers in Finnish and Swedish that 'when the train is passing through the PORKKALA AREA, it is STRICTLY FORBIDDEN to stand in the front of the carriage or at the carriage entrance or to make any attempt to view the landscape outside the train'. Berndt now spoke up again and revealed that he had travelled frequently through Soviet Porkkala in his mother's womb. His mother later told him what a hostile experience it was. Once when pregnant she was sitting beside another pregnant woman who suddenly went into labour. Anywhere else along the route, the train would have stopped quickly so help could be summoned. But in Porkkala that was impossible. The train trundled on until it had safely exited the Soviet territory with Berndt's mother doing her best to calm the panicking woman. All the while she was thinking that she must not find herself on this train when her own baby – when Berndt – decided to arrive.

On 5 March 1953 Stalin died and the whole world waited to see what could possibly fill the enormous vacuum he had left. In Porkkala there were only small changes to start with. In certain places the border became more porous. This did not yet mean

A bilingual sign from a Finnish train carriage, warning passengers that it was forbidden to look outside while transiting Soviet Porkkala.

that trains could go through with their blinds raised. Rather, it was black market commerce that initially flourished, made possible by the diminishing culture of fear among Soviet troops. At isolated stretches of the frontier Soviet cement and vodka were now traded for Finnish cigarettes and food.

This continued through the rest of 1953, all of 1954 and the first half of 1955, but during that time there was no hint that the USSR's wider commitment to occupying Porkkala was wavering. Then quite suddenly, in August 1955, Finland's Soviet ambassador made a trip from his huge Helsinki embassy building – to this day a Stalinist edifice that takes up an entire block of the city centre – to the presidential palace and told the Finnish president, Juho Kusti Paasikivi, that the Soviet government was ready to return Porkkala if a broader settlement could be reached about Finland's future relations with the USSR.[4] Paasikivi was astonished by the news which was completely unexpected to him. He and his prime minister, Urho Kekkonen, then travelled together to Moscow in mid-September for bilateral talks. They had planned for an attritional battle that might last months and might easily end in failure. But after just a few days the entire proceedings wrapped up with both sides declaring themselves satisfied with the results.[5]

According to the two treaties the Finns and Soviets signed on 19 September 1955, Finland could have Porkkala back as soon as the end of January 1956. In return, Finland agreed to remain neutral and unaligned with the USA or NATO for at least twenty years. All Soviet military personnel would leave Finnish territory and the country would be allowed to join the Nordic Council, a body that was fostering co-operation between the democracies of northern Europe. The whole of Finland was jubilant. The most gaping of the country's Second World War wounds could now begin to heal. The political manoeuvrings that had brought this about were richly rewarded by Finnish voters both immediately and long into the future. When

Paasikivi retired as president in 1956, Kekkonen succeeded him and remained in post until 1982.

The achievement had the biggest impact on the thousands who could now go back to their homes in Porkkala. For Bengt, in his mid-teens, the day the deal was done was unforgettable. He recalled to me how it coincided with his sister's tenth birthday. The whole family, except his mother who had died a couple of years earlier, was gathered in the farmhouse as the news broke on the radio. Looking around the room, Bengt saw shocked faces. All of them knew instantly that they would move back to their own farm, back to a place that only one of them, Bengt's father, could really remember. They had spent eleven years improving a new property and fashioning a new livelihood for themselves, and they had absolutely no idea what would await them. But, like so many exiles in other times and places, they were determined to return.

Why did the USSR's new leader, Nikita Khrushchev, let go of Porkkala with such apparent ease? There are two reasons, one specific and one general. First, the exclave's specific strategic value had dropped. It was no longer so important to ensure that Soviet ships and submarines could sail freely in and out of Leningrad, because the country's vital theatres of operations had shifted. The relative importance of ports in the Barents Sea was growing and there were new naval bases on the Baltic coast of Latvia and Lithuania, well away from the bottleneck of the Gulf of Finland. Secondly, Khrushchev was keen to change the nature of the USSR's buffer zone generally. From his point of view a wide buffer remained essential to Soviet security, but he and his advisors thought they had spotted a clever way to reduce the costs of maintaining it.

For the most part, the Soviet Union's buffer was comprised of countries with friendly communist regimes – Czechoslovakia, Hungary, Poland, and so forth. In such countries the possibility of hostility towards the USSR was precluded by every aspect of state law and culture, beginning with the occupying Red Army and the close ties that existed between local secret police forces and the Soviet KGB and ending with widespread pro-Soviet propaganda targeted at local populations from nursery school onwards. In just a small number of places the situation was more complex. In parts of Finland and Austria the Soviets had an occupying army, but the state itself was a multi-party democracy with a free press and a capitalist economy. In Germany, meanwhile, the two types of system co-existed uneasily, with a one-party communist state in the East and a multi-party democracy in the West, and a divided old capital, Berlin.

Hawks in the Soviet elite always argued that any territory the USSR possessed should never be given up. But Khrushchev knew that he needed to save money and, no less importantly, try to alter international attitudes towards the country he ran. Hence he adopted this new strategy which historians have called 'neutralism'. Returning Porkkala entailed a long-term agreement which had the effect of turning the whole of Finland neutral. Finland got its territory back, but it also had its foreign policy choices meaningfully curtailed for at least twenty years: no NATO membership and not even the possibility of NATO members carrying out operations or exercises on Finnish soil.

Khrushchev achieved something very similar in Austria the same year. Again at his instigation, a new treaty was signed between the Austrian government and the four powers that had run the country since 1945. Finnish historian Risto Penttilä has written that the 1955 withdrawals from Austria and Porkkala were together 'an integral part of a long-term Soviet effort to turn "neutralism" in Europe to its own advantage'.[6] Khrushchev seems to have hoped to tempt other states that were already in NATO away from the Alliance in return for a quieter life. At the same time, he beefed up the multinational defence arrangements that existed between countries the USSR fully controlled: the Warsaw Pact, a direct counterpart to NATO, was created in May 1955.[7]

The Soviet leader envisaged a two-tier buffer, with a primary layer of fraternal states protecting the USSR's main border in continental Europe and a second layer of neutral countries keeping the Americans still further at bay. The ultimate goal may have been to see Germany reunified on the condition that the whole country became neutral. It was, after all, the NATO bases in West Germany that Moscow feared the most. Abandoning the fraternal state of East Germany might have been a price worth paying as far as the Kremlin was concerned if such an outcome could be achieved.

Up to this point almost all Cold War diplomacy had involved threats of escalation – and actual escalation – from both sides. Khrushchev's 1955 change of direction deserves attention because it was an attempt to do something different. Even if it was applied inconsistently and did not succeed in its ultimate aims, in Finland its effects were enduring.

The Soviet exodus from Porkkala proceeded with exceptional haste. On 24 January 1956 the occupying forces threw a farewell party in the exclave's one guesthouse. Kekkonen himself attended and much vodka was drunk and many toasts raised. Just two days later the Soviets had gone and Finns re-entered what had for over a decade been hidden from them behind fences and train blinds. From what Berndt and Bengt said, it wasn't so much a case of the coffee still steaming on the stove as of the smoke still rising from the wreckage.

Bengt said that almost nothing of his family home and outbuildings survived. The transformation was so great that his father could not at first be sure where the structures had been in 1944. 'We started again like pioneers,' Bengt went on. 'We had to make a fresh start twice.' A huge cast-iron kettle was the only sign of recent habitation they found on the farm. Then, a few weeks after moving back, Bengt's father discovered the family's sauna intact but transported to another property. For two years they laboured to reconstruct the family home. 'We did a good job,' Bengt says. 'I'm still living there today.' All the while other families were returning and uncovering their own surprises. As well as the vipers and the areas that had been shelled, ten corpses had been left behind in the former Soviet military hospital. Berndt's shock at this was still fresh after all these years. 'How could they depart without giving their comrades a decent burial?' he asked. 'How could they?'

Porkkala recovered and reintegrated with the rest of Finland relatively quickly. The whole country meanwhile settled into its new relationship with the USSR. I have spoken to many Finns about this relationship over the years. Overwhelmingly they see the exchange that Paasikivi and Kekkonen made – guaranteed neutrality for territorial integrity – as a sensible one, a pragmatic recognition of Finland's strength relative to the Soviet Union and an achievement that left the country free to pursue democracy and increase its prosperity. Berndt and Bengt both agreed.

Yet the Finnish template did not strike everyone as a good idea and was not always plain sailing either. A pejorative term, 'Finlandization', was coined to describe any country that enjoyed technical independence but had to abide by the USSR's rules. Critics said that Finlandized states accepted they could play no meaningful part in global superpower disputes, irrespective of the moral or strategic issues at stake. When the West German government pursued rapprochement with some Eastern European countries in the 1970s, it was accused by some in NATO's camp of flirting with Finlandization. In the 1980s, when politicians and peace activists in a slew of nations demanded their countries go nuclear-free and send resident US forces home, they too were warned that the result could be the zombie condition of Finlandization. The Finnish political scientist Mika Aaltola likened it to being a well-fed lion caged in a zoo.[8]

There is something to be said for both sides of this argument, depending on which feature of the Cold War you focus on. Finland or Austria were never going to be able to stand up to the USSR alone. With the Soviet army already *in situ* they were also never likely to be allowed to join NATO. In such circumstances, being permitted to pursue an autonomous domestic policy free from forces of occupation was positive. On the other hand, if the Soviet Union had managed to woo just a few NATO members to accept the same settlement, the Alliance's overall impact would have diminished markedly. In a context where the Warsaw Pact continued to be strong and united, that would have meant a major tilting of the balance in Moscow's favour. One can see how President Putin's recent calculations have trod similar intellectual ground but he seems constantly to reach different conclusions to Khrushchev about the relative merits of inducements and threats.

To idolize Finland's post-1955 situation would be wrong. A pro-government Finnish election broadcast in 1967 said the country had chosen to be 'a doctor rather than a judge', suggesting somewhat piously that it had deliberately opted for a higher path than those nations that regularly opposed the Soviet bloc.[9] Day-to-day reality was grubbier. The self-censoring, lip-biting, non-judgemental approach was the only one the USSR allowed. Neutrality meant constant effort to remain in the USSR's good books. According to the Finnish political scientist Tuomo Martikainen, Finland's entire political elite from the 1950s to the 1980s 'went overboard in terms of friendliness to the Soviets'.[10] Any ambitious Finn in politics, in the media or in the trade unions made sure to befriend a Soviet diplomat in order to avoid hitting a Kremlin-imposed glass ceiling. These Soviet connections became known as '*kotiryssä*' or 'home Russians'. Naturally enough, a significant number were spies, meaning that, consciously or not, many Finns ended up acting as informants.

The best evidence that Finlandization was no picnic is the collective sigh of relief the nation exhaled at the end of the Cold War. People were glad to be free of what had been a bearable but nevertheless troubling period. But, to this day, the legacy of compromise remains only partially worked through. The bestselling novelist and critic Sofi Oksanen has made Finlandization a focus for her work. With a Finnish father and an Estonian mother who fled the USSR in the 1970s, Oksanen sees the phenomenon from both sides. For her it is the censorship, self-censorship and promulgation of myths that is most striking and may have done greatest long-term damage inside Finland itself.

'The Ministry of Education prevented the spread of negative information about the Soviet Union, especially in history books,' she writes. 'The Soviet Union always had to be described in a flattering way. Schoolchildren were, for example, taught that agricultural collectivization in the Soviet Union took place entirely on a voluntary basis, that the Prague Spring was caused by "a counter-revolutionary threat", and that socialism in the Soviet Union worked well . . . According to the school books, "The Red Army liberated the Baltic States from German occupation and these states joined the Soviet Union as its new republics." None of this was true, but we were taught that it was.'

In recent years she felt Finland continued to let Russia off the hook despite the great escalation in Kremlin provocations. This was because appeasement had become second nature: 'The long-term work of Finlandization ate away at our ability to take a stand against Russia . . . The language of that time seemed to hail from a toothless mouth with no tongue. The Soviet Union trained Finland to become a country in which we obediently dodge inappropriate expressions towards Russia; this approach is now wedged in our subconscious . . . Finlandization still generates our reality.'[11]

*

As I left Mustio railway station the morning after my tour with Berndt, I headed first for the tip of the Porkkala peninsula. It was a crisp morning and the previous day's snow had been replaced by bracing wind and razor-sharp visibility. This part of Porkkala was the reason the Soviets had wanted the territory in the first place. Near here, the huge anti-submarine nets had once been tethered. It is now a well-tended nature reserve. On my way from the car park to the coast I encountered other Sunday walkers, many with Nordic poles. At the place where the land meets the sea there was yet more evidence of purposeful leisure: a large group of Finnish scouts was on a weekend camping expedition. A few scouts were cleaning up after breakfast, sorting rubbish into recyclable and non-recyclable piles and washing saucepans with water from canteens. Others were collaborating on a new wooden shelter that was being built directly on the rocks. It was made of bright yellow pine cut into geometric blocks, and the effect in the bright sunshine was similar to an M. C. Escher drawing.

My mind went back to the start of 1956. I tried to imagine the scene of chaos that the USSR had left behind. Perhaps there had been ordnance strewn over the rocks. Perhaps I would have seen vipers in the woodland I had just walked through. Now all was neatness and peaceful order. The Cold War was out of sight and out of mind and the Iron Curtain was a phantom presence, only revealing itself to those, like me, who deliberately went in search of it. Even contemporary Russia, troublesome and perplexing, was just far enough off to be forgotten most of the time.

Berndt would no doubt have been thrilled at the scouts' tidy industry, I thought, and all the pristine nature in this once devastated landscape. I suspect he would also have used it as yet further illustration of the essential differences between Finnish and Russian culture. But the question of who is civilized and who is wild is truly a vexed one. To me it didn't seem particularly helpful to divide the world into goodies and baddies, however tempting or even pressing it can sometimes feel to do so. I could already see that in matters pertaining to the Iron Curtain there could be no definitive answer to the question of who was right and who was wrong. But was admitting this my own kind of self-imposed neutrality, I wondered. My own Finlandization? Or was it just the relativism and equivocation that comes with specific examples and extra detail? Nervously anticipating my own first encounter with the Russian frontier for thirteen years, I could not reach a conclusion there and then. There would be plenty more time to decide whether I wanted to be doctor or judge or someone else.

4

Vyborg, Russia

The Allegro train departed Helsinki at 11 o'clock in the morning and spent the next ninety minutes making rapid progress across the east of Finland. It was busy: a mixture of local Finns and Russians and some big foreign tour groups as well as a scattering of backpackers and solo travellers like me. I had opened a book on my lap but was paying it little attention, preoccupied instead by the border ahead and the vast country beyond, a place that constantly took up space in my mind but that I was now about to visit for the first time in ages.

After their rapprochement in 1955, the border between Finland and the USSR was technically open. Train and road crossings existed for those with visas, and the number of people transiting increased over time. Nevertheless, it remained a tense Iron Curtain frontier, highly militarized and comprised of a series of windswept checkpoints where travellers felt literally and metaphorically exposed. On the Soviet side, transit times were random, questioning abrupt and intrusive, and processes intentionally opaque. Individuals were meant to feel that they had had a brush with a mighty, all-knowing superpower. If the border guards had a softer side – which, of course, many must have – they were well schooled at hiding it. All who came into contact with them met grim poker faces locked beneath iconic wide-brimmed caps.

In the summer of 1986 Mark Kramer, who is now a Harvard academic specializing in the Cold War, can recall taking a train from Helsinki to Leningrad and grinding to a halt on the Soviet side of the frontier. When border guards reached his carriage they proceeded to check his luggage item by item. They said they were worried he might be smuggling Bibles. They found none but went on to dismantle his entire compartment as well, just in case he had managed to stash banned books or other contraband in its walls during the short journey. The operation took ages. For the sake of a few pages, as late as 1986, an entire international passenger service was delayed.[1]

Fast-forward fifteen years to the start of the 2000s, and the USSR was long gone. The border infrastructure had significantly deteriorated, which seemed to suggest, at least at a glance, that there had probably been some relaxation in procedures. The border guards had new uniforms which looked of exceptionally poor quality; they definitely lacked the visible menace of former times. And yet when I crossed the border several times in 2002 and 2003 I experienced it much as Kramer had. I could have brought in as many Bibles as I liked by then, but the air of acute suspicion and the willingness to delay a train indefinitely had persisted.

I can still hear the wheels screeching to a halt in that clearing in the birch forest. The spot was parallel with an old one-storey office block set well back from the tracks. As we would stop, a detachment of border guards, both male and female, would always start walking towards us in a long straggly line, picking their way across the weeds, rocks and disused platforms, all the while taking long drags on what would probably be their last cigarettes for an hour. They would board the train at several points and work systematically through. All surly, they would shout for each passenger to sit with his or her luggage, and bark still louder if someone seemed not to understand. Occasionally they instructed passengers to unpack everything. They would then watch as the person held up each item in turn, sometimes demanding to know what it was. In the case of bottles of perfume or alcohol, people always had to remove the lids. Alsatian dogs sometimes boarded. On one occasion, as a dog ran through my carriage he halted at the rucksack of an American student and turned his head towards it, signalling drugs. The rucksack was seized along with the student and her three companions, all removed from the train and conveyed back over the scrubland to the office block. Our train finally began moving a few minutes later but my mind stayed with the students all the way to St Petersburg, and I wondered about them often in the days that followed.

I was thinking about them again as I braced myself for the border, now almost three decades since the USSR's collapse. I had got my documents ready. Procuring a visa for this leg of the journey had been one the most difficult parts of my preparation. Utility bills, bank statements, a tourist voucher, print-offs of my travel insurance terms and conditions, and several hundred pounds in fees had been required, along with an in-person appearance at a processing centre in London. No other country I was going to, including Albania, Turkey and the former Soviet republic of Azerbaijan, had had anything like as much bureaucracy. I was only too aware that the more complicated the paperwork, the more chance there was I would have made a mistake.

As the frontier approached I was also reflecting on how Russia's relations with most of the rest of Europe had deteriorated since my last visit in 2006. Putin's regime had become markedly more hostile towards the nations of the old West and towards its own near neighbours than it had been back then. There were cases like Frode Berg's and Thomas Nilsen's to consider, and I also found myself worrying about the negative assessments of Putin and his government that I had made in my book about the Beslan school siege. Until just before boarding I had told myself that I could miss out this stage of the journey and visit Russia at a later date. But I knew that was wrong. The point of the trip was to experience the former Iron Curtain as it was today, for good and ill.

Finland's border guards boarded the train first, at Kouvola, and swiftly went about their business. The train kept moving as they performed their checks. One briefly glanced at my passport and waved it under a handheld scanner. They all disembarked just shy of the border at the tiny Finnish station of Vainikkala. We then rolled slowly forwards. An announcement in three languages stated that we had now entered the restricted zone and would soon be crossing into Russia. The WiFi signal would drop, it said, and we would need to register our mobile phone numbers in order to regain access. (This is a key surveillance feature of the Russian regime.)

I watched through the window as the train drew near to and then ran parallel with the border for a few hundred metres, the blue-and-white and red-and-green border posts aligned on my right. We then took a sharp right turn and cut through the posts. Finland was behind us and we were in Russia. I kept waiting for the train to stop and looking out for the old office block, which did not appear. The train was picking up speed again. Then it seemed to be back at full speed. How could this be? There had been no Russian checks of any kind. I realized I had been holding my breath and clutching my documents so tight that my fingers hurt.

After a few more minutes, we pulled into the station at Vyborg, the first city inside Russia. This was my destination and so, completely uncertain about what to expect, I took my bags from the rack and headed towards the doors. Here finally I saw, through the glass, a dozen or so Russian border officers gathered on the platform, kitted out in uniforms that were much smarter than the ones they used to wear. When the doors opened, they stood back to let me and a handful of other passengers pass. One even nodded at us in what seemed to be a friendly gesture before they all got on the train. Up ahead on the platform, another official indicated to us where we should enter a door marked 'Passport Control'.

Only now did the penny drop. The Russians had abandoned the old office block and moved their railway checkpoint to Vyborg. Passengers disembarking at Vyborg now passed through the checks inside the station building itself. The vast majority of passengers, who were headed for St Petersburg, would have their documents checked *en route*, in the same way as the Finnish controls operated.

Would a difficult interrogation now ensue for me, I wondered. Not at all. In just a few minutes my passport and visa were checked and stamped by an officer who even smiled as he handed them back to me. Then the customs official didn't bother to glance at the screen as he put my bag through his scanner. And before half past one in the afternoon, I was shaking hands with Varvara, the owner of the flat I had rented, and we were stepping out into the bustling streets of Vyborg while she chattered about the difficult morning she had had at the kindergarten where she works.

My entry into Russia was only the first of many ways in which I found the country changed since my last visit. As Varvara and I walked and talked, I instantly saw other differences. High-polluting Moskvich and Zhiguli cars had been comprehensively replaced with Western makes. The tattered plastic bags Russians of all ages used to carry were now almost absent. People sported designer handbags and branded rucksacks. There was even the occasional cotton tote bag. Everyone had smartphones. The generalized crazes for barista-made coffee and coffee-to-go were taking hold. I could remember when Nescafé was the new kid in town.

As the visit went on I became aware of bigger shifts. I noticed how the professionally friendly norms of Western service culture had made inroads. If you have never experienced the offhand hostility of a Soviet-trained *offitsiant* or *offitsiantka*, you cannot fully appreciate how nice it is to be greeted with stock phrases and broad, insincere smiles when you enter a Russian restaurant.

And in a country where authoritarianism had definitely gained ground, the streets were paradoxically freer than previously of police and other uniformed personnel. In towns and cities across Russia in the 2000s, I would walk down the street and expect to see traffic police flagging down cars, regular police at the entrances and exits of metro stations checking people's documents, and detachments of OMON riot police in armoured jeeps waiting for trouble. On the face of it – and even in 2019 I knew it was only on the face of it – Russia now seemed less policed and people abler to go about their daily business unmolested.

What unmistakably accompanies these developments is the establishment of a millions-strong middle class with upgraded expectations about living standards and an excitement for consumerism. These are not the notorious billionaire oligarchs. They are regular people, making spending and other lifestyle choices to suit themselves, using their limited but meaningful disposable income. Their fashion preferences, exercise regimes, social media fixations, and much else, usually originate outside Russia. A nation that became accustomed to setting norms – political, economic, social and, yes, even aesthetic – now cleaves to an international mainstream that is made elsewhere.

Of course, the legacy of communism lingers. On certain days, in certain places, in the minds of certain people, one feels it acutely. The main square in Vyborg is called Red Square and Lenin still stands at the top of it silently hectoring passersby. Varvara and I walked past his feet on the way to the flat. Later in the stay, when a contact emailed me and suggested we meet 'near Lenin on Red Square', I laughed: this was exactly the sort of phrase we had learned in the Soviet-produced textbooks of my youth.

As a rule of thumb, the further one goes from the centre of towns and cities, and the further away one gets from the big metropolises, the more Soviet it still feels. Eventually you reach places where the big changes seem not to have changed much at all. Puzzling over this reality – the self-contradictory reality of where Russia has taken herself since the USSR's demise, and what it means for ordinary Russians – occupied me a lot in Vyborg. Contradictions are a feature of any complex society, yet somehow it did not feel like the contradictions in Russia could safely go on co-existing.

Vyborg was the second biggest city in newly independent Finland in the interwar period, but the Soviet army seized it in June 1944 and it has been part of Russia ever since. Unlike Porkkala, Vyborg's annexation was always presented as a permanent one, and in 1947 Helsinki recognized this painful fact and relinquished all claims to it and the surrounding territory. As an entire population of Finns departed, a city's worth of new residents arrived. Being so close to the border, Vyborg developed large standing garrisons of Soviet troops too, and became a closed city. Stalin's regime promulgated ideology with particular ferocity here because it needed to ensure the loyalty of its borderlands.

Lenin still stands in Red Square in Vyborg but around him many aspects of life had changed greatly.

I got a glimpse into one part of what this had entailed at the small Lenin House Museum. It commemorates one of the places Lenin hid before the Bolshevik Revolution of 1917. When I went, a temporary exhibition was showing artefacts of everyday Stalinism. Among them a 1949 essay by an eleven-year-old local girl marked the occasion of Stalin's seventieth birthday. At the top was its title, 'Stalin, our leader, teacher and friend', alongside a picture of the man himself, cut from a magazine. The essay was fanatical throughout and built up to the following crescendo: 'On the day of comrade Stalin's seventieth birthday, I somehow feel my love for this wise man with special strength. If I could give my life to secure the eternal continuation of his life, I would consider it my duty. T. Mashanina, Year 4, Vyborg.'

It was only after 1953, when Khrushchev took over, that some metaphorical light and air began filtering into postwar Vyborg. The immediate threats of denunciation and imprisonment passed for most Soviet citizens, and the economy gradually began to make more modern consumer goods available. A mass programme of house-building commenced as well, resulting in the five-storey apartment blocks, nicknamed *khrushchyovki*, that still litter most former Soviet cities today.

Vyborg, like other closed places, benefited disproportionately from these developments. By some measures, it became one of the best places to live in the Soviet Union. My mental image of a closed Soviet city had once been one of restriction and greyness. I imagined people caught in dingy snow-globe existences, their eyes cast permanently downwards and their lives spent endlessly queuing for public transport that could only take them as far as the city limits. But Vyborg was not alone in being a place of significant privilege. Loyalty was especially important in closed cities – due to the sensitive scientific or military research that people carried out, or, in the case of Vyborg, the proximity of the border. After Stalin the Soviet authorities realized it was at least as important to give residents positive reasons to be loyal as well as threats and brainwashing.

When today's Russian pensioners look back on their own childhoods and young adulthoods, they often feel great nostalgia for the Khrushchev period in which they grew up. This is especially so in formerly closed places. At Vyborg Slot, the city's principal landmark, I encountered my first nostalgic person of the trip. The Slot is a Swedish castle dating from the thirteenth century. It occupies its own islet on the edge of the city centre and has a splendid main tower which gives panoramic views over Karelia and the Gulf of Finland. At the time of my visit the thick walls were also host to a perfectly preserved Brezhnev-era museum, complete with quotations from Engels carved on the walls.

I had just gingerly walked to the top of the tower, and even more gingerly back down, on a metal staircase that hung over a huge void, when I met Tatiana, a room attendant. She was probably in her mid-sixties and had the sort of dyed hair in a neat but severe crop that was common in the USSR of the 1980s (think Raisa Gorbachev).

'How did you like it up there?' she asked with a smile. I replied that it had been wonderful if a little windy and asked in return if she had noticed many changes in Vyborg over the years.

'They've ruined it,' she replied instantly. 'It was better when it was closed.'

She told me of the Vyborg she had grown up in and still loved. 'It was ours,' she said simply. This was clearly the best encapsulation she had found for the dislocation she now felt. After pausing she added, 'It was so clean and tidy.' The mayor himself used to walk the streets on foot apparently – '*on foot*,' she repeated for emphasis – checking that everything was in order. 'There was no rubbish in the park. Beautiful plants were put in the flowerbeds each spring, not the cheap stuff they chuck in them now. And there weren't all these people everywhere. We had exactly what we needed. We wanted for nothing. They were kinder times.'

We talked on. The list of things she missed grew longer. Bills for food and electricity were cheaper. People went to the theatre whenever they wanted. They had a holiday at the seaside each year. It did sound nice, and I could see she really felt that the new Russia had taken many of these benefits away from her or spoiled her enjoyment of them in some way.

She added that there were lots who felt like her, and she is right. In recent surveys more than two thirds of Russians aged fifty-five and over report that they regret the USSR's collapse. Among the most common reasons given are sadness about the loss of social trust after 1991, and the sense that society has become harsher ('they were kinder times').[2] Others cite nostalgia for the fact the USSR was a great power, and many say the country's break-up has separated them from family members and loved ones. If one were to consider only the crimes of the USSR – especially its crimes against its own people – or some of the things it banned people from doing or punished them for, one would struggle to understand why anybody could miss it. But that is not what people like Tatiana dwell on.

Nostalgia is a potent force across much of the world today, but particularly in Russia. It forms a major part of many Russian politicians' appeal to voters, none more so than the most important politician of all. I had no idea who Tatiana voted for, or even if she voted, but I did know that Putin had used nostalgia relentlessly over the years to try to hold onto the support of people like her.

Famously, he told the nation in 2005 that he viewed the collapse of the Soviet Union as 'the greatest geopolitical catastrophe of the century'. He personally experienced the draining away of Soviet power in East Germany in the late 1980s, and by all accounts it devastated him. In a chaotic Dresden in 1989 the young KGB officer called for Soviet military assistance to suppress protests. But the local Soviet garrison refused to assist him after the Kremlin did not indicate its support. 'Moscow is silent,' the garrison commander informed Putin.[3]

Tens of millions of Russians agree that the USSR's collapse was a catastrophe. Putin wants them to believe that he is the only person capable of preventing further catastrophic decline and also that he is uniquely willing to do what it takes to make Russia great again – doggedly, deviously, impressively. His audacious foreign policy serves this end. The 2008 invasion of Georgia and the 2014 incursion into eastern Ukraine were ways of showing that the Russian government still believed in the borders of the old Soviet Union. The annexation of Crimea literally proved Russia could still grow not just shrink. The superpower drug was highly addictive and the manner in which Russians were withdrawn from it at the start of the 1990s savage: 150 million people forced to go patriotic 'cold turkey'. Putin's overarching demand that Russia be shown more respect almost always plays well with these recovering imperialists. But, just as in the days of Soviet stagnation when Leonid Brezhnev was tempted into the quagmire of Afghanistan, there is the ever-present danger of self-delusion and overreach.

The moments from Soviet history that Putin has long chosen to emphasize are designed to appeal to Tatiana's generation. First among them is the victory in the Second World War. Known in Russia as the Great Fatherland War, it has been central to Soviet and Russian culture ever since 1945 – both because of the scale of the human sacrifice and because of its importance during the rest of the Soviet period. Most people agree that defeating the Nazis was the USSR's greatest feat. Any talk of Soviet war crimes – such as the Katyn Massacre or the systematic sexual violence that Soviet soldiers unleashed as they moved across Europe in 1944 and 1945 – is liable to see the speaker branded not just unpatriotic but a fascist sympathizer or neo-Nazi.

Of late, Putin's regime has supercharged its commemoration of the war. The generation that fought in the conflict has almost died out, yet official acts of remembrance have increased in scale and number. Some sceptics speak of victory mania (*pobedomaniya* in Russian). But the generations that recall attending mass acts of remembrance in their youth when veteran fathers, grandfathers and uncles were still alive welcome the renewed focus. As recently as 2010 the government made Vyborg a City of Military Glory and installed a major new war memorial here. Tatiana recommended I go and see it.

The role of Stalin in the 1945 victory was long downplayed, and for good reason. First, the dictator's wider record was appalling. Secondly, his 1939 pact with Hitler was one of the reasons the war started when it did. And thirdly, Stalin failed to prepare the USSR for Germany's 1941 invasion, making the scale of the country's human sacrifice much worse. Under Putin, however, the Great Leader has been benefiting from a steady rehabilitation. Stalin's positive achievements have increasingly been pushed to the forefront of public discourse, while his errors and crimes are clumsily concealed. Just a few months before my visit hundreds of people had gathered on Moscow's Red Square to mark the anniversary of the dictator's death. It is not easy to get permission for public demonstrations in Russia today but this one was allowed. When two activists approached the crowd and shouted that they were honouring an 'executioner of the people' and 'a murderer of women and children', it was they who found themselves detained by government security forces while the pro-Stalin demonstrators were allowed to continue.[4]

More sinisterly, in the Karelian town of Medvezhegorsk, a few hours from Vyborg, a local museum director, Sergei Koltyrin, was arrested on charges of child abuse when he objected to official attempts to reinterpret a historic site used under Stalin for mass burials.[5] The charges were widely believed to have been invented but Koltyrin was convicted and sentenced to nine years in prison and died there in 2020.[6]

It is increasingly easy to see why Putin wanted to rehabilitate a taboo figure like Stalin. He built an empire that subsequent Soviet leaders could only maintain or retreat from. He ruled for a very long time. He often got the better of foreign governments. And he was a leader for whom settling scores, uncovering conspiracies and governing by fear were second nature. The current ruler's most direct comments about his predecessor, made in a 2017 interview with the film director Oliver Stone, included the statement that 'excessively demonizing Stalin [was] a means to attack the Soviet Union and Russia' and shouldn't be done.[7] He went on to compare the dictator to Oliver Cromwell and Napoleon Bonaparte, suggesting that these historical figures were often celebrated in their home countries despite having blood on their hands. (Of course, no one alive now was personally harmed by either the British or French dictator.) An important strand of Putin's message has become that there is no shame in feeling nostalgic for, or even inspired by, Stalinism.

The general public, young and especially old, have seemed to respond to the new mood. In 2019 fully 70 per cent of Russians said they felt positively about the earlier dictator's role in Russian history, and 51 per cent said they felt excitement, respect or sympathy for him. These were Stalin's best ratings in at least twenty years. Then by 2021 60 per cent were saying they supported the creation of a new Stalin museum, and almost half said they wanted a new statue to him in a prominent place.[8] Perhaps with his own bloody wars of conquest and expansion in mind, Putin's PR machine has worked wonders for the old mass murderer.

Away from geopolitics, the nostalgia for simpler, more austere times is genuine for many older Russians. Putin genuinely misses the power and control of the Soviet Union's glory days, but his commitment to a simple, austere life is more doubtful. When I was at the top of Vyborg Slot's tower, with its panoramic views, there was one landmark in particular I was trying to pick out. The Villa Sellgren is a large mansion on a spit of land jutting into the Gulf of Finland. It became famous in the 1980s when a popular Soviet film, *The Adventures of Sherlock Holmes and Dr Watson: The Twentieth Century Approaches*, was shot there. Built in beautiful art nouveau style, the house fell derelict in the immediate post-Soviet period and the authorities gave permission for it to be re-zoned as private land and transformed into a luxury residence with tight security and high fences.

Scores of similar mansions have been built on formerly public land across the country, but the allegation with the new Villa Sellgren is that it belongs to Putin himself, held for him in secret through a warren of third parties and complex legal structures. Russia's most famous opposition politician, Alexei Navalny, and an independent television news company scored a viral internet success in 2017 by managing to source pictures of the 'improved' villa. It had tripled in size through the renovations and ended up with interiors shorn of all period detail.[9]

I could not locate the house from the top of the tower, and people I mentioned it to were tight-lipped about Putin's potential ownership. One quipped that she found it hard to imagine the president wanting to holiday much in western Leningrad Province. But the villa now has a private helipad, so it is unlikely local residents would see any presidential motorcade as he came and went. Whatever the truth, these claims and others like them do resonate with millions of Russians who feel they are at the mercy of greedy masters whose main interest is in feathering their own nests. A similar video in 2021, also from Navalny's movement, showed drone footage of an alleged private palace Putin had had built on the Black Sea. It gained 120 million views during its first nine months on YouTube.[10]

Putin has worked hard to remain untainted by the avarice

of the elite generally, cultivating the image of an ascetic public servant who deplores, and occasionally even punishes, his more grasping minions. When his own exorbitant tastes surface they risk damaging one of the cornerstones of his appeal. Society was stratified in Soviet times too, but the gap between top and bottom was much smaller. For many back then the main points of distinction were whether they were well-enough connected to get into a foreign currency shop or enjoy an annual trip to a spa. By contrast, the glamorous lives of their rulers today look absolutely otherworldly, and often grotesque, to average Russians.

Anyone determined to rule without end is walking a tightrope above the heads of the people they dominate. Their time in power can end very suddenly if enough of those down below decide to shake the pillars that hold the tightrope up. For most of his more than twenty years in power Putin has given his subjects some important reasons to avoid shaking the pillars: a restored sense of national pride; a return to the good old days of Russia being respected and feared on the world stage; an increased standard of living without the currency devaluations and savings wipeouts of the chaotic 1990s; and less everyday criminality. But Putin has also long been planning for the day when some of these tangible and intangible benefits disappear, or when they are no longer enough to keep the tightrope steady.

A new apparatus of terror has grown up inside Russia, intended to deter public opposition. Like other aspects of Putinism, this new police state borrows heavily from the old Soviet system and particularly the practices of the KGB. Alexei Navalny was meant to be dead and in his grave long ago, poisoned with a banned nerve agent that security officers smeared on his underpants. Instead, at the time of writing, he is languishing in prison. Others who looked like they might become lightning rods for dissent suffered similar fates. One of the earliest, the billionaire Mikhail Khodorkovsky, spent ten years in jail. Another, Boris

Nemtsov, was assassinated just metres from the Kremlin in 2015.

In Vyborg I spoke to a supporter of Navalny's opposition movement, who wished to remain anonymous. I am calling him Kolya. We met by prior arrangement in a large expanse of scrubland that wraps itself round one edge of the city centre. Kolya had just picked up his daughter from school and she played on her bicycle while we sat and talked. The wind was blowing strongly off the Baltic that day and as Kolya smoked one cigarette after another I could see his hand turning blue.

'Putin thinks he has everything stitched up in the country right now, and maybe he has,' Kolya said. 'Far too many people here are bewitched by his patriotism and most of the rest are terrified of what would come next if he left. We wouldn't get Gandhi or Merkel, not in Russia. We would just get someone even greedier and more corrupt. And all the oligarchs would fall out and we might end up with a civil war. That's what they think.'

What Kolya thought was that most Russians still hadn't noticed how unfree they were. A bit like the frog in the adage, they hadn't realized that the water around them had started to boil because the temperature had been increasing only gradually. '"So the government attacks the gays and the Jehovah's Witnesses," they say to themselves. "I do not want to be a gay or a Jehovah's Witness. So I am still fine." Only when they decide they are not fine will they see the situation they are in,' Kolya had concluded.

He had been feeling increasingly desperate. 'Even jokes have become dangerous again, like in Soviet times.' He related the story of Maria Motuznaya, a twenty-three-year-old from the Siberian city of Barnaul who was arrested for sharing light-hearted memes on VKontakte, Russia's equivalent of Facebook. One joke showed a group of nuns lighting cigarettes above the caption, 'Quick, while God isn't looking!' For this, Maria was accused of insulting the feelings of Orthodox Christians and placed on Russia's official list of extremists and terrorists. She has since fled the country.

'Living conditions have deteriorated a lot too lately,' Kolya went on. He described how the price of everyday goods had increased without wages keeping pace. In many countries if this happened people would protest in the street or change their government, he noted. 'But when even quite small numbers of people protest here, the government attacks them savagely, with sticks, tear gas and rubber bullets, and then with arrests and imprisonment.' With each year, the scale of the sacrifice ordinary Russians would need to make to achieve change would only grow. 'I worry by the time they wake up to the situation most people won't have the strength necessary to remove Putin and his cronies.'

Kolya said Motuznaya was by no means alone in deciding to leave. Increasing numbers of liberal Russians, especially younger ones, had been voting with their feet because voting at the ballot box was not a meaningful proposition. 'You hear about the millionaires in "Londongrad",' he said. 'But actually when my friends go they tend to choose the capitals of the Baltic states or Berlin or Prague. It isn't yet like in the Cold War when it was impossible to get out. For now Putin seems happy to let people go.'

Kolya must have thought about leaving too, I said. 'For now I will stay. My salary is only 34,000 roubles a month. That's less than €500 and I have no savings. I don't think I am ready to take my daughter away from her grandparents.'

So what did he hope for inside Russia? Strangely enough, and with what now feels like prophetic force, Kolya had come to the view that only war would be sufficient to get rid of Putin – not war waged on the regime by its opponents, he was quick to add, but some war that the president would foolishly take the country into. Up to that point, Kolya explained, Putin's belligerence in Georgia, eastern Ukraine and Syria had not cost many Russian lives. 'One day he will be tempted to do something bigger, and the dead bodies will pile up and the mothers of those dead bodies will come out onto the streets. Russians want their peace and quiet. They want their holidays in Turkey and their evenings with Netflix and their loved ones close beside them. I wonder if they will not be able to accept what Putin one day demands from them.'

It was a fascinating, chilling, theory. I could see the logic in it and wondered if Putin himself had spotted the same logic: his people's unwillingness to suffer for his regime's expansionist ambitions. Kolya hoped the leader would miscalculate and in so doing overreach himself. That seemed desperately bleak to me. How devastating that the best a young Russian of mild political aspirations could dream of was a full-scale revolution precipitated by war, just as in 1905 and 1917. We parted at the edge of some woodland, Kolya and his daughter walking further out of town to their home, me heading back into the centre.

I had pondered before coming to Vyborg how much today's citizens knew of its Finnish heritage. Places that change countries often experience a conspiracy of silence about their previous incarnations, especially where mass movements of people are involved. So I was pleased to learn that over the past fifty years, starting back in Soviet times, Vyborg has increasingly valued its Finnish connections.

Finns started visiting Vyborg regularly for day trips in the 1970s. Their movements were tightly controlled and they were not allowed to stay the night, but nevertheless their presence became a tangible link with the past, especially because many who came were once residents. More recently, large numbers of Finns have visited, and restaurants and hotels have enthusiastically catered to their needs. In the castle museum a wide-ranging exhibition explores aspects of interwar Vyborg, which was then known as Viipuri. Dozens of black-and-white photographs depict a vibrant city of luxury hotels, dance and fitness clubs, and bustling trade and commerce. As I went round I heard

The remarkable Alvar Aalto Library, built for Finnish Viipuri in the 1930s and lovingly restored for Russian Vyborg today.

some Finnish tourists exclaiming in delight at what had once been.

However, for today's Finnish visitors there is one building above all others that acts as a bridge back to the Finnish past. Vyborg's central public library, often referred to as the Alvar Aalto Library, was a beacon of international modernism when first erected in the mid-1930s and was celebrated by architects across the world. After the border shifted in 1944 and the Iron Curtain descended, hardly anyone except local residents saw it for forty-five years. Architects and architectural historians in the West even wrote that the landmark had been destroyed by wartime bombing. But, in fact, it clung on and has now been lovingly restored to sit proudly and simply at the heart of the city.

Alvar Aalto first designed the library in the late 1920s.[11] The city's authorities were investing heavily in infrastructure at that time and wanted a bold building to serve as a statement of their belief in progress and the confidence they felt in their young nation. Aalto would go on to become Finland's most famous architect, but he was still just in his twenties when he won the commission. Like a growing number of others in his field – including many Soviet architects of the same generation – he was committed to ridding architecture of inherited rules. In particular he wanted to build functionally, without superfluous ornamentation.

The library structure is a long series of dazzling white cubes and cuboids set in a restful urban park. It is ruthlessly minimalist but at the same time has everything an excellent library needs. Instead of elaborate plasterwork, light is used to create visual effects. In the lecture hall a wall of windows gazes onto the park, but the main reading room is lit from above rather than the sides in order to reduce distraction for readers. (The circular skylights were pioneering in their day and still feel futuristic now.) In what was for me the most exciting touch, a single curved bannister winds through the reading room, naturally directing visitors to the issue desk when they exit. When I sat there each morning during my stay, writing up my travel diary, I felt a deep sense of calm.

After completion Aalto's library stayed in Finland for just ten years. In 1944 it joined the rest of the city inside the USSR, and until Stalin's death it lay closed and in disrepair, losing parts of its roof. An initial plan for renovation would have seen the structure defiled by High Stalinist pillars, cornices and capitals. For such a high price Aalto might have preferred it to collapse, but fortunately the plan did not come to pass. Then, under Khrushchev, lighter-touch repairs were made which allowed the library to survive until the end of the Soviet period. In recent decades a fuller makeover has been undertaken, funded in large part by Finnish and international donors.

The library today is free for all to use, and concerts and other events are regularly held in the lecture hall. As the sun blazed through its windows one evening, I attended a recital there of piano music by the Finnish composer Sibelius. The pianist, who was from St Petersburg, played beautifully and I allowed my mind to wander through the century the library had seen, including the period when it had lain empty and its later resurrection. I felt the old and new worlds intermingling in strange ways. The building is old itself now but still feels new. It was as if I could see the different visions of the good life that had driven

Europeans onwards in modern times, present in the room. Some of them now utterly discarded, some still mourned, some in the process of being rediscovered. How dear such visions can be to people. How tragic it can feel when they have to surrender them or admit they were never what they seemed.

Did any memories of this library form part of Tatiana's beloved childhood, I wondered. She would have been a girl when it first reopened after the war. Was she pleased it now looked so well again? Out in the park there were lots of children with their parents, people stopping for a few minutes to chat to acquaintances, and others sitting alone to eat sunflower seeds and watch the world go by. I tried imagining how the space would have looked when Tatiana's beloved mayor had policed it more diligently. In my mind's eye I put him into the scene, a man in a black Soviet suit walking through the park and gathering up stray leaves and litter. In all honesty, I did not think he could have made the place look any better than it did now.

I left Vyborg as I had arrived. My next destination was Riga, but the easiest way to get there was back through Finland. The border procedures at Vyborg station were as smooth on the way out as they had been on the way in. That had been no aberration. Polite, efficient customs and border guards scanned my luggage and stamped my passport. A short time later the same was true for me and other EU citizens when the Finnish guards inspected our documents just over the border inside Finland.

But the Russians in my carriage had a different experience. As they entered Finland and the Schengen Area they were extended a frosty welcome. It wasn't quite a repeat of the old third degree that used to await travellers heading eastwards, but it wasn't far off. The Finnish guards gruffly demanded document upon document, speaking only in Finnish or English. From some passengers they insisted on proof of hotel reservations and the production of particular credit cards.

A glamorous Russian woman in her fifties was sitting at our table of four. She was visibly shocked by the manner of the guard who dealt with her and, in particular, by having to submit herself to a fingerprint scan. When the ordeal was over I wanted to show sympathy. I said to her that I had found the Russian officials in Vyborg much friendlier and that there had been no sign of these high-tech scanning machines. Her expression changed in an instant. She sensed a slight. 'Of course Russia has fingerprint machines like that,' she said. 'Russia has everything. Everything.' I was going to try to explain myself but decided against it. It was easier just to let the veil of misunderstanding hang between us.

5

Riga, Latvia

As I flew into Riga I was watching a film on my tablet. Despite being mostly in black and white it was from the 1980s and was about everyday life in and around the Latvian capital at the end of the Soviet period. The communist state always placed huge emphasis on childhood and youth. A regime dedicated to controlling people's minds and fashioning a new kind of human made sure to get in early. The idea was that each new generation of Soviet youth would be more loyal and grateful to the system than the last. But, as the film powerfully showed, that was not how things had played out.

Is it Easy to Be Young? – Vai viegli but jaunam? in Latvian – was made during 1985 and 1986 by Juris Podnieks and released at the start of 1987. From the first frame the standoff between young and old is unmissable: the exuberance of youth pitted against an ossified, restrictive bureaucracy in every area of life. One immediately senses a situation that cannot persist much longer. The film opens with footage of thousands of teenagers at an outdoor music concert. They jump up and down, cheer and laugh and clap their hands above their heads in time to the driving rhythm. The band is Pērkons, a rock group whose name meant 'thunder', and which operated on the fringes of legality. Its songs have a strong beat and sound a bit like Status Quo only with more anarchic lyrics. The song 'Noise', which plays at the film's start, includes references to sinking ships and – significantly for Soviet ears – crumbling stars. The crowd dances ecstatically and screams along when the band reaches the chorus: '*I can't, I can't, I can't, I can't, I can't.*'

We cut to a shot of a youth in a quiet classroom. We have just been watching the same boy in the concert crowd. Now he is leafing through a pile of photographs and talking to an off-camera interviewer. He says he does not recognize any individuals in the photos but is unsurprised to learn that there were arrests after the event. It was what his father said would happen.

We dive back into the music briefly before the film's title fills the screen. What then follows is a series of candid interviews with concert attendees and others, all in their teens and early twenties. Gradually we discover more about the arrested youths. We attend court with seven of them to see them tried for vandalizing the train they caught home that night. Apparently they smashed its windows and light-fittings, tore vinyl from its seats, and shouted what the authorities call 'slogans'. These included nihilistic phrases like 'Let there be darkness, darkness!' We see the mother of one defendant sob as she pleads with the judge to show leniency to her son. Then we watch the group sentenced, two to lengthy stretches in prison. The concert, a moment of intense pleasure, has laid bare fundamental fault lines in Soviet society, fault lines the film suggests may be unbridgeable.

Is it Easy . . . ? was big news in the USSR upon release; nothing like it had ever been shown in Soviet cinemas before. It still packs a punch now, in a world newly concerned with intergenerational inequality and estrangement. I was travelling to Riga to search both for the film's history and its afterlife, and to see how Latvia's current youth were faring thirty years after the country broke free from the Soviet Union.

On my first morning in the city I headed to the trendy, ultra-modern headquarters of Tet. Tet is Latvia's former state tele-communications monopoly and continues to provide mobile, television and internet services to a large proportion of the country's population. As I sat in its reception waiting to be collected, I was treated to clips of films, music videos and basketball games, all shown to me on an enormous wall of screens. The employees who were walking in and out seemed as fashionable as their surroundings: Adidas trainers, Lacoste polo shirts, Levi's, designer glasses.

I had come to meet Juris Gulbis, who was at that time Tet's chief executive. He was the first boy Podnieks interviewed in *Is it Easy . . . ?* and stood out in the film as a whole as one of the only participants to resemble a model Soviet youth. While other interviewees were seen in courtrooms or squatted buildings or alongside rubble heaps – one even conducted his interview in a morgue – Juris, then sixteen and neatly dressed with fair hair and chiselled good looks, was shown at school and performing guard duty at one of the most important communist statues in Riga, the memorial to the Latvian Riflemen. Early on, he is even heard to criticize the kind of young person who would vandalize a train. 'These guys haven't really got anywhere,' he says. 'They don't have ideas. They just go wild and have fun. They want to do something, so they break something.' It was exactly what a Soviet authority figure would have wanted a young man to say.

But when the director asks him, perhaps provocatively, how he manages to juggle the demands of being an A-grade student with the everyday desires of youth, something unlocks in Juris and we discover that he has no love for the system either. 'I am one person at school and completely different outside,' he says. When he grows up he wants a wife and an interesting job – so far, so Soviet – but also 'a lot of money', enough, he explains, for 'a car, an apartment, nice clothes, and a summerhouse'.

But what of socialist values? the director probes. 'I am not fighting for anything. I have no ideals,' he replies. The Latvian Riflemen who helped defend the Bolshevik revolution after 1917 are from 'a lost period' as far as he is concerned. 'They mean nothing to my generation. Now, there is nothing to fight for, nothing to die for and nothing to live for. Sometimes you wonder what it is all about.'

Juris's frustrations, delivered in a matter-of-fact tone, resonated with millions of young people who watched the film across the USSR, as did his individualistic life ambitions. No matter how long he spent guarding huge monuments or saying the right things in political education classes, there would be no winning this young man back to the Marxist cause. For him, it was irrecoverably tarnished. It was how many others felt too.

The statue of the Latvian Riflemen, erected in 1970.

After about ten minutes in Tet's foyer I was collected and conveyed to a stylish boardroom by a secretary who brought me coffee. Juris himself entered minutes later, a man in his early fifties in a suit and open-necked shirt. He was still slim and clean-cut and, though older looking, instantly recognizable from the boy of thirty-five years before. At first he seemed oddly nervous. 'I'm not a big talker about general things,' he said. I thought I sensed the caution of a prominent business leader worried about being drawn into areas of controversy. But I also remembered the boldness with which he had spoken back in 1986. How, I asked, had the director got him talking so candidly in what was still an authoritarian state?

Podnieks had a special rapport with young people, Juris said. He came to Juris's school a few months after the Pērkons concert looking for students who appeared in his footage. Juris identified himself without being sure what would happen next. 'Podnieks was fantastic because, as you know, as a teenager you don't typically trust someone who is twenty years older than yourself. But he was able to build that trust fast. Probably I was more honest than I should have been. I didn't realize, because at a very young age you don't always count the risks associated with things you do.'

He paused and in so doing looked uncannily like the boy in the film. 'Maybe I already knew it was okay to be honest,' he mused. Despite the continued restrictions in Soviet society in 1986, it was already pretty clear there would be few ramifications from just speaking one's mind. 'I was actually secretary of the Komsomol organization at school. Obviously you had to do your duty on the political side, but that was only secondary. I took the role because it gave me an opportunity to organize parties and stuff. By then it was fairly relaxed. I think everyone expected something would have to change.'

Looking back at the goals Juris set in the film – a wife, an interesting job, a lot of money – I told him it seemed that he had never faltered in his pursuit of them. He corrected me. Before he could really advance, he first had to endure eighteen months of military service on a Soviet army base in East Germany. It was like being forced to press pause on his life. Though technically in a friendly socialist country, Juris had almost no interaction with the local Germans and was permitted just three days off base during the entire posting.

Only when back in the newly independent Latvia could he begin to realize his ambitions. He secured a job with Coopers & Lybrand, then one of the 'big six' global audit firms. Like scores of other Western businesses, it rushed to establish offices in the former Eastern Bloc. Juris shone and his manager selected him for a two-year training contract in London. It was his big break. British values and the British approach to business suited him perfectly. He learned an immense amount in London, he tells me, but he did struggle with the hierarchical working culture of the City of the mid-1990s. 'The Soviet system wasn't good for much,' he said, 'but it was pretty egalitarian.'

In Latvia once more, he began working at LatTelecom (Tet's old name) and rose to be its chief executive while still in his thirties. In a 2006 television interview, he said that getting to the top had been surprisingly easy. At the time of our meeting his annual salary was reportedly in the region of €400,000, 'a lot of money' by any standard.[1] He also had a wife and two children and, of course, the car he had sought as well as the ability to go on holiday wherever he wanted.

The Juris I interviewed in 2019 was leading a modern European life in a plural democracy where he was resolutely plugged into the moderate mainstream, just like hundreds of thousands of his fellow citizens. He believed in capitalism and markets but did not come across as a neoliberal purist. He seemed to understand that his preferred system, just like any other, sometimes failed. He had maintained contact with a few of the other interviewees from *Is it Easy . . . ?* and he said some had led very hard lives. 'There is an old Soviet joke about Kremlin propaganda,' he said: '"They lied to us about communism. But everything they said about capitalism was true."'

In commercial terms, Gulbis's company partly depends for its success on the cacophony of voices, interest groups, fads and crazes that make up the contemporary social media whirl not just in Latvia but in most countries around the world. How would he respond to the suggestion that this kind of communication was by its nature damaging, both because it destroys social cohesion and because it is a breeding ground for misinformation?

He answered quickly. Instinctively he disliked the idea of people in power 'prohibiting something' on the grounds that they wanted to keep other people safe. The kind of free expression that the modern age has encouraged was indeed a business thing for him, but it was not solely a business thing. It was also tied up with his childhood memories of the top-down monoculture of Soviet life. 'I lived in a country where people told us what to watch and what to listen to,' he said. 'Nowadays, because of social media, society is more fragmented. You can create your own bubble, your own society, your own values; you can live within it and adhere to it. If it doesn't interfere with other people, then that's okay as long as you don't get aggressive or push one ideology over another.'

Juris has had a significant role in the making of modern Latvia. Tet provides the connectivity that links many Latvians with family, friends, employers, their sources of income and entertainment, and the wider outside world. The company also employs more than a thousand people. It was therefore a major national news story (and a shock to me) when, at the end of 2020, Tet's board sacked its chief executive following allegations of financial misconduct – allegations that at the time of writing remain unproved.[2] Gulbis has since ended up in a lengthy court battle, fighting to prove his innocence alongside several other businesspeople and politicians, including a former prime minister.[3] The wheel of fortune has finally turned for the confident boy who had such a clear idea of what he wanted. But, as he once said himself, 'The only guarantees in life are birth and death. For everything else a person must strive.'[4]

I walk across town after the interview to meet another person whose life has been touched by *Is it Easy . . . ?* Alise Podniece is Juris Podnieks's granddaughter, and, although she has no personal experience of the Soviet period, she has lived with his famous film and its legacy since birth. I found Alise, who is in her mid-twenties, through Facebook, and we corresponded online in the weeks running up to my visit, exemplifying some of the positive possibilities modern communications and the connected world bring. She had agreed to meet me in a neighbourhood café a few streets from Tet's headquarters. We arrived separately and each ordered flat whites. We laughed at the coincidence when they were both delivered to us a few seconds apart.

'I feel you can really sense in that film how the Soviet system is about to end,' Alise says, adding that each time she watches it she is struck anew by the strength of the stories her grandfather unearthed. The character she remembers most vividly is Agnija, a young woman whom Podnieks filmed at the concert and then, as with Gulbis, interviewed at length some months later. By the time he tracks her down Agnija has had a baby. She speaks to camera while cradling the tiny infant and says that she is frightened to bring another human being into the world so soon after Chernobyl. The nuclear accident had happened just weeks earlier. 'I truly hope my daughter will be able to play in puddles barefoot,' she says. 'That she can pick apples from a tree without risking her life. Now the nuclear plant has exploded I am terribly scared.'

No event damaged the image and reputation of the Soviet Union after Stalin so much as Chernobyl. What Alise finds impressive about her grandfather's take on it is how in the space of just a few frames he communicates a person's deep anxieties about the disaster and also manages to make them speak for society as a whole. 'He shows, without exaggerating, that both Agnija and her daughter are at the mercy of a huge and dangerous state, and somehow also suggests that everyone else is actually in the same position.'

The USSR's collapse came only a few years after Chernobyl and *Is it Easy . . . ?* It was much less violent than it might have been but definitely not bloodless. 'Juris quickly got involved with the independence movement,' Alise tells me. From 1988 Latvians began holding street protests about various issues of concern. Most of the demonstrations included calls for greater autonomy from Moscow or even full independence, and then, in May 1990, a new Latvian legislature formally declared its intention to take the country out of the USSR. The population waited uneasily to see what the Kremlin would do.

'My grandfather was here in January 1991 when the people got their answer,' Alise recounts. 'The Soviet tanks turned up in Riga and people began to erect barricades.' They were determined to resist the overthrow of the local pro-independence administration. Gorbachev had won the Nobel Peace Prize only a short time earlier but that did not stop the troops opening fire on the civilians. Six Latvians were killed. Many believe the death toll would have been much higher had Podnieks and other filmmakers not placed themselves directly in the line of fire to record what was going on and make the Soviet commanders fear they might subsequently be held to account for their actions.

These brave chroniclers turned themselves into sitting ducks in order to get a clear view of what was going on. Two members of Podnieks's crew were shot and wounded, picked off by Soviet marksmen. Juris himself was unhurt but his friend and fellow filmmaker Andris Slapiņš was gunned down. As others in the crowd attempted to resuscitate him, Podnieks grabbed Slapiņš's dropped camera and used it to film the last moments of his life.

Independence was a historic achievement but it left many problems unsolved and created new ones as well. Alise tells me that many Latvians faced terrible difficulties after 1991. 'In Soviet times everyone had a job. They didn't even have to be good at their jobs. They just had one. Life, in a way, was calm. There were a lot of people who wanted Latvia to be free but afterwards, once they had freedom, they didn't know what to do with it. They ended up slipping behind.'

I mention that Juris Gulbis had said something similar to me. She smiles, 'Gulbis is well known in Latvia and many people, not just me, remember his special contribution to my grandfather's film. He stood out in 1986, but if you watch the two follow-up documentaries you really do see what an exception he became.' The programmes were made for Latvian television in 1996 and 2006. As I would discover, they showed many of the original participants struggling with depression, alcoholism, poverty and unemployment. Others seemed to suffer what we would now call post-traumatic stress disorder, a result of their military service in Afghanistan. The boy Podnieks interviewed in a morgue had committed suicide. 'He took many sleeping tablets. He thought he wasn't needed in this life. I think he was overtaken by a bottomless feeling of hopelessness,' his young widow says.

In Alise's own family circle there were plenty of tales of hardship too. The good life many young Latvians enjoy now is built not just on the ruins of communism but on the ruins of post-communism as well, she suggests to me. Even Podnieks struggled with stress after the independence struggle. He would not direct the follow-up programmes to *Is it Easy . . . ?* because he would not live long enough.

'My grandfather was such a hero in books and articles and press releases, but he was a human being too,' Alise says. A man in great demand, he travelled to many European countries lecturing about his craft and his crusading journalism. He also kept on documenting the seismic shifts that were happening inside the new Latvia. But, although he loved and believed in what he was doing, the result was burnout.

Podnieks seemed prematurely old, people who were with him around that time have told Alise. His family life suffered, including his relationship with his wife, Alise's grandmother. The experience of being shot at and seeing fellow cameramen injured and killed also cast a traumatic shadow. In June 1992, when still just forty-one, Juris Podnieks took a day off work to go scuba diving in a lake. He drowned. A great talent had been snuffed out at the peak of his powers.

As one of Latvia's most famous people, Podnieks's sudden death was understandably the subject of much speculation. Everyone knew the KGB was capable of staging such 'accidents' – a leading Latvian poet, Klāvs Elsbergs, was widely believed to have been pushed out of an upstairs window back in 1987 as punishment for his anti-Soviet writings. Conspiracy theories proliferated about Podnieks too. There are those who still believe them, but Alise says that for her and the rest of her family there was never much doubt that Podnieks's death, though tragic, was not suspicious. 'To be honest, I think there's a logic to him dying around that time. Knowing that he was very, very tired. He'd done all those big movies. I'm not a fan of all the conspiracy stuff and I don't even think it's necessary to know. A dead person's a dead person.'

We had both been growing cold sitting in the draught of the café's open door, and now the recollection of Alise's grandfather's death deepened the chill. I suggested we walk through Riga's art nouveau streets for a bit. I asked Alise to tell me more about her own life in the city. '*Vai viegli but jaunam?*' I repeated the title of her grandfather's film with a smirk, deploying the only Latvian sentence I am ever likely to know.

We walked past neighbourhood cafés and bars, the one-time home of the philosopher Isaiah Berlin (an especially beautiful building with sphinxes outside) and an ornate cinema, the Splendid Palace, which Alise used to visit as a child. We then stood looking over a flat expanse of city parkland towards the impressive spires of Riga Old Town. 'Riga is my playground,' Alise says. 'I'm lucky enough to know lots of artists and creative people here, just as my grandfather did.' She and her friends go to restaurants and nightspots and visit exhibitions and installations. Her generation was the first to be born with a little money behind it, she says, and large numbers of Latvians today still feel that they are climbing.

So it is easier to be young now, I say. Alise initially agrees with the statement but then hesitates. She says Latvians generally consider themselves a depressive bunch. The relative optimism of the present, fuelled by high educational standards and inward investment and other new opportunities from the EU, cannot completely erase a national tendency towards fatalism, even among young people.

Some of her friends and acquaintances talk about feeling burned out or complain of their low salaries or long waits for promotion. Most are thoroughly disengaged from politics. In the part of town she lives in, she daily sees young people she doesn't know struggling with poverty, alcoholism and homelessness. Yes, life in Riga today is by any objective measure better than it used to be. But telling people that things were worse before or, as would be true for most young Latvians, that they've never had it so good, does not necessarily make everyone feel bright and happy. The relationship between freedom, opportunity and happiness is complicated. Is it ever truly easy to be young, Alise wonders, whatever the time or place, whatever the conditions?

Where does she think she will find happiness in the future? At the time of our meeting, her main job was in the communications team of one of Riga's major hospitals, but she was also increasingly involved in doing PR for Latvian films. I ask her if she has any thoughts of becoming a filmmaker herself. 'I don't even know,' she replies. Clearly it is a question she puzzles over. She tells me she has received some cinematographic training and enjoys taking photographs and making video clips. She sometimes feels she has a knack for composing a shot, perhaps inherited from her grandfather. But she senses that people only want to be entertained by 'really dark stories' today – murder, horror, blood, guts and gore. 'That's not what interests me,' she says.

Alise Podniece, granddaughter of film director Juris Podnieks, with me at the end of our walk through the streets of Riga.

6

Liepāja, Latvia

The next day, I hired a car and headed west to the city of Liepāja. Juris Gulbis had told me I would enjoy the drive, and he was right. Outside of the capital, Latvia's main roads are high quality, recently upgraded with EU money, and largely empty. It was a pleasant day and I found the endless forest restful. Eventually, the landscape changed to flat coastal plain and, at Liepāja itself, I was back by the waves. Riga is in a natural bay sheltered from the main expanse of the Baltic. But Liepāja's coast faces directly onto the open sea, Sweden lying due west across the water. In Cold War times it meant that both Liepāja city and the surrounding region were treated as militarily important and vulnerable.

My first stop in the area was about 30 kilometres north of the city, where I wanted to find the site of a small miracle that once gave locals hope in the face of overwhelming Soviet hostility. Ziemupe is a tiny, unremarkable village where people subsisted for centuries on cattle farming and sea fishing. The Soviets took it over with the rest of Latvia in 1940 and, until 1945, battled the Germans for control of it. Then, in the immediate postwar period when locals sought a return to normal life, Stalin's regime started applying its tried and tested approaches to security and control. First, in 1949, the village's wealthier and more successful farming families were deported *en masse*. Then, over the next twelve years, its fishermen had their right to live off the sea challenged and ultimately removed.

For Soviet strategists, sea borders were a key location. In addition to specific naval and other bases the entire Soviet coastline was treated as a restricted zone, accessible to the general public only by exception. Swimming in the sea and even walking on beaches were strictly controlled, limited to designated fenced-off stretches of coast and daylight hours, even at resorts. Raked strips of sand and sometimes tripwires were installed to detect infringements. Zenith rocket launchers were stationed at 25-kilometre intervals along the seaboard and manned twenty-four hours a day, ready for deployment in the event of a foreign attack.

A Latvian film made after the Soviet collapse, *Kurpe* (1998; in English, *Shoes*), attempted to satirize the Soviets' coastal paranoia through a fictional but credible story of a shoe on a beach whose discovery causes a manhunt.[1] Reality could be just as absurd but usually with less comic potential. The biggest negative effect was felt by those who put out to sea each day. They were suspect by nature: men who regularly sailed away from Soviet territory and who might therefore be in contact with the USSR's enemies or helping other citizens to escape.

The fishermen of Ziemupe had seen their freedom initially curtailed in the late 1940s, when they were told they could only go to sea with an armed Soviet border guard on board. Though this change made the fishermen feel like prisoners on a chain gang, for a few years they made the system work. (What choice did they have?) But one day in the 1950s a vessel capsized in a storm and several crew and a guard died. Without further explanation the authorities banned fishing altogether. The villagers' boats were confiscated, dragged up off the beach and piled high beside the fence of the local military compound.

For several years at the end of the 1950s and the start of the 1960s locals could only look longingly at their vessels as they walked past the compound, hoping that someday they might be returned. Then, one night in 1961, out of vindictiveness or at the conclusion of a drunken party or as a calculated way of removing the problem once and for all – no one was ever quite sure – a member of the border troops set fire to the boats. Seeing smoke, villagers rushed to the scene but there was nothing to be done.

Grown men had to watch as their livelihoods turned permanently to ash. They wept. The jobs and skills they had inherited from fathers and grandfathers were useless to them now. The Soviet system and its border paranoia had done their worst.

I came to Ziemupe because of what happened next. I was looking for the fire's precise location. It has achieved some fame of late and I was hoping for a road sign but saw none. I ended up stopping at the village hall. A small monument outside it commemorated the Ziemupe residents who were deported under Stalin. I saw a door propped open in the side of the building, which gave access to a steep flight of steps (more a ladder than a staircase). At the top was a dark book-lined room. Here was Ziemupe's library. Suddenly a door further inside creaked open and a woman in her early sixties, the librarian, stood looking back at me with a quizzical expression. It took me a couple of minutes to explain why I was there. Fortunately the woman spoke Russian and said she would be happy to direct me to the place where the boats burned. But first I should sit down and join her for coffee. She had been there that night, though still a babe in arms; she would tell me what she knew. I couldn't quite believe it.

Daina Vitola has ruddy cheeks and the kindly, patient demeanour of a countrywoman who has spent her life helping others. In addition to being Ziemupe's librarian, she is the self-appointed local historian, a custodian of stories and collector of artefacts in a community that has been shrinking for as long as she has been alive. She sees it as her duty to remember things that Ziemupe would otherwise forget, and to teach them to its few remaining children.

'The boats were covered in tar which had all dried out. That's why they burned so quickly,' Daina begins, while gently rocking a little filter coffee machine to make the water percolate faster through it. 'A man who still lives around here and is a bit older than me remembers standing beside his granny and not understanding why she was crying. Their family didn't have a boat so he didn't know what the fuss was about. As a youngster, he couldn't grasp that it was the whole point of our village that was going up in flames, a village that had always had its face to the sea.'

The site of the fire was considered cursed in the immediate aftermath but then the miracle happened. Over the next couple of years, a dense grove of juniper trees grew up there. Previously, there had been no trees at all. Some local people saw it as a divine intervention, like the biblical rainbow God sent after the Flood. The new juniper wood was always known locally as the Fishermen's Tears. Some years ago, Daina says she participated in a survey which counted more than 500 separate plants.

The villagers of Ziemupe in the late 1930s posing on one of their fishing boats. In 1961 a Soviet border guard burned all the boats.

Official paranoia continued after the fire, Daina adds. The Soviet security apparatus would have preferred no civilians at all to live so close to the maritime border. In other parts of the USSR, as also in East Germany, villages were sometimes emptied and inhabitants forcibly relocated, but for some reason this was not done at Ziemupe. Instead, locals were tolerated but deeply mistrusted. Daina remembers how, every so often, a male border guard would don a woman's patterned headscarf and walk through the fields. 'It was a test,' she says. Residents were supposed to spot the headscarf-wearing figure, establish they were a stranger, and report them to the border post, all within a few minutes. Failure to do so led to compulsory training and further drills.

One day in the late 1960s, Daina and her friends were playing hide-and-seek. They were using a stick and an old tin bath to beat out the time people had left to hide: 'Ten – BANG – Nine – BANG – Eight – BANG. From the border post, the guards heard the noise and mobilized. They actually thought an invasion had started,' she chuckles. 'They arrived and fired shots in the air. We played hide-and-seek a bit quieter after that.' Daina makes a face indicating that she recognizes the ridiculousness of this. 'We were so jumpy about strangers,' she says. 'Even after Latvia regained its independence, locals here would sometimes call the police if they saw outsiders walking on country lanes or picking flowers in meadows.'

We are standing beside my car now. The wind is rustling in the tall beech trees over towards the sea. I say it sounds a bit like living in Ziemupe was a kind of house arrest during Soviet times. Daina thinks. People did feel great bitterness about what happened to their boats and all the other restrictions placed on their lives, but they got on with life and it wasn't all bad. 'We didn't simply shun the border troops in our midst,' she adds. The personnel changed regularly and came from all across the USSR. Plenty of them didn't want conflict; they were just doing a job. 'We continued to live alongside them. We had to. And we were able to be friendly with a few of them. They were people too, after all.' In the hall beneath her reading room dances used to be held. The troops got invited along with everyone else, and local girls, herself included, danced with them and sometimes went on to date them. 'Their uniforms were attractive. How could we just ignore them,' she says with a twinkle in her eyes.

She gives me the directions to the Fishermen's Tears. It is only about 500 metres away but I would not have found it on my own. A few minutes later, I stand among the junipers. These short bushes are small and insubstantial but somehow sturdy and noble. It is thought that birds most likely deposited the seeds that they grew from, seeds that went on to thrive in the fertile ash. I touch the bushes' spiky leaves and the berries that grow in tight to their branches. Little trees, nothing more. And yet within them, in the soil under them, are the atoms of the boats that were once a community's pride and joy, existing still in new form.

Daina was balanced, even charitable, I felt, in her assessment of relations between Ziemupe's residents and the official representatives of Soviet power. 'They were people too, after all' is a phrase I have found myself repeating ever since. It is probably worth recalling in any situation where one set of humans has behaved badly towards another, and I hope I would remember to say it if I were the injured party. But of course not everyone in Latvia feels able to be so kind to those who have made their lives difficult. Latvia today is a country divided between people who identify as Latvian and people who identify as Russian or Russian-speaking. Some in the former group continue to dwell on their status as victims of a concerted attempt to wipe out their culture during Soviet times. Many in the latter camp feel deliberately and punitively marginalized in the new country they have ended up in. It has made for a vengeful atmosphere which has been exploited by state-sponsored actors from across the border.

Soviet propaganda promoted an idea of communist states as communities of equals. But, to paraphrase George Orwell in a book that communist governments mostly banned, some were more equal than others. The USSR's primacy among the nations of the Warsaw Pact was never in doubt. Likewise, inside the Soviet Union, Russians were privileged above all other nationalities. Latvians thus endured decades of systematic discrimination – sometimes bureaucratic, sometimes cultural, sometimes violent.

I had spoken to a member of the Latvian Historical Society,

Reinis Lazda, while in Riga. Over a dinner he made of foraged mushrooms and pearl-barley porridge, I learned of the struggle that most 'indigenous' Latvians had endured just to get decent jobs and housing after 1945 and to keep their culture alive. Preferential treatment was invariably shown to the 800,000 Russians and other migrants who came from elsewhere in the USSR. Reinis said schoolteachers were instructed to promote Russian as the main language and even to warn parents not to let their children learn Latvian because, so the authorities alleged, 'bilingualism harmed brain development'. Age-old traditions got sidelined. There were bans on Latvian festivals, songs, symbols and literary works.

After 1991 the tables turned. Independent Latvia inherited a very large Russian-speaking minority. Estimates vary but even now perhaps as many as one quarter of the population identifies as 'ethnically' Russian. This minority has seen its once-privileged position eroded as Latvian-speaking Latvians have taken over running the country and re-established the primacy of their culture and language.

My next stop after Ziemupe was Karosta, a suburb of Liepāja that is effectively a Russian town. Karosta is a palimpsest of the different phases of Russian power in Latvia. The core is a crumbling military city built for the Tsar's imperial navy in grand style at the start of the twentieth century. Several massive redbrick barracks still survive along with a splendid manège for training horses, a military prison and, at the centre, an ornate Orthodox cathedral which would not look out of place in a capital city. Slotted around these, often with the maximum of architectural insensitivity, are military buildings of the Soviet era: a 1981 monument to nuclear submariners, a school, a polyclinic and many modern housing blocks.

For over thirty years Karosta was off-limits to the inhabitants of the rest of Liepāja, and it did not feature on any published map (replaced by a fake extension of the Baltic Sea). It was the home of the USSR's Baltic fleet of nuclear-armed submarines and a place of extreme security. In the 1980s some 32,000 personnel and their families lived here, mostly Russians. The shops were always well stocked, even when there were shortages elsewhere. Residents had their own clubs, a cinema and the grandly named Vsevolod Vishnevskii Drama Theatre, which staged everything from light-hearted farces to Shakespeare plays.

By the time of my visit, Karosta had rematerialized on maps, but was otherwise still quite overlooked. The population had slumped to just 7,000 mostly elderly Russians who stayed after the Soviet navy left. Early post-Soviet problems with drug dealers, prostitution and squatters had largely been addressed. The NATO School of Diving had taken up residence in one part of the old base. But across such a huge depopulated space an air of neglect predominated.

I spent a morning walking Karosta's wide streets and exploring its ruined, roofless buildings. I visited the former military prison, now a museum, and then approached the cathedral. The building's colossal domes had been glittering at me from afar, taller than any other nearby structure, but when I was only metres away I still could not see the rest of the structure as it was screened by blocks of flats. These had been erected uncomfortably close on all four sides. Right up against the cathedral's railings there was also a line of rusting metal garages.

Beside one of the garages two figures were at work, a man and a woman, both pensioners. I walked over and, after saying good morning, asked if they could remember Soviet Karosta. The man was chopping old furniture up for firewood. He paused and said sullenly that of course he remembered it, but immediately went back to his work. The woman, whom I will call Anna, was dragging extra pieces of furniture over to him. She looked up and, smiling broadly, said to me that she thought about Soviet Karosta every day because it had been 'my lovely home'. She dropped what was in her arms and headed back into the garage, emerging seconds later with two rickety kitchen chairs, which she proposed we sit on.

Anna turned out to be a pressure cooker of memories. I made what was just the tiniest of openings and the anecdotes burst forth. 'Where should I begin?' she asks, but it's only a rhetorical question, for, without drawing breath, she proceeds to share her wide-ranging take on the USSR and its aftermath.

'People back then were different, you see. Society was different. Our laws and principles of life were different. We were open and kind. We were more humane. We drank together. Chatted. Danced. Sang songs. We lived better.' Suddenly she is back in her childhood in a Siberian city in the 1950s. 'We lived in a communal apartment. The women came together each week to make the food. They would pool their money and buy meat and flour to make *pelmeny*' – a Russian dish like ravioli – 'No one had fridges back then but, when it was cold, they would take the *pelmeny* to the balcony and throw them over into the snow. They froze instantly and it was our job, as children, to go down and put them into sacks. The sacks would sit on the balcony all week, and when husbands and wives came home from the big factory for lunch or dinner they would go to the sacks and take as many *pelmeny* as they needed. The attitude of people back then was all about mutual assistance.'

What did she think of Karosta when she first came? Anna says she instantly fell in love with the place. It was the 1970s and she and other residents felt united by a great sense of purpose. 'It was a military city. At one point I was head of the military construction committee. I co-ordinated the work of the penal battalion that built these very houses.' She gestures at the flats all around, clearly proud of the labour she extracted from the soldier prisoners under her control. Perhaps sensing my unease, she adds, 'You know, there are excesses in any system. There are those at the top who look after their own interests. It's the same in your system. It was the same in ours.'

Karosta's cathedral is hemmed in on all sides by modern blocks of flats, some built by prison labour. They were once sought-after dwellings for Soviet naval officers.

As a mother, she loved the safety and community of the military town. 'I want to say that I had two children and I was able to feed and clothe them easily. Of course, I was younger and stronger than now. But that's not the point. I could ask people to look after my kids. We didn't fear letting our children out, even at night. I remember – I was twenty-nine years old in 1977 – there was a particular restaurant we loved to go to. We were peaceful, happy, golden, beautiful young people. We got drunk. We stayed sober. We had energy. We didn't fear anything.'

Seemingly out of nowhere, Anna emits a huge sob and her eyes well up with tears. I am surprised and so, evidently, is the old man, for he looks up from his chopping and warns her that she is saying too much and will regret it.

Life didn't feel restrictive here? 'It wasn't at all bad,' she replies. 'Access to the West has increased the material level of our lives a bit, of course. But look at it philosophically. Material wealth is not the main thing. Back then we had certainty. Salaries were lower. But for rent we paid one eighth of what we earned. I received 100 roubles in pay and all I paid for my flat was 12 roubles, and that included water, heating and everything.' The old man pipes up: 'In the USSR you could buy a Zil for the equivalent of 50 to 60 Euros. Now you pay thousands and thousands for some horrible little car. It's true we couldn't go to Sweden or other Western countries, but so what?'

Anna nods. 'If you're a family person, with a wife, a husband, children and a flat, where do you need to go? The "Iron Curtain" [that] people talk about with its "uncrossable borders" – it wasn't a curtain as such. It was just two completely incompatible systems. I don't care what you say, capitalism dictates that money is truth. But in the USSR people lived by completely different values. The system that existed here allowed us to take joy in the little things. Springtime, you'd go to get new clothes for your kids and you'd find some item with a picture of a strawberry on it and you'd be happy for a whole week. People were materially less well off. Light industry didn't operate so well. But this thing-ism, this chasing after things, has had a bad effect on people. We were able to find joy in other ways back then – in flowers, in youth.' She is crying again.

I mention my meeting with Daina the previous day and the Fishermen's Tears. Were they aware back then that many Latvians were unhappy inside the Soviet Union? 'A lot of Latvians moan now about their experiences under communism,' Anna says, 'but it isn't right.'

'Relations were excellent back then,' the old man comes in again, while prising his axehead out of a table leg. 'We can take you right now and show you Latvian villages where the local Latvian old people still say Soviet power was good. Back then, they had asphalted roads and gas. But now . . .'

'Russians and Latvians lived together absolutely fine,' Anna says. 'Relations were peaceful. He' – she points at the man – 'was married to a woman with five sisters. One of them was married to a Latvian. The families were close. The father of the Latvian family once guarded Lenin. He was a Latvian Rifleman. They were good people. But now some Latvians want to pretend all the Russians were KGB informants and no Latvian played any part in the system. And the language thing is nonsense too,' she continues. 'Latvian is all well and good, but it isn't a world language. *That's* why people were encouraged to learn Russian in Soviet times. The Russian language unites people. I think it's stupid to put pressure on people *not* to learn Russian and then encourage them to learn English. England is so small and far away. Russia is right here and it's enormous. And what has the West brought us? Homosexuals. In general, our young people are dirtier, more vulgar, more cynical, harsher than they were before. Frankly, I'm frightened. I often wish I had copied other people in the 1990s, packed my bags and left for Russia. But it is too late for me now. I am too old to start again.'

On the subject of the Second World War, Anna says she believes the local city authorities in Liepāja have banned Victory Day commemorations in recent years because they view the Red Army victory as a defeat, the start of an occupation. 'Latvians sympathized with the fascists,' she explains.

I thought of how much Anna had in common with Tatiana in Vyborg. They would have enjoyed a very harmonious conversation, even if Anna might not have listened to everything Tatiana said. But Tatiana was actually living in the place Anna felt was better, and she was dissatisfied too. The truth was they both longed for a place that no longer existed, and for a version of it that had only ever been half the story.

I remembered a deaf-mute man I once met in a bathhouse in a non-Russian part of the former Soviet Union. I asked him where he came from and, without apparent irony, he used a finger to etch the letters C C C P in the air. Tatiana and Anna came from there too. On Latvia's Russian-language talk radio stations, which I listened to while driving, people like them seemed to be on air constantly. They bolstered one another's pro-Soviet worldviews, a form of nostalgia that made clear demands on the present. (We are learning more all the time about just how costly those demands can be.) I also heard time and again of the noble values of Soviet society. I heard of the state-sponsored degradation of Latvia's Russian community and the terrible scourges of homosexuality and transsexuality which had been imported from the EU. I heard of official pressure to prevent Latvia's Soviet veterans commemorating their victory over the Nazis.

There was a fair amount of pro-Russian graffiti around Karosta as well. I walked the beaches of the adjacent Ziemeļu Fort complex, surely one of the most stunning stretches of coastline anywhere in Europe. An enormous, Russian-built coastal defence network now lies broken and partly submerged in the sea, like a supersized Duplo Lego set swiped by a giant toddler. The scene could be an embodiment of Russian retreat, and yet much of the graffiti on the structures indicates Russia's continued attractiveness: 'Libava is Russia' (Libava is the Russian name for Liepāja); 'President Putin is our President'.

What happens next in a place like this? Many Latvian-speaking Latvians have behaved in ways that suggest they are not overly concerned about the unhappiness of the people in their midst who identify as Russian. They have in many cases chosen to see it as a protracted but ultimately passing hangover of the Soviet collapse, and point to the fact that younger members of the Russian community now grow up bilingual and tend to be happy living in a democracy that is part of the European Union. A Russian-speaking waitress I talked to in a restaurant seemed to confirm this: 'Our parents are trying to teach us things we don't need to know. Their minds are from a different world that doesn't exist any more. They will go and things will change.'

But the idea that it is only a matter of time before tensions abate worried me. First, it felt bleak. Abandoning the likes of Anna and her wood-chopping friend to the vagaries of time requires no actual violence but is indicative of great hostility and disregard. They were people too, after all. Secondly, it seemed naïve. Yes, mindsets change with changing generations. But it

The Ziemeļu Fort complex, closed to the public for half a century, is a magnet for graffiti artists today.

is also true that injuries and prejudices may be inherited, and people frequently start to think more like their parents as they age. Russia's current government has actively sought to drive wedges between Russian and Latvian speakers in the country today. Its television and radio channels, which many Latvians watch, have reinforced daily the narratives of oppression and supposed cultural genocide. These things resonate, and not just with the elderly.

I thought of Northern Ireland. When I was a teenager in the 1990s I was certain that sectarianism would die out as younger people replaced older generations. But time has passed and, although the violence has in large part ceased, the province's two communities are as polarized as ever. Old community divisions have turned out to be useful for explaining new problems and mobilizing people. In Latvia's case sadly there are dangerous people just across the border who would love to exploit those divisions to the point of open conflict.

My last day in Liepāja was Victory Day, 9 May. Just before eleven o'clock in the morning I made my way to the Soviet war memorial. From about 200 metres away I could see that Anna had been misinformed and there were actually several hundred people who had gathered on this most important of Soviet holidays.

At just after eleven the speeches started. Everyone spoke in Russian, but among the speakers were representatives of Latvia's Russian, Ukrainian, Belarusian and Lithuanian communities. There was much talk of the spirit of common endeavour the war had brought and of how fascism would never have been defeated without the sacrifice of so many Soviet heroes. One speaker, himself a veteran, said if we all paused in silence for just one minute for each of the twenty-seven million Soviet dead, we would still be standing there fifty years later. Someone else noted that it would soon fall to the next generation to keep the flame alive and celebrate the centenary of victory in 2045. The crowd listened attentively and, when prompted, shouted *Ura!* and *Slava!* (the Russian words for 'hurray' and 'glory').

Two young Latvian police officers had been sent to police the event – a man and a woman who stood at the edge of the group

Several hundred people attend a Victory Day commemoration in Liepāja.

looking impassively on, respectful but completely disengaged. Were they thinking of the very different narrative their parents, grandparents and schoolteachers had taught them about the war? A narrative that might recall Hitler 'giving' Latvia to Stalin in 1939? Or the Soviet army occupation that was actually crueller on many Latvians than the Wehrmacht's? Or the thousands of Latvians who took to the sea to escape in little boats to Sweden on the night of the final Soviet 'liberation'? Or perhaps like the waitress I met, they were thinking of a time, not far off, when no one would seek to commemorate this complicated war at all?

As I listened I looked round the crowd. The majority were pensioners, and there were few children. In Latvia, 9 May is now a normal school day. But there were still plenty of people in their thirties, forties and fifties. Many carried red tulips and other flowers, which they would later lay on the main memorial or take to other burial sites. The final speaker ended with an old rallying cry: 'Our cause is just!' There was not a hint of doubt in his voice and he got the loudest *Ura!* of all.

PART II

The Baltic Sea

NORWAY
Oslo

SWEDEN

DENMARK

Copenhagen

NORWAY
Oslo

Stockholm

Gotska Sandön

Fårö
Visby · Slite
Gotland

Ziemupe
Karosta
Liepāja

LAT.

LITH.

Baltic Sea

Kaliningrad

(Soviet presence between
1945 and 1946)
Allinge · Bornholm
Rønne
Dueodde

Słupsk

Mukran/Sassnitz
Rügen

POLAND

Travemünde
Priwall
Lübeck   Boltenhagen
GERMANY   Szczecin

——— Iron Curtain

7

Gotland, Sweden

One man frantically pulls a gas mask away from his face to reveal streaming eyes. He clutches his throat, gasping for breath. Nerve agent has penetrated his protective equipment and poisoned him. Another man chokes too, an expression of horror etched on his face. He knows he will not survive. A different pair take turns to sweep radioactive waste from their uniforms using bundles of leaves. And a fifth man sits briefly to jab himself in the leg with an antidote of some kind.

I had thought little about the human reality of a Third World War until confronted by these images at the Gotland Defence Museum (Gotlands Försvarsmuseum). I had imagined either total obliteration of mankind in a series of nuclear strikes, clinical and instant, or lines of tanks, probably seen from above, advancing towards one another over a barren landscape. But these Swedish army manuals of the 1960s and 1970s brought home some grim truths about what the next global conflict might be like. With their luridly memorable pictures, they were probably an attempt to underline to recruits the importance of training hard and learning the correct procedures. But in the process they also demonstrated the certainty of great suffering and many painful deaths.

The Iron Curtain was one of the most likely places where a fresh global conflict would have started between 1945 and 1989. Infringements and provocations that might be smoothed over elsewhere could not be easily dismissed on Europe's East–West fault line, where the military might of the world's two great systems was constantly primed for action. Among all the places I was visiting, however, I had not expected Sweden to display such heightened anxiety about invasion. Its state was officially neutral in the Cold War and did not belong to NATO. It lacked a land border with the USSR or any other Warsaw Pact nation. Sweden, however, did sometimes get very anxious – particularly so when it came to Gotland, its largest island.

Gotland sits in the middle of the Baltic. Its population of just under 60,000 is separated from the Swedish mainland by 90 kilometres of water. To glance at it on a map is to see a place exposed. The Soviet coastline was only 130 kilometres away, a journey of a few hours by boat or submarine and – as I had experienced – a few minutes by plane.

Images in Swedish army training manuals suggested dire consequences if the Cold War turned hot.

Sweden and Russia have a history of enmity. Once, in 1808, Gotland itself was occupied for a month by a Russian invasion force of 1,800 men. When the island's defenders saw what they were up against they surrendered immediately at a country pub, a defeat that has been remembered ever since. But what really concentrated minds in the Cold War was the possibility of the Soviet Union seizing Gotland as a bargaining chip in bigger battles. This is something strategists have called 'the Gotland Gambit'. It might have been a way to test NATO's resolve. Would the Alliance ride to the rescue of a small island that was not even part of a member state? Or it might have been the basis of a ransom demand: withdrawal from Gotland in return for other Western powers making concessions, for instance over the status of West Berlin or about troop deployments in Turkey or the Caribbean. How to make Gotland unattractive to would-be Soviet invaders was an issue that constantly concerned Stockholm.

So seriously did Sweden's military planners take the threat that the island became one of the most militarized places in Sweden. Before going to the Gotland Defence Museum I drove from the capital, Visby, to the large zone in the north-east which was under permanent military control in the Cold War. Foreigners were banned from this area and roadside signs in English, German, Russian, Polish, French and Finnish warned them to keep out. My landlady later told me that the Gotland police also maintained the cordon stringently, stopping cars at entry points and demanding to see the identity documents of everyone inside. (The same rules applied on the smaller neighbouring islands of Gotska Sandön and Fårö, where Ingmar Bergman had his home.)

Cold War Gotland teemed with soldiers. The island was home to a multipurpose force of 20,000 troops, which swelled the resident population by some 40 per cent.[1] They used the restricted landscapes for covert surveillance on the country across the water and also for combat practice. Regular forces and conscripts were taught the dangers of chemical, biological and nuclear weapons, and then sent into war games in the controlled zone's fields, forests and beaches, simulating fighting at close quarters, often with live ammunition, repelling amphibious attacks, and operating in hazmat suits.

The much-feared invasion never materialized, but there were enough scares over the years to keep the military vigilant. In June 1952 Soviet jets shot down two Swedish aircraft near the island. The planes crashed into the sea, killing eight crew members. The Catalina Affair, as the episode was known, was a murky Cold War skirmish in which no side covered itself in glory. The first downed aircraft had been secretly conducting surveillance on behalf of NATO in spite of Sweden's non-aligned status. The Swedish government hid the fact for forty years but it is likely what provoked the USSR to attack. The second plane, a Catalina flying boat, was on a search-and-rescue mission, looking for survivors of the first crash, when the Soviets blasted it from the sky. The USSR denied involvement in both incidents right up until 1991 and refused to make any other comment. This left the widows and families of the dead wondering whether their loved ones had perished at sea or been picked up and spirited into Soviet captivity. For people on Gotland the episode was a powerful reminder of their position right up against the maritime Iron Curtain.

Soviet fishing trawlers were another visible sign of proximity and frequently got too close for comfort. In bad weather it was accepted practice under international law that fishermen of any nation could shelter in any calm water. But Soviet trawlers were particularly quick to head for the inshore waters of Gotland. On several occasions, the Swedish coastguard detected a dummy trawler among their number, most likely laden with surveillance equipment. The submarines were harder to spot but were assumed to be sailing in the sea near the island constantly. Gotlanders out on coastal walks or sailing in their yachts sometimes reported periscopes breaking the surface of the waves. It was always hard to know, of course, to which nation a periscope belonged.

A Soviet navy ship, the *Smolny*, did sail right into the harbour of Slite, the main port on Gotland's east coast, early one morning in April 1961.[2] The event caused pandemonium on the island but not in the way that people worried about an invasion would have predicted. At dead of night the ship – a submarine tender on a mission from Klaipéda to dump chemical waste at sea – had weighed anchor off Gotland's coast and sent up distress flares. Its captain and another sailor then rowed ashore in a lifeboat, reaching land close to a lighthouse. They were promptly detained by armed Swedish security personnel, at which point the captain immediately claimed asylum. 'I can no longer live in a liars' world' were the words he spoke to the policeman who asked him to explain himself.[3]

It transpired that Jonas Pleškys, a twenty-six-year-old Lithuanian, had singlehandedly navigated his ship to Gotland without the knowledge of his crew. He then lied to them about the vessel being in distress. Even the sailor who had come ashore with him was in the dark about Pleškys's motives and had not even known that the landmass they were approaching was Sweden. The authorities permitted Pleškys to stay so he could apply for refugee status, but the other crew member vehemently wanted to return, so they provided him and his lifeboat with an armed escort back to the *Smolny*. It was at this point that an already strange incident had turned downright weird.

The *Smolny*'s crew were pitched into crisis by Pleškys's defection, so much so that they seemed incapable of sailing away. Perhaps they were contemplating the welcome that would await them after such an act of treachery. Perhaps – as many Swedish officials suspected at the time – they were collectively not competent to operate the vessel on which Pleškys had sabotaged the compass. In the end a waiting Swedish coastguard vessel intervened and took the difficult decision to escort the *Smolny* into Slite harbour.

Swedish military commanders had already been informed of the events and were determined that all necessary precautions should be taken at Slite in case the debacle was some kind of elaborate Soviet ruse, a sort of maritime Trojan horse. When the *Smolny* reached the port its sailors saw a dense cordon of armed soldiers gathered on the land to keep their berth separate from the rest of the harbour area. The ship was then hemmed in on the sea side by ships from the Swedish navy, and military helicopters and aircraft took up positions hovering overhead. By lunchtime on the same day, a number of senior Swedish military officials had arrived over from Stockholm, as well as three shocked Soviet diplomats from the embassy. Scores of Swedish and European journalists were also racing to get to the tiny town as news broke on the wires of an unusual Cold War standoff.

I drove to Slite to see for myself where this circus had occurred. A more incongruous setting for an international altercation it would be hard to imagine. The few narrow streets cluster round the harbour and the only buildings of note are a windmill, a quaint wooden swimming club, and the pretty Slitebaden hotel. The *Smolny* was moored right beside the Slitebaden, which enjoyed its two best days ever as Soviet diplomats used it for emergency meetings and dozens of representatives of the press set up temporary offices in its rooms. Standing on the hotel steps late in the evening of the first day, the Soviets told waiting journalists that they had wired to Moscow for instructions and were expecting answers by morning. They could give immediate assurances, they added, that the USSR had had no sinister intent when it came to the *Smolny*'s sudden appearance in Gotland. Walking the few steps down to the harbour, the Soviet military attaché had then boarded the tender and spent the night there, interrogating its crew as he tried to piece together what Pleškys had done. The other two diplomats actually took officers of the Swedish military out for dinner. It was partly a gesture of thanks for their calm reaction to events but partly in the hope of pumping them for information about Pleškys.

At 4 p.m. the next day, the *Smolny* sailed away accompanied by a Swedish navy ship as far as international waters. The military attaché sailed with it all the way back to Karosta, the nearest Soviet port. The crew could no longer be trusted on their own. One of them, the man who had joined Pleškys in the lifeboat, later said he was kept under KGB surveillance for the next twenty years. Meanwhile, Pleškys himself received a death sentence *in absentia*, but with support from the CIA moved to the United States and lived between there and Guatemala until his death in 1993. He worked a variety of jobs but never again captained a ship. After 1961 he said he always felt like he had to look over his shoulder. Without knowing it, tens of millions of people have encountered Pleškys's tale as one of two true-life stories that inspired Tom Clancy's *The Hunt for Red October*.

Escaping to Gotland from the Soviet Union was not a common occurrence. As I had discovered at Ziemupe, the authorities made it as hard as possible for people living near the coast to access any mode of transport that might be used for a getaway. Nevertheless, there were a few more men like Pleškys who found themselves both desperate to leave and able to do so.

In 1983 and 1987 two agricultural crop-sprayers successfully crossed to Gotland in small planes. By coincidence they arrived on the same day, 27 May, four years apart. The second man, Roman Svistunov, was twenty-four and had dreamed of escaping for all his adult life before drumming up the courage for an attempt. Creeping to the aerodrome in the middle of the night, he took off just before dawn, hoping to evade Soviet air defences. He knew that agricultural planes carried only small quantities of fuel. This was specifically to prevent their use in escapes (a measure introduced after the 1983 incident). For his entire journey he was terrified the plane's engine would cut out, ditching him into the water. But luckily it failed only at the last moment, with Gotland already in sight. Svistunov brought the plane down safely in the sea and swam ashore. Unlike Pleškys he would make his home on the island, mostly working as a chef at a local pizza restaurant. Asked in a magazine interview what had gone through his mind as he flew away from the USSR, he replied, 'I wasn't thinking anything. I just wanted to survive'.[4]

At an earlier point in time, in the mid-1940s, escaping to Gotland was briefly very popular indeed, as large numbers of people fled the advancing Soviet army. A replica of the boats they used – similar to the ones later burned at Ziemupe – now stands in Slite harbour. Then, soon after the USSR's collapse, a new mass exodus commenced. These refugees crossed the same stretch of water, putting to sea from a variety of Baltic ports. But this time they came from much further afield. Most had been displaced by the Gulf War and were fleeing from the regime of Saddam Hussein. They made their way up through Turkey and Russia into the newly independent Baltic states on their long trek to Western Europe. Once at the coast, they used small fishing vessels to escape, sometimes piloted by hired locals and sometimes purchased and operated by the refugees themselves. The usual rules about the grave dangers of such crossings applied. In one widely reported episode, on a cold January morning in 1993, the Slite coastguard was called to a ship in distress and found 391 people hiding in terrible cramped conditions in its cargo hold.[5]

Gotland and Slite have not been untouched by the recent great waves of unplanned migration to affect Europe, starting with the influx of refugees in the summer of 2015. On that occasion the needy came not by boat but were allocated to the town as part of a planned Swedish government dispersal policy.

I went into the Slitebaden hotel and met its current owner, a cheerful man called Peter. I wanted to talk to him about Pleškys and the *Smolny*, but he knew little of the episode. Instead, he wanted to speak about the recent refugees. The Slitebaden had closed down as a hotel some time before 2015 and found itself pressed into service as temporary accommodation for the arriving Afghan and Syrian families. Peter explains that when he took over the building a year later, with plans to turn it back into a hotel, he discovered it in a very poor state. Another nearby hostel which was exclusively used by young male refugees was basically left in ruins, he adds, with its doors kicked in and holes punched in walls. He is among the majority of islanders who were pleased to do their bit for these people in difficulty, he says. But a significant minority, as in other places across the continent, felt it was not their problem and created risks for local residents.

Peter has now opened the Slitebaden again, after an elegant renovation involving muted Swedish paintwork and some simple mid-century modern furnishings. 'We're still posting big red numbers,' he admits as he shows me round. But 'like the Soviet commissars of old', he jokes, 'I have a five-year plan.'

All trace of Iron Curtain tension disappeared from Gotland almost immediately after the USSR fell apart. The island seemingly had nothing left to fear. Russia was set on a course for democracy and, anyway, the coastline across the sea mostly passed to other successor states, the small friendly countries of Estonia, Latvia and Lithuania. Only a short stretch around Kaliningrad remained under Moscow's control. New ties and relationships quickly developed and Gotlanders stopped thinking of themselves as a people marooned on the edge of the West.

Inside Visby's stunning medieval walls I paid a visit to Lena Pasternak, director of the Baltic Centre for Writers and Translators, to ask her about the years after the Cold War ended. Lena is a relative of the author of *Doctor Zhivago*. She chose Gotland as her home in the 1990s. Soon afterwards she began establishing the centre that has become her life's work. Its vision is inspired by Gotland's position at the heart of the

The Slitebaden hotel which sits beside the harbour where the Smolny *was impounded in April 1961.*

Baltic. She has made a retreat for writers from any country with a Baltic coastline. They may apply for bursaries to spend time there, away from the pressures of daily life, focusing on their novels, poems and translations. The building, which includes a library and lots of individual writing spaces, is located on a rocky plateau overlooking Visby's majestic twin-towered cathedral and, beyond it, the sea. Lena welcomed me in on a chilly Friday morning when the wind seemed to be blowing straight from Siberia. She led me upstairs for coffee and a chat.

We started by talking about the good years. Multinational co-operation on equal terms had been the name of the game during the centre's first two decades. Writers' unions and arts councils in every eligible country collaborated with Lena and her team to identify promising authors and publicize the centre's grants and fellowships. There was sufficient funding thanks to support from the Swedish government and many others. Efforts to integrate the old East and the old West were an acknowledged priority for every nation in the region.

Things had been trickier of late, she said. Money was more of a struggle. Some funders had come to believe that the centre's integrative work was done, after most former Eastern Bloc countries joined the European Union. There were newer needy causes. Yet, simultaneously, the urgency of the centre's mission actually increased as writers in Russia began to face growing persecution again. The retreat found itself becoming a sanctuary in a way that Lena would not have predicted back in the 1990s.

Integration was something people started taking for granted, she told me. She felt a constant duty to remind them that co-operation between cultures is always fragile. 'The situation in Russia is especially worrying,' she said. The centre could still assist many Russian writers each year, but increasingly it was doing so by word of mouth or through direct relationships with the individuals concerned. Official Russian literary organizations could not be relied upon to make fair, nonpartisan decisions about funding applications because they had been so thoroughly captured by the state. Unquestioning patriotism was once again the only route to government support as a writer in Russia.

Lena worried about the willingness some Russians displayed to swallow the leader's rhetoric. Too many were happy to see their country bullying other nations once more. Too many were excited at the prospect of settling old scores. And, conversely, too few felt moved to fight for their own liberties. 'What strikes me,' she said, 'is that back in the late Soviet period there was a doubleness in most people's attitudes towards the regime. What the regime said was not really truth; it was a kind of fable. But now I sense that many Russians really want to believe what's being said, really want to believe in this imperialism of Putin's.' The Visby centre had explicitly started to try to support the other voices, some of them political and some not, so that they would be available for Russians as and when they wanted and were in a position to hear them.

Does Gotland itself feel bullied by Moscow again? I asked. The short answer was yes. Back when Lena was first setting up the centre, Gotland was demilitarizing at breakneck pace. The Swedish armed forces had pretty much gone by 2010. A walk around Visby's main garrison complex had already shown me this: the barracks, offices and messes of the old Gotland Regiment had been transformed into a business park of accountancy firms, burglar alarm suppliers and massage salons.

Yet no sooner was the change complete, Lena explained, than many people began questioning the wisdom of leaving the island unprotected. In the first half of the 2010s Russian submarines started to test Sweden's defence and surveillance capabilities much more keenly, just as Soviet ones had during the Cold War. In the autumn of 2014 the Swedish navy spent a week hunting a Russian mini-submarine that had been sighted in the country's territorial waters.[6] Naval commanders were sure there was something down there but could not find it – a situation that was partly blamed on Sweden's decision to sell its submarine-hunting helicopters. Russian fighter jets also began infringing Sweden's airspace more regularly, and there were signs of the now-familiar softer taunts: an alleged increase in espionage activity by resident Russian diplomats; suspected hacking efforts from Russian IP addresses; and rumours of online misinformation campaigns. Ever since Russian forces annexed Crimea and occupied eastern Ukraine the Gotland Gambit has seemed a realistic prospect again in a way that it did not for thirty years.

By 2018, there was no trust left between Stockholm and Moscow, and the Swedish government performed an apparent 180-degree U-turn. It reintroduced conscription and posted some of the new conscripts, along with regular personnel, back to Gotland. Just eight years after being abolished, the Gotland Regiment was re-established and plans were hatched to build a major new military complex. Like citizens in the rest of the country, Gotlanders also received a Cold War-style booklet in the post, *If Crisis or War Comes* (in Swedish, *Om krisen eller kriget kommer*). Although it did not mention Russia by name, it dropped pretty big hints about the reasons behind the shift in official thinking: 'For many years, the preparations made in Sweden for the threat of war and war have been very limited . . . However, as the world around us has changed, the Government has decided to strengthen Sweden's total defence.'[7] There was a short chapter on public shelters too, although no pictures of people choking on nerve gas or administering antidotes to themselves.

Lena did not think Gotland was next on President Putin's list of desired acquisitions. She, like others I spoke to, also felt there might be something a bit cosmetic about Sweden's enhancement of the island's defences. The new garrison, which was under construction on the outskirts of Visby during my visit, was mainly remarked on for its lavishness, having been designed by a famous architect. And the new unit's focus on high-tech warfare had left some wondering whether its location on Gotland was

The fantastical medieval walls of Visby, Gotland's capital.

merely a matter of political expediency. But Lena said there were other locals who were pleased Gotland was 'not just left alone to face Putin'. The old divide clearly had much more life in it than people once thought. Whatever that may bring Sweden in reality, when you find yourself on the edge again it can be good to know that the centre hasn't forgotten you.

8

Bornholm, Denmark

5 May 1945. In Denmark the Nazis had just surrendered. After five years of German overlordship, British troops were streaming into the country through Danish ports and along Danish roads. No sooner had news of the defeat broken the night before, announced by the BBC's Danish Service, than families everywhere began tearing blackout blinds from their windows and coming out into the streets to celebrate. As the echelons of Allied soldiers made their way towards their designated muster points, they were mobbed by happy crowds. The joyous festivities would continue for over a week.

Yet there was still one part of the country where the Third Reich remained in control. On the small isolated island of Bornholm, far out in the Baltic, 180 kilometres east of Copenhagen, the German naval captain Gerhard von Kamptz continued in charge. Von Kamptz knew the game was up and had despatched telegrams to the Danish capital to ask for a single British officer be sent to the island to take his surrender. But because of Bornholm's location the British were deliberately not sending one. This far east, by prior agreement, it fell to the Soviet Union to end the war.

In recent weeks Bornholm's population, usually around 40,000, had grown to over 70,000 as German-speaking refugees fled there from Prussia and other lands the Soviet army had liberated. Having heard the stories they brought and, no doubt, knowing something of the brutality with which the Nazis had occupied the USSR, von Kamptz was desperate to avoid either himself or his men being captured by the Soviets. For days, Soviet commanders had issued regular ultimata demanding his complete capitulation. Von Kamptz had ignored them all.

On 9 May Churchill belatedly reconsidered and authorized British forces to send a detachment to Bornholm, but by that point time had already run out.[1] Von Kamptz had stood his ground and on 7 May the USSR lost patience. During that day and the one following, Bornholm endured a ferocious assault. Ten Danes died, as did many hundreds, possibly thousands, of German soldiers and refugees. A large proportion of these are known to have been civilians blasted off boats they were living on in the island's harbours. On 9 May the Soviet troops finally came ashore. After a small battle with the remnants of the German garrison, they declared Bornholm free.

For the first time in history, and with most Danes completely unaware of it, a part of Denmark was now controlled from Moscow. So began what the Danes call 'the Long Liberation' (*den Lange Befrielse*), a surprising and largely forgotten episode in which Denmark found itself in the front line of the incipient Cold War. The Soviets established control over Bornholm quickly. As von Kamptz had feared, they carted him and his surviving forces, and the German refugees, into captivity in the USSR. On Bornholm they settled in for the duration.

Even if you arrive from Gotland, Bornholm feels tiny. Rønne is small in the way Scottish fishing towns are small. There is rigour and single-mindedness in its streets and its modest, often charming buildings. Most of the latter date from the 1940s, for the reasons just set out, but hark back to older styles. The island's villages usually cluster round a solitary centre of economic life, typically a harbour with a smokehouse. The sea is almost always visible, often in multiple directions.

On a gin-clear Monday morning – the island is reputedly Denmark's sunniest place – I walked over to the Bornholm

Museum to talk to its curator, Jakob Seerup. I was early for the interview, having woken at 5 a.m. when the first shafts of light broke through my flimsy Scandinavian curtains. Waiting for the museum to open, I found myself sitting by a hillock with a door in its side. I later discovered it was one of many bunkers the townspeople had used to shelter from the 1945 bombing.

Jakob walked up to me with his hand outstretched and soon we embarked on a wide-ranging conversation about the island's unique postwar history. It would take up the rest of the morning.

Denmark escaped fairly lightly for most of the Second World War, Jakob begins by telling me. Undoubtedly there were instances of great hardship and the distressing fact of the occupation itself, but there had been much normality. The tongue-in-cheek nickname German personnel gave the country was the 'whipped-cream front' (*der Schlagsahne Front*). It was seen as a good posting to have.

'This was where lucky Germans ended up,' Jakob says. 'It was the front where you ate cake and had a jolly time. And most Danes, Bornholmers included, were probably pretty content much of the time. They were aware of the bombings of other European cities. They were aware of the sufferings of the Norwegians and the Dutch. And here we were making money from the war, trading with the Germans, selling them wheat and pork.'

The events on Bornholm in May 1945 were definitely more shocking because of the quiet that preceded them. When the Soviets landed, they spread out across the island. Rønne itself had been destroyed by the air bombardment, so while locals cleared the rubble and disposed of the corpses, the Red Army made a headquarters at the little resort of Allinge and the nearby medieval fortress of Hammershus. More than 7,000 Soviet soldiers came in total, many ending up billeted in Allinge's seafront hotels.

Locals were instantly anxious. The new masters' reputation

preceded them and they gave no explanation for the buildup of forces at a time when Bornholm no longer faced any threat. The demeanour and conduct of the first Soviet arrivals did nothing to help. They were a disorderly bunch, exhausted, brutalized and traumatized by their experiences on the Eastern Front. Both Jakob and Klaus Linnert, whom I would meet at the nearby Bornholm Defence Museum (Bornholms Forsvarsmuseum), tell me there were several cases of rape in the early days and that more than anything else these fuelled the islanders' fears of a terrible ordeal ahead. Some Bornholmers also found themselves threatened at gunpoint, and a few may even have been killed for getting on the wrong side of groups of soldiers.

Quickly, however, the situation began to calm. The first arrivals were rotated off the island and their replacements were generally friendlier and more disciplined. Order within barracks was reinforced: as in Porkkala, the authorities put up exemplary slogans and gave lectures about good conduct. They also began to crack down harder on misdemeanours.

The greatest and most intractable evil for both Bornholm's population and Soviet commanders was alcohol. The troops couldn't get enough of it, drinking their way through the island's entire stocks of beer, wine and spirits in a matter of weeks, before turning to more dangerous sources of intoxication. Klaus's museum preserves a letter from 1 August 1945 in which local authorities forbade Bornholm pharmacists to sell surgical spirit to Soviet soldiers. Klaus tells me the soldiers then moved on to aftershaves and perfumes. A majority of the twelve Red Army personnel who died during the USSR's time on the island were victims of alcohol poisoning.

By late summer 1945 life on Bornholm was settling into an uneasy but tolerable pattern. The islanders were working out how to coexist with the new military interlopers, and the interlopers in turn were placing progressively fewer restrictions on daily life (the aftershave shortage notwithstanding). There were even instances of friendly cultural exchange. On hot days the army's bands would come out of their barracks to play for the public. A card I saw advertised a 'Russisk Koncert' that took place one evening at seven o'clock in the square in front of Rønne's main church. A London friend with Danish relatives told me how her elderly stepmother-in-law had visited the island at this time and watched her mother dancing with a Russian officer. Klaus says that several consensual Soviet–Danish romances blossomed. 'There are still half-Russian children on Bornholm today.'

For Soviet soldiers who could handle their drink Bornholm seems to have been a comparatively relaxed posting, their own version of the whipped-cream front. Surviving panels from hastily erected Soviet buildings show paintwork rendered in hopeful shades of light blue and cream, naïve stars and hammers and sickles stencilled on them. An irreverent sign, probably from a bathhouse, indicates the location of a '*rastrusochnaya ploshchadka*', literally 'a place to take your pants off'.

A 1945 advertisement, now in the collection of the Bornholm Defence Museum, publicizing a Russian concert.

One of the richest insights into the Soviet presence on Bornholm comes from a stash of photographs taken by Alfred Kjøller, who ran Allinge's photography studio. Having snapped the Kriegsmarine and Wehrmacht during the German occupation, Kjøller immediately offered his lens to the Soviets after May 1945. Officers and squaddies alike were keen to pose for portraits, often sending them as keepsakes to far-off family members and sweethearts. The results are spellbinding.[2] The glimpse I'd had back in Porkkala of Soviet troops at rest, enjoying downtime with friends, was hugely expanded by this collection. I was particularly struck by the portraits of female soldiers. Around 500 were stationed on Bornholm at any one time and Jakob tells me they were treated as 'a real peculiarity'. They were part of the more than 800,000 women who served in the USSR's armed forces during the war, a higher proportion of whom spent time at the front line than those of any other country.

Portraits of Soviet soldiers from Alfred Kjøller's studio in Allinge.

On each leg of my journey so far I had confronted Soviet power in a different guise. The usual depiction of the USSR as a monolithic giant imposing identical harsh conditions and unbending ideology everywhere it went simply didn't hold. To be sure, the Soviet paradigm was severe, but within it there was room for nuance and responsiveness to circumstances. I asked Jakob whether the Soviets had ever reached out to resident socialists on Bornholm or engaged in communist propaganda. He laughed. The historical record proves that all problems with propaganda came in the opposite direction. In October 1945, after several complaints from Hammershus, the Rønne police chief banned evangelical missionaries from handing out Christian tracts to Soviet soldiers.

How long would the USSR remain on Bornholm? That was the question that everyone on the island and elsewhere in Denmark was asking themselves as 1945 turned into 1946. Politicians in

Britain, France and the United States were also watching with growing apprehension. A lasting Soviet occupation would have repercussions for the balance of power across northern Europe. Would the Soviet Union really dare to separate Bornholm permanently from the rest of Denmark, as had happened with East Prussia, which would become the USSR's Kaliningrad Province? Or might it insist on renting the island, as it had Porkkala? Might the local population be expelled? Precedents existed for all manner of outcomes but the longer the Long Liberation continued the more likely it seemed that the USSR would not leave.

Both the resident forces and leaders in Moscow were giving nothing away. London's MI6 had scored what it thought was an early victory when it recruited the chief Danish official on the island, the *Amtmand*, to be its informer. (The fact only came to light recently when a journalist turned up at Klaus's museum with a cache of documents that contained the *Amtmand*'s reports.) Codenamed 'HANSEL' and always referring to himself in the third person, Poul Christian von Stemann sent weekly despatches to the UK. But, while they contained much fascinating local colour, they were frustratingly silent on the subject of Soviet intentions. Addressing the House of Commons in October 1945 the British Foreign Secretary Ernest Bevin could only say that 'Soviet forces [were] still in occupation of Bornholm' but that he had 'no information as to the tasks on which they are now engaged or the date on which they are to be withdrawn'.[3] Four months later, in February 1946, George Kennan, the United States's deputy ambassador in Moscow, wrote in his famous Long Telegram that he worried Bornholm would be one of the places where the USSR found it 'timely and promising . . . to advance [the] official limits of Soviet power'.[4]

It is impossible to say what the Western Allies would have done if Moscow had decided to annexe Bornholm. So stretched were their resources and so relatively insignificant was the island that the truth is it would probably have been left to its fate.

Only a short time later, in 1948, it would take massive, almost superhuman efforts to retain control of the western sectors of Berlin – and Bornholm was no Berlin.

But to the great relief of all Danes and many in Europe's Western capitals the question did not arise. Suddenly, in March 1946, the Soviets began making arrangements to leave, and by 5 April they had gone. 'On the day the last ship departed, everybody came to the harbour here in Rønne,' Jakob tells me, 'and there was a mighty gun salute that no one ever forgot. The Russians didn't have blanks for saluting purposes, so they just used up all their live ammo. It was a terrific noise. You really can say they came in with a bang and went out with a bang as well.'

But why did they go? Jakob thinks the Soviets 'would have preferred to stay but decided it wasn't worth it'. They would have known that 'a time had come when it was difficult to explain what they were doing here without declaring a proper occupation'. But a proper occupation would have meant partition, effectively penalizing a country that had been one of its allies in the Second World War, not an opponent like Germany, Austria or Finland. Given all the opprobrium that would have attracted, it seems it was not a step Stalin was prepared to take.

The Soviet exit did come with significant terms and conditions attached, however. To secure full control of Bornholm, Copenhagen had to promise never to allow foreign troops onto the island again. Apparently the Soviets explicitly threatened – in a text that neither side has ever published – that any infringement of this would be tantamount to a declaration of war. Jakob tells me that USSR diplomats in the Danish capital policed the stipulation meticulously. 'Even as late as 1983,' he says, 'there was an American Marine brass band that was invited to play at a country fair here. The Soviet embassy learned of it and protested. To them it was simple: you just couldn't have American soldiers on Bornholm. The band never came.' There were incidents that slipped by without the Soviets noticing, of course. Once or twice early in the Cold War, MI6 smuggled agents into Eastern Europe by despatching them in boats from Bornholm harbours. NATO ships on exercises sometimes berthed overnight in Rønne. But even then, Jakob adds, the Danish authorities were quite strict about not allowing any sailors to come ashore.

Moscow reserved for itself the exclusive right to bring non-Danish military personnel onto Bornholm. For a full NATO member, it was really quite remarkable to have to adhere to such a concession. In practice it took the form of annual, and sometimes more frequent, pilgrimages to the graves of the Soviet dead, which had been gathered at a cemetery in Allinge. I drove there during my trip and sat looking at the black granite obelisk which declares 'Eternal Glory to the Russian Heroes', and an adjacent red granite monument imported from the USSR in 1986, and, beyond them, the sea. It is a beautiful spot.

Jakob tells me that right through the Cold War, no matter how sour relations were, the Danish army always provided an honour guard for these military visits. In a symbolic show of respect, the Danes presented arms to the Soviets, and they all lunched together afterwards. The Russian army took the tradition on after 1991 and, more recently, for unexplained reasons, representatives of a Kaliningrad yacht club have joined the small ceremony each Victory Day. (Their lavish wreath was still propped against the obelisk when I visited.) In a mark of how relations between Russia and the old West have deteriorated of late, however, no Danish honour guard has come since 2014, when President Putin annexed the Crimea – and it is very hard to imagine that any will return soon.

The USSR left its dead on Bornholm, and some children who never got to meet their Soviet fathers. But its most important legacy was probably an enduring sense of bitterness. Everyone I met mentioned it: bitterness not at the Red Army itself, but at how Bornholm's plight was ignored and downplayed in the rest of the country. 'While Denmark was having a huge party,

Rønne and other parts of Bornholm were being levelled,' Jakob said. Over the next eleven months the Red Army's presence was treated as a fait accompli. 'The perspective of people on Bornholm to this day is that politicians in Copenhagen didn't do enough and weren't quick enough to say, "Thank you very much, Soviet soldiers, now you can go back home."'

The enormous bombardment and the ensuing Soviet occupation are always referred to by mild-sounding euphemisms like 'the Soviet presence' and '*den Lange Befrielse*'. But Bornholmers number themselves among the Second World War's forgotten victims. Another local said to me, 'This is really a big part of Bornholm's identity. We were occupied for a year longer than the rest of Denmark, and somehow it was forgotten. The rest of Denmark abandoned us.'

Through their 1946 agreement with Denmark the Soviets effectively neutralized Bornholm as a launching point for any future attack, but the island's location meant they could not stop it having other kinds of involvement in the Cold War. As divisions between East and West strengthened, it became an important destination for Eastern Bloc refugees. It was temptingly close to both the German Democratic Republic and Poland – just 90 or so kilometres north-east of the East German island of Rügen and around 120 kilometres north-west of the Polish city of Słupsk. We know from firsthand accounts and other research that a lot of Eastern Europeans saw Bornholm on maps and toyed with the idea of escaping there, hatching plots only to realize that the odds would be steeply stacked against them. A few thousand probably went further and actually set off, though only around a hundred and fifty are known to have actually made it across.

The star among this select band was Franciszek Jarecki, a twenty-one-year-old Polish fighter pilot who stole a plane from his base at Słupsk and flew it the short distance to Rønne on the morning of 5 March 1953. Coincidentally, Jarecki was taking to the skies just as Stalin, in his dacha outside Moscow, was breathing his last. Even the shock of the Great Leader's death could not eclipse entirely the crisis the Pole's escape caused because Jarecki's chosen vehicle was a MiG-15 jet, the first intact example to fall into Western hands. The Danish government returned the MiG on a ship some weeks later, but the communist governments knew the damage that had been done. A team of aeronautical experts had swiftly come to Bornholm and dismantled and reassembled the plane in order to gather a complete picture of its design and potential vulnerabilities. Here was one of the best examples of the impact a single defector could have. In the USA Jarecki was rewarded with an audience with President Eisenhower and a cheque for $50,000.

Most other arrivals made do with much less, both in terms of how they travelled and the welcome they received. As Patrick Wright describes in his excellent book, *Iron Curtain: From Stage to Cold War*, fugitives 'set sail in canoes, reconditioned amphibious vehicles, and catamarans improvised out of old kayaks' and a few even took to the high seas 'on resort-style pedal boats and perilous rafts made of inflatable mattresses'.[5] Jakob showed me one such vessel and it was immediately clear to me that it was not the kind of thing you would want to sit in for a 90-kilometre crossing of the Baltic. Narrow and flimsy, it was powered by a single oar made from a broom handle with two wooden seat backs for paddles. This was the dinghy in which twenty-one-year-old Bernild Casper escaped East Germany in 1979.

It was more than a coincidence that Jarecki and Casper were 21, Jonas Pleškys 26, and Roman Svistunov 24. Escaping across the Iron Curtain was a young man's game, particularly when it came to making a successful crossing of the sea. 'We talk a lot about the Wall. The city of Berlin has become this symbol for Cold War brutality in general because of the people who were shot there,' Jakob says. 'But a big number also died on this big wet wall called the Baltic.' Estimates vary, but it is thought that

Bernild Casper's dinghy on which he escaped from East Germany to Bornholm in 1979.

at least 174 East Germans drowned in maritime escape attempts, while more than 4,500 were picked up by their own authorities. Youth could be helpful in giving an escapee the edge to succeed. It also likely increased their sense of desperation in the first place, spurring them on to actions that older and equally disillusioned citizens would have considered foolhardy. Research indicates that, contrary to the propaganda, most refugees were not spies or even military employees. A large number were young manual labourers.[6]

Every successful attempt was a combination of bravery, re-sourcefulness and luck. As early as 1950 two pilots from the Polish national carrier LOT plotted an escape by air but were unable to work out how to steal one of their employer's planes. Instead, they ended up fashioning an ingenious pedalo from a spare aircraft fuel tank and pedalling their way to Bornholm. In 1970 five Poles seized a civilian aircraft by threatening the pilot with a hand grenade. They made it to Bornholm but found themselves jailed for hijacking; later, one would commit a bank robbery and actually end up being deported back to Poland.

'Just this past December,' Jakob says, 'two men in their sixties came into the museum. They were two of the six Ciborowski children who had escaped in a group of ten back in 1968. Their father had captained a ship while their mother hid with them – their ages ranged from eight to eighteen – in a tiny storage space created behind some fish boxes. It really was an amazing feat. You couldn't just leave an Eastern Bloc harbour without being checked by the authorities, so just imagine how absolutely silent they must have been and the stress of that.'

It is stories like these – of ordinary people risking everything – that resonate most with his visitors today, Jakob says. It has become harder to interest some of them, particularly the young, in the details of the capitalist–communist standoff, but the human drive to seek a better life really grabs them. 'That story is something our young people seem to understand intuitively,' Jakob says. Immigration has become a hugely divisive issue for Danes. Many schoolchildren and students are ashamed of the restrictions and barriers the Danish government places on asylum seekers and of the populist anti-immigration rhetoric that circulates in politics and the media. Consequently they are keen to learn how the communist refugees of old were treated. It surprises them to discover that the Eastern defectors were often received with open arms.

Of course, the two situations are different in key respects – particularly the smaller numbers involved in the Cold War, and the fundamental closeness of Danish and Eastern European cultures compared with, say, Danish and Middle Eastern cultures. But Jakob says there is no doubt that both official and public attitudes have hardened enormously. 'Back then, once they made it to Denmark, they were automatically accepted as political refugees. Not like if you come from the war in Syria when they'll be like, "Bah! Are you really a refugee?" For these guys' – he gestures at a display of black-and-white photographs of successful escapees to Bornholm in the Cold War – 'there was no problem at all.'

I walked back to my flat reflecting on the fact that it really was very rare for countries in the West to try to send people back over the Iron Curtain during the Cold War. Irrespective of any burden they might place on their receiving countries, it was simply accepted that refugees from the Eastern Bloc should not be returned. The exceptions were people who robbed banks or committed murders. For today's asylum seekers from outside Europe, it is often enough to fail to fill in a form properly or, in some cases, just to turn eighteen. Racism and religious prejudice have clearly played a part in modern-day intolerance. But is it also partly the fact that Cold War defectors represented a kind of victory over an enemy that made them more acceptable to their hosts? Would the same calculation hold, and to what extent and for how long, if Putin were to create large numbers of new defectors and refugees from his own or another European country today?

Moscow's intention was that Bornholm should have no military role after 1946, but in fact the island carved out a new strategic niche for itself, one which exploited its geography without breaching the letter of the Soviet deal. As you drive east from Rønne the terrain briefly rises before falling away towards the windswept beaches of the south-east coast. From here southwards, there is first sea and then the Great European Plain, with scarcely any high ground until one reaches the Tatra mountains of Czechia and Slovakia. To the east it is the same story right to the Urals.

Electronic and radio signals travel well over such landscapes, and during the second half of the twentieth century interception technologies improved rapidly, meaning that things said in offices, bunkers or aerodromes in one country could be picked up with a minimum of distortion or interference in places thousands of kilometres away. From the 1950s onwards the Danish government and NATO developed Bornholm as a kind of gigantic ear for permanently listening to sensitive exchanges across the Eastern Bloc.

The eardrum was located in a former lighthouse at a place called Dueodde on Bornholm's southern tip. Danish intelligence agencies took out a lease on the building in 1958 and spent three years kitting it out. Then in 1961 the listening devices were switched on and a detachment of intelligence officers and engineers moved into the old lighthouse keeper's cottage. They were one of many links in a chain of NATO surveillance stations that included more famous locations like Fylingdales in North Yorkshire and Teufelsberg in West Berlin. As NATO's easternmost listening station, however, and the one best situated to get clear uninterrupted signals from multiple directions, little Bornholm's electronic ear was always among the most important.

Many of Dueodde's intelligence achievements remain shrouded in mystery. But one tantalizing revelation to emerge is that, during the Prague Spring of 1968, operatives at Dueodde listened in real time to conversations between Soviet tank crews on the streets of Czechoslovakia. When the base's future was considered at some point in the late 1970s, NATO decided not just to keep it but to expand it greatly. Alongside the old lighthouse they added a much taller concrete tower with a huge heavy-goods lift that could be used to move satellite dishes to the optimum location for spying on different targets.

I visited on a blustery day and, while still some way off in the car, was struck by both the architectural beauty of the 1980s structures and their incongruity. The main tower was a giant military beanstalk rising up out of an otherwise gentle landscape of woods and farmland, a space shuttle primed for lift-off.

After surviving earlier rounds of post-Cold War defence cuts Dueodde listening station finally succumbed to the same fate as Gotland's military installations, closing for good in 2012. At that point seventeen people lost their jobs, and an 80-metre radio mast was dismantled. It was absolutely no shock to discover that this decision was quickly regretted and has subsequently been reversed, once again because of President Putin's combativeness.

Just four years after the closure, a new 80-metre mast was erected a few kilometres away from Dueodde at Østermarie. It replicates exactly – at least as far as locals and experts understand – the capabilities so recently switched off.[7] I drove to see it, in a field on the relatively high ground in the middle of the island. This time it seemed that all supporting equipment and offices had been hidden discreetly underground or at a remote site (unless the adjacent farm machinery showroom is a cunning front).

The listening station at Dueodde was one of NATO's most important bases.

I circled the mast for a while on a series of deserted single-track roads, stopping occasionally to get out and take photographs. At one point a silver Audi came towards me at speed. It contained a man and woman, both wearing black business suits (the only people I saw dressed like this during my entire stay on Bornholm). My pulse quickened. They could have been ordinary Bornholmers on their way to or from a funeral or wedding, but I couldn't help seeing them as intelligence officers, perhaps despatched from Copenhagen to check that the mast was working properly, or perhaps even spies from Russia or another of the countries that NATO still listens to. I got back in my car quickly and motored home to Rønne, my mind buzzing with plots.

An overactive imagination was something that afflicted some Bornholmers during the Cold War too, probably a natural result of their exposed position right up against the maritime Iron Curtain and their experiences in the mid-1940s. Back at

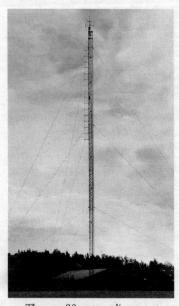

The new 80-metre radio mast at Østermarie.

the Bornholm Museum, Jakob had ended his tour by taking me into his office. There he had reached down to a low window ledge and brought up a black leatherette box. 'Now I will show you something that only very few people have ever seen,' he said. 'This is our Cold War Object Number One. This is a little bit toxic.' For a split second I wondered if the box actually contained something toxic, like nuclear waste, but he lifted the lid to reveal an inner compartment filled with pink and yellow index cards.

Jakob explained that this belonged to a local man who had served at the army barracks in Rønne in the 1960s and 1970s. He was a major who had been seconded from army intelligence – there was always at least one at the barracks whose job it was to spot conscripts with pro-communist or pacifist sympathies and kick them out. The particular major in question had gone well beyond his remit and ended up spying on the island's entire civilian population. The card index was the fruit of these labours, a personal repository in which he noted every suspicious act that came to his knowledge, and cross-referenced suspects one with another. Over twenty years he built up an ever-more elaborate picture of conspiracies and subversive networks both real and imagined.

'I am quite sure he was acting in a personal capacity with all this,' Jakob says. 'That's what will make it such a good object for teaching people about the Cold War, about the atmosphere, the paranoia.' He starts plucking out cards at random. 'This one is a harbour worker, born circa 1915,' he translates. 'He lives with an uncle who was earlier the chairman of the Rønne Communist Party. It says he's married to a woman from East Germany and that he must be regarded as an active communist and "a dangerous type".' Jakob chuckles. A majority of the cards seem pretty clearly to relate to people who posed no real threat, he tells me. 'But by sheer coincidence I know that this guy was, well . . . He went to evening school and learned Russian, and in the 1970s and 1980s he was in every delegation to the Soviet Union as a translator and political aide. Maybe the major got this one right.'

Jakob picks another. 'This one. She had a restaurant, and was connected with one of the local conscripts that the major sent home.' The next few cards were all signatories to a petition against nuclear weapons and nothing else was noted against them. 'That was enough to get you included,' Jakob says. Then there is a man of Polish birth who worked as a fisherman in Nexø, the main town in Bornholm's east. 'He sails out with his boat each evening and returns in the morning with a catch even though his nets are dry. The major must have thought he was sailing to meet East German or Polish secret police, maybe couriering letters or photographs to them and receiving the fish in payment and as a cover. Something fishy may well have been going on, as you say in English.'

The museum acquired the box when the major died a few years ago. His widow had asked a volunteer to come over and take away anything of historical value. Apparently she had no idea there was this 'unexploded bomb', as Jakob describes it, among his belongings. Why isn't it on display? I ask. Jakob says that many of the people named in the cards are still alive and so the object raises ethical questions. Moreover, unlike in the UK and some other countries, Denmark's secret services have never declassified any archives, so the box really is unique. Exhibiting it could be controversial. But one of the most troubling things is that the

*'Cold War Object Number One' at the Bornholm
Museum, a card index of local suspicious behaviour
kept by an army officer between the 1960s and
the 1980s.*

major could never have observed all these people singlehandedly.
He must have had a network of his own, informing him about
the goings-on in Bornholm's towns and villages, and, presumably,
acting on tip-offs he provided perhaps to deny people jobs or
even to have them placed under official surveillance.

I had flown into Bornholm and also used planes between most
of my destinations in northern Europe, but I would not now
take another flight until I reached Trieste on the southern side of
the European mainland. My means of transport from this point
would be cars, trains and buses and, first of all, the ferry from
Rønne to Rügen. Standing at the top of the 1980s listening
tower in Dueodde the previous day, I had realized for the first
time what a significant junction point Bornholm was on my
journey. Up to now I had focused on the fault line that ran
directly between the capitalist West and the Soviet Union.

From here on, as I travelled further south, I would be exploring the Iron Curtain that ran along the edge of the buffer of new communist states that Stalin forced into existence at the end of the Second World War. I would only return to the USSR's own frontier at the very end of my trip, when I reached the Turkish–Azerbaijani border.

As I walked into Rønne harbour at 7 a.m. on another sunny morning, I spotted my Bornholmslinjen catamaran in the distance. Before I reached it I had to walk past another, much grander vessel that had not been present when I bought my ticket the evening before. It was a huge vintage yacht, painted gleaming white and cream and with polished woodwork and lots of gold leaf. *HDMY Dannebrog*, I read on the side: the Danish royal yacht, which first entered service in 1931. While the UK had decommissioned the Royal Yacht Britannia back in 1997, Denmark, it seems, has kept her equivalent, and the Danish Royal Family still uses it.

I was now being watched. Two sailors stood at either end of a gangway, both in crisp parade uniforms and with shining silver cutlasses. They nodded and smiled. Was the Queen herself on board? I asked, feeling a bit stupid as the words left my mouth. Not the Queen but the Crown Prince, one replied, being far more forthcoming than a British equivalent would have been. The ship had sailed into the harbour overnight and Prince Frederik was now having breakfast before a day of engagements.

I thanked the sailors and walked on. As I queued for my own much more humdrum ship, I found myself wondering if Frederik would get through his day without anyone mentioning the Long Liberation to him. Probably not. Even after almost eighty years Denmark's neglect of the islanders was still strongly felt. Bornholm's Iron Curtain experience has become integral to its selfhood as a whole.

9

Rügen and Priwall, Germany

The crossing to Rügen is short, but the sea felt choppy even on a mild spring day and a large passenger ferry. I sat on the open deck and found myself contemplating the emotions that refugees must have experienced as they made this perilous crossing, having ditched their old lives and put themselves in harm's way in hope of something better.

In just a short while I would set foot on the territory so many had found intolerable. About an hour before arriving I could already see it clearly up ahead: cliffs on the right of my field of vision and a wide, curving bay on the left, both gradually growing in size. It was the first place on my journey that had been part of the German Democratic Republic. Here was a state that was designed as a permanent expression of Soviet victory and of the Soviet army's reach into the heart of capitalist Europe. Here too was a territory that ended up being infamous for the thoroughness of its tyranny.

I am not alone in seeing the Soviet Union and the GDR as the two great poster children of the communist world, but my knowledge of the two powers was uneven. At the start of this project I knew much less about the GDR. Apart from the fall of the Berlin Wall, my only personal memory of the country dates from when I was ten. In 1988 I spent weeks glued to the television screen watching the Seoul Olympics. East Germany won 102 medals at the games, including thirty-seven golds, and I was left with a strong, if immature, impression of a deter-mined small nation punching far above its weight. It was just what the leader of the GDR, Erich Honecker, would have wanted me to think.

In the years that followed, of course my thoughts darkened, specifically through watching the GDR's collapse a year later and, sometime thereafter, learning of its massive state doping programme. Like most people, I have picked up a sense of the GDR's notorious surveillance culture: for me, books like *Stasiland* and films like *The Lives of Others* have lingered long in the mind. More recently I have become aware of the disproportionate appeal that right-wing populism holds for some former East Germans and have wondered about what this means.

I was now about to spend a fortnight travelling through the lands of East Germany and along its one-time frontier with West Germany. As our ferry manoeuvred awkwardly into a berth at Mukran harbour and I queued to disembark, I was excited, but not a little daunted.

Mukran and the island of Rügen initially made it onto my itinerary because of travel logistics alone. The coastal meeting place of East and West Germany, where I was heading, was some 200 kilometres to the west. But the more I looked at the history of this island that lies right up against the German coast, the surer I felt that I should linger a little while there rather than just jump in a car.

As an aside, one can make a case for Mukran's sister port of Sassnitz (just a couple of kilometres away) being key to the very origins of the Cold War. It was here, in April 1917, that Vladimir Lenin spent a night after journeying across Germany in a sealed train on his way to revolutionary Petrograd. Without the German Empire's support Lenin might never have got out of Switzerland and Bolshevism really might not have taken hold in Russia.

But what piqued my interest most was discovering that Mukran had been the GDR's last great construction project, partly built using conscripted labour. It was conceived as a new deep-water port after the 1980 Solidarity protests in Poland, a way to keep shipping running between East Germany and the USSR should the Polish communist regime ever collapse. Much of the heavy work was done by East Germany's despised conscientious objectors, the small group of people brave enough to refuse service in the armed forces.

I had arranged to interview a former conscientious objector in Prora, just a short bus ride from Mukran and within sight of the port around the long crescent-shaped bay. On my way I passed enormous lorry parks and storage warehouses, and a huge field given over to segments of the Nord Stream 2 pipeline, the controversial under-sea gas connection which was then still under construction between Germany and Russia. The industrial installations soon gave way to bright, cubic apartment blocks with neat balconies and off-road cycle paths. Everything seemed plain and neutral, as is often the case in Germany; it was at first hard to see the history and complexity all around. But back at the coast the unbelievably long buildings of Prora's infamous Nazi holiday camp suddenly came into view. I realized that it was in one of these that my interview was to take place.

Christian Schmidt first struck me as burly and stern-looking, dressed in a duffel jacket and flat cap and standing tall and tipped back slightly on his heels, rather like a policeman surveying a crime scene. But then he smiled broadly and extended a big welcoming hand. We talked for two hours, partly in English and partly through a translator, the historian Katja Lucke whose own work has sought, among other things, to gather and preserve the memories of Rügen's conscientious objectors.

'The term they used in GDR times was *Bausoldat*,' Katja explains up front a word that I will hear a lot. Literally translated as 'construction soldiers', *Bausoldaten* were frequently employed on building projects and other manual labour while still being subject to full military discipline. 'This was military conscription without weapons,' Katja continues. 'The men still had to wear military uniforms and live in barracks. And they were trained by National Volunteer Army officers. They often worked in gruelling conditions.'

The creation of the *Bausoldat* cadre was a concession the East Berlin authorities granted in 1964. They were reluctant to do so and even though they grudgingly stuck with the policy for the next quarter of a century, being a *Bausoldat* was never presented as a valid alternative to mainstream military service. Indeed, it was never advertised and only rarely mentioned in public. One first had to summon one's own courage to refuse army service before the route to *Bausoldat* status was pointed out. Even then objectors faced immense pressure. They were warned (truthfully) that they might struggle for the rest of their lives, perhaps finding it impossible to go to university or be considered for good jobs. 'A *Bausoldat*'s period of service was also explicitly structured as a punishment,' Katja says. A 1980s exposé in the West German magazine *Stern* bluntly quoted an anonymous *Bausoldat* as saying, '*Wir sind der letzte Dreck* (We are the lowest of the low).' Or maybe, 'The GDR treats us like the scum of the earth.'[1]

With a population of over 16 million, East Germany only had around 16,000 *Bausoldaten* in total in a quarter of a century, just 650 a year. For Christian, as for most, it felt like no choice at all. His father was a priest and a life-long pacifist. Having been born in Dresden in the 1920s, he had survived the Allied bombing of the city in 1945 but was then forced into the army of the Third Reich just three days after his sixteenth birthday. These experiences shaped his views of war and he passed them on to his son.

'I was a bit nervous when my time came,' Christian tells me. 'I suspected the authorities might put pressure on me and I wasn't sure I'd be strong enough. Nobody else I knew was choosing this route.' He realized quickly that the whole thing was designed to feel like 'a kind of revenge'. 'I began my experience

Christian Schmidt poses with photographed pages from his Bausoldat *service book.*

in a notoriously polluted chemicals town called Bitterfeld,' he says. 'By the late 1980s the levels of chemical contamination [from the factories] there meant it was hard for the state to get ordinary workers to go, so *Bausoldaten* were made to fill the empty posts. If a *Bausoldat* refused a particular posting, he would be jailed for up to two years.' The conditions were awful. He and other *Bausoldaten* – and presumably many of Bitterfeld's 20,000 ordinary residents – regularly woke in their sleep because of the concentrations of poisonous chemicals in the air. It was with relief that he learned one day that he would be moved to Rügen, even though he did not know what work awaited him there. He supposed that at least the air would be cleaner.

Christian was immediately put to work on the sprawling Mukran port project. The site managers at Mukran had been instructed to make sure they used the *Bausoldaten* for the heaviest work. 'It was backbreaking,' Christian says, and made worse by the fact that, as in Bitterfeld, the men were treated like criminals. 'We were always watched very closely by officials who wanted to be sure we weren't going to sabotage the harbour.' At the end of each working day the *Bausoldaten* returned to barracks, where there were very few options for relaxation, let alone fun. Although they lived right beside one of the longest sandy beaches in Europe, this was also an Iron Curtain frontier and completely out of bounds.

Declassified documents have subsequently proved what the *Bausoldaten* always knew: surveillance of their lives was constant. The walls of every room in their barracks had microphones in them, and Stasi officers and informers were always nearby listening to conversations, intercepting mail and hiding in the ranks of the *Bausoldaten* themselves (and even among the local clergy) in the hope

Bausoldaten unloading concrete slabs from a goods train at Mukran in 1983. In heatwave conditions, they had been allowed to shed their uniforms.

of catching the men off guard. 'We adjusted our conversations accordingly,' Christian says. 'But we also all distrusted each other.'

Bausoldaten were entitled to just one day off a month. Technically conscripts were free to use the time as they wished, but it was hard to do much except hang around the barracks. Punishments for arriving back late were severe. At some point, most men attempted a quick dash back to see relatives or friends elsewhere in the country, but this was always fraught with risk. Leave could be cancelled at the whim of officers, and another favourite trick was to delay the *Bausoldat* at the beginning of a day off, thereby making him miss the only train he could catch back home. Christian clearly counts it as among the greatest achievements of his life that he managed to use one of his own brief spells of leave to rush back to his fiancée in Gera, over 500 kilometres away, and marry her.

By the end of the 1980s, when he was doing his service, the cracks in the communist regime were becoming clearer by the week. By then Gorbachev had unleashed *glasnost* and *perestroika* in the USSR, and other socialist countries had begun taking their own tentative steps towards liberalization. With rare exceptions, however, the government in East Berlin had been deaf to these developments and had instead doubled down on its long-standing instinct for total control. In words I would hear repeated many times during my journey through Germany, Christian says that, despite the signs, he completely failed to foresee communism's collapse in November 1989.

'Something was fishy that summer,' he says. Activists, including some of Prora's own *Bausoldaten*, had publicly accused the government of ballot-rigging in local elections that May (as usual, government-backed parties had claimed 99 per cent of the votes cast). Then, when East Germans were returning from summer vacations, they brought news of demonstrations in Hungary and other places. 'But still we did not think it was so close here.' Christian's service as a *Bausoldat* ended on 26 October 1989. 'If someone had told us that the Wall would fall exactly fourteen days later, none of us would have believed it.'

After Christian left, I asked Katja about the building in which we were standing. Prora is dominated by some of the world's largest totalitarian structures. This *Bausoldat* barracks was one of eight enormous, identical edifices that the Nazis had constructed along the coastline in the late 1930s. Intended as a holiday camp and stretching almost five kilometres from end to end, this remains the longest man-made complex in the world, with the exception of walled fortifications. Katja says that, along with the Nuremberg rally grounds in Bavaria, the Colossus at Prora, as the site is often called, is the most important surviving example of National Socialist architecture (though she adds that it is now threatened by modern refurbishment that seeks to efface its difficult past and turn it into luxury flats and hotels).

The Colossus was the brainchild of Robert Ley, a key element in his Strength Through Joy (*Kraft durch Freude*, KdF) movement which offered German workers subsidized holidays and other benefits as a way of bolstering loyalty to the regime. It was never finished and never received a single Strength Through Joy tourist. By 1939, at the outbreak of war, it was still just a shell. The accommodation blocks had been erected, all of them facing out to sea. Work had commenced on the vast central complex of cinemas, dancehalls, swimming pools and canteens. And two enormous brick piers had been built to allow the KdF's cruise ships to dock and use the facilities. But the war saw construction cease and the existing structures quickly got pressed into service as education centres for Nazi police battalions that were preparing to serve, and often to commit crimes of mass murder, across occupied Eastern Europe.

The Colossus passed from the Nazis to the conquering Soviets in 1945 and returned to German control in the early 1950s. One block then became a training terrain for National Volunteer Army paratroopers; others served as offices for parts of the army and the police. And one even approached its original purpose when it was refurbished as a holiday home for retired military personnel. In the 1980s the block closest to Mukran was reserved for the *Bausoldaten*, including Christian.

Katja talks with passion and precision about the many different meanings that are imprinted in these structures. Comparisons between the Nazi regime and the East German dictatorship often get made. Prora, in particular, would seem to invite them. Yet from Katja's perspective the important thing is not to try to rank these very different systems in a hierarchy of evil but rather to learn the specific ways in which each sought to control humans and punish difference and dissent.

We walked together onto the beach and came to a standstill beside the great brick piers. Katja gestured out to sea, asking me to imagine the cruise ships that were once supposed to dock here. Unlike the resort, KdF cruise ships did operate for a time before the war and thousands of Third Reich citizens enjoyed holidays on them. One of the ships was called the *Robert Ley*

The Colossus at Prora, partly as it was in GDR times and partly modernized.

while another was the *Wilhelm Gustloff*, named for a Nazi Party official whom a Jewish man shot dead in 1936. When Katja mentions the second ship to me, it rings a bell somewhere in my mind. It takes a few minutes to work out where I have heard of this vessel before: oddly, it was back in Porkkala.

Like Prora, the *Wilhelm Gustloff*'s association with leisure was tragically undermined by subsequent events. On 30 January 1945, while carrying some 9,000 Germans fleeing the Soviet army, it sank, killing almost everyone on board. This remains the deadliest maritime disaster in history. The sinking was caused by a torpedo from a Soviet submarine, the S-13. That submarine had put to sea just a couple of weeks before from the USSR's newest base, Porkkala.

This palimpsest of historical darkness marked a sombre beginning to my time in Germany. Everywhere I had been so far, starting with the ferry terminal at Mukran, seemed to have a sinister underside. I headed on foot to Binz, the next town along the coast, and hired a car for my onward journey to the old inner-German frontier.

*

The first time I became aware of the vanished Iron Curtain land border was when I was already crossing it. A few kilometres before reaching the city of Lübeck, formerly in West Germany, I saw a large brown sign that had been placed by the roadside to remind drivers this was where the country was once divided. It is one of hundreds of such signs across the network, giving the precise day and hour when a particular route reopened following the 9 November revolution. It can only be a good thing for people to be reminded so frequently, and in the course of their daily lives, that something as natural as moving from one part of Germany to another was for a long time impossible; and good, too, for them to recall the hundreds of separate moments of joy when citizens of each side walked towards one another for the first time.

West Germans could always get as near as they dared to the border, and in many places flights of steps and viewing platforms were erected to allow them to peer into the shady state on the other side. But for East Germans, as for Soviet citizens, even to see the dreaded frontier was rare. The GDR border system began several kilometres away from the actual boundary and intensified in stages until the final, almost impassable barrier.

I was approaching from the eastern side, through the modern-day German state of Mecklenburg-Western Pomerania. I had actually hit the start of the former restricted zone some 5 kilometres before the sign, somewhere outside a village called Niendorf, near a spot on the A20 autobahn that now boasts a Shell garage and a McDonald's. Before the end of 1989 I would have encountered a permanent roadblock there with uniformed personnel demanding to see documents. From then on, as I advanced through the zone, I might have met further detachments of troops combing the territory but few if any civilians. This broad swathe of land, amounting to millions of acres across the state as a whole, was sacrificed to security. It was systematically depopulated by waves of forced internal migration: first one household, then another, and occasionally entire villages were deemed unsafe and moved to less sensitive areas, at least 11,000 people in all. Farming continued but many of those labouring in the fields were bussed in daily. The empty homes stayed empty and often became derelict despite the GDR's chronic housing shortage. Those who remained inside the controlled zone were reminded constantly that they lived in no man's land.

The last 200 or 300 metres of the country was like an enormous modern moat. Signs along its inner edge instructed people to go no further, and were followed by a first fence that, if crossed, led to a ploughed, raked strip which showed the footprints of anyone who stepped on it. Either side of that strip the trees were uprooted and replaced with low-growing plants that afforded fugitives no cover. Finally, several metres before the actual international frontier, the highest fence of all constituted the ultimate obstacle.

Signs, strips and fences: the age-old border technologies that, along with watchtowers, floodlights, armed patrols and bloodthirsty dogs, provided the backbone of East German territorial defence. The state perfected their use and also progressively augmented them with the most advanced forms of surveillance and deterrence available. What was most unusual was the thoroughness with which the GDR applied all these precautions. Measures that were employed only sporadically along other countries' borders (even on the Iron Curtain) were used across the entirety of the GDR's frontier with West Germany. Nothing was left to chance.

The country was among the first to make widespread use of closed circuit cameras at its frontier. It also installed signal wires on long stretches of the inner fence to alert the nearest troop detachment when an escape was attempted. From the late 1960s, the original outer fence – made of barbed wire and measuring up to 2.5 metres in height – was replaced with a much higher fence (up to 4 metres) made of sharp metal mesh that cut the fingers of anyone climbing it. After 1966 much of the border was mined and, between 1970 and 1984, 60,000 automatic firing devices, *Selbstschussanlage*, were installed. Triggered by sensitivity wires on the fence itself, they shot eighty steel projectiles in the direction of would-be fugitives. It was a formidable assault course, all the more so because most escapees encountered each part only once and typically in darkness.

I spent the next night in Travemünde, the Lübeck seaside resort renowned for its bourgeois gentility. In the Cold War both the city and the resort lay just inside West Germany. While I was there, walking through its refined, monied streets and on the beautiful beach with its distinctive covered chairs, I found it impossible not to think of how different the place's experience of the second half of the twentieth century would have been had the frontier followed even a slightly different course.

Early the following morning I headed to where the Inner German Border had hit the sea. The frontier copied the route of the age-old boundary between Schleswig-Holstein and Mecklenburg. This meant it terminated in a historical eccentricity, one that was barely noticed for centuries but then suddenly became unmissable through the introduction of massive Iron Curtain infrastructure.

The division between the north of Schleswig-Holstein and the north of Mecklenburg seems obvious if you glance at a map. The wide estuary of the River Trave would appear to mark the spot, with Schleswig-Holstein on its western bank and Mecklenburg on its eastern one. But right at the point where the Trave meets the Baltic, a narrow sliver of land on the eastern bank actually belongs to the city of Lübeck, and thus to Schleswig-Holstein. This has been the case since at least 1226. It is the Priwall peninsula. No one is quite sure how the anomaly first arose. It may be that Priwall was once an island and only became joined to Mecklenburg through land reclamation. In any case, it means the north-eastern tip of West Germany was located on a tiny exposed peninsula, just two kilometres in length and less than one kilometre wide, stuck to the GDR and with no land connection to the rest of the Federal Republic (the FRG). Getting into Priwall in the Cold War involved a short ferry ride across the Trave, where a single road started at the ferry ramp and ended a short distance later at the Iron Curtain.

That ferry still exists today and just after 8 a.m. I found myself queuing for it along with other early morning commuters. When I had first noticed Priwall on a map, I assumed it must have been closed to the general public before 1989. I imagined some kind of concentration of troops there, perhaps a naval base or a listening station. But, in truth, it was always what it still is today: a holiday destination where a small number of Lübeckers own summerhouses and where a great deal more come for day trips. That is why the ferry kept running through those years, allowing West Germans to assert their rights to this outpost by means of simple everyday use.

The ferry takes only two minutes to cross the Trave, and, when you stand at Priwall's little harbour and look back, Travemünde still seems within touching distance. But as soon as you go a few metres along Mecklenburger Landstrasse the resort disappears and you find yourself hemmed in by a corridor of trees with small cottages and bungalows peeking out on either side. The sea is just to the north, on the other side of dunes. I soon parked up and walked across one of the boardwalks.

During the Cold War the eastern extent of Priwall beach was demarcated by a low chain-link fence, which also denoted the territorial limit of West Germany. It was the kind of fence that might more typically be found in a municipal park, dividing a pathway from a lawn, and at high tide it extended right into the sea where it slowly merged with the Baltic waves. On land, just a metre or so beyond, the official red, yellow and black concrete border posts of the German Democratic Republic were sunk at regular intervals in the sand. Then several metres further east the main GDR security fence loomed up. East Germany hadn't run its fence into the waves but instead used it to divide the land from the sea for several kilometres along its own coastline. From the vantage point of Priwall, this made the GDR look like a place encaged. By the 1980s fully seven GDR watchtowers overlooked the West German beach, the result of successive bouts of fortification.

The states' starkly different attitudes towards their shared border were further underlined at Priwall by a Travemünde council decision, in 1975, to open a nudist beach right up against the chain-link fence. Tempting as it is to see this as a grand prank, the main justification seems to have been sparing the blushes of non-nudist West German bathers. There would be no inadvertent passersby on a stretch of coastline that terminated in the Iron Curtain. (Ironically, whether the Travemünde councillors knew it or not, nudism was actually much more widespread in the GDR than in the West: the East German government had attempted to ban it in the 1950s but had had to perform a rare climbdown in the face of mass public disobedience; it then became the norm for East Germans to take off their clothes at any tourist beach or beauty spot.[2])

West Germany's *Der Spiegel* magazine ran a tongue-in-cheek article about Priwall's new amenity soon after it opened. It was titled 'The Naked and the Red' and revelled in the site's peculiarities: 'A red and white chain fence marks the border of the newest nudist beach in the Bundesrepublik . . . If the wind blows cold from the East, windbreak sheets may be attached to this fence. And if the sun shines, bath towels might

Priwall beach was once the place where the Inner German Border met the sea. From 1975, it was reserved for nudists on the West German side.

be found dangling from one of its iron posts, or maybe even the occasional bra. But this red and white fence also marks the point where all West Germans, whether naked or not, have to come to a halt because the GDR begins five steps after the chain.'[3]

Even in this extreme location nudists' perennial bugbear, voyeurism, had not been banished entirely. From time to time West German 'textiles', as non-nudists are known within the community, still wandered over to gawp. And then there were the men with binoculars in the nearby watchtowers.'*Vopos* in the east, voyeurs in the west,' was how Heike Diestler of Hamburg described it, using the slang term for East German border police (*Volkspolizei*). A local customs officer said there had definitely been 'a lot more movement' in the GDR towers of late. It even seems the arrival of the nudists may have led some Eastern soldiers briefly to let down their guard. West German nudists had watched in amazement one afternoon when three GDR troops came down from their watchtower, opened a gate in the fence, and stripped off to skinny-dip.

More generally, however, bathing at Priwall was a bit like dancing on the edge of a volcano. Over the years several incidents demonstrated the proximity of danger. One day in the late 1970s, for instance, a British nudist who didn't understand the seriousness of the situation ran around to the other side of the West German chain-link fence at low tide and entered East Germany. He was immediately detained at gunpoint and made to stand, naked and with his hands up, for more than half an hour before being released back.

Later, in September 1989, when the communist regime had just weeks to live, twenty-four-year-old Mario Wächtler swam for nineteen hours from the East German town of Boltenhagen to get to Priwall, a distance of some 38 kilometres, further than swimming the English Channel. When on the brink of crossing the international border and within sight of the beach, he was spotted by GDR troops who despatched a police ship to detain or drown him (they did not care which). A West German ferry, the *Peter Pan*, had also noticed him and managed to launch its lifeboat and rescue him despite direct interference from the GDR vessel. It was to be the last ever successful maritime escape from East to West Germany.[4]

I had imagined interviewing real nudists during my own time at Priwall, perhaps even someone who had bathed there while the Iron Curtain existed. I had even been ready to get undressed to prevent accusations of gawping. But the sea mist lay heavy on the coast that day and the temperature was only about 10°C, and felt colder. I ended up being more or less alone, with just three dog walkers and a group of cyclists on a windswept picnic for company. All, like me, were well wrapped up.

I did walk across the invisible line into Mecklenburg-Western Pomerania, of course, and in a copse of trees behind the

'Never again divided', the message on a boulder at the eastern edge of the Priwall peninsula, where West and East Germany once met.

beach, where the watchtowers used to stand, I found cut-off stumps of old fencing posts and discarded clumps of metal wire. These seemed to be all that remained of the fortifications. Back on Mecklenburger Landstrasse, right at the point where the barricades used to be, there is nothing but a change in the colour of the tarmac on the road today (in Germany, this often turns out to be the best way of determining exactly where the old international border ran). Some time in the 1990s, however, a great boulder was placed in the verge. On it are carved the words '*Nie wieder geteilt*', 'Never again divided'.

PART III

GERMANY

DENMARK
Baltic Sea
Rügen
Rostock
Priwall • Bad Doberan
Lübeck Dassow
Hamburg Schlagsdorf
Bröthen
POLAND
Lübbow
Bonzenghetto
Zicherie/
Böckwitz Berlin • • Strausberg
Potsdam •
Helmstedt • Marienborn
• Hötensleben
Harz Mountains
Leipzig •
Dresden •
Chemnitz •
Plauen •
—— Iron Curtain Hof •
Selb • Aš CZECHIA
• Prague

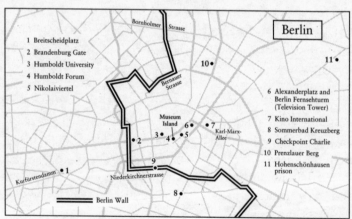

Berlin

Bornholmer Strasse

1 Breitscheidplatz
2 Brandenburg Gate
3 Humboldt University
4 Humboldt Forum
5 Nikolaiviertel

10 •
11 •

Bernauer
Strasse

Museum
Island
3 • 4 • 6 • • 7
• 5
Karl-Marx-
Allee

2 •

6 Alexanderplatz and
  Berlin Fernsehturm
  (Television Tower)
7 Kino International
8 Sommerbad Kreuzberg
9 Checkpoint Charlie
10 Prenzlauer Berg
11 Hohenschönhausen
   prison

Kurfürstendamm • 1

9 •
Niederkirchnerstrasse

8 •

—— Berlin Wall

10

Schlagsdorf and Helmstedt, Germany

One night in March 1976, around 3 a.m., thirty-two-year-old Michael Gartenschläger parked his car on a quiet country road and walked with a friend towards the Inner German Border near the West German village of Bröthen, a few dozen kilometres south of Lübeck. When he reached the frontier – in those parts a wooden rail at waist height – he tied a fishing line round his body, said goodbye to his friend, and ducked under the rail into the GDR. From there he crawled across an area of low grass for 30 metres to arrive at the East German fence. As he crawled he was dragging with him a ladder, a length of rope and a collection of wire cutters, spanners, flashlights and sticking plasters. He was also pausing every few metres to sprinkle pepper on his traces in the hope of confusing any guard dogs sent to hunt him.

Michael got back to his feet at the fence. He had studied this stretch of border for many weeks and had selected the spot carefully: Border Post 231. The fence took a sharp right-angled turn here, meaning he could carry out his operation with unusually good sightlines and hopefully get advance warning of any approaching East German guards. His friend was watching from the safety of West Germany and was to tug on the fishing line if he saw anything untoward. Michael placed his ladder against the concrete post and climbed up. He then used one of the flashlights to locate the object for which he had come. He set to work.

Using just a single hand, which he stretched as far as he could over the fence, Michael Gartenschläger spent the next two hours painstakingly cutting wires and unscrewing bolts. Eventually, with dawn breaking, there was only one bolt left to unscrew and he tied the rope he had brought around the object in preparation for lifting it over. As it came free, it swung dangerously and might easily have dropped. But Michael succeeded in bringing it over and carried it safely, along with everything else he had brought, back into West Germany. A fortnight later *Der Spiegel* published an exclusive story about the spoils of that night, the first automatic firing device ever to reach the West.[1]

Since installing the weapons in 1970 the GDR had continually claimed they were only sirens or loudspeakers. West German activists had managed to detonate a few by poking sticks through the border fence and pressing their triggers. In January 1973 an East German twenty-six-year-old, Hans-Friedrich Franck, had died of devastating wounds a few hours after dragging himself into West Germany. The doctors who treated him said he had incurred shrapnel injuries as if from a bomb blast and they blamed an automatic firing device. Yet, until Gartenschläger's raid, no specimen of the weapon had made it out of the Eastern Bloc.

Der Spiegel's scoop caused an international sensation. It was exactly what Gartenschläger had wanted: to show up the GDR for the barbarous, cruel, deceitful state he thought it was and embarrass it globally. He hoped to inject fresh energy into the campaign for change at the border. 'I was convinced that sensible resistance to this unjust system was not just a right but a duty,' Michael wrote at the time.

A surviving automatic firing device (Selbstschussanlage) mounted on a stretch of reconstructed border fence at the Schlagsdorf Grenzhus Museum.

'I believe that the illegitimate character of the GDR is particularly evident in the automatic firing system. Since there was no example in the Federal Republic . . . I decided to get a complete unit for demonstration purposes . . . The risk seemed worthwhile.'[2]

Gartenschläger might well have left this dangerous business alone at this point. But instead he returned to the same stretch of border on 23 April 1976 and stole another device – the very one the East Germans had

Michael Gartenschläger on one of his visits to the Inner German Border.

put up to replace the first. This one he sold to the famous Checkpoint Charlie Museum in West Berlin, for use in educating visitors about the brutality of the Eastern border.

A week later, on 30 April, he returned for his third foray, with the aim of bagging yet another device, possibly for installation across the street from East Germany's Permanent Mission in Bonn. This time Michael's luck ran out. Aware the risks were mounting he had brought two friends with him as lookouts, and all three men were armed. But as soon as Michael dipped below the West German rail he was hit by heavy fire and fatally wounded. Nine bullets entered his body, and the GDR border troops fired a further 100 rounds into West Germany as they unsuccessfully attempted to kill his friends.

Michael Gartenschläger's dying body was quickly transported through a gate in the fence and conveyed to the nearest East German guardhouse, where he was declared dead a short time later.

Grizzly photographs were taken for the record and, on 10 May, his remains were cremated without ceremony (the crematorium was told he was an unidentified corpse the authorities had found in a river). His ashes were then scattered to the winds. East Germany had caught its culprit by posting a team of twenty-one marksmen on a round-the-clock watch. The marksmen were honoured for their service. The operation, which avenged the huge damage Gartenschläger had done, was declared officially 'very good'.

Michael Gartenschläger's remarkable, tragic story was often in my mind as I motored along the northern sections of the old Inner German Border. His life had been ruined by the GDR long before the state actually killed him. He had grown up the son of restaurant owners in the East German town of Strausberg, a few kilometres east of Berlin.[3] As a teenager, he had fallen in love with rock and roll music and, along with a few friends, had founded a fan club for the West German star Ted Herold, who sang Elvis Presley covers. Before the Berlin Wall was erected in August 1961, Michael and his friends travelled regularly to West Berlin to buy banned Western records and music magazines. When that outlet for their youthful energies suddenly closed, they protested, daubing graffiti on buildings around Strausberg (slogans included *Today Red – Tomorrow Dead* and *Open the Gate!*) and one night setting fire to a local barn.

Gartenschläger was arrested and in a show trial in September 1961 the seventeen-year-old found himself sentenced to life imprisonment. Had he been a year older he would have been executed. He spent the next decade in East German prisons. His freedom, and with it a transfer to the West, came only in 1971, not as a result of any internal leniency but thanks to a campaign by West German human rights activists, and oiled by a hefty cash payment from the West German government.

At liberty once more Gartenschläger found work at a Hamburg petrol station. But his rage at the GDR regime always endured.

It is said he helped more than thirty-one other East Germans to escape in the five years he spent in the Federal Republic. In some cases, he personally drove back into the East, along the protected transit routes to West Berlin, and hid escapees in the boot of his red Opel. In many ways, and ultimately even in his death, Michael Gartenschläger never really managed to leave the GDR at all.

Today the border infrastructure that so obsessed him is just a memory in most places. Yet every so often as I drove, an old watchtower would pop up in a field, as at Dassow, near Priwall, or beside a river, as at the village of Lübbow. Even stripped of their context, these relics continue to cast claustrophobic shadows over the landscape. The more sustained stretches of border, kept for the purposes of education, do the same, making today's visitors wonder how they might have responded to such categorical and aggressive restrictions on their freedom.

Would I have tried to escape the GDR? What risks would I have been willing to take? Might I have contemplated leaving loved ones behind? And would I, like Gartenschläger, have gone back in just to help someone else get out? The Iron Curtain is a structure that, even when long gone, still poses difficult questions.

The communist government of East Germany knew from the start it had a people problem. Europeans fled in all directions at the end of the Second World War, but mostly they went from east to west out of fear of the advancing Soviet army, which came with many understandable scores to settle and a grim, ever-increasing reputation for rape. Wilhelm Pieck and Walter Ulbricht, the GDR's first leaders, may have hoped that by establishing a socialist regime in Germany's Soviet sector in 1949 they would tempt ordinary Germans back, but in reality it achieved the opposite. Then, with every step the sector took towards communist statehood in the 1950s, more residents voted with their feet and left.

Leaving was initially a reasonably easy thing to do because the early Inner German Border was porous. It was never the Allies' intention, at least not their stated intention, to partition Germany in perpetuity. Stalin no doubt had his own undeclared ideas about the shape of the USSR's sphere of influence when designing the postwar settlement at the Yalta and Potsdam Conferences in 1945. But officially the plan was to de-Nazify, demilitarize, and reconfigure the country to make a non-threatening, but still unified, nation state. The sectors of occupation, based on Germany's pre-existing administrative boundaries, were supposedly just a means to that end.

To start with, therefore, citizens with the right paperwork could cross the inter-sectoral boundaries with relative ease – to go to work, for instance. Among these 'commuters' there were always people attempting a permanent move, and even with the border under Allied control such permanent moves were frowned upon. If Allied soldiers suspected people of moving sectors without justification they arrested and fined them and returned them to their sector of residence. A few were even imprisoned, which is why migrants began using clandestine routes, through the mountains or across isolated stretches of countryside far from checkpoints. This subterfuge was inherently dangerous because, if caught, the escapees risked being branded smugglers or fugitive Nazis. (It was also terrifyingly exploited by a certain Rudolf Pleil, 'the Deadmaker (*der Totmacher*)', a serial killer who offered his services as a guide through the Harz mountains in 1946 and 1947 and murdered at least nine women there.)

Between 1949 and the end of 1952 it is estimated that 100,000 West Germans made what now seems like the strange choice to move to the GDR. But over the same period fully 675,000 East Germans fled the other way. East Germany was gradually tightening its border regime throughout these years but, before 1961, each tightening only made matters worse, as more people took fright and left. During just the first four months of 1953, when there was a particular crackdown, 122,000 East Germans departed for the West. The majority now went for explicitly political reasons. A few feared for their lives; many more had simply had enough of state intrusion along the lines of restrictions on their business activities, the destruction of their professional bodies, the collectivization of their farms, and the persecution of their faith groups.

As Anne Applebaum has written, leaving was an option for East Germans of the 1950s in a way that it was not for many disgruntled inhabitants of other Eastern Bloc countries: 'Poles who left Poland or Hungarians who left Hungary left not just their homes and families but their language and culture.'[4] Citizens of the GDR knew they could exist in the Federal Republic in the sense of being able to shop or study or understand instructions at work; many also had readymade support networks. The emigration figures climbed ever higher until, by the start of 1961, more than one in seven of the GDR's entire population had departed; a total of 2.5 million people.

My first stop south of Priwall was Schlagsdorf, a tiny village that once lay just inside the GDR. It was a cold, wet morning and I was there to meet Andreas Wagner, the head of the Border House Museum (Grenzhus Museum), which tells the story of the Inner German Border between Mecklenburg-Western Pomerania and Schleswig-Holstein.

Andreas greets me at the door and ushers me upstairs to a conference room where coffee and biscuits are already laid out. An immensely knowledgeable man, he is measured in all his words and, while making no attempt to minimize the enormity of what the GDR did, he never seeks to exaggerate either. Birds chirp noisily outside the window as he starts telling me of how in 1961 East Germany faced ruin. The millions of citizens it had lost were disproportionately men and women of working age and well educated, the kind of people any state depends on to staff its hospitals and schools and run its factories, never mind a state rebuilding after a terrible war. Among the leavers were no fewer than 17,000 teachers, 4,700 doctors and dentists, and 800 judges and lawyers.[5] All steps taken to strengthen the border had failed, mostly because freedom of movement continued between East and West Berlin under rights that the four Allies had guaranteed back in 1945. (Once in West Berlin a person could get to West Germany without further hindrance.)

Andreas talks of the unthinkable solution that formed in the minds of some members of the regime: the idea of hermetically sealing the entire country so that escape became not just difficult but physically impossible. The Soviets had wanted the GDR to halt the exodus for years. From Moscow's point of view the economic situation was secondary to the terrible embarrassment of a country in the socialist camp being unable to keep its own people. Early in his leadership Nikita Khrushchev considered abandoning the GDR's experiment in socialism if the West could be persuaded to agree to a neutral reunified Germany. When that plan went nowhere, the Soviet leader also toyed with authorizing a Warsaw Pact invasion of West Berlin. In the end, however, it was Ulbricht's audacious upgrade policy that won the day. On Sunday 13 August 1961 East Germany commenced construction of what may legitimately be called Europe's first total border system: an impassable wall to seal off West Berlin from the GDR, and an upgraded high fence to separate the rest of the country from West Germany.

Andreas has artefacts at hand to show me how the regime sold these developments to its own people. In GDR leaflets, posters, newspapers and books, the Berlin Wall was always the 'Anti-Fascist Protection Rampart (*Antifaschistischer Schutzwall*)'. Both it and the wider border were said to be measures to buy the country time in the inevitable invasion to come. West Germany was supposedly the fascist state in question. The Wall and the fence were also repeatedly described as means of stopping massive infiltration by Western secret agents. Of course, most people never believed this (with the possible exception of indoctrinated schoolchildren). The truth was only too clear from the events of the preceding years: the Berlin Wall and the border fence were about keeping people in.

Pausing for a moment, Andreas asks if I am aware that the post-1961 border's true purpose was actually encoded in its physical structure. He says it will be easier to show me what he means, so we put on raincoats and walk through the damp village to a stretch of fencing that is an exact replica of what once ran alongside Schlagsdorf. 'What you must never forget is that *this* is the important side of the border,' he says, standing on the eastern side. 'This is the only important bit of the fence, not what's on the other side.' What he goes on to tell me is in one way blindingly obvious, yet still chilling.

Every defensive measure the GDR took at its western border – the automatic firing devices, the anti-vehicle traps, the mines, the raked strip, the signalling equipment – was intended only for use against GDR citizens. Despite mostly locating the fence several metres inside its actual international boundary, the East German regime did not use the remainder of the territory for anything more menacing than well-tended lawns. As Gartenschläger had done, a person could easily approach the fence from the West and not encounter a single obstacle. It was also easy for a Westerner to climb the fence. The layers of steel mesh were arranged so the upper ragged edge always faced the western side, creating natural footholds. The rivets joining the sheets also protruded to the West. And the concrete posts holding the fence up were covered with fencing in the East but bare in the West. Still more conveniently, the occasional gates were constructed with an ingenious hinge that meant they could not be forced open from the East but would easily give way under pressure from the West. The fence's designers knew that their sole objective was to prevent escapes.

According to its own grim logic, the new border system succeeded. After haemorrhaging hundreds of thousands of people annually before 1961, the GDR lost just a few thousand through illegal emigration each year for the rest of the 1960s. By the 1970s, when new measures such as the automatic firing devices were introduced, this dropped still further: 610 escapees in 1976, with 3,620 failed attempts; only 288 in 1987, with 3,006 failed attempts.

For a while, thanks to the border, the East German economy revived. Many people who would have left the country stayed put and worked. Yet this was an enormously expensive intervention, and the costs never stopped. Andreas says the exact figures are not known but some information has come to light. Aside from ongoing maintenance costs, enhancements to the border were priced at more than two million marks per kilometre of fence in the 1980s; a vast sum for a perennially cash-strapped country, especially when many components came from abroad (ironically, often from the West) and had to be paid for with hard currency. And then there was the human toll: not the deaths at the border, about which the regime didn't much care, but the

Andreas Wagner shows me the unclimbable finish on the eastern side of the border fence, which contrasts sharply with the western side's many footholds.

spreading sea of resentment as each new generation woke up to the reality that they had been trapped by a government that distrusted them. 'More and more installations and more and more effort to avoid every escape – that was the mindset,' Andreas tells me, his face pursed with regret. The regime set itself a Sisyphean task and exhausted itself in pursuit of it.

As we wrap up, Andreas

asks me where I am going next. My destination by evening is Helmstedt, about 200 kilometres south, where one of the major East-West checkpoints was located. He says it is a great place to get an understanding of the GDR's paranoia in action. But he also recommends a stop along the way at the village of Zicherie and a little detour beyond Helmstedt to one of the largest surviving stretches of border at Hötensleben. Both places in their different ways will show me, he says, how the frontier simultaneously blocked centuries-old norms of human interaction and attacked the European landscape.

By the time I reached Zicherie the sun was out and I had the car windows down to enjoy it. I was not clear what to aim for in the tiny village but I suddenly spotted an old GDR border post in the verge and parked up. When you plan a trip carefully genuine surprises are rare, but Zicherie provided one.

It turned out that the village was not one but two settlements – Zicherie and Böckwitz – grown indistinguishable over time, so that anyone walking through them before 1945 or after 1990 would think them a single place. Zicherie is located in Lower Saxony and Böckwitz in Saxony-Anhalt, two German provinces that became separated by the Iron Curtain. From 1961 they were subjected to the full force of the new East German border policy, which meant that for twenty-eight years a huge concrete wall divided them and a watchtower stared down on them, both installations of identical size and design to the ones around West Berlin. Lots of people think the only wall was in Berlin. But in fact there were twenty-nine mini-Berlins, mostly villages, split apart by a staggering 105 kilometres of wall.

The surviving GDR border marker here indicates the spot on which the defences were focused, the old east–west road that the Cold War had closed. Apart from the marker all that remains is a large West German boulder carved with the words

'*Deutschland ist unteilbar*' ('Germany is undivided') – exactly the same sentiment as in Priwall, and the same rendering in rock, but this time dating from 1958. I walked back and forth between Zicherie and Böckwitz (between the old FRG and the old GDR) wondering what the daily reality of living with a wall here had felt like. I really wanted to talk to someone. When I saw a woman feeding horses in a paddock on the Böckwitz side I waved to her and walked over. She said hello.

'You look at our border.'

'Yes,' I replied. 'Do you remember when it was here?'

'Of course I do,' she said. 'I grew up in Zicherie.' She pointed back up the road. 'Back then, it was our normal.' I reckoned she was in her early fifties, which would have made her a teenager in the 1980s.

'How soon did you come over when it opened up?' I asked.

She laughed. 'I came just as soon as I could. And I came back a few days after that and walked up to the farmer here and asked him if I could pay to keep my horses in his field. I was always looking for places to put my horses, and I've used this field ever since.' The transaction had been humdrum but she was aware of it as a moment in history too. Something so mundane that had been impossible for decades.

We introduce ourselves. Her name is Ulrika and she is the local florist. She asks me if I have seen the nearby monument to Kurt Lichtenstein. Of course I have not and she says that I must. After trying unsuccessfully to give me directions, she throws her hands in the air and says she will take me herself. I wait for her to spread the rest of the hay and lock the paddock gate.

'Those were strange times indeed,' she says, once we are driving. Her car is littered with the tools of her trades: bits of horse tack, bunches of flowers, gift tags and raffia. 'In Zicherie we could only stand and look as the border defences got larger. We thought they would last for ever, of course. Everybody did. When I was young I rode along the side of the wall, right up against it. I said hello to the GDR guards up in their watchtowers. They never spoke back but one or two did sometimes give a little smile. Mostly they did not. That was my only experience of the GDR before the wall came down. Our family had no relatives over there so we never went. We just saw the soldiers and said hello.'

It was a wicked system, Ulrika adds, because it divided people for no good reason and mistreated its own citizens. Zicherie was divided from Böckwitz, of course, but it was subsequently to emerge that even in Zicherie the GDR had sown discord. When a particular set of Stasi papers was released, a West German border guard who had lived and worked in the village turned out to be an East German spy. 'He's not in Zicherie any more,' she says.

We pull up at the roadside in a small wood about two kilometres south of the village. Beside the car are an information board and a cross. 'This is where a man called Kurt Lichtenstein was murdered,' Ulrika says, as I look at a black-and-white photograph of a kind-faced man about her age. 'He parked his car here one day, exactly here. I think it was in 1961. Anyway, it was before they had the time to put up the really big border fence. He walked over and spoke to some farmers in the fields in the East. He was a journalist making some kind of story about the border. But the guards spotted him and shot him. He was killed and his body fell in a ditch, half inside the GDR and half inside the West.'

Lichtenstein, a former communist and veteran of the Spanish Civil War, had lost both his parents to the Holocaust. In the autumn of 1961 he had set out to drive the full length of the Inner German Border, beginning, like me, in Lübeck. By all accounts, he had had no particular axe to grind but was interested to document the recent changes at the frontier and the everyday lives of the people living along it. Some think the gunmen deliberately targeted him, as they later would Michael

Gartenschläger. His red Ford Taunus was certainly conspicuous and would have been noticed by guards further north on previous days. Others speculate that his killing was ordered by the very top of the regime because he was a lapsed communist. But it is just as likely that he fell victim to the general policy of maximum harshness that was then becoming the norm. Again, like Gartenschläger, Lichtenstein was carried dead or dying back into the GDR and cremated. The regime's only concession to decency in his case was to post his ashes to his widow in the West.

I thanked Ulrika for allowing me to interrupt her day and motored on to Hötensleben. Andreas had told me that this was probably my best chance to get a sense of the physical scale of the border – better even than any surviving remnant in Berlin. The stretch of wall was only added in 1976, a strengthening of security for no particular reason, because Hötensleben had been cleansed of suspicious elements back in the 1950s. Officials referred to the new wall, and other upgrades around the same time, by the euphemistic title 'the pioneering development of localities'.

I arrive as the sun is setting. The preserved wall does indeed look momentous here, forced through a pretty meadow and propelled by its own paranoia to the top of a hill. A watchtower still stands there and the anti-vehicle barricades are laid out just as they would have been in 1989, along with the raked strip. I stay till dark, aware of my freedom to sit on this dewy grass in what was once a death strip. I see people coming and going in the first row of houses in Hötensleben; houses that were kept empty for the best part of four decades because of their proximity to the border. When the moon is bright overhead I walk back to the car, appreciating and yet not really able to appreciate how unimaginable these few steps would have been during all those years.

After 1961 it was border guards who were among the likeliest people to flee. They had time to study the total frontier up close and gradually to identify weak spots. Even they were frequently caught, however; either because of the blanket surveillance, or because of the sheer amount of time it took to get through the various layers, or due to the fact that some measures were kept secret from all but the most senior officials. In Schlagsdorf Andreas told me

The preserved East German watchtower at Hötensleben.

of one former guard, Harry Weltzin, who launched a bid for freedom in 1983. He made it through the first fence with wire cutters and then across the death strip undetected. But as he was digging to get under the second fence he triggered a self-firing device and was killed. Andreas said the sad irony was that Weltzin had evidently not known that the second fence had deep concrete foundations, specifically to prevent tunnelling. Even if shrapnel hadn't got him, he would likely not have made it.

For most who succeeded in leaving after 1961 it was not a case of sprinting across the border under the searchlights' icy glare, or paddling over the Baltic, but an intricate exploitation of the few legitimate exit routes that the state continued to permit. A small number of people were exiled by government order; these were generally individuals who had made a nuisance of themselves but whom it was deemed too dangerous to lock up (singers, prominent writers, and the like). Another group were defectors whom the state wrongly trusted with the privilege of foreign travel: representatives at trade fairs, or participants in sporting competitions or arts festivals. After 1964 pensioners could visit the West for a defined period each year – a sign of their reduced economic value to the state – but they could only take ten East German marks with them (equivalent to just $20 today).

Then there were the ransomed, an astonishingly large number of people whom West Germany took in after the early 1960s – perhaps as many as 250,000 in all – who were sold on a grey and secretive market for hard cash or payments in kind. These were people who wanted to leave but whom the GDR would not allow to do so on their own terms. They were instead traded away when it suited the GDR like a toxic export or dangerous cash crop. Martina and Rüdiger Schmidt were one couple who made it out this way. I met them one evening in their stylish suburban house in Stockelsdorf, in Schleswig-Holstein, both now in their sixties but looking younger: Rüdiger tall and poised, Martina blonde, alert and thoughtful.

Rüdiger says his sense of alienation from the GDR began early. He remembers a primary school teacher confronting his class with the question 'Who believes in God?' He and three others said that they did and were made to stand up and face ridicule from their twenty-six other classmates who told them they were 'backward, unenlightened and ignorant'. Martina's first awareness of these issues came on a school outing, aged seven or eight, when she was overheard admiring an ornate medieval statue of the Virgin Mary in Doberan Minster. A home visit by a teacher followed, inquiring about the family's attitude towards religion.

After they married in the late 1970s, Martina and Rüdiger ran a church youth group together.[6] This activity was officially frowned upon but tolerated. As they suspected at the time, however, the Stasi infiltrated the group and kept track of everything that went on there. 'The youth circle of the St Petri and St Nikolai community in Rostock, led by Sch[midt] Rüdiger, with the help of his wife, comprises about twenty young people between the ages of fourteen and nineteen,' a report they have since seen said. 'As leader of the youth circle, Sch[midt] Rüdiger exercises a politically negative influence on the young people. In particular, he inspires them to pacifist thinking . . . he voices doubts about the correctness of party and government policies, specifically in relation to military service legislation, socialist military education, socialist education [and] the implementation of socialist democracy.'

By early 1984 the couple had become determined to get out. Their young daughter would soon reach school age and they feared putting her into an education system with such strong pro-war and anti-religious ideology. They knew the state viewed them as undesirables and hoped this would be enough to secure them a passage out. However, their successive requests for visas were turned down. They then wrote a letter to the leader of the West German state of Bavaria and had it hand-delivered. In it, they sought an outside intervention. Although it was not advertised anywhere, many dissidents in the GDR knew that West German political leaders and institutions sometimes paid money to secure their release. Often these people were prisoners, as was the case with Michael Gartenschläger, but in many other instances they were everyday citizens who were subject to religious or political persecution.

For months the Schmidts heard nothing, but in the background wheels were turning. They had actually entered an extremely well-regulated and sophisticated clandestine system in which deals were constantly being struck. West Germany's first ransom payments to the GDR came at Christmas 1962, when the East released twenty prisoners and twenty children in return for (literally) three lorryloads of potash. The justification for this and thousands of subsequent exchanges was never made explicit by either regime. It seems, however, that the West was motivated by a combination of humanitarianism and *Realpolitik*. This unorthodox method of barter turned out to be one of the only ways to stage a meaningful, non–military intervention in the authoritarian East. For East Germany, the theoretical defence of the deals was that they allowed the country to rid itself of undesirables and extract compensation for the education they had received or the damage they had caused. In reality, the attraction was simpler: precious Deutschmarks and Western goods that were in short supply.

Deals were often sealed at the two countries' trade fairs, especially the one held annually in the GDR city of Leipzig. Contracts were signed for orders of Volkswagens or Western radios or fruit like oranges and bananas, and, alongside them, West German negotiators would provide lists of the names they wanted released. Alternatively, cash settlements were reached by lawyers. Prices per person ranged from about 50,000DM to 150,000DM (equivalent to $100,000 to $300,000 today).[7]

Since the payments were a direct result of the post-1961 frontier, they could be viewed as yet another benefit of the reform. But they actually locked the East into a moribund cycle of needing a constant supply of the thing it hated most, people who wanted to leave. The ransom was like a narcotic and had the unintended effect of making the country dependent on its Western nemesis. The West, for its part, could be accused of propping up the East, perhaps even of prolonging its existence – particularly during the 1980s when the GDR once again became mired in economic difficulties. It was a murky business and neither side came out of it looking good, which is why it was kept largely secret. Nevertheless, thousands of people did escape persecution as a result.

In May 1986 the Bavarian government secured the Schmidt family's release. Martina and Rüdiger were delighted but also apprehensive. They wondered whether, when it came to it, the GDR would actually allow them out, and they also did not know what awaited them in the FRG. The news came with a warning that they should not talk to anyone about their upcoming departure, and there were also strict instructions about listing every item they wanted to take with them. This was an exhausting process. Even books had to be listed separately – by title, author, publisher, edition and publication date. The full list had to be approved, item by item, by the city council's culture department. Finally, on their daughter's sixth birthday, the family handed in their GDR identity cards and received expatriation certificates in return. 'You must now leave the GDR within twenty-four hours,' they were told.[8]

The Schmidts built a second life in the West but it took time. Their new land welcomed them in certain ways but not others. Soon after arriving they received an official welcome from the Bavarian State Chancellery, effectively a reply to their own secret communication of two years' earlier. They made new friends but they also experienced discrimination, which is something that almost all East German emigrants to the West describe. There was general wariness about refugees in the West following the huge influxes of the 1940s and 1950s, and also snobbery. Refugees' skills were considered worthless. Even those with advanced professional qualifications had to work in menial jobs or start afresh with full retraining. The West really was more hierarchical, Martina says, just as Eastern propaganda had asserted – a place where 'many judged a person's value according to his professional position or income'. Martina and Rüdiger were perhaps most shocked by how little people used their intellectual freedoms: 'They could read anything they liked but they had no books!'

Right to the bitter end, in 1989, the Stasi watched and listened to the Schmidts and kept a list of their addresses in the West – 'We don't know why and we don't know who told them', Rüdiger says. It also bugged the telephones of their loved ones in the GDR. 'A few days after we left, two men in white coats rang the doorbell of our old flat, where Rüdiger's mother was now living,' Martina says. 'They told her they had come from the telecommunications office and needed to check the phone. We were suspicious when we heard about this and, sure enough, after the Wall came down we learned that the Stasi was not only listening to our telephone calls but also using the microphone in the telephone to listen to everything else people said in our old flat.'

At this point Rüdiger goes upstairs to fetch the couple's Stasi file, and Martina explains that, like thousands of other Germans, they requested this documentation under legislation that allows people to see what the Stasi had collected on them. 'There wasn't so much,' she says, just as Rüdiger arrives back in the room with a lever-arch file containing several hundred photocopied pages.

Martina and Rüdiger Schmidt with their Stasi files.

We sit together on the sofa as they flick through a version of their earlier lives that they never asked to be compiled. They point out some reports on their Rostock youth group, and the list of their West German addresses, and also a document ordering their arrest if they tried to leave the GDR even for a holiday in another socialist country. Martina tells me that once they fled, and until the regime collapsed in 1989, neither she nor Rüdiger ever went close to the Inner German Border again: 'I suppose we just didn't want any more confrontation. We stayed away.'

Rüdiger and Martina's caution was entirely rational. The Schmidts feel they got away lightly, because the GDR regime had a pronounced vindictive streak and could sustain grudges seemingly without end. We discussed some operations the Stasi mounted against former citizens abroad. One in particular left an indelible mark on my mind.

Lutz Eigendorf was a top East German footballer who played for Dynamo Berlin. He decided to defect on an official trip, a friendly fixture against the West German club Kaiserslautern in March 1979.[9] The regime's rage was great when any sporting star defected, but it was more acute in Eigendorf's case because his club was officially under Stasi patronage. The footballer went on to play for Kaiserslautern and Eintracht Braunschweig but was under constant surveillance by Stasi informants, one of whom was an old friend sent to the FRG as a fake defector. Eigendorf had left behind a wife and baby daughter in the East. Perhaps he hoped they could join him at some point, but instead his wife divorced him and married another man. It then turned out that the other man was a Stasi agent too, deliberately tasked with winning her affections and monitoring whether she was still in touch with Eigendorf. Finally, in March 1983, poor Lutz was assassinated in a staged accident. Driving at night on a quiet West German road he was blinded by headlights from a strategically positioned lorry and swerved and hit a tree. It is possible, but has never been confirmed, that the death squad had first drugged him to make his death more likely. The blinding technique, known in Stasi jargon as *verblitzen*, was used in other cases as well.[10]

What was it like to cross the Inner German Border legally, as an ordinary traveller or tourist? The ongoing existence of West Berlin after 1961 and the Allied agreements protecting it meant that the GDR had to accept a huge quantity of movement over its borders, amounting to many millions of journeys a year. Of course, East Germany would have preferred it if West Berlin had not existed but for as long as it did the postwar settlement required the GDR to maintain transit corridors linking West Germany to its Berlin exclave. The distance was substantial, around 160 kilometres by the shortest route. Air travel was possible too but only ever accounted for a minority of trips. The East German response to this ongoing imposition was to maintain the most hostile and intrusive checkpoints imaginable. The largest was the combined road and rail crossing at Helmstedt–Marienborn. It was here that I would make my final stop before heading for the German capital itself.

For decades the names Helmstedt and Marienborn were synonymous with the miserable experience of waiting to get in or out of the GDR and the associated rituals of intimidation and humiliation. But they were also real places where real people lived. As Bettina Akinro, whose home was in Helmstedt throughout the 1980s, told me, no local was left untouched by the looming frontier. Now in her seventies, she met me in a car laden down with books about the Inner German Border and the two Germanies, and folders of her own photographs of both countries. For good measure she had also brought a picnic of sandwiches, biscuits and tea – so we would not be distracted from the task in hand, a tour of important border sites.

Bettina's English is beautiful. She had taught the language in local schools throughout her working life. 'The border put Helmstedt on the map,' she says, 'and increased our population with British, French and American troops – and in the case of the Americans, with their wives as well.' She remembers one wife confiding in her that she feared she and her husband were being sent to a 'sentry box in the desert' when she heard Helmstedt was to be their home. It was only when they actually arrived that they realized the town was an affluent place with plenty of community spirit.

The foreign troops' main duty was to guarantee the security and integrity of the West German crossing point, but most of the actual work was done by West German guards and customs officials. Consequently, there was lots of free time. 'They often arranged festivals and games evenings,' Bettina recalls. She produces a photograph of a khaki-coloured train carriage parked in a siding at Helmstedt station. 'Can you guess what this was?' she asks playfully. 'It was the US army's private carriage. Under the rules of occupation both German governments had to connect this to any train the Americans wanted, and no one could search it. It was used for official business but they also regularly took it from Helmstedt to West Berlin for theatre excursions and things like that. Once a week the American wives had exclusive use of it for a shopping trip to the Ku'damm [the Kurfürstendamm avenue].'

At Helmstedt station, Bettina Akinro shows me a photograph of the US army's private railway carriage which officers' wives used for shopping trips to West Berlin.

Of course, most people weren't lucky enough to have untouchable private train carriages. For them, the East German checkpoint which lay just a few minutes east of Helmstedt was a fearsome prospect. Bettina tells me she personally got anxious just thinking about it. Whatever actually happened, each time was an ordeal of nerves and stress. 'The railway checkpoint station was all of two kilometres from Helmstedt but so different from any station in West Germany,' she says. 'It was a mass of mirrors and fences and security personnel. There was a special set of tracks where they could divert the train at short notice if they suspected it of carrying an escapee.'

Guards performed detailed checks on every passenger in every service. Silence reigned, Bettina says. The trains were often travelling between major international destinations – Paris–Moscow; Leningrad–Hook of Holland – and were timetabled to clear the eastern border in six or seven minutes. But until GDR officials were satisfied, no train moved. I thought of those great sleeper services, many in existence since the nineteenth century, all brought to a standstill by this awesome frontier, all made to thread themselves through this eye of a needle.

The road checkpoint was close by. Unlike the rail crossing, much of it still survives. It covers a vast space, meaning its visual impact remains considerable as you approach along the thundering A2 autobahn. Bettina handed me over to Justin, one of the official guides at the checkpoint's museum. Though just eighteen he had an impressive knowledge of what had happened here, events far removed from his own life.

'I find it hard to grasp from a modern standpoint just how observed you were,' he says while finishing a cigarette. 'The surveillance was total. Human eyes and camera lenses. Thermal cameras. X-ray machines. Two-way mirrors. There was even a dedicated morgue.' He looks up to see the effect this word has on me. GDR guards prised open coffins on their way to family burial plots. 'They wanted to be sure people

The vast GDR checkpoint at Helmstedt–Marienborn as it looks today.

inside were really dead and that there was no contraband.'

Justin takes me first to the main control tower, which rises high over the rest of the site, just like an air traffic control tower at an airport. From here, guards monitored and controlled everything. Justin points to a bank of switches that could be flicked to flood the entire terrain with super-bright light or to plunge it into darkness. If a vehicle made a bid for freedom, the people in the tower could activate one of numerous spring-loaded barriers to stop it. These were made from steel and weighed six tonnes and had been tested to prove they could stop a 40-tonne truck travelling at 80 kilometres per hour. Justin describes a gruesome incident in which a West German couple got fed up with the slow-moving queue one day and decided to abandon their trip to West Berlin. When guards in the tower saw them driving back into the FRG, they assumed they were fugitives from the East and deployed a barrier. The couple were decapitated by the impact.

Later, we walk from building to building, along corridors decorated in the strangely domestic style that Eastern Bloc officialdom liked – a result, perhaps, of how the GDR and other socialist states did not differentiate between furnishings for the workplace and furnishings for the home. As Justin unlocks occasional doors and we step in to look around, the visuals often jar with his words. A room kitted out like a 1970s suburban lounge, complete with boldly patterned wallpaper, is a director's office. The main passport-checking area has linoleum flooring similar to what we had in our kitchen in the 1980s.

For vehicles that raised no concerns the passage through the checkpoint could be fast or slow. It depended on factors ranging from the local (volume of traffic; the mood of a particular checkpoint chief on a given day) to the geopolitical. A favourite tactic was to order go-slows on days when major public events were to occur in West Berlin: a sporting fixture, maybe, or one of the periodic symbolic sessions of the federal parliament at the Reichstag.

For those warranting additional scrutiny, waits were potentially unlimited. Justin shows me the rooms used for strip searches and a garage where cars were dismantled in the hunt for secret passengers and smuggled goods. If you were unlucky enough to end up with a dismantled car the GDR border mechanics would not help you put it together again, even if they had found no evidence of wrongdoing. Instead, they gave you a business card for a Helmstedt mechanic who had special permission to cross the Iron Curtain and reassemble vehicles. No civilian East Germans were trusted to do such work, so it was the very definition of a captive market. Unsurprisingly, the mechanic charged steep fees.

X-ray scanners were first installed in 1982 to allow the authorities to look for concealed humans in a greater proportion of cars. Selected cars were directed through an X-ray channel and brought to a halt for a period of time so a scanner could make an image. The fact that scans were being made was kept secret, and for good reason. The dose of radiation car occupants received was massive. GDR authorities knew this and may even have used it as a kind of targeted nuclear weapon. Multiple reports now attest to the cars of known dissidents and anti-GDR campaigners being subjected to the longest scans. It seems likely that this was a deliberate attempt, sometimes successful, to give them cancer. Many past employees who worked the equipment have also subsequently died of radiation-related cancers.[11] Tellingly, unlike almost everything else at the checkpoint, the X-ray machines were removed before the site was abandoned.

Visitors were meant to feel menaced at Helmstedt–Marienborn. For those lucky GDR citizens who were granted permission to cross the border the experience could be profoundly disillusioning, a moment when they were confronted with the full truth of their country's paranoia. In his memoir of growing up in East Germany Maxim Leo writes of a road trip he and his grandfather made to France in the summer of 1987 (his grandfather was a national hero who had worked with the French Resistance during the war; he was going to meet old comrades): 'The closer we get to the border in Marienborn, the emptier the autobahn gets. There's a sign saying that this is the last exit in the GDR. We drive on, there are no more Eastern cars, even though we are in the East. At a walking pace, we drive past the barbed-wire fences and anti-tank barriers, the soldiers with submachine guns . . . How barricaded our country is. What became of a dream of Socialism?'[12]

Finally, it is time for me to drive the transit route for myself. On a sweltering Friday lunchtime I am heading to Berlin, the city that for decades was the Cold War's tightest knot.

11

Berlin, Germany

As I drove along the A2 my thoughts turned to the hundreds of thousands of men and women who ran the border system and generated the secret police files in East Germany and other communist regimes. After the fall of the Iron Curtain these people mostly kept quiet about their old jobs. Only a small number have ever chosen to speak out, and usually only after exposure in the media. The defences of their actions that they mount usually centre on familiar themes. They were just following orders. What they did was legal at the time. The context required it but everyone has conveniently forgotten the context. Sometimes they used their positions for good, to show leniency.

I had tried without success to find a former Stasi officer or similar official who would grant me an interview. All the emails I had sent had gone unanswered, except for one where the man had initially agreed to meet but then withdrew the agreement half an hour later. As I was travelling through Germany I had been reading books about informants, collaborators and operatives – the worker bees of the Eastern Bloc's fear-generating system.[1] I had been left with the sense that some were definitely sadists or even psychopaths. But this was not nearly as common as one might expect. The difficult truth was that most of the people were decidedly humdrum. If patriotism was a motivation for many, they also seem to have been driven by baser day-to-day impulses: responding to blackmail and fearing the consequences of refusal; also pleasing their bosses, achieving promotion, protecting their organization's reputation, or simply churning through the work that crossed their desk.

I found myself imagining what it would have been like to order the installation of the deadly X-ray machines back at Helmstedt–Marienborn. I tried to see myself as an informer in Martina and Rüdiger's youth group in Rostock. I thought of fitting microphones in the walls of the *Bausoldaten* barracks in Prora. When my mind reached poor Lutz Eigendorf I made myself flash my headlights, imagining that as I did so I was blinding him, sending him off the road to his death. A shiver ran through me. I knew I was incapable of such things, would not be able to do them. And yet. And yet. For every ninety-nine realities in which I withstood, there was surely one in which I might have complied.

Never to be ordered to harm another human being is good fortune indeed.

The wonderful capital of the reunified Germany creeps up on you nowadays. Situated in the flat centre of Europe, it does not have the kind of skyline or surrounding landscape that makes it visible for miles around, though eventually the syringe-like television tower does shimmer into sight. When arriving from the west there is no longer the huge Wall and associated checkpoints to bring you to a standstill and make you supplicate for entry. Instead, pretty woods and lakes begin to acquire summerhouses, then the leafy suburbs begin. And eventually the suburbs turn into the large quarters of plain apartment blocks where most Berliners live. Berlin is modest in one way but packs a punch in others. A big reason for that is the knowledge most people carry of how the place suffered during the twentieth century and in particular of how it was marooned, besieged, divided and rusticated by the Cold War.

I was starting my week in Berlin in the former West and would move back and forth between it and the former East.

West Berlin really was a place of contradictions. It was denied the right to lead the Federal Republic after the war, and in constitutional terms was not even part of the FRG but a special occupied territory, divided into American, British and French sectors just as West Germany itself was. West Berlin's two million inhabitants could not vote in federal West German elections, while the demi-city's unenviable location prevented it becoming a major industrial centre like Munich or Stuttgart, or taking on any other functional role in postwar Germany. And yet West Berlin was of central importance in world affairs. Its purpose in this regard was simple and unrivalled: to go on existing as a vital beacon of the West in the East, physical proof of the West's determination to stand firm.

Those who lived in West Berlin had to come to terms with a certain claustrophobia while developing reserves of courage. This was already the case before the Wall went up, but the situation became much tenser thereafter. 'Berliners show a peculiar fearlessness which excites the almost unbelieving wonderment of the world,' the poet and critic Stephen Spender wrote in 1961. 'That is because they have reached the place on the far side of fear, where, being utterly at the mercy of the conflict of the great powers, they feel there is no use being afraid and therefore they have nothing to be afraid of.'[2]

To get by day-to-day West Berlin ended up falling back on the whole city's former reputation for entertainment and consumerism. It marketed itself without irony as a place where you could forget your cares, a kind of reincarnated Weimar, an invitation to party on the exact spot where the end of the world was most likely to occur. Tourists came for two main reasons: quickly to look at the awful Wall and then to let their hair down at their leisure. Sprinkled among them were always West German schoolchildren, millions of whom moved through on subsidized pilgrimages each year.

West Berlin had lost out to the East when it came to Berlin's historic centre. It had to create a new hub at Breitscheidplatz, which had the famous ruined Kaiser Wilhelm church in the middle. Abundant West German subsidies paid for new shopping and entertainment venues.[3] Many people I met on my trip told me of visits they had made before 1989: of late nights, of bars and even sex clubs, of big shows and concerts and conference dinners till dawn, and, always, of shopping. You can still catch a glimpse of this glitzy, slightly trashy West Berlin past today in the occasional faded shopfront or abandoned neon sign, but the aesthetic is hardly distinctive; in fact, it feels almost intentionally generically Western.

People who chose West Berlin as a permanent home often prized something quite different about the place. Of necessity a backwater, it became after 1961 a seedbed for fringe lifestyles. As the geographer T. H. Elkins wrote in 1988, 'West Berlin more than any city of Germany is the place where there is a non-violent search for alternate living. The principle is to opt out of the cash economy by the formation of collective or co-operative groups. There are collectives for craft and repair services, health-food shops, self-help, communication skills, residential management, medical services, legal services, ecological groups, actors, and many more.'[4] Two features in particular attracted counter-cultural pioneers. First, state subsidies meant that rents were unusually cheap: the West was determined that West Berlin should not become an empty shell. Secondly, young men who moved from the FRG automatically became exempt from military conscription.

Alongside old ladies with little dogs and old men who drove the trains and buses, an enormous youth population grew up.[5] The journalist and former DJ Tobias Rapp called the West Berlin of the 1980s a 'village in the shadow of the Wall' and added that it was a village where some of the villagers were pretty strange. 'If you were clever, you finished school in West Germany and just left your hometown and went to West Berlin. That created a situation where you had all these people here who had problems with authorities; who didn't want anyone to shout at them. All of these anarchists, left wingers, dope smokers. [They] came to Berlin because they were looking for something else. This had a huge impact on the atmosphere of the Western half of the city. Thousands of people would move to Berlin every year. Add that up over thirty years, and that's a lot of dope smokers.'

Many elsewhere in West Germany thought of West Berliners as spoiled rotten.[6] And politicians in the GDR frequently condemned the city as decadent even by Western standards, because of both the fleshpots and the dropouts. But West Berlin developed an impressive tolerance for niche groups, alternative cultures and people living in self-made communities – and in that sense it highlighted the intolerance of both the systems it coexisted with. In the shadow of the Wall, many in West Berlin succeeded in not being defined by the macro-political craziness all around, or indeed by any state-endorsed ideology. Magically they found a way to live on their own terms.

After checking into a flat in Kreuzberg I headed out to swim. I swim almost daily in London and had missed this part of my routine. The Barents and Baltic seas had been too cold and the weather too bad. But on this sunny Friday I found a nearby open-air pool, Sommerbad Kreuzberg, which turned out to be a glorious stainless steel construction, on whose base and sides the sunlight and water created constantly shifting patterns.

Both pool and adjacent park have been popular since Cold War times, when they were favourite places for sunbathing and partying just three blocks from the Wall. After drying off, I sat in the spectator seats and fell into conversation with Heinrich, a local man who had been coming here for over forty years. He told me he had first moved from Cologne to evade military service. 'It was 100 per cent its own place,' he said. 'The Wall made the city in a way, but actually we paid very little attention to it.

By the 1980s it was a kind of natural phenomenon, like a hill or a cliff. Of course we wished it would go away but somehow it also helped us have the life we wanted. Nobody cared what you did here as long as you didn't start shooting into the East, or something.' He lit up a post-swim cigarette. 'Our life was truly simple then. You had your friends. You had a little job, maybe. And you could do your art or make your music or just do drugs.'

Heinrich himself combined being an artist with work as a care assistant in an old people's home. In recent years, he has united the two endeavours by teaching art to children with learning disabilities. He tells me he still comes to the Sommerbad every day it is open. 'Sometimes, my friends and I are like them,' he says, pointing at two young men a few rows beneath us, who are playing a dice game and drinking bottles of beer. 'What is the game?' I ask. 'It's Kniffel,' he replies. (Kniffel, I later discover, is a German version of Yahtzee.)

'So, how did it feel when it all came to an end in 1989?' I ask.

The dominant mood in West Berlin on the evening of 9 November was one of rejoicing. But for Heinrich it was a strange time. He was personally delighted to see Easterners regain their freedom. But his girlfriend was traumatized. '"Now they will ruin us all," she said. "West Berlin will be no good any more. They will come here with their Stasi and their neo-Nazis. There will be pogroms."' She even threatened to throw herself out of the window of their flat in a moment of angst. At the time Heinrich felt she was wrong, and still thinks so today. 'But,' he says, 'it shows you how we alternative thinkers and dropouts became dependent on a particular, very unusual situation.'

I enquire what a typical night out would have been for him back before the Wall came down. 'We would never go up to the Ku'damm; it was terrible over there, so cheap and kitsch,' he tells me. 'Maybe we would take some wine at a neighbourhood bar or maybe at a friend's flat. Sometimes there were parties in squats. Often we just sat right over there on the grass. Of course those were good times and of course everything then changed,' he continues. 'Berlin now has gentrification, like in London. We still do things like this. We find a way. Berlin is still a village sometimes.'

As I prepare to go, he adds, 'You should learn Kniffel. Kniffel, I think, is very West Berlin.'

The dissenting, free-spirited cultures of the Western city had their equivalents in East Berlin, particularly from the early 1980s on. But the thing that struck visitors most was the monolithic official culture the GDR imposed over on its side of town.

East Berlin *was* a capital city, the *Hauptstadt der DDR*. The country was perennially short of money and slow to clear away the rubble of 1945. But there was never any doubt about communism's delight that it had dragged so much of one of Europe's greatest cities into its orbit. The famous Museum Island was entirely within the GDR, as were the Humboldt University and the Brandenburg Gate, Nikolaiviertel, the kernel of medieval Berlin, and Alexanderplatz, the hub of interwar city life. I have wandered round Berlin's central Mitte district many times now but I will always remember the dominant impression of my first visit: the East Germans got so much.

This part of Berlin made for a wonderful trophy and would be the regime's principal stage throughout its four decades. To get a sense of what the dictatorship did with these cultural riches one need only look at photographs and film from the period. East Berlin's historic structures and thoroughfares are constantly bedecked in red banners, triumphant slogans and Marxist-Leninist portraits. These form the august backdrop to countless marches and demonstrations, all of them arranged by the state, up to and including the most splendid of all, the fortieth anniversary celebration on 7 October 1989, a final hubristic blowout just a month before the Wall split open.

Like previous autocracies, the GDR wanted to leave its mark

The Fernsehturm, Berlin Television Tower, was built in the 1960s to a design partly inspired by the USSR's Sputnik satellite.

on the capital. The Wall was its most obvious imposition of course, and, at least officially, a source of pride. Nikolaiviertel received a makeover in time for Berlin's 750th anniversary in 1987, its medieval buildings quite sensitively restored and in some cases reimagined, even if they did end up interspersed with modern pre-fabricated (*Plattenbau*) apartment blocks. On a much larger scale the nearby Berlin Television Tower, or Fernsehturm, became (and remains) the tallest structure in all Germany. It was explicitly intended to be a statement building, containing a visual reference to the USSR's pioneering Sputnik satellite, and a vertical message of progress to contrast with the horizontal Wall underneath. The Fernsehturm's construction required many vestiges of old Berlin to be swept away along with a centuries-old street plan, and the same was true of an earlier project, Karl-Marx-Allee, which stretches for two kilometres from Alexanderplatz in layer upon layer of monumental Stalinist architecture. This was called Germany's first socialist avenue at its opening, and for its first decade was known as Stalinallee, even boasting a statue of the man himself.

My favourite Berlin walk leads, in just twenty minutes, from Café Moskau on Karl-Marx-Allee to the Fernsehturm and through Nikolaiviertel to Museum Island. It was here that the crowning glory of GDR buildings, the Palace of the Republic, was situated. A structure with both violence and virtue in its DNA – and an awful lot of asbestos – the Palace, like the regime, has disappeared. It was the communists' main addition to Museum Island. To build it, East Germany first had to remove the extensive remains of Berlin's City Palace, a Baroque masterpiece that had been the Kaiser's historic seat. The City Palace could have been saved, but its connection to Prussian militarism was deemed too toxic and the visual metaphor of demolishing it too tempting. During the early 1950s gelignite destroyed what was left of the building, and volunteers from the Free German Youth bagged up the rubble. Work on the emptied plot was supposed to continue apace but stalled for twenty years, as no one could agree about what to put in such a special place.

Only in 1972 did Erich Honecker give approval for his people's palace to be built. The Stalinist 'birthday-cake' aesthetic (used in similar projects in the Eastern Bloc like Warsaw's Palace of Culture and Science of 1952–55) was out of fashion by then. The Palace of the Republic that went up between 1973 and 1976 was a low-slung, modernist structure that had more than a little in common with Alvar Aalto's Vyborg public library. It had acres of windows, which allowed occupants to look out on what some might have felt were more distinguished structures nearby. The glass in its windows was tinted bronze – a look that did not age well but which was intended to be warm and inviting (in photographs, the colour rather reminds one of a villain's sunglasses in a 1970s thriller). Unusually, the building combined the roles of rubber-stamp parliament, theatre, bowling alley and discotheque, as well as having several art galleries and thirteen restaurants.

It is all but impossible to recover what the Palace of the Republic looked like when you visit Museum Island today. It closed its doors in 1990 and suffered demolition between 2006 and 2008. In a slow-motion rewinding of history, the site is now occupied by the Humboldt Forum, which is an exact replica of the City Palace on three sides with a bland modern office facade on its fourth. Five thousand tonnes of asbestos was the practical justification for destroying the GDR's most important building, but the decision to do so also involved many subjective moral

The fourth side of the reconstructed Berlin City Palace, while still under construction. It now houses the Humboldt Forum.

judgements about progress and beauty, just as much suffused with the spirit of triumphalism as the GDR's plans had been back in the 1950s and 1970s.

I had become interested in the vestiges of the Palace of the Republic, in particular a cycle of sixteen paintings that had been commissioned for its opening. All were supposed to be inspired by a lesser known utterance of Lenin's, the question 'Are communists allowed to dream?' Taking the answer as yes, the paintings were supposed to show how three decades of socialist rule had led to flourishing creativity in East Germany. Each canvas was by a different GDR artist, and they really were given considerable freedom to create what they wished – except for any self-censorship they may have applied.

The artworks had hung in the building's main foyer throughout its life and were seen by millions of citizens and visitors, but the majority are not on display anywhere in Germany today. Indeed, they were entirely off limits from 1990 until 1995, when they were stuck inside the boarded-up building. After being shown for just thirty-nine days in 1996 they were again packed away for twenty-one years, until a new gallery, the Museum Barberini in Potsdam, dedicated an exhibition to them in 2017 as part of a more general attempt to rehabilitate East German art. Many people came to see the old curiosities but afterwards they disappeared once more, into the vaults of the Deutsches Historisches Museum.[7]

The cycle may easily be dismissed as simple propaganda – the general charge that people level at any non-dissident art from the Eastern Bloc. But what the paintings actually show, in my view, is that official art is not always propaganda and propaganda is not necessarily simple. Even as late as 1976, the obvious choice for an East German committee charged with decorating a major public building would have been to commission murals depicting some aspect of society's linear progress towards socialism. A popular alternative would have been art celebrating a major socialist achievement: Sputnik and Gagarin's space flight were go-to favourites. But here, in the largest public space in the most important building in the country, something more complex and edgier was attempted; something that lacked a clear pro-regime narrative.

Six of the sixteen canvases show a society where humans wear no clothes. Some of these scenes are idealized and Edenic, but Hans Vent's *People at the Beach* shows a group of naked bathers on what seems to be a contemporary East German beach, exposing in an official space a pastime that was popular but frowned upon. Other artists depicted human faces and bodies in ways that are reminiscent of Bosch and Bacon: meaty, visceral and sometimes pained. In *Ikarus*, Bernhard Heisig chose a theme that was especially hard to square with straightforward progress. Heisig's tragic hero is seen looking nervously to his wings. Perhaps we are witnessing the moment when he first realized the wax was starting to melt. Was this a daring commentary on the GDR's own ascent?

My favourite painting from the cycle, both as a visual object and because of its ambivalence, is Wolfgang Mattheuer's *Guten Tag*, or *Good Day*. In its centre, a modern family (father, mother, young son) walks through grass towards the viewer. Their reaction to what lies ahead of them (which we cannot see) is decidedly uncertain. On their left, a thick wooden fence runs into the distance, and on the other side of it an old man looks on sadly. A huge city sprawls in the background. The real Wall was only a couple of kilometres away from this canvas in three directions, so it was certain that many visitors would interpret the painting as a version of divided Berlin. What was Mattheuer trying to say? It is by no means clear that the grassy (eastern) side of the fence is really the better one. The only tree in the field has been chopped down and has no leaves. Flowers grow only on the other side of the fence even if a few of their blooms do protrude through. The young son, the clearest symbol of the future, brandishes a bow and arrow. Such lack of clarity, such potential for pessimism, was most un-communist.

It would have been the job of a heartbeat to withhold these pictures from display or relegate them to some provincial museum or the director's office of a collective farm. But back in 1976 I think the commissioners were inviting East Germans to take pleasure in the level of sophistication their country had reached. Though it could never be said explicitly, for fear of offending the Kremlin, the GDR's ruling elite saw themselves as the most mature of all socialist states: the most orderly, the best educated, and also the most willing to address life's genuine complexities. This theme comes through strongly in some GDR literature, for instance the novels of Christa Wolf, in which tortured souls wrestle with impossible moral conundrums. Many in the intelligentsia disliked aspects of the regime but

Wolfgang Mattheuer's Guten Tag *(Good Day), one of sixteen surprisingly ambivalent paintings commissioned for the opening of the Palace of the Republic.*

simultaneously saw the country as less shallow than the West and less intellectually dishonest than the USSR. 'Are communists allowed to dream?' was a cycle of paintings that seemed to prove that point.

I had booked myself on a tour of Hohenschönhausen, the Stasi's main political prison located in Berlin's north-east, about eight kilometres from the centre. Surviving members of the East German regime sometimes decry the fact that so much of what gets remembered about their country relates to its repressive and punitive aspects, while positive achievements like the Palace of the Republic have been destroyed. (The historian Clare Copley has described a perception among former East Germans of a concerted campaign 'to erase the traces of the GDR from the built environment' and 'to conflate it with National Socialism through reducing its legacy to its most repressive elements'.[8]) But in truth even while East Germany existed it was overshadowed by its addiction to secret surveillance and repression. The sad fact needs to be recognized.

Hohenschönhausen was where one could make one's career as an ambitious young officer enforcing the state's norms. It was where many thousands of psychologists began their careers, deploying their knowledge of the human mind as fearsome interrogators. And it was where some 7,300 people spent months of their lives on remand and under investigation for all manner of crimes, from plotting escapes over the Wall to owning a copy of 1984 to saying the wrong thing to a neighbour.[9] Grey and beige throughout, the prison utters a long stifled scream at visitors today, trying and failing adequately to explain itself.

The Stasi was established in 1950 as part of a wider transfer of power from Moscow to East Berlin. The KGB was withdrawing, at least partially, but something very like the KGB was to be left in its place. The Stasi's workforce then went on to double for each decade that it existed, so that it ended up larger by an order of magnitude than the Gestapo. Its wide-ranging powers basically amounted to being able to intervene in any citizen's life at will, to spy on them, threaten them, investigate them, punish them and occasionally to kill them.

Hohenschönhausen was the black jewel in the Stasi crown, the place where it perfected its trademark approach of committing violence without leaving bruises. My guide was not a former inmate, though twenty-five one-time prisoners do still show people round. On our way to the main detention block, Christoph led me through a succession of courtyards, one of which included an incongruous collection of rose bushes. These, he quickly explained, had not been planted for detainees (who could only get fresh air in walled-in cages which had no view) but for the staff who at some point had complained of growing depressed in the bleak surroundings.

At the main detention block, Christoph ran through the many facets of the horrific regime. On arrival, often in police vans disguised as delivery vehicles, prisoners were stripped, searched and made to stand naked for between one and two hours. The uniform they received was always a shapeless tracksuit deliberately selected to be too big or too small. Mugshots were then taken, which sometimes also involved irradiating the subject. And then in spartan cells the prisoners' long confinement began. Most inmates confessed at their very first interrogation, but irrespective of when they talked they would be held for nine months. They had to sleep in a special control position, on their backs and with their hands on their thighs. Falling asleep in some other position inevitably meant being woken up by guards banging on the door. (This point struck me particularly because I have never been able to sleep on my back.)

Dehumanization was as near to total as possible. It wasn't a tyranny that treated enemies like animals; rather it treated them like robots, denying many of their most basic social and emotional needs. Inmates were always addressed by number not name. A series of red and green traffic lights regulated corridors so that no prisoner ever saw another. Even in interrogation rooms, prisoners were seated at right angles to their questioners, on backless stools. There were padded cells and a Kubrick-esque CCTV control room. A multipurpose basement was used by Soviet occupying forces for water torture between 1945 and 1951. (It subsequently became a sauna for Stasi officers.) Between 1960 and 1990 Hohenschönhausen held a small town's worth of people, but over that period there was just one recorded outbreak of prisoner violence. The regime they lived under made clear to detainees that resistance was pointless.

'Democracy is not a gift but an achievement,' Christoph says. I'm sure he says it on each tour but it sounds like a fresh reaction to what we are seeing. The manifestations of oppression are always subtly different wherever they occur, he adds, but as

Europeans we need to acknowledge that our own societies are only ever a few steps from replicating this kind of nightmare. 'It should surely be the work of everyone, every day, to prevent this short distance being covered again.'

We end up at the museum's permanent exhibition, which helps me to put the prison into its wider context. There are photographs of the gala dinners that management held inside the complex – all the guests men, all of them thoroughly locked into the regime in their own way. There are pennants for sporting associations that the Stasi sponsored, among them the football team that Lutz Eigendorf once played for. And there is even a bizarre selection of LPs, albums of socialist marching tunes which seem to have been produced specially for the security service market. They have titles like 'Weapon Colour RED: No Chance for the Enemy' and 'Our Singing Must Be a Battle Cry'. It really was a total system, whichever side of it you wound up on.

Surveying a room of mugshots, I instantly see how young people dominated among the inmates, just as they did the ranks of escapees. Men and women, mostly still in their teens or twenties, were photographed by the Stasi lens at moments of supreme vulnerability. They could not even have begun to adjust to the fact of their impending incarceration, but somehow their eyes show that they knew they were already trapped: Matthias Melster, locked away in 1987 during the city's 750th anniversary celebrations; Matthias Bath, taken out of action in 1976 just before the opening of the Palace of the Republic; Ulrike Poppe, founder of the Women for Peace network, detained in 1983 and again in 1984. Christoph says the museum would only need a very small display to show the mugshots of former Stasi operatives imprisoned for their actions. Of some 250,000 men and women who served the organization only two have ever gone to jail.

I devote a day to walking the Berlin Wall, both its few surviving stretches and other places along its route which are now carefully marked out with a line of bricks in the ground. Today's Berlin crowds in everywhere. On the banks of the Spree, looking from east to west across the old river border, my view is interrupted by a *bateau-mouche*-style boat offering '*Mörderische Spreefahrt*' nights (whodunits with dinner and a cruise along the river). By Friedrichstrasse station, whose checkpoint became widely known as the Palace of Tears because of the terrible partings that occurred there, a billboard outside a lunch venue advertises '*Salat Macht Sexy*'. Near Checkpoint Charlie an escape-room experience cashes in on the location's notoriety, and a new block

Murder on the Spree, now a fun way to spend an evening on the old east–west river border.

of luxury flats promises 'Charlie Living', whatever that might be.

I end up walking for kilometres through the city following the former border's twists and turns, crossing some of the 192 Berlin streets it used to block off. Tourists cluster in some places – in particularly large numbers on Niederkirchnerstrasse, where a long expanse of Wall still stands. This is beside the Topography of Terror museum, making for a gathering of darknesses. Although I have my doubts about the decision to demolish the Palace of the Republic, I can see that removing the Wall was essential. It is good some bits remain, of course, and also that so much information is available in other places where it ran. But it is

'MADNESS': graffiti on the surviving stretch of Berlin Wall on Niederkirchnerstrasse, a particularly popular spot with tourists today.

also good that its physical reality has disappeared. The wound it constituted was too large, a disfiguring scar after a botched operation.

Away from the crowds it is easier to reflect on what the Wall actually meant. The Mauerpark in Prenzlauer Berg is now a green space where parents push prams and skateboarders attempt tricks, but it used to be the death strip that kept East Berliners away from the border proper and, at quiet times of day, one can still get a sense of how much of central Berlin the GDR authorities had to wreck in order to drive the Wall through the city. Nearby, on Bernauer Strasse, the Wall infamously ran right up to the doors of houses and blocks of flats. This was due to a deal two city boroughs had done back in the 1930s to move their shared boundary from the middle of the street to its edge in order to make street sweeping and bin collection more efficient.[10] The alteration of just a few metres gave rise to many of the most shocking stories of escape in 1961, with people jumping from their Eastern windows onto the West Berlin pavement and digging tunnels out of their basements.

The buildings quickly got bricked up and sealed off once the authorities got wise to what was going on. Many were subsequently destroyed. But the street today still bears witness to the suffering of those years. One commonly sees visitors crying as they read the information boards there. I stood for the longest time at a board dedicated to Ida Siekmann, the Wall's first victim. The words on it have a simple poetry as they conjure up the ghost of an ordinary woman in a state of frenzy: 'Ida Siekmann was deeply affected by the consequences of the closed border. Her sister lived in West Berlin. This unbearable situation led the fifty-eight-year-old woman to flee on the day before her birthday. On August 21, 1961 the East Berlin police locked the front door of her apartment building that opened to West Berlin. It was probably then that she decided to flee. She had seen the West Berlin firemen catching neighbours who had jumped from their windows into rescue nets. Misjudging the danger, on the morning of August 22 she threw her bedding from her third-floor apartment onto the sidewalk below. For reasons that are not known, she jumped out the window before the firemen were ready with their rescue net. When she hit the ground, she was badly injured and died on the way to the hospital. Ida Siekmann was the first person to die at the Wall. Her death sparked outrage. After the funeral service wreathes and flowers were placed in front of her apartment building. The Wedding district erected a monument in September.'

Other escapes were more successful. There were tunnels through which dozens passed to West Berlin before the authorities shut them down, or rising groundwater made them impassable. There was the young officer of the *Volkspolizei*, Conrad Schumann, who took his chance and vaulted over freshly laid barbed wire on 15 August 1961, just two days after the Wall's construction began (though his experience is yet another reminder of how physical flight does not guarantee full freedom: Schumann's escape continued to haunt him throughout his life and he committed suicide in 1998). A world of pain on a single street. The jaws closing, and then staying closed for twenty-eight years.

When confronting the East's enormities, it is easy to let the West slip from your mind. Freedom and justice were absent in East

Germany, but they were only ever partially achieved in West Germany and the West generally. A favourite strategy of Western politicians in the Cold War was to rank the two systems and declare theirs the winner – in terms of absolute wealth, in terms of living standards, and in terms of human rights. Not everyone in the West could agree to this outlook, and West Berlin was frequently a focal point for rage against Western complacency and hypocrisy. West Berlin's unique circumstances and population ended up casting unforgiving light in both directions.

Local tensions really first began to intensify in 1967, when the police in West Berlin killed Benno Ohnesorg, a twenty-six-year-old student. Ohnesorg had been demonstrating against a visit to the city by the Shah of Iran, a tyrant who was one of the West's key Cold-War allies. Anti-Shah demonstrators clashed with pro-Shah supporters, and amid the chaos Ohnesorg was shot dead. The policeman who killed him, Karl-Heinz Kurras, argued that he had done so out of self-defence, but many onlookers said it was a premeditated, unjustified attack. Kurras, like many violent police officers before and since, was acquitted. (It subsequently emerged that he had once been an informal collaborator with the Stasi and some have speculated that the GDR may have ordered Ohnesorg's shooting to provoke rioting, but no proof has ever materialized.)

During subsequent protests in 1968, West Berlin students organized some of Europe's largest demonstrations. The targets of their ire were what they saw as the bastions of Western injustice: capitalist inequality and corruption, a rigged economic system, police brutality, colonialism, racism, misogyny, and a generalized traditionalism that was resistant to all change.

Prevalent among the younger generation in West Berlin was the sense that the legacy of West Germany's unique right-wing past had not been adequately dealt with. A specific concern was the number of former Nazis in positions of power. At the end of the war, the Nuremberg trials had dispensed justice to a select few Third Reich politicians and officials. But, partly due to the onset of the Cold War, hundreds of thousands of others were quietly rehabilitated. Many then went on to flourish without ever apologizing for or even acknowledging their previous actions. The tendency seemed to reach a shameful apotheosis in 1966 when Kurt Georg Kiesinger, a one-time Nazi Party member, became West German Chancellor. At the Christian Democrats' party conference in West Berlin in 1968, the young activist Beate Klarsfeld mounted the stage and publicly slapped Kiesinger across the face, calling him a Nazi and telling him to resign. At moments like this it felt like West Berlin was functioning not so much as a beacon for the West, but as a kind of detached conscience, at one remove from the rest of West Germany and able to communicate some difficult home truths.

12

Potsdam, Germany

For twenty-eight years after 1961 the Berlin Wall had an air of permanency that has eluded many older structures and institutions. Very quickly people became convinced it would be around for a long time. The impression only intensified over ensuing decades as barbed wire gave way to concrete, and concrete to still thicker and higher concrete and the Wall's many other embellishments. John le Carré, in a novel set in 1963, observed that 'the Berlin Wall had been up two years and by the looks of it would stay up for another two hundred'.[1] In 1983 the Iron Curtain traveller Anthony Bailey said he could not 'imagine Berlin as one city. It is as if the wall has been there for a thousand years'.[2] People I had met on my own journey confirmed this was no writerly hyperbole. Martina and Rüdiger Schmidt felt sure the Wall would be in place for their whole lives. Andreas Wagner also 'didn't expect a change'. When Ronald Reagan stood at the Brandenburg Gate exhorting 'Mr Gorbachev' to 'tear down this wall', in June 1987, most listeners endorsed the sentiment but doubted anything would happen soon.

The events of the summer and autumn of 1989 were one of history's true surprises. The GDR regime excelled at look-ing strong. At showpiece events it continued to present an adamantine face to the world right to the bitter end. But despite public appearances, the socialist dictatorship actually entered the 1980s with several serious illnesses that, after wholly inadequate treatment, proved fatal. I left Berlin and doubled back to

Potsdam, to meet a man who had had a remarkable vantage point during the last years of the East German dictatorship as the cracks began to show.

In economic terms, the Wall and the fortified Inner German Border at first helped the GDR to right itself – so much so that in the 1960s some experts began speaking of an East German economic miracle to rival West Germany's 1950s *Wirtschaftswunder*. But the tacit bargain the regime struck with citizens was costly. Not only did the border infrastructure cost a lot, so too did the promises of improved living standards that were effectively issued as compensation for the population's incarceration. The GDR spent big in the 1970s to provide more citizens with new consumer goods and housing. The bill was well beyond what the country could afford. While Western banks initially made up the difference, they became notably stingier after global recession kicked in in the early 1980s, and specifically after another communist country, Poland, defaulted on its loans in 1982.

Officials thought they would have time to put these and other problems right and were nothing if not creative in their efforts to increase the supply of hard currency. Upping the number of citizens who got ransomed to the West was one tactic. Others included turning the GDR into the premier destination for West German toxic waste, and enrolling East German patients in lucrative medical trials for experimental Western pharmaceuticals that the West would not test on its own sick.

But while these brought in some more money they did not stop living standards stagnating and then slumping. The shops and restaurants of East Germany became increasingly empty and the waiting lists for cars, televisions and other modern essentials hopelessly long. Countless East German jokes described the situation with pithy sourness. 'A man comes into an East Berlin department store, looks around in desperation, and asks a saleswoman, "Have you no shoes?" Her reply: "No shoes is on the first floor. This floor is no bed linen."[3]

The gap between the standard East German car or television and its West German equivalent was also widening rapidly at this time. East Germans, almost all of whom watched West German television, could see that they were being left behind. Meanwhile, foreign consumers became less likely to purchase outmoded GDR exports, further compounding the economic crisis. The GDR, like the Eastern Bloc generally, was woefully slow to adopt new technologies. Automation in heavy industry was, in many cases, impossible because of a lack of investment capital, but it also raised difficult ideological questions because of the imperative for full employment. Personal computing was another thing that confounded the GDR. It could see the potential, but desktop computers were expensive and also brought security problems. When groups of young programmers started to meet up in the 1980s to play computer games and write code, the state's principal response was to infiltrate them.

And herein lay the key to East German weakness by the 1980s: the immense distrust that had developed between rulers and ruled. Over four decades of relentless propaganda, state surveillance and, at times, notable rises in living standards, the populace had not become happier and more biddable. Instead, they had become disillusioned and apathetic. Many simmered with anger. An eloquent sign of the general desperation was that, by 1989, the GDR had the highest per capita consumption of beer and spirits in the world – twenty-three bottles of spirits per person per year.[4]

Although East Germany avoided the USSR's fate of losing three superannuated leaders in the space of thirty months (Leonid Brezhnev, Yuri Andropov and Konstantin Chernenko all died between November 1982 and March 1985), it too had an ossified elite who were detached from reality. They mostly lived in a leafy compound – ironically, behind high fences – on the outskirts of East Berlin: the *Bonzenghetto*, or Ghetto of the Bigwigs, as it was disparagingly known. They did not realize the extent to which, back in the real world, people no longer believed in the goals they set, and thought the propaganda absurd and the surveillance frightening.

All over the country citizens had begun to establish their own kinds of community. They came together to speak about their actual needs and interests and to help one another, focusing on the things that were true and important to them, rather than the matters the party instructed them to care about. The punks of East Germany were the most famous of these new countercultures, but there were many others. Citizens who objected to the growing pollution and environmental degradation in their neighbourhoods came together to campaign. Others who hated the increasing importance placed on military education in kindergartens and primary schools started to argue for change. These and other groups found safe havens in the Lutheran church. Its most forward-looking congregations began to make their buildings available following concessions about freedom of assembly that they had won in the 1970s, a key chink in the state's armour.

But even the most innocuous gatherings attracted Stasi attention. Just the fact of coming together was suspicious and could have nasty consequences for those involved. For a paranoid regime anything except active support meant attack. Consequently, it took great courage to protest about acid rain or a poisoned river, or to say out loud that the GDR should live up to its rhetoric of peace and friendship, or to dye and spike your hair, or even to play 'The Last Ninja' with your mates on a bootlegged Commodore 64: hundreds of thousands of acts of courage that were undertaken not to destroy the regime but to make life more bearable and liveable.

*

I took the train from Berlin to Potsdam. Dirk Kummer met me at the station in his Audi and drove me back to his house on the beautiful Weißer See lake, a few kilometres from Potsdam city centre. Before we even left the station car park, he started talking about my project, enthusiastically sharing some snippets of his memories. A warm and gentle man, now in his fifties, he has devoted much time to reflecting on the GDR and what it did to the people who lived in it.

Dirk was born in 1966, in an East German town that lay close to the border with West Berlin. Interested in acting from an early age, he became involved in one of the GDR's many children's theatres and was selected, aged thirteen, to act in his first movie. This taste of the silver screen proved addictive and he decided there and then to try to make a life in cinema. While still in his teens, towards the end of secondary school, he also had another, more difficult, revelation: he was gay.

East Germany was unusual in the Eastern Bloc for ceasing to enforce its laws against homosexuality in 1957 and then formally decriminalizing homosexual acts in 1968. (As Josie McLellan observes in her excellent study on sex in the GDR, 'this was good for the modern, progressive image the [country] strove for', particularly since West Germany maintained its ban for a full year longer.[5]) Nevertheless, actually to live as gay in the country was far from easy. Homosexuality was frowned upon by most people. Many still viewed it as a mental illness, and no major public figure was out. Indeed, there were no depictions of normal gay characters on television or in the press, and the Stasi saw gay men and lesbians as legitimate targets for enhanced surveillance.

Intuitively understanding some of the problems his orientation could bring, Dirk fell into a deep depression shortly after his eighteenth birthday in 1984. He was struggling in particular with his looming national service. It would be double the normal length – three years instead of eighteen months – because that was the minimum necessary to earn him the chance to apply to the prestigious Potsdam film school.

'I was so afraid of the army and coming out,' he tells me as we talk in his front room over coffee and apricot cake; his partner, Ingo, having briefly stepped in to say hello, was now busy elsewhere in the house. 'What happened to my favourite teacher was also much on my mind. She was really a lovely woman. Young, blonde. We went to the theatre with her and she kept in touch with us outside class. After one summer vacation, we came back to school and learned that she jumped off her balcony because of some kind of love problem. Her death was probably partly what put the idea of suicide in my head.'

Dirk went into the kitchen at home one day, opened the oven door, and turned on the gas. He lay down on the floor and waited. He thinks now that it was probably a cry for help: 'I suppose I did hope people would find me.' It was just that every route through life seemed filled with problems. Fortunately, Dirk was found. He then attended a psychiatrist for a time, a fact about which, he tells me, the Stasi was informed. A few months later he started his dreaded national service. He served for most of the time on the Inner German Border. It was a low point but somehow he found the strength to get through: 'The crazy thing is: I don't remember much about those three years at all. It's like a kind of trauma. I didn't have any particularly dangerous situations to deal with, but the pressure and the constant political education – it was miserable. I didn't make a single friend and I felt I always had to hide the fact I was gay.'

Dirk was finally discharged in the middle of 1988, aged twenty-one. He applied to the Konrad Wolf University of Film and Television in Potsdam's Babelsberg and was offered a place on its directing course, provisional on submitting a showreel. It was at this point that he made what appeared to be a huge error.

Demob happy and suddenly hopeful, Dirk decided to enter

a showreel that spoke of the reality of his life. After leaving the army, he had started frequenting Prenzlauer Berg, the part of East Berlin where a few gay bars existed and a supportive community of gays, lesbians and others who didn't fit into the GDR mainstream had grown up. Filming in black and white on Super 8, he shot a ten-minute short that showed this version of the East German capital. He called it *Berlin: Pink Clouds and Me*. 'I mistakenly thought the film school would understand,' he says. 'That it would be an island of tolerance in my intolerant country.' But the showreel was far too radical. There were plenty of gays at Babelsberg, but they were almost all closeted, and the management was still trying to maintain the party line, particularly when selecting trainee directors. 'After seeing my film, the entrance committee declared itself shocked. They asked what I meant by it and what was wrong with me. Was I gay, or something?!' Dirk lets out a throaty laugh.

His provisional place was withdrawn and suddenly he was jobless. He took to sitting in the bars of Prenzlauer Berg day and night. (What else was there to do?) One day, he got into conversation with a man who introduced himself as Wolfram Witt. He said he was in the film industry and this led Dirk to share his tale of woe. 'They will never let you study there after that,' Wolfram confirmed. But he then revealed that he had just finished his own screenplay for a gay film and that to his huge surprise the authorities had passed it for production. 'I am going to talk with the director and see what he can do for you,' Wolfram promised and took Dirk's address.

A few days later Dirk had the very strange experience of receiving a visit from Heiner Carow, one of the most celebrated film directors in the GDR. Heiner confirmed that he and Witt were making the GDR's first ever gay feature film. It was to be called *Coming Out*. Upon seeing Dirk's Super 8 film, Heiner turned to him and said, 'From tomorrow, you will work with me. You will be my Second Assistant Director.' Dirk's eyes still

Dirk Kummer, standing on the right here, saw his life change forever when celebrated GDR director Heiner Carow asked him to work on East Germany's first gay feature film.

fill with wonder as he recalls those words. 'My life changed from one moment to the next.'

It is now clear that the GDR regime was incapable of systematic reform, but that does not mean that reform was never attempted. The problem was that each time someone in authority decided to try to take the country in a new direction, someone else, usually more senior, blocked the move. This was arguably the story of the Palace of the Republic's difficult modern art, which failed to spark a more general renaissance in East German creativity. It had also been the story of Heiner Carow's career.

Carow had first made films that pushed the boundaries of official taste in the 1970s. The most famous was *The Legend of Paul and Paula*, a wonderfully bleak evocation of young love in East Berlin that highlighted the city's ruined buildings and the population's emotional angst. The film had to be personally cleared by Erich Honecker and had many detractors. Consequently, for a prolonged period through to the mid-1980s, DEFA, the state film company, did not allow Carow to produce any films. He only came back into favour with *Coming Out*. Pressure groups had begun lobbying for greater acceptance of gays and lesbians. They wanted the age of consent equalized for gay and straight relationships and also for gays and lesbians to be permitted to add wreathes at Holocaust memorials in memory of the Nazis' homosexual victims. In this atmosphere someone at DEFA decided that the moment had come to give a measure of official recognition to the GDR's gay citizens. This decision was then ratified by the Politburo member for culture.[6]

Dirk tells me that for him the film was an amazing apprenticeship. They shot on location in his local bars (the Burgfrieden and the Schoppenstube) and at DEFA's studios in Potsdam, the celebrated place where Fritz Lang's *Metropolis* and Josef von Sternberg's *The Blue Angel* had been made. In addition to the assistant director role, Carow ended up casting Dirk as one of the film's stars: 'We made all these casting calls with young German actors all over the country, in Leipzig, Rostock, all the schools and theatres. In screen tests I always played the other part. Then one day – I remember it happened to be my birthday – Heiner said, "Now you go in front of the camera and do it." He had watched me reading the roles for months and said he hadn't seen anyone better. I got cast as Matthias.'

I ask Dirk if Heiner was gay. I suppose I was partly wondering if some sort of sexual relationship had developed between them, but he tells me it did not. At first Dirk assumed that Heiner was straight. He was married with two children. The director was curious about gay life but Dirk assumed this was because of the film. 'He was really a bit of a crazy guy. He rang the doorbell of my flat very early one morning, like 7 a.m. I had a boyfriend and Heiner asked if he could come up and see how a gay flat looked first thing in the morning. My boyfriend was lying there in bed. That was what Heiner wanted to see. He repeated the set-up in the movie.'

But then one day a make-up artist remarked to Dirk on set, 'Heiner's wife doesn't have it easy, does she?', and went on to tell him that Heiner had a hidden gay life. Apparently his wife knew about it. Dirk suddenly understood that for Heiner *Coming Out* was much more than an outsider's attempt to help a marginalized group or make groundbreaking art. It was a personal contribution to giving people of the future a more honest, less shame-ridden life than he had had.

Dirk decorated the cover of his shooting script for Coming Out *with good-looking men and an Oscar statuette.*

By the start of 1989 *Coming Out* was ready to show to officials. The permission to make it did not include permission to release it; for that, fresh approval was needed. Carow submitted the film to DEFA in early spring and waited. For months there was only silence, and he and the cast and crew worried that *Coming Out* might never, well, come out. Heiner learned through his contacts at the studio that the general director was refusing even to view the film and had reputedly said, 'I will not be the first leader of a socialist film studio to make a gay movie.' But the film's existence was already common knowledge among East Berlin's cultural elite. In mid-September Heiner decided to ratchet up the pressure on DEFA by taking a risk and privately screening *Coming Out* at his sixtieth birthday party. 'It was a deliberate tactic to try to make it harder for the authorities to block us,' Dirk says. And it worked: just a few days later, but still without the general director having viewed the film, *Coming Out* was passed for release. Its première was scheduled for 9 November 1989.

I have now watched *Coming Out* many times. A complex, nuanced, often beautiful film, it is undoubtedly an important artefact of the late Cold War and cannot but cause viewers to reassess their conception of the GDR – of what happened there, of what was possible there. It shows authentic gay men living three-dimensional lives in a community that is not obsessed with sex but has wide-ranging interests and concerns. Arriving in 1989 it came only a few years after similar trailblazing films in the West such as *My Beautiful Laundrette* (1985). The fact the East German authorities allowed it to be made and released was progressive. But, as you may already have worked out, the film's content is only half its significance. The other half is a coincidence of history. On the night it premièred, the Berlin Wall fell and the GDR effectively ended. I ask Dirk to tell me the story of that astonishing evening.

'The première happened at the Kino International on Karl-Marx-Allee,' he says. 'Where all East German feature films had their premières.' For the director and lead actors such events invariably began in a large room at the back of the cinema known as the Honecker Lounge. There they would meet and be congratulated by the GDR's top brass, not just DEFA's management but members of the Politburo and typically the leader himself. 'This was the first time the crew for a movie wasn't invited backstage,' Dirk says. He is pretty sure the cold-shouldering was planned – of a piece with the DEFA head's refusal to view the film – but he admits that East Germany's leadership already had a lot on their minds at 6.30 p.m. that night.

The tensions had been mounting all year. There had been the falsified local elections in early summer, which had stoked anger. Then, in August, hundreds of GDR citizens had occupied West German embassies in Czechoslovakia and Hungary demanding asylum. The GDR government had made some limited concessions but still refused to grant genuine freedom of expression, assembly or movement. Viewed on state television, the celebration of the country's fortieth anniversary, on 7 October, looked impressive, but it actually made a bad situation worse. A large number of citizens were sickened at the triumphalist display. We now know Gorbachev used his attendance to warn Honecker that the one-party state urgently needed radical change if it was to survive. He famously told the ageing leader, 'Life punishes those who come too late' – and also signalled that the thousands of Soviet troops in the country would not get involved if social unrest did break out.

Major street demonstrations had begun the very same day, in the southern town of Plauen where a crowd of 10,000 refused to disperse even when confronted with water cannons and police dogs. A day later 20,000 protested in Dresden, and a day after that 70,000 in Leipzig. By 18 October Honecker had resigned. And on the Saturday before the première of *Coming Out* one of the largest demonstrations in East German history took place on Alexanderplatz, demanding wholesale political reform. Dirk attended it and says that by then people knew something would have to happen, but still no one expected the regime to disappear. Many instead worried that East Germany might copy the Chinese Communist Party, which had brutally quashed protests in Tiananmen Square a few months earlier.

The cinema was packed for the Thursday night première. 'Everyone was talking about this film,' Dirk recalls. Many who had seen it at Heiner's birthday came to watch again on the big screen. Among them was the author Christa Wolf.[7] Members of East Berlin's gay community were also present in large numbers, and there were a few gays, journalists and critics who had made the journey from West Berlin too. The demand for tickets was so great that, in a break with tradition, the cinema decided to screen the film twice, at 7.30 p.m. and 9.30 p.m.

A short time after the start of the second screening, Heiner and Dirk slipped out of the auditorium to smoke and talk in the cinema bar. It pleased them to think of the hundreds of people on the other side of the wall who were now experiencing their creation. For Dirk, still just twenty-three, the night had already seen the fulfilment of many dreams. As they stood talking by the enormous plate glass windows that overlook Karl-Marx-Allee, they noticed how on one side of the wide Stalinist boulevard a large number of cars had started to queue up. As in most communist cities, the streets were normally empty by this point on a weeknight. People tended not to hang around in the centre after work. There were few bars and restaurants and, anyway, in recent times they had had little with which to tempt customers in.

'Something has happened,' Dirk said, but neither of them knew whether it was something good or bad. Dirk suddenly remembered how the film's female lead, Dagmar Manzel, had run into the cinema just before the start of the second screening and muttered something about a decision to open the checkpoints from East to West Berlin. In the rush he thought he had misheard her or, as had always been the case in the past, that she was talking about something that might happen in the future, and then only with many restrictive conditions attached. But perhaps these cars were linked to what she had said; they were all heading towards the Wall.

The end of the film saw the audience, cast and crew pile out onto the street. Everyone could now see the huge stationary traffic jam. They ran round trying to discover what was happening from drivers and passersby. What they learned was that an official regime spokesman had stated on live television just before 7 p.m. that East Germans would be allowed to cross into West Germany without restriction and with immediate effect, including at the crossings in the Berlin Wall. They then heard how the crowds had immediately started gathering along the routes leading to the crossing points, but the crossings had remained closed. (We now know this was because the 7 p.m. announcement had been an error: the new policy was only supposed to come into force the following day, though surely there would have been chaos then too.) The atmosphere of anticipation among the crowds steadily turned more militant. Then, at around 11 p.m., just as *Coming Out*'s second screening was finishing, the commander at the nearest crossing to the cinema, at Bornholmer Strasse, ordered the gates to be opened.

As traffic started to crawl forwards Dirk, Heiner and others crammed into Dirk's car and joined the jam. They were not heading to the West but to *Coming Out*'s after-party, which was very close to the Bornholmer Strasse crossing, at the Borgfrieden. Approaching the bar, Dirk's car was hemmed in on all sides. 'It was completely crowded with cars and people and I couldn't get across the lanes of traffic to park. I was so frightened we would just be swept into West Berlin almost by accident.' What worried him most was that if they crossed out of the East they might never be allowed back. Still locked in the norms of the past, Dirk also feared that if it was discovered he had visited, his sister, who had a good job at Interflug, the state airline, would be sacked.

The party was strange beyond all imagining. People were dizzy with the success of the film and also with the momentous events going on all around them. After downing a few drinks a group decided to join the throngs walking up to and through the Bornholmer crossing. One was Charlotte von Mahlsdorf, a transgender woman who had played a barmaid in the film. Some time in the early hours, Dirk recalls Charlotte returning with a West Berlin bottle of beer and a newspaper, like the dove that brought the olive leaf to Noah at the end of the Flood. 'You realized in that moment,' Dirk says, 'that this socialist part of Germany was going to end. You knew it. It was clear. It was over.'

I asked Dirk when he made his own first journey to the West. I expected him to say he had gone at dawn. I already had a sentimental image of him and fellow cast members, their arms linked, striding over the border. But, like many people, Dirk took time to believe in the change. The writer Jenny Erpenbeck, with whom Dirk went to school, has described how for decades East Berliners had 'learned there were paths beneath our feet that were not meant for us . . . airplanes flying over our heads that we would never set foot in . . . an entire world that seemed so close [but] could still be out of reach'.[8] On 9 November the physical barrier was lifted, but the barriers in many minds remained.

Dirk finally ventured across three days later. He went to a West Berlin gay bar and then to his first gay sauna. 'I had never seen something like that,' he says. In East Germany there were no licensed venues for people to have or view sex – no strip bars or erotic cinemas – and there was hardly any printed pornography, straight or gay.[9] Wrapped in a towel, he saw through the steam that most of the other clientele were on similar day trips: 'I met only people from East Germany, all these people I already knew. It was so funny.' Overall, his verdict was that West Berlin was not as different as he had expected. 'It wasn't so exotic. The main difference was you could buy something for your money. In East Germany there was nothing to buy.'

For Dirk the first real sense of being overwhelmed occurred not in West Berlin but West Hollywood. *Coming Out* turned into one of the arthouse cinema sensations of late 1989 and 1990, and the West German Goethe-Institut put up funding for it to tour the USA. Dirk travelled with the film to New York, San Francisco and Los Angeles. The constant round of screenings and lavish functions and parties finally showed him how different the West could be. The Hollywood correspondent of *Stern* magazine, Frances Schoenberger, offered to take the twenty-three-year-old under her wing. 'I went to her house in Beverly Hills and she promised to introduce me to all these LA actors and producers.' It was a stunning time. Exactly a year earlier Dirk had been in uniform defending the East German border – but now, as Hollywood beckoned, he faltered. 'At that moment, I became afraid.' In this new world, he worried about failing but also about how success might change him; he suddenly felt very alone.

On his return to Europe Dirk did not stay in Berlin for long. The city he knew was changing before his eyes, in good ways and bad. The immediate cause of his departure was financial hardship: 'For the first time in my life, I lived in fear of not being able to pay my bills. I continued working as Heiner's assistant but I also had to work nights as a hotel receptionist. It was all frightening – learning to feel free, the safety net gone. This was the same for most people. I actually think it was in those months that people first started feeling what they now call *Ostalgie*.'

Dirk lived away for two decades, in Frankfurt, Vienna, Bern, and finally Baden-Baden. There, he became a successful director of television films. His sense of dislocation never really disappeared, however, until, aged forty-five, he returned to live and work around Berlin and Potsdam. What brought him back? I ask. 'I don't call it *Ostalgie*,' he says with a smile. 'But lots of people like me, people who fled – we're sometimes called the "lost sons and daughters" – have come back. And it does feel like coming home. I loved Baden-Baden and being close to France. But I did not hear my language there, my German. For some years I put it from my mind but then I realized what was missing. Now, I love just standing in the garden and hearing my neighbours talk. I suppose that's what it was for me. I realized how much I missed my language.'

It is understandable that Dirk resists labelling his homesickness *Ostalgie*. The term originally denoted a kind of kitsch longing for objects and rituals associated with the GDR. But in recent years it has become connected to extremist right-wing political movements like Pegida, Alternative für Deutschland (AfD) and the Nationaldemokratische Partei Deutschlands (NPD) and the mindsets of the people who support them. For them the GDR's end was too abrupt and fundamentally illegitimate. Reunification with West Germany, in October 1990, occurred on unfair terms that rejected and derided the GDR's achievements over forty years and shortchanged its population. East Germany's tough approach to law and order and conservative social attitudes are often missed too.

But for Dirk this is not the case, and nor does he see the past as a blueprint for the future. Rather, memory is something he uses to try to understand himself and the people around him. Returning home and falling in love with Ingo (whom he had first met at a screening of *Coming Out* in Leipzig in 1990) have helped him to feel comfortable in his own skin. He has done some of his best work since returning too. His acclaimed 2017 film *Zuckersand* explores the paradoxes of East German life through the unruly and dangerous imaginations of children. 'Across the whole of Europe, across the world,' Dirk says, 'there are lots of people my age who miss their past. That is part of life, not just the GDR. But it shouldn't be how you do politics. What would I like from my own past? I would like to be able to remember how it felt to get up in the morning in East Berlin and walk up the street. In some ways I can remember, but in other ways it is gone forever.'

Dirk drops me back to Potsdam station. In the car he says I must return to Berlin to join him and others at a screening of *Coming Out* at the Kino International on 9 November. This is an annual event that commemorates the original première on the night the Wall fell. But this year's showing will have a special significance because it is the thirtieth anniversary.

Back in Berlin a few months later I find little islands of commemoration all over the place: a massive sound and light show on the side of department stores in Alexanderplatz; detailed information displays about 1989 at every important landmark; clusters of memorial candles outside most East Berlin churches. At the Kino International both exterior and interior remain unchanged since communist times, so the building continues to project a hopeful, modernist vision, the 1960s dream of a now vanished state. The big signboard above the entrance advertises tonight's 8.30 p.m. showing, *Coming Out*. The words '*30 Jahre Mauerfall*' are written underneath.

Dirk had told me to expect a festive atmosphere. Many of the surviving cast and crew have reassembled and are kissing and hugging one another, promising to catch up properly soon. There are also younger people who will see the film for the first time. Some in the audience have brought bottles of champagne. Corks go off regularly during the screening. When one pops at exactly the same moment as a bottle in the film, the whole auditorium cheers. At the end Dirk and his co-stars Matthias Freihof and Dagmar take to the stage for bows and interviews, happy to reminisce about the première, about that epic moment of progress and rupture, when the old was not yet dead but the new was already being born. Everywhere I look, through my own teary eyes, I see others crying.

PART IV

Central Europe

GERMANY
POLAND

• Jáchymov
Selb • Aš
• Cheb
• Mariánské Lázně
• Prague

CZECHIA

GERMANY

SLOVAKIA

Devínska Kobyla
Vienna •
Bratislava
Petržalka
Sankt Margarethen
im Burgenland
Pan-European
Picnic site
Sopron

Budapest •

AUSTRIA

HUNGARY

Lake
Balaton

13

Selb, Germany, and Aš, Czechia

It was time for me to move south again. I had inched my way from Prora to Berlin, but my journey would now pick up pace, covering the 350 kilometres between the German capital and Czechia in just a day. I boarded a morning train at Berlin Hauptbahnhof and let the views direct my thoughts for the next several hours.

In the countryside of Brandenburg and Saxony, whenever the train slowed, I saw political posters affixed to most lampposts. The elections to the European parliament were about to happen and the AfD and NPD were focusing their advertising on these parts of the country: 'Protect your home'; 'Vote out of love of your homeland'; 'For a Christian Europe'; and 'Secure borders', the posters said. In Dresden, Saxony's capital, I remembered how the city and its environs had been known as the Valley of the Clueless (*Tal der Ahnungslosen*) because it was one of only a couple of parts of East Germany that did not receive West German television and radio. In Chemnitz I thought of the ugly race riots of 2018, while in Plauen I recalled the happier protests that had kicked off the unrest that precipitated the GDR's 1989 collapse.

Eventually – invisibly – we crossed out of the old East Germany and into Bavaria. I made it to a cheap hotel in the city of Hof early that evening. After a meal in the hotel's overlit dining room, I went quickly to bed. The next morning, I headed for the Bavarian–Czech border.

*

Czechoslovakia was one of the great innovations of the Treaty of Versailles but the Western Allies, who always felt very proud of their creation, betrayed it in the 1938 Munich Agreement and again in 1945, when they ceded it to Stalin's sphere of influence. The postwar Czechoslovak government was initially a broad church that tried to keep all sides happy. But Moscow had it on a tight leash. When, in June 1947, the leader, Edvard Beneš, signalled his intention to accept American Marshall Aid, Stalin immediately wired him to say, 'It is necessary for you to cancel your participation.'[1] Beneš complied, but just eight months later Moscow yanked Czechoslovakia fully into its orbit by means of a coup. Beneš was lucky enough to die from natural causes, but others who threatened USSR dominance were despatched more forcefully. The famous foreign minister, Jan Masaryk, was almost certainly thrown to his death from a third-floor window by a Soviet intelligence officer.

Gulag-style camps quickly housed tens of thousands of supposed counter-revolutionaries. Some had previously been active politicians but many were incarcerated for the typical Stalinist crimes of family background or guilt by association with friends and acquaintances. The most feared of all camps were located around Jáchymov, close to the borders with East and West Germany. Prisoners there were forced to mine uranium without protection. Miners tended to die quickly – one source says average life expectancy was just forty-two.[2]

It was unsurprising that some citizens rushed for the exits. Increasingly through 1949 and into 1950 security at the borders with Austria and West Germany was tightened so that fugitives were shot on sight and anyone caught assisting them was sentenced to death. These dangers discouraged many, but others were spurred on to feats of ingenuity. I was about to meet a ninety-year-old eyewitness to one of the most impertinent escapes of the entire Cold War.

*

It was blustery and drizzling by the time I turned my car off the road onto a pitted track on the outskirts of the Bavarian town of Selb, the home of the fine German porcelain maker Rosenthal, just 4 kilometres from the Czech border. At some point in the 1970s a local farmer had evidently decided to try his hand at property development, and a single line of bungalows and some sports pitches now sat adjacent to the lane to his farm. I was aiming for the penultimate bungalow. As my car came into view a woman looked up from her kitchen sink and waved at me energetically. This was Hilde Swart. Her husband Rolf appeared at the front door a few seconds later, raising his own arm and simultaneously bowing his head.

Hilde and Rolf Swart – she in her eighties; he, then, just shy of his ninety-first birthday – have led cosmopolitan lives that have taken them far from this part of Germany. Hilde lived in Canada for several years earlier in life and together they holidayed all over the world until creeping infirmity confined them to Selb. When I tell them of my own trip, they look envious. 'We live off our memories now,' Hilde says. But for Rolf it was an incident that occurred just a stone's throw from here, on a September afternoon in 1951, which was by far the most exciting, and the most international, of his life. With Hilde acting as translator, Rolf agreed to take me to the places where it happened.[3]

We drove towards the border and Rolf reminded us of the spirit of that time. Bavaria was just starting to get back on its feet after twelve years of National Socialism and the subsequent military defeat. Under American occupation Rolf actually felt his life was more normal than it ever had been. For young men like him there was no longer the imminent threat of death. At sixteen he had been press-ganged into the Wehrmacht during the Nazis' desperate last stand. In 1951, aged twenty-two, he had a respectable job on the railways, certifying goods wagons that passed through Selb and forwarding information about them to West Germany's tax and customs authorities.

Rolf says that on the afternoon of 11 September 1951 he and his superior Max had left the station at Selb for a while to stretch their legs. They ended up strolling towards the frontier. They knew they had a couple of hours to kill before the next service requiring their attention, and Max often liked to walk this way because it allowed him to look over at the town of Aš, in Czechoslovakia, where he had previously lived and worked.

Max was a Sudeten German, one of a million or so who had had to move out of western Czechoslovakia in the second half of the 1940s. They were compulsory expellees, an entire ancestral population of German speakers collectively punished for their support and encouragement of Hitler's 1938 annexation. Exile was traumatic and sometimes violent: those who had once been the Third Reich's biggest winners were now dispossessed. But after the Czechoslovak coup in 1948 a growing number began to realize that expulsion might actually have been a blessing in disguise.

Max certainly did not want to go back to Czechoslovakia under current conditions, even if he still pined for his old home and old job running Aš station. Together he and Rolf climbed a hill from where they could easily see the Iron Curtain just 300 metres away, and beyond it the roofs of Aš. Hilde and Rolf tell me to stop the car at the exact same point. 'We were right here when it happened,' Rolf says.

The border is almost invisible now, but in 1951 barbed wire cut right through this landscape. Rolf sweeps his arm from left to right. The only exception was a tightly guarded opening where a single set of railway tracks crossed from Czechoslovakia into West Germany. This was the link between Aš and Selb. It had been a bustling passenger line until the end of the war (when it had all been in Greater Germany) but services had then dwindled, ceasing altogether in 1948. Only freight still passed this way on a number of specially permitted trains, freight that Rolf and Max often verified as it came through Selb.

The pair stood looking over the border and noticed a passenger train moving some distance away in the Czechoslovak countryside. There was nothing remarkable about this: Max knew it was the regular afternoon express service from Cheb to Aš, a train popular with housewives returning from shopping trips, children coming back from school, and usually a few people who had been for cures at the nearby spas of Mariánské Lázně (the famous Marienbad) and Františkovy Lázně.

They watched the train disappear into the trees on the outskirts of Aš, which was its final scheduled stop. They were still looking down into the valley a minute or so later – at exactly 15:04 – when it unexpectedly hoved back into view. Put simply, it should not have been where it now was – on the tracks on the other side of Aš, on the line reserved for freight, and heading into West Germany. With incredulity the two colleagues saw how the train was actually gathering speed. It dashed through the gap in the barbed wire fence into the West, and a few seconds later there was an almighty screech as the driver slammed on the brakes and brought it to a halt.

Rolf and Max sprinted down the hill. Rolf remembers wondering, as he stumbled over the ground, if this might be an international service deliberately redirected away from the mainline, which had the official border crossing for railway passengers. But he quickly discounted the idea. This train only had three carriages, far too small for an international service, and anyway he and Max would have been notified of any diversion in advance. Could it be an accident? 'It really was as if they had fallen from the clouds,' he tells Hilde and me, reliving the moment.

Rolf directs me to drive to the bottom of the hill where tracks still elegantly curve between one country and the other. We get to a certain point and again he tells me to stop. I am amazed to see that the back of the final carriage really did only clear the frontier by a hundred metres at most.

In 1951 Rolf saw, as he approached the train, that some of the people on board looked clueless about what had just happened to them. Some apparently did not even know they had just crashed out of Czechoslovakia. Others were beginning to panic as the reality dawned on them. As Rolf watched, a group of three men in suits leaped out of one wagon and ran full pelt back up the line and into Czechoslovakia.

Some on board were clearly showing signs of jubilation. Among them was the driver. Max could hardly believe it when he saw that this was František Konvalinka, an old acquaintance from his days in Aš. The two hugged by the side of the tracks. After a few minutes, Konvalinka deputed another man to walk along the line to a nearby emergency telephone box. From there he called Selb station and asked for local border guards to attend. These would be Americans. As everyone waited, Rolf and Max tried to learn more about what had just gone on.

There were four key conspirators, it turned out: the driver Konvalinka, a former train dispatcher called Karl Truksa (also known to Max), a dentist called Jaroslav Švec, and Karel Ruml, an underground opposition figure who until recently had been

Rolf stands at the exact spot where the runaway train from Cheb came to a halt, just a few hundred metres inside West Germany.

a law student in Prague. They had planned the escape meticulously. The vulnerability they exploited was the fact that the track outside Aš was often left connected to the West German line even when no special freight services were scheduled. At lunchtime that day the dentist Švec had gone in person to check that the line remained connected to West Germany, and this was the signal for the others to put the plan into action.

The train departed Cheb as normal at 14:12, already with several of the plotters aboard – not just the four men but also their wives and children and a couple of other dissidents and members of the underground. A few more escapees joined at subsequent stops. At Hazlov station Konvalinka held the train for an extra four minutes to allow himself and Truksa to walk the length of it disabling each carriage's emergency brake.

As they approached Aš the engine at first slowed down, as if preparing to stop at the station. But then suddenly Konvalinka pulled a gun on his stoker, who was the only other person in the cab, telling him to lie face down on the floor. He then sped back up to 70 kilometres per hour. From that point on the whole episode was over quickly – it took just two minutes to pass from the outskirts of Aš to the final stopping point inside West Germany.

In the passenger carriages the main conspirators were also armed. Karel Ruml later remembered seeing 'machine-gun towers, minefields with barbed wire around them [and] all the beautiful sights of a police state' flashing past. Then he had his very final interaction with Czechoslovak officialdom when one of the three men in suits attempted to overpower him. Ruml showed his gun and the man quickly relented. 'The guy turned cowardly like all the defenders of totalitarianism,' Ruml later told a Czech oral history project. '[He] just stood there giving me a horrible look of hate. I could smell beer, onion and sausages on his breath, and that's how I crossed the border.'[4] It would subsequently emerge that all three suited men were actually members of Czechoslovak state security. It was their job to ride these near-frontier services and prevent escapes. From their perspective, 11 September 1951 had not been a good day.

The attending Americans quickly gave orders for the train to be driven into Selb. By this point it was clear that most passengers had not been trying to flee to the West. There were 113 people on board and only twenty of them knew about the plan. Mostly, people just wanted to get back to their families, dinners and homework. Nevertheless, the Americans offered everyone the chance to claim asylum. The twenty conspirators said yes without hesitation, as did seven others who took a spur of the moment decision. But eighty-three people went back home later that evening.

By the next morning the 'Freedom Train' was headline news around the world. At a particularly tense moment in the Cold War the fugitives were celebrated in many Western nations, especially the USA. They were on the front page of the *New York Times* and dozens of other American papers. Konvalinka was quoted saying, 'We did it because it is no longer bearable to live in an East European state.'[5] It was the perfect message when communism still seemed to be on the rise in many places and Americans were dying to combat it in the Korean War. The choice that the eighty-three made to return to Czechoslovakia and the fact they had been the unsuspecting victims of an armed hijacking were scarcely mentioned.

By the end of 1951 a majority of the refugees had moved to America or Canada. Arriving at New York's main airport in late November Konvalinka and Truksa were greeted by the owner of the Lionel Corporation, the largest toy manufacturer in the world. If this seems odd, it may help to know that the Lionel Corporation specialized in model trains. In the best tradition of American consumerism, Lawrence Cowen had spotted what he thought was the photo opportunity to end all photo opportunities. He also arranged for Konvalinka and Truksa to commence their new lives with a six-city welcome tour. (When I learned this I thought of how the pair must at times have felt overwhelmed like Dirk Kummer did on his American tour forty years later.)

The Czechoslovak heroes were celebrated elsewhere in less flamboyant ways. The BBC broadcast a radio play about them in January 1953. *Suspense: 9.15 to Freedom* (the time referred to an earlier connecting service on which some conspirators travelled from Prague) featured Trevor Howard, the star of the railway film *Brief Encounter*, as the narrator. The *Radio Times* said it was 'the dramatic story of the people who plotted this fantastic mass escape and of the thrilling journey that brought them through the Iron Curtain to freedom'.[6]

Meanwhile, back in Aš and the surrounding towns and villages, the returning passengers were able to resume their daily lives after only cursory investigation. Czechoslovak state security concentrated instead on hunting down all the hijackers' alleged accomplices. One man was sentenced to death in the resulting trials and nine more received a total of 162 years in jail, an average of eighteen years each.

I assumed that following the escape the old train line between Aš and Selb must have been sealed completely. But, as we walk along the platform of today's Aš station, Rolf tells me that the Czechoslovak authorities built a new set of tracks for passenger trains from Cheb, tracks that were entirely separate from the ones leading into West Germany. Freight trains then continued to come across to Selb as before – just like the East Germans, the Czechoslovaks needed their hard currency. Right through to the end of communism the Aš–Selb line remained freight-only. Even after Czechoslovakia's Velvet Revolution in 1989 the passenger link did not return. But Rolf and a small group of committed campaigners, both Germans and Czechs, argued ceaselessly for investment to allow cross-border passenger services to resume. Finally, in 2015, almost seven decades after the last – illegal – passenger train had raced through, the Aš–Selb line reopened to the public.

We stand on Aš platform as one of these trains sets off on its little international odyssey, charting exactly the same path Konvalinka and Truksa took. Rolf points the train out to me but says nothing further. But Hilde, full of pride, says, 'Rolf was so hardworking in getting this service open again, you know? Deutsche Bahn is closing stations all over Germany and even selling off the buildings in lots of little towns and villages, but not in Selb. Selb and Aš now have great friendship and the train is a big part of that. And of course nobody wants to look at our passports any more. That makes us very happy.'

I drive them home. I tell Rolf and Hilde that I next plan to travel by train to Bratislava, and have deliberately decided to begin my journey on the Selb to Aš line. They are delighted, and Rolf wants to know the exact time of my connections, at Selb, at Františkovy Lázně, at Mariánské Lázně, and finally at Prague. Hilde advises me to use my two hours in Mariánské Lázně to explore the town – 'Lots of Russians visit,' she says – and Rolf commands me to buy plenty of alcohol before I board the night sleeper in Prague. I sense they would both still love to be heading off on a journey like this. The travel bug has not left them.

14

Bratislava, Slovakia

My own past travels were calling to me as I neared Prague. In September 1996 I went inter-railing around Eastern Europe with two friends. Like thousands of other Western European youths at the time, we were seeking an encounter with something exotic, something that had been truly inaccessible until a few years earlier. The three of us had just finished history A-level, in which a key element of the syllabus had been Stalin's postwar takeover of this part of the continent.

The trip helped to shape our views of ourselves and the world. Travelling on a shoestring, we spent a month sitting beside a series of great landmarks and talking about the burning issues in our lives. Back then I was wrestling with how to come out as gay and had brought a copy of E. M. Forster's *Maurice* along for the ride. I used to sit reading it to my friends and explaining why Forster's descriptions of the closeted queer life felt so accurate and poignant.

Even if we lacked knowledge to put it in these terms, this was our Grand Tour. Just like the Grand Tourists of old, however, the encounter we had with the cultures we were moving through was pretty slight. Over four weeks, we took in Czechia, Slovakia, Hungary, Poland and Austria. We confirmed a lot of things we had learned back in the history classroom and saw much that was beautiful and new. But in a way it was all 'Eastern Europe' to us, and most of the people we spoke to or made eyes at or got drunk with were foreigners like us. We met very few local people and spent too little time noticing the differences between the places we were visiting. Vienna was the outlier, a ridiculously wealthy Western city where we never seemed to be done visiting cash machines and revising ever downwards our budget for the rest of the holiday (I have a memory of reaching the impossible figure of $8 a day at one point, including accommodation). Everywhere else was the old Eastern Bloc: a single space, we thought, with a single set of historical and cultural experiences.

Looking back on my younger self I can now see that the trip was more about self-discovery than gaining a deep understanding of a different part of the world. On this new journey, I was actively trying to listen to, and learn from, those who really understood their own countries. But I was aware that I was still only passing through and always destined to see things from the outsider's perspective, applying my own lens, spending too much time dwelling on how places and stories made me feel. It is, I suppose, an inescapable fact of travel.

Communist Czechoslovakia came closer than any Soviet satellite to finding a form of top-down socialism that worked with people rather than against them. After the 1948 coup and the Freedom Train incident, the state's defining act of Stalinist excess came in December 1952, when the second most powerful man in the country, Rudolf Slánský, was subjected to a show trial and hanged with a dozen co-conspirators. After 1953 there was a gradual softening of tone and policy, much as under Khrushchev in Moscow. At that point the Soviets still thought of Czechoslovakia as their loyalest fraternal state, mostly inhabited by people who were sincerely grateful for their liberation from the Nazis and who had fewer historical hang-ups about Russian domination than others (having never previously been part of the Russian Empire).

In the mid-1960s, however, the two regimes started to diverge radically. The Soviet 'thaw' ran out of steam at just the same time that Czechoslovakia moved towards greater liberalization.

Many experts believe that the first seeds of the Prague Spring were sown as early as 1963, at a scholarly conference on Franz Kafka, but the specific events that led to the transformation of Czechoslovakia's leadership commenced in the summer of 1967. That was when a group within the Central Committee of the Czechoslovak Politburo mobilized against their leader, Antonín Novotný, because of concerns about the weakness of the Czechoslovak economy. Novotný responded by urgently wiring the Kremlin and asking Leonid Brezhnev to visit (like a beleaguered teacher who frantically summons the headmaster to help him regain control of a class). It was a decent enough stratagem in the odd logic of the communist world and Brezhnev duly appeared, but the tactic backfired because the Soviet leader left convinced that Novotný was indeed part of the problem.

No one in Moscow objected on 5 January 1968 when Alexander Dubček succeeded Novotný as leader. In fact, they were initially pleased. Dubček, at forty-six, would be a fresh pair of eyes and might inject new dynamism into the economy and wider Czechoslovak society, but with a Soviet education and seventeen years of living in the USSR behind him he was not expected to give trouble. 'Our Sasha' was apparently how the KGB referred to him at that time (the Russian, 'nash Sasha', sounds even more patronizing than the English).[1]

Dubček quickly turned out to be deeply problematic for Moscow. Instead of instigating only technocratic initiatives, efficiency drives and industrial restructurings, he homed in on the true source of Czechoslovak communism's weakness: its lack of legitimacy due to the needless restrictions it imposed on people. Deploying the slogan 'Socialism with a Human Face' he launched a wide-ranging reform programme that sought to reduce state repression, increase the space for freedom of expression, and build forms of social life beyond the confines of the one-party system.

It is impossible not to admire Dubček. He must have known

from day one that he was playing with fire. And yet he pressed ahead because he believed it was the right thing to do. His opposite numbers elsewhere in the Eastern Bloc worked tirelessly to hide the same flaws he exposed. Dubček's famous slogan was an insult to the Kremlin top brass at whose pleasure he served. It implied that socialism with a human face was something that still had to be created in 1968. During a visit to the USSR in May 1968 he was apparently asked repeatedly by Brezhnev, 'What's with this human face? What kind of faces do you think we have in Moscow?'[2]

Inside Czechoslovakia people felt as if the windows had just been thrown wide open. They began to meet up and discuss all manner of subjects that had previously been banned. Journalists wrote the news they wanted, not what apparatchiks demanded. With surprising speed, fear dissipated. For me, one of the neatest encapsulations of the change comes from a July 1968 edition

Alexander Dubček shows his freedom of spirit on a visit to a swimming pool in Czechoslovakia in July 1968.

of the youth magazine *Mladý Svět*, which gave over its front page to a most un-communist photoshoot of Dubček. He is shown wearing swimming trunks and making elegant dives into an outdoor swimming pool in the Czech countryside, not something any previous socialist leader had been seen doing. Superficial though it was, it spoke volumes about the tone he was striking: greater informality, greater accessibility, the spirit of freedom. 'A day off, plucked out from the meetings, speeches, public appearances, discussions and official visits, is a kind of miracle,' the article says. 'In his own slightly beat-up car, he and his wife Anna went out to a small swimming pool . . . hoping for a few hours of privacy. This, however, lasted only a few minutes. As soon as he was spotted by the autograph hunters, he was literally blockaded by children and adults.'[3] For his willingness to take Czechoslovakia in a new direction, Dubček had instantly become a star.

As my train moved through the Czech countryside, I had on the table in front of me *The Unbearable Lightness of Being*, Milan Kundera's famous novel about 1968. Between spells looking out of the window I dipped into it, reminding myself how its characters, like the author himself, thrived in that period and then tried to keep warm in its afterglow.

For Kundera the Prague Spring was a kind of carnival, a short-lived moment when the normal rules were suspended. The fun concluded dramatically when the armies of the Warsaw Pact invaded Czechoslovakia on 21 August. Moscow had finally woken up to the impossibility of allowing Prague to go its own way. Seven months, two weeks, and two days was long for a spring but the winter that followed was much longer. Around 140 Czechoslovaks were killed as the USSR reimposed what it considered order. Officially, the Soviet army and the armies of the three other invading nations (Bulgaria, Hungary and Poland) were responding to a request for assistance from Czechoslovak hardliners, but really the invasion would have happened anyway.

Dubček and a number of other likeminded politicians were spirited away, first to Poland and then to Moscow. Brezhnev himself asked the First Secretary to recant. There is little doubt he would have had him shot but for the fact that doing so could have caused more trouble. Dubček reluctantly agreed to return to Czechoslovakia and oversee a reversion to the communist norm in order to spare more of his countrymen's lives. Many Czechoslovaks saw this as betrayal. But they also felt betrayed, just as in the 1930s and 1940s, by the fact that Europe's other democracies all stood idly by as their democracy was once again crushed. 'No carnival can go on for ever,' Kundera wrote in *The Unbearable Lightness of Being*. 'The compromise saved the country from the worst: the executions and mass deportations to Siberia that had terrified everyone. But one thing was clear: the country would have to bow to the conqueror . . . Workaday humiliation had begun.'[4]

My hours in Mariánské Lázně, waiting for the connecting train to Prague, were dominated by thoughts of 1968. In Kundera's novel the main protagonists visit an unnamed spa a couple of years after communist order has been restored. It may be Mariánské Lázně or Karlovy Vary or an amalgam of the two. At first the place seems unchanged, but then the characters become aware of an insidious transformation: 'What had once been the Grand now bore the name Baikal. He looked at the street sign on the corner of the building: Moscow Square. Then they took a walk . . . through all the streets they had known, and examined all their names: Stalingrad Street, Leningrad Street, Rostov Street, Novosibirsk Street, Kiev Street, Odessa Street. There was a Tchaikovsky Sanatorium, a Rimsky-Korsakov Sanatorium; there was a Hotel Suvorov, a Gorky Cinema, and a Café Pushkin . . . Tereza suddenly recalled the first days of the invasion. People in every city and town had pulled down the street signs; sign posts had disappeared. Overnight, the country had become nameless. For seven days, Russian troops wandered the countryside not knowing where they were . . . Hindsight now made that anonymity seem quite dangerous to the country. The streets and buildings could no longer return to their original names. As a result, a Czech spa had suddenly metamorphosed into a miniature imaginary Russia.'[5]

Kundera was exaggerating for effect but his broad point was true. Czechs passively resisted the invading armies in any way they could. When the takeover was complete, however, the Soviets ensconced themselves far more thoroughly than before. The anomaly of Czechoslovakia being the only satellite state without a Soviet army presence was rectified. In the 1970s and 1980s Soviet forces were permanently billeted at thirty-three bases across the country.[6]

I thought of what Hilde had said about Russians being everywhere in Mariánské Lázně today. To judge by the voices I heard and the hierarchy of languages in shop signs and on restaurant menus, she was right. They seemed to be the resort's main foreign visitors, but coming now in executive taxis and hire cars from Munich and Prague airports rather than in tanks. I knew their presence still rankled for some. Once a country has invaded you in order to change your government, it is very hard to forget about it.

Sleeper trains were a staple of life in the Eastern Bloc until much later than in Western Europe. This was partly because of the greater distances travellers often had to cover, especially in the USSR, and partly because commercial air travel was poorly developed and high-speed railways like the TGV never appeared. The cramped multi-day isolation Eastern Europeans periodically experienced inside sleeping compartments or, worse still, sat bolt upright in ordinary carriages could be seen as a metaphor for their more general sequestration behind the Iron Curtain. But sleepers were also hives of enforced sociability.

As I waited for the platform to be announced at Praha Hlavní I remembered other sleepers I had taken. With the exception of one from Paddington to Penzance, they had all been in Eastern Europe: from Budapest to Warsaw, between Moscow and the Caucasus, and frequently between Moscow and St Petersburg. They had been characterized by unsolicited intimacy: the smell of other people's food, shared vodka when I didn't want to drink, and unexpected confessional conversations. On one service I befriended a group of Portuguese travellers and we stuck together for two weeks after the journey before staying in touch for years. One summer in Russia I had policemen among my compartment companions on four successive sleeper trains, and began to wonder if I was under surveillance. Once, on a two-night service from Vladikavkaz to Moscow, I met a mother and daughter. The mother, in her late eighties, was moving from the Caucasus to live with her daughter in Blagoveshchensk in Russia's Far East. The daughter had travelled a dozen nights to collect her and now, together, they had a dozen more nights of train life ahead. The mother had never left the Caucasus before and this would probably be the only long journey of her life. All her worldly possessions were stowed in canvas bags under our bunks.

The sleepers that now run between Prague and Bratislava are modern trains with onboard showers and lots of other clever fittings. My companions in a three-berth compartment were two young men: one a student heading home for the weekend, and the other a professional with a day of meetings ahead in the Slovakian capital. The student was new to sleeper trains and, being tall, found it difficult to bring his elbows and knees under control. The professional, who instantly set out his toiletries and hung up his suit ready for the morning, told us that he made the journey regularly: it was much more convenient, he said, than bothering with airports.

We chatted on for a bit. I told them about the last time I had taken a night train from Prague, back on that 1996 inter-railing holiday. Trusting to guidebooks, my friends and I had assumed we would find accommodation easily on arrival. The write-ups said that poor residents would be waiting at the airport to offer us their spare rooms at low cost (a kind of analogue version of Airbnb). But on the night we arrived there was no one to be seen. A local English-speaker saw us downcast at the airport's exit and explained that we were unlikely to find a bed that weekend because Prague was holding Michael Jackson's first-ever concert in Eastern Europe. We decamped immediately to Bratislava (only circling back to Prague at the end of the trip). The student lying two bunks above me now said, 'Wow.' I think he was most amazed by the fact that there was no internet to warn us of the Michael Jackson event in advance. He added that he thought his mum might have been at the concert. I felt very old.

I woke once during the night as the train came to a halt in a siding for a few hours. Stops like these are normal on sleeper services between places that are close together; otherwise passengers would reach their destinations at 2 a.m. The rhythmic noises of the engine and the rattling tracks suddenly ceased, replaced by intermittent creaks. For a second or two my sleepy imagination saw us suspended over a cliff but I then fell back into my deep sleep. At just after five the train manager woke us and handed out boxes of breakfast rolls, jam, cheese and orange juice. He followed up with coffee and tea. Only the most organized of us – the professional, of course – managed to squeeze in (and squeeze into) the shower before Bratislava. At 5.50 a.m. we were all emptied onto a cold dawn platform. I had three hours to kill before my professional guide arrived.

Bratislava was in Prague's shadow for as long as Czechoslovakia existed. Demand for Slovak self-rule was an important aspect of the Prague Spring and led to the city being granted the status of second capital. But charges of 'Prague centrism' persisted right up until the country split in the early 1990s. Czechs and Slovaks, who could never have been described as enemies, have become even better friends since the division, and Bratislava has shed some of its old inhibitions and emerged a bit from its shell. I had come to the city because, with the exception of Berlin, it was the closest major urban settlement to the Iron Curtain. The Austrian border runs less than 3 kilometres from the centre.

My guide arrived at the station in a small Peugeot just before 9 a.m. and I piled in with my bags. Peter had offered to bring one of his company's communist-era Škodas but added that (as was infamously said to be the case) it might struggle with some of the hilly terrain we were due to cover. All smiles, he started by handing me a bottle of Kofola, a Czechoslovak fizzy drink that was created in 1960 and continues to be more popular than Coca-Cola or Pepsi in these parts.

Peter told me his own family's story. Some of it sounded very familiar after my weeks on this Iron Curtain road. In the early 1950s one of his grandfathers had been exiled from Bratislava because of political unreliability. He was forced to move with his family to a provincial backwater and work in a quarry for several years. Life then became a bit easier but the false dawn of 1968 was keenly felt. The regime's eventual collapse was not mourned. Peter was still a boy when he stood with his father on Bratislava's SNP (Slovak National Uprising) Square in the Velvet Revolution in 1989. He asked what was happening. His father said, 'It's hard to explain but one day you will understand that this was a big moment in your life.'

Peter was driving us to Petržalka. A maze of concrete flats, it had been just a village as recently as the 1970s but then grew rapidly into Bratislava's largest borough and the densest residential district anywhere in Central Europe. In many respects the place could not have been more ordinary. Governments everywhere undertook mass housing projects in the 1960s and

1970s in their quest to keep pace with rapidly growing urban populations and give people modern accommodation. But Petržalka was different. It lies right on the Austrian border and consequently might well have been considered out of bounds for an Eastern Bloc government. (Think of all those emptied villages on the GDR side of the Inner German Border and the demolished flats in Bernauer Strasse in Berlin.)

The decision to pack Petržalka with people was, Peter says, part of a wider modernizing crusade that was unleashed after 1968. This led to the destruction of much of Bratislava's medieval centre, the creation of a brutalist inner-city motorway, and the erection of the SNP Bridge, colloquially known as the UFO Bridge because of its famous revolving restaurant. Perhaps it was the fact that Petržalka had once been Slovakia's own miniature Sudetenland that tipped the balance in favour of the development. Here was a piece of territory that the Nazis had not just occupied but had fully incorporated into their Greater Germany. Settling tens of thousands of Czechoslovaks there may have been an attempt to prevent the land ever being taken from the country again.

Peter suggests we stop for morning coffee. He has brought me to Meteor, an original Petržalka bar that is spaciously arranged over the ground floor of a huge apartment block – the kind of expanse that might more typically be given over to a furniture showroom. A sprinkling of elderly locals are already in position, most on their first beers of the day despite the early hour. Rolling news unfolds silently on two mounted televisions as from his rucksack Peter produces a book of photographs of Petržalka. It clearly shows how the barbed wire and watchtowers were sited just metres from the accommodation blocks. Literally thousands of living rooms looked out over the Iron Curtain and the West, all created as a matter of policy in communism's final years. It was strange to me. And despite the regime choosing to send its citizens there, Peter explains that trust was predictably in short

Petržalka's development in the 1970s and 1980s took Bratislava's city limits right up to the Iron Curtain. Shown here is the famous 'UFO Bridge' that connected the new district with the city centre.

supply in Petržalka. As in other places I had visited, it was hard to bring visitors into the borough during the communist era. The Iron Curtain was so near that for a time even close relatives needed special permission.

At the border itself the Czechoslovaks did not go in for four-metre-high fences and automatic firing devices, but they still had much heavier frontier infrastructure than Western nations, and they were prepared to mete out summary justice at a moment's notice. A local innovation was the half-wolf half-German Shepherd hunting dog known as the Czechoslovakian Wolfdog (*Československý vlčiak*). This was the product of deliberate experimentation at military kennels in the 1950s; a dog bred with the express purpose of finding escapees and hunting them down. Peter says, 'It is definitely not the kind of dog you should pet unless you're its owner.'

Wolfdogs mostly only injured their prey, but there is a recorded case of one killing someone at the border, and it happened here in Petržalka in 1986. The victim was eighteen-year-old Hartmut Tautz, an East German born in Plauen.[7] With his compulsory military service looming, the same kind of depression hit Hartmut as did Dirk Kummer, and he resolved to escape. He chose Petržalka as the spot to make the attempt and travelled in secret to Bratislava, telling his mother that he was on an organized tour of Leningrad instead.

The few published photos of Tautz when he was alive show him looking thin and vulnerable. He spent a week in Bratislava, staying in a student dormitory. On the day of his bid he crossed into Petržalka shortly after dark. As television screens flickered above him in those thousands of identical flats, he then walked to the edge of the suburb and kept going onto a small expanse of waste ground that led to the first border fence. He cut his way through it and hurried on. Unknown to him he had triggered an alarm in the guard station and two soldiers set off with their guns and Wolfdogs. But Tautz was quick, clearing two further obstacles in the time it took the authorities to give chase. And the soldiers were still far away from him when he approached the frontier itself. The dogs were quicker, however. They pinned him down just 22 metres short of Austria and tore him to shreds.

Images of Tautz's corpse show terrible injuries to both his face and body, including chunks missing from his scalp. He was still alive when the border guards arrived on the scene and they must have noticed his desperate condition, yet they willingly admitted in the subsequent investigation that their first act had been to demand that he tell them the names of his accomplices. His only reply had been a weak, 'Help.' It was almost midnight before he was finally delivered to the nearest hospital, where he was pronounced dead shortly afterwards.

A group of activists succeeded in 2016 in getting a memorial to Tautz erected on the site of the dogs' attack. These same activists have also established the names of all those involved on the Czechoslovak government side. They hope that someone will eventually be brought to justice for the crime of murdering Hartmut. But Peter thinks it unlikely. So few people have faced justice for any of the dictatorship's wrongdoing, he says. There continues to be a culture of impunity with regard to that era.

*

We stay in the suburbs. Peter parks up briefly so we can walk across Freedom Bridge, a pedestrian and cycling bridge that now connects the city – without any checks – to Austria. On the Slovakian side a short stretch of Iron Curtain fence has been re-erected to show the contrast with former times.

Freedom Bridge is beside Devínska Kobyla, the hill Peter had worried about a vintage Škoda struggling with. We climb in the car for several minutes and then continue on foot, hiking past 'No Entry' and 'Danger' signs in a landscape of dense forest. Peter has been secretive about why we are here, so it is a moment of theatre when we round a corner and are confronted by a large modernist building, partly on stilts and partly recessed into the hillside, resplendent in a glittering costume of smashed glass and graffiti.

The Soviets were not the only ones to increase their military presence in Czechoslovakia after the Prague Spring. The Warsaw Pact's junior partners, like NATO's, were expected to spend big on their own defences rather than only relying on the USSR and USA. The Czechoslovak authorities built Devínska Kobyla between 1979 and 1983. From afar the hill looks like any other. Close up, however, along with the now-dilapidated headquarters building, it resolves itself into a maze of bunkers and silos that were maintained at high readiness by a rotating staff of 150 soldiers. Even if little is known about the precise rationale for this vast missile complex on Austria's doorstep, the planners' minds were clearly fixed on the potential for World War Three to break out.

Peter says ordinary Bratislavans knew nothing about the base during the Cold War. He adds that it was actually quite easy to keep its existence secret. Although the hill had long been a popular hiking spot until the military closed it in the mid-1970s, the authorities were forever putting places out of bounds, so that did not particularly raise suspicions. From the 1990s on, there has been speculation that Devínska Kobyla was actually a covert nuclear site, secretly controlled from Moscow. But Peter finds this implausible. Perhaps it could have been quickly reconfigured to hold nuclear weapons, he says, but its principal role seems to have been anti-aircraft and anti-missile defence – the missiles here were probably intended to shoot down other missiles before they penetrated deeper into socialist territory.

We walk through the deserted headquarters, glass crunching under our feet. It is a strangely beautiful building given its purpose and the fact that so few people were ever meant to see it. The unknown architect seems to have had fun responding to the strictures of the site. A cascade of freestanding staircases (now shorn of handrails) flows from top to bottom along a back section deep in the hill. What was once a canteen or officers' mess has a screen of windows that would give people inside a glorious forest view without allowing them to be seen by anyone beyond the base.

Right on the hill's summit we encounter a metal structure

Hidden from view, the Czechoslovak government built a vast missile complex right on the Austrian border at Devínska Kobyla late in the Cold War.

that looks a bit like a submarine conning tower. Peter helps me to climb it. Once on top we balance on narrow strips of rusty iron where the floor has fallen away. Austria is before us, as is a huge expanse of sky through which enemy aircraft and missiles might have flown. Peter points out another tower, a couple of kilometres over the border. 'They say that was the CIA's.'

The silos lie beneath us and we descend into them through a network of tunnels and woodland corridors that Peter navigates expertly. Each silo is enormous. Hollowed out of the hillside, they have hemispherical openings to the outside world but are otherwise shrouded in darkness. One's imagination readily puts back what is missing. Sixteen missiles were stored here, four of them held at high readiness at all times. An atmosphere of paranoia seems to linger. The concept of Mutually Assured Destruction hangs in the air.

We see the usual signs of military abandonment: upended shelves and tables, mouldy instruction manuals, telephones left dangling forever off the hook. Peter shows me how most pieces of equipment still have a metal tag that gives the exact date of their manufacture: December 1979; November 1982; June 1983. These dates call to mind some bad times in the superpower standoff. Relations deteriorated quickly in the space of just a few years because of the Soviet invasion of Afghanistan and Ronald Reagan's bellicose rhetoric. Then, in early September 1983, the USSR mistook a South Korean passenger aircraft for a spy plane and shot it out of the sky, killing 269 people.

A few weeks later, on 26 September, a Soviet satellite appeared to detect that the USA had launched a nuclear attack. The signal was transmitted to a computer in an airforce bunker near Moscow and, by rights, should have led to instant retaliation – if this really was an atomic assault, the Soviets only had minutes to respond. In an amazing stroke of good fortune for the planet, the duty lieutenant-colonel at the Soviet bunker that night, a man called Stanislav Petrov, concluded that he was seeing a system malfunction and overrode the signal. He had to make the same assessment for a second time just minutes later when the system showed four more nuclear missiles heading for the USSR. How the adrenalin must have throbbed in his veins at that moment. Had Petrov acted in line with his orders none of us might be here today.[8]

My evenings in Bratislava were spent at pavement cafés, drinking excellent Slovak wine and watching the city's fashionable people share space with the inebriated hen- and stag-party revellers who now regularly visit from Germany, Sweden and, pre-eminently, the UK. Bratislava felt worldly in a way it did not on my first visit in 1996. A significant segment of the population now has enough money to engage in conspicuous consumption and they no longer have to flee the city to do so.

But Bratislavans have also had to confront some of the negative features of post-communist democracy in recent years. Corruption and organized crime, often linked to the country's elected representatives, have become increasingly brazen. The populist prime minister Robert Fico was kept in power for many years by the votes of rural Slovaks, despite plentiful evidence that he was principally motivated by feathering his own nest. (Peter disparagingly pointed out his huge hilltop mansion to me at the end of our tour and told me that some called him 'Slovakia's little big man'.)

Fico finally resigned after a young journalist was murdered. Twenty-seven-year-old Ján Kuciak had been investigating connections between Fico's ruling party and various mafias. In February 2018 he and his fiancée were gunned down in their home in a contract killing that shocked the country. For many students and young professionals in Bratislava it was a clarifying moment and, in the months that followed, they took to the streets in numbers not seen since 1989.

The avoidance of showdown moments tends to be a priority

for today's strongmen leaders. If something like a murder happens, the domestic temperature can suddenly rise and there is a risk that previously unsuspecting citizens may wake up to the harsh realities of their society. Chaos can ensue and leaders can be forced to contemplate still greater violence to avoid removal. The problem for those who ordered Kuciak's murder, as in numerous other cases, was that he had become too dangerous to be allowed to live. Killing him seemed a gamble they had to take. The same was true of Anna Politkovskaya and, perhaps, of Boris Nemtsov in Russia. Their murders were risky too, even if it now seems like a foregone conclusion that Putin's rule would continue unchecked. In Slovakia the story developed differently. Just a few days before I arrived Slovakians had voted for their first female president, Zuzana Čaputová, who had stood on an anti-corruption platform promising to clean government up.

Kuciak had been dead for just over a year but I could see that his memory and image were still casting a long shadow over the city. A representation of his face with an iconic, somewhat Che

Guevara look had been stencilled onto many walls and on the backs of many road signs. Several women had pendants bearing the slogan '#AllForJan' on their handbags.

The Kuciak graffiti often has the words 'Ján Hus; Ján Palach; Ján Kuciak' painted underneath, explicitly ranking him with famous namesake martyrs from the Bohemian and Czechoslovak past. Aged just twenty Palach burned himself alive in Prague's Wenceslas Square in January

The face of murdered journalist Ján Kuciak was a common sight during my time in Bratislava. Gunned down in 2018, he is explicitly likened to namesake martyrs of the past, Ján Hus and Ján Palach.

1969 in protest at the Soviet invasion. A public letter, which was circulated just before his death, claimed that he belonged to a clandestine organization of others who were preparing to die in the same way. Historians now think this was untrue, even if two other individuals – Jan Zajíc and Evžen Plocek – were inspired to their own acts of public self-immolation in the months that followed.

Societies tend to have a limited supply of people who are willing to undertake acts of extreme bravery, and the world's authoritarian and corrupt regimes know it. If they can make enough arrests, fire enough rubber bullets, and let off enough tear gas, they always hope the populace will be cowed into submission and go back to their everyday existences.

One of the poignant long-term effects of the Prague Spring was a sustained period of national soul-searching in Czechoslovakia about the right way to live under the continuing dictatorship. Should people continue to resist in any safe way they could? Should they sacrifice themselves? Or should they just accept the regime and try to get on with their lives?

Post-1968 Czechoslovakia did not boast the café culture and consumer choices of today's Prague or Bratislava, but it was still a place where one could live comfortably, and that is what many people decided to do. For some this felt natural, but for others it was a source of personal and national dishonour. They had abandoned the Prague Spring under a hail of bullets, but their docility afterwards was enforced by much lesser kinds of repression as well as the promise of a nice flat, nice holidays and a new car for those who obeyed and complied.

Czechoslovak life in the 1970s and 1980s was exceptionally well documented by the generation of writers and other intellectuals who suffered most in the Soviet crackdown. After 1968 they often had to perform menial physical labour in conditions of internal exile just to eke out an existence. While some found ways to flee, and some nobly endured, others ended up cracking and compromising in order to get back some semblance of their previous lives. Those who continued to fight often felt resented by their fellow Czechoslovaks: prophets in their own land, distrusted and seen as pot-stirring troublemakers and moralists.

Milan Kundera departed for France in 1975. *The Unbearable Lightness of Being* describes the country he left behind, a place where the leading personalities of 1968 were humiliated in the media and forced to recant their previous statements. Kundera felt that most who remained had no choice but to knuckle down to a life of 'totalitarian kitsch' in which 'all answers are given in advance and preclude any questions'.[9] But Czechoslovakia's most famous dissident (who eventually became the president), Václav Havel, did try to continue his life as an agitator. He found work in a provincial brewery for a time and endured several spells in prison but managed to organize the powerful Charter 77 manifesto, which exposed the Czechoslovak government's many abuses and failure to live up to its own constitution and the international treaties it had signed.

In Havel's dramatic work, which circulated in clandestine samizdat form and was frequently smuggled to the West, he put his finger on some deep truths about post-1968 life. Even characters who were doing the right thing were riven with doubt, questioning both the point of their actions and the motives behind them. It was as if the shame the Soviet Union should have felt for invading Czechoslovakia – which of course it did not feel at all – had been outsourced to the country itself and distributed among the population.

15

Vienna, Austria

Vienna's Cold War reputation principally rests on two pillars. Rather like *The Sound of Music* neither is actually Austrian but, nevertheless, they have had a big impact, speaking as if on behalf of a place that is often reluctant to speak for itself, a place that has developed a knack for flying below history's radar. The first pillar is the British novella and film *The Third Man*, written by Graham Greene and directed by Carol Reed in the late 1940s. The second is the 1961 superpower summit between John F. Kennedy and Nikita Khrushchev, which was the two men's only meeting and a key stepping stone on the route from the Bay of Pigs to the erection of the Berlin Wall and ultimately the Cuban Missile Crisis.

In their different ways, *The Third Man* and the 1961 summit ignored Vienna's famously glittering charms. The protagonists of these episodes had no time for stucco and Sachertorte because of the difficult business they had to transact. Greene has his jaded narrator admit as much early on in the novella: 'I never knew Vienna between the wars, and I am too young to remember the old Vienna with its Strauss music and its bogus easy charm; to me it is simply a city of undignified ruins.'[1] For Kennedy the grandeur was merely a backdrop to humiliation. He privately told someone at the end of his bruising encounter with Khrushchev that it had been the 'worst thing in my life; he savaged me'.[2]

I arrived in the City of Dreams on a steamily hot afternoon at the start of a heatwave that stayed with me all the way to Turkey.

I deposited my bags at the railway station and, beginning as I meant to continue, set out immediately to hunt for two of the city's neglected historical features. As is so often the case, I had been told I would find them hiding in plain sight.

I crossed the Ringstrasse and entered the Innere Stadt. After passing the front of the massive Hofburg palace and the entrance to the Prunksaal (a library so distractingly baroque that it is hard to imagine anyone ever reading a book in there), I arrived at the Spanish Riding School in Josefsplatz. I had been told to stand in the square and look for some unexpected writing. My informant had said no more, and I genuinely had no idea what I was supposed to see. I found a spot out of the way of the crowds and studied each of the square's sides in turn. There were posters and street signs but all seemed unremarkable.

After some minutes I was on the point of giving up and heading to the second location. But then I saw something that seemed worth approaching: a small rectangular patch of wall at head height on a building I would later learn was the Palais Pallavicini. The patch was a slightly different colour from the rest of the wall and had some indiscernible writing on it. When still a few steps away, I was already coming to the conclusion that it was just some old business name. But then the faded white lines resolved into Cyrillic: '2/18 КВАРТАЛ ПРОВЕРЕН'. No further explanation, no tourist gloss, and there was no one else in the vicinity paying the rectangle any attention. My contact had told me this would be so, and she also said I should seek out both pieces of writing before reaching a view on what they were.

The second was on the exterior of the great St Stephen's Cathedral. I thought I knew what I was searching for by this time but it still proved elusive. Only on my second circuit did I notice it – higher up than the first sign and looking even more insignificant among the grand funerary monuments, an oblong of black paint with some faded writing, this time in red: '3/18 КВАРТАЛ ПРОВЕРЕН'.

In April 1945 the invading Soviet army divided central Vienna into eighteen subdivisions. The signs were painted up when each subdivision had been checked for enemy fighters.

'2/18 QUARTER CHECKED'; '3/18 QUARTER CHECKED'. Together these signs are rare relics of one of the darkest times in Viennese history, the days in April 1945 when the Soviet army invaded, occupied and liberated the city. The conquerors divided the Innere Stadt into eighteen subdivisions, each of which they systematically checked for enemy fighters and booby traps. It was when these checks were complete that an army officer in each subdivision gave the order for these signs to be stencilled in a prominent place.

For my Austrian informant the two signs are a painful reminder of the Soviet army's conquest of the city, taken block by block over the course of a month, and of the organized plunder, rape and other violence that accompanied it. As I was to find, for the small number of Russian tourists who have written about the signs in blogposts, and on review sites, they bear witness instead to the USSR's selflessness. Some see evidence of an effort to de-mine central Vienna, making it safe for everyone. One man writes that while he stood alongside the Josefsplatz sign (and ran his fingers over it) he could see in his mind's eye the Red Army soldiers dancing waltzes with the happy Viennese. Those made of sterner stuff say they immortalize a more ruthless de-Nazification, searches of every building, the liquidation of all fascist elements.

For me, on this brightest and hottest day of the trip so far, I saw a curfew descending on a bruised and battered city, with palaces on fire, and men young and old being prodded through the streets at gunpoint.

Vienna was another of those places where the end of the Second World War was immediately followed by a prominent role in the new Cold War. The city was completely occupied by the Soviet Union, yet, just as with Berlin, the Allies had agreed in advance to control it jointly through a system of zones. Due to a quirk of geography, Vienna also shared with Berlin the fact that it was fully located inside the Soviet sector of the country as a whole. For Berlin, these conditions led fairly quickly to complete breakdown. Yet in Vienna, the city and country managed to remain unified and the inter-Allied institutions continued to function for a full decade before being disbanded by mutual consent. Why were the cities' fates so different?

The relative importance of the two locations played a part in this. Quite simply, the erstwhile Allies cared less about Austria than Germany. The latter was the war's great prize; the former was a staging post on the way. Most Allied officials felt Austria bore some responsibility for the war and knew that individual Austrians had played key roles in the Nazi administration. But they agreed that Austria's culpability paled before Germany's, and thus the desire for vengeance was less. It was also generally accepted that a recovered, independent Austria would be much less threatening to their own future interests than a recovered

Germany. Consequently, developments in Austrian politics did not typically rise to the top of in-trays in Moscow, Washington, London or Paris, and the actions of any one power in its sector were less prone to provoke immediate reactions by the others.

But there was a further factor. Superficially the zoning of the Austrian capital was a carbon copy of Berlin's, but there were actually significant differences. Berlin's four sectors were geographically distinct, meaning it was relatively easy for the USSR to isolate its eastern section from the rest. In Vienna the Soviets controlled two different districts which were separated by British-run territory. Still more important, while the Soviets had complete control over Berlin's central district, the Mitte, in Vienna the equivalent Innere Stadt was an international zone that the Allies shared together. In Berlin, sharing meant side-by-side coexistence. In Vienna, it meant actual sharing.

Vienna's international zone was first proposed by British diplomats in a paper of January 1945, but objected to strongly in counterproposals from the Soviet Union. Predictably Moscow wanted a similar outcome to the one it had for Berlin.[3] There was diplomatic back and forth through the spring and early summer (long after the Soviets had actually occupied Vienna and after Berlin's zoning was settled), then finally, on 9 July 1945, an agreement was reached which for once saw Stalin back down.

In hindsight the details look in some ways sensible and in some ways ridiculous. Austria was to be overseen by an Inter-Allied Commission, which would scrutinize and ratify all laws passed by the elected Austrian parliament. Vienna was in turn controlled by an Inter-Allied Command, which reviewed the laws of the Vienna City Senate and co-ordinated the activities of the individual Allies in their sectors. In addition this Inter-Allied Command also directly ran the Innere Stadt, where the parliament, presidential palace and government ministries were located.

The Command comprised four commanders, one from each

Allied nation. The chairmanship rotated monthly, and these regular transfers were accompanied by pompous public ceremonies involving uniforms, flags and military music. Actual power was vested in the Inter-Allied Military Patrol, which was an institution that Graham Greene brought to worldwide attention in *The Third Man*. This unique military police force moved through the city in groups of four, first in jeeps and later in regular cars. A Frenchman, a Brit, a Yank and a Russian, all official representatives of their countries, all armed and crammed into a single vehicle. To this day it sounds like the stuff of fantasy, or perhaps the first line of a bad joke.

Before arriving in Vienna I had made contact with Paul Rachler, who had agreed to talk to me about the period when the Innere Stadt was under international control. On my second day in the city I walked to meet Paul, the in-house historian at the Haus der Industrie, out of whose palatial building both the Inter-Allied Commission and the Military Patrol operated for a number of years.

Just across the road I was waylaid for a few minutes by the enormous Soviet war memorial in Schwarzenbergplatz. As elsewhere, the Soviets were quick to erect a monument to their dead in Vienna. (In fact, the competition to design the edifice began in February 1945, when the 17,000 men whose deaths it memorializes were still alive.) It still boasts gold-leaf quotations from Stalin himself, and once also had a real decommissioned tank on it and some graves of actual soldiers. Vienna City Senate also renamed the square Stalinplatz as its own mark of respect, a name that remained in place until 1956.

Whether planned or accidental, it would have pleased the USSR that Austria's inter-Allied administration was carrying out its work on Stalinplatz under the gaze of a huge Soviet memorial. But Paul Rachler tells me that, day to day, the Inter-Allied Commission was surprisingly collaborative. The Haus der

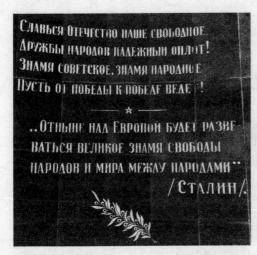

СЛАВЬСЯ ОТЕЧЕСТВО НАШЕ СВОБОДНОЕ,
ДРУЖБЫ НАРОДОВ НАДЕЖНЫЙ ОПЛОТ!
ЗНАМЯ СОВЕТСКОЕ, ЗНАМЯ НАРОДНОЕ
ПУСТЬ ОТ ПОБЕДЫ К ПОБЕДЕ ВЕДЕТ!

— ☆ —

„ОТНЫНЕ НАД ЕВРОПОЙ БУДЕТ РАЗВЕ
ВАТЬСЯ ВЕЛИКОЕ ЗНАМЯ СВОБОДЫ
НАРОДОВ И МИРА МЕЖДУ НАРОДАМИ"
/СТАЛИН/.

The Soviet war memorial on Schwarzenbergplatz, formerly Stalinplatz, still includes this quote from Stalin about world freedom and peace.

Industrie had been purpose-built for Austria's national association of industrialists around 1910 but became the headquarters of the Commission in 1945 and, from the early 1950s onwards, of the Military Patrol as well.

'Perhaps it was the famous Viennese *Gemütlichkeit*,' Paul says, referring to the cosy ask-no-questions hospitality the city is renowned for. 'Or perhaps it was something else. But right through that decade up to 1955 they all found ways to work together. Despite the nuclear race. Despite the Korean War. Despite Berlin. Despite everything else.'

We walk through the building's ornate corridors and past its rare paternoster lift on our way to one of the main salons. Paul pauses to tell me that the Soviets stationed here used to enjoy playing on the lift, jumping in and out of the open compartments as it moved slowly from floor to floor in an endless loop. They had never seen anything like it before, he says. But then he checks himself. It is always important to try to avoid easy stereotypes, he says: backward Russians; casual Americans; stiff Brits. 'There is often some truth in it but always a lot of fiction too. Take the rapes as an example,' he continues. 'Rape was certainly not

(l) The palatial interior of one of the grand rooms of Vienna's Haus der Industrie, home of the Inter-Allied Commission and the Inter-Allied Military Patrol.
(r) The rare paternoster lift on which Soviet soldiers, and presumably those of other nations, liked to play.

a privilege only of Russian soldiers in Vienna but that is what history has chosen to remember.' And, while many think Soviet commanders must have pressured the Viennese into calling the square Stalinplatz, Paul says his research indicates that 'actually it was the city council that decided to do it on its own'. There had been an epidemic of renaming in Vienna ever since 1918, when the Habsburg Empire collapsed: 'Streets, squares, institutions. They were all switching their names constantly. In that context, it didn't mean all that much for the authorities to name a single square after Stalin. It was just a small thing to try to keep the Soviets happy.' *Gemütlichkeit!*

The Haus der Industrie itself was something of a fortress between 1945 and 1955. Paul says it was almost impossible for an Austrian to enter. Inside, most of the space was divided into separate offices for the four powers while the grandest rooms were reserved for joint meetings, which happened regularly to ratify or challenge Austrian laws or deal with other problems.

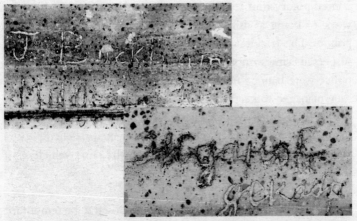

Buckham and Zhdanov, presumed British and Soviet members of the Inter-Allied Military Patrol who scratched their names in the stonework of the Haus der Industrie in the early 1950s.

The Military Patrol took over the ground floor when it moved in (apparently its members were banned from so much as ascending the stairs to the fancier offices and state rooms of the Commission). Outside, a road was blocked off to create a parking lot for its fleet of Chevrolets. Paul says one can still see evidence in the building's fabric of how the policemen spent long hours hanging around during their shifts: 'They ate here. On night shifts they slept here too. And of course they got bored. Like bored people everywhere, particularly before smartphones, some made graffiti.' Paul shows me some of the names they carved into the wooden panelling and stonework. Together we also discover a scrawl in German which says 'Long live Stalin. Long live Mao. Long live Communism (*Es lebe Stalin. Es lebe Mao. Es lebe Kommunismus*)'. 'Ironic?' I ask. Paul says, 'Probably not.'

Graham Greene's *The Third Man* depicts the military patrol as a blundering, slightly comic organization in which the Soviets, because of their great deviousness, had the upper hand. But Paul says that the 'Four in a Jeep' ('*Die Vier in Jeep*' was the standard Viennese nickname for the patrols and also the title of another contemporary film featuring them) mostly just got on with the work of being a visible armed presence in the city, free from politics. The trickiest duty they had, he adds, was investigating suspected crimes among their own nationals; the regular Austrian police were banned from such cases.[4] But even in these matters they managed to keep the show on the road.

The Inter-Allied Military Patrol was a kink in the Iron Curtain like no other: ordinary men from all the principal Allied powers co-operating with one another, often in the same vehicle, as if the Cold War was not happening.

The four-power regime was only ever supposed to be temporary. Negotiations on a permanent settlement opened immediately after the war but, although they did not rupture like in Germany, soon got bogged down in points of detail. As the years passed, a stalemate developed that became difficult to see beyond. The USSR was the main block to progress, but then a couple of years after Stalin's death it suddenly became the main promoter of a quick settlement. Khrushchev had new priorities: saving the USSR money by reducing its military footprint, and lowering the international temperature by finding more conciliatory ways to protect his country's vital interests. Just as with the Finnish leadership over Porkkala, he summoned Austria's most senior politicians to Moscow in early 1955 and proposed a complete withdrawal of Soviet forces (provided the other Allies also withdrew) in return for a permanent Austrian guarantee of neutrality. Julius Raab, the Austrian Chancellor, and Leopold Figl, the foreign minister, gladly agreed.

The Haus der Industrie became the forge in which the Austrian State Treaty was made. Diplomats first worked inside it to get most of the treaty's content in place, and then the ambassadors of the four Allied countries met there for a week to resolve outstanding sticking points (details such as how many military aircraft and what kind of weapons a neutral Austria would be allowed to have). For the first time since 1945, a delegation of Austrians was invited into the building.

On 14 May 1955, the day before the treaty was signed, the four foreign ministers – Vyacheslav Molotov, John Foster Dulles, Harold Macmillan and Antoine Pinay – flew to Vienna and gathered in the Haus der Industrie to close the deal. Sometimes such events are formalities but on this occasion important business was done. Most significantly, the Austrian foreign minister, Figl, unilaterally declared that he would remove from the treaty text the lengthy reference to Austria's guilt for the Second World War. The four foreign ministers and their delegations looked at one another waiting to see who would object first, but no one did – not even the Soviets, Paul tells me, who debated briefly with one another but then nodded the change through.

I later saw a copy of the draft treaty Figl had been using that day (now on display in the House of Austrian History museum (Haus der Geschichte Österreich). It was possible to follow each historic manoeuvre: a pencilled list of the parties to the treaty; two red 'Xs' made with a secretary's lipstick to indicate the expected objections from the Soviet Union; and finally the whole guilt paragraph excised with jubilant pencil strokes.

The Austrians were by all accounts shocked at this concession. I was shocked too, having never heard of the episode before. Paul explains that it was more complicated than it appears. Figl himself had spent five years in the Dachau concentration camp and a further period in Mauthausen. He felt strongly, and could argue from personal experience, that it was wrong to burden the entire Austrian people with war guilt. But, of course, a great many Austrians *were* complicit in the war and the wider Nazi regime, and this alteration to the State Treaty helped cement in place a partial view of Austria as the first victim of Naziism ('*Erstes Opfer des Nationalsozialismus*' is the oft-cited phrase).

'Figl had the right to say what he said for himself, but not for the whole country,' Paul says. 'It really had an effect on the

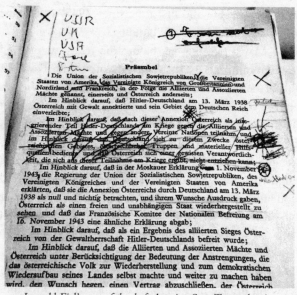

*Leopold Figl's copy of the draft Austrian State Treaty, showing
the crossed out paragraph referring to Austrian guilt for the
Second World War.*

self-understanding of this country. The whole issue would be
bottled up again until Waldheim.' (Austrians and the wider world
finally faced the country's easy amnesia about the war in 1986,
when the chancellor Kurt Waldheim – who had also served
as United Nations Secretary-General – was exposed as a one-
time member of the Sturmabteilung, or SA, and a Wehrmacht
intelligence officer who almost certainly had known about war
crimes.)

The Austrian State Treaty was actually signed at Vienna's
Belvedere Palace on 15 May 1955, a still grander location
than the Haus der Industrie and the place that most Austrians
associate with the achievement of postwar independence. But
when I visited the Belvedere later that day, the spot where the
treaty was signed was being used for the queue to see the Gustav
Klimt collection. Tourists of all nations shuffled over it seemingly

without any awareness of what had happened here. I was glad to have met Paul and seen where the treaty was actually created.

The settlements reached in Vienna and at Porkkala did not turn out to be the template for other places the Soviet leader had hoped for. At the superpowers' 1961 summit in the Austrian capital, the American president called 'neutral Vienna' a symbol of 'the possibility of finding equitable solutions' within the context of the Cold War.[5] But in reality neither the Americans nor the Soviets were willing to do what was necessary to replicate the arrangement. In particular, they remained faithful to their client states in Bonn and East Berlin, thereby continuing with the approach of maximum proximity and maximum hostility in a divided Germany.

A plaque in the floor of the Belvedere Palace marks the spot where the USSR, the USA, the UK, France and Austria signed the 1955 Austrian State Treaty. At the time of my visit, the plaque was overshadowed by the queue for the Gustav Klimt collection.

But, even if it wasn't a universal blueprint, the existence of neutral countries on the edge of the Iron Curtain did turn out to be useful for both sides, facilitating a wide range of contacts, public and clandestine, that would otherwise have been difficult. Vienna, to an even greater extent than Helsinki, became notorious as a city of espionage.

This reputation had already started to develop in the occupation period. As the historian Siegfried Beer has said,

'Within just a few months and years of the end of the war, and in total disproportion to the size and significance of the country, [Vienna had] become an international centre and stomping ground for agents, informants, provocateurs and spies.'[6] KGB officer Peter Deriabin, writing in 1959, similarly singled out 'the comparative looseness of the four-power occupation scheme, by contrast with the rigid sector demarcations in Berlin'.[7] This might actually have diminished after the State Treaty was signed, had it not been for Austria's decision to develop a new string to its bow. Banned from NATO, the country instead offered itself, and specifically its capital, as a home for international bodies.

Michael Platzer, who worked for United Nations agencies in Vienna during the Cold War, told me, 'Austria never wanted to join NATO anyway, so being neutral was no big hardship. But after 1955 the country spent large amounts of money attracting and creating facilities for the UN and other international organizations, starting with the International Atomic Energy Agency.'

After a few decades the list of bodies had grown long, including the International Atomic Energy Agency, the UN Industrial Development Organization, the UN High Commissioner for Refugees, the Organization of the Petroleum Exporting Countries, and the Organization for Security and Co-operation in Europe (originally called the Commission on Security and Co-operation in Europe), to name only the most prominent. The SALT talks on strategic arms limitation also took place partly in Vienna, with the second SALT treaty being signed there in 1979. During the 1970s Austria built a new quarter in its capital to house the multinational institutions and their workforces: Vienna International Centre. It was granted extraterritorial status, meaning that it was, and remains, outside Austrian law. Rather amazingly, this designation necessitated the re-founding of a kind of Inter-Allied Military Patrol, the UN Security and Safety Service (SSS), which to this day has a remit that would be recognizable to the 'Four in a Jeep' patrolmen of old.[8]

I ask Michael why Austria embarked on this line of business. 'There was an explicit Cold War dimension to it,' he says. 'The Austrian government felt it would make the Soviets think twice before invading Vienna if all these international organizations were based here. However,' he continues, 'in practice it led to the development of colonial-style administrations around the Austrian capital, thousands of administrators and diplomats, helping to make Vienna the spy capital of the world.'

Vienna seems to have been a particular favourite with KGB officers looking to meet up with Western moles. These moles sometimes worked in the city but often flew in specially. Vienna was the sort of place one could easily find a pretext for visiting, especially for people working in the fields of intelligence and foreign affairs: some conference or convention or, failing that, an opera trip or Danube cruise.

Two cases give an insight into this clandestine world. David Henry Barnett worked for the CIA until 1970. After leaving his job and getting into debt, he began trading his old knowledge to the KGB. At regular meetings in the USSR's Vienna embassy between 1976 and 1979 – apparently there was no need to be more cloak and dagger – he is thought to have revealed the names of around thirty CIA officers. He also handed over classified intelligence about what the US knew about major Soviet weapons programmes. His payment, in addition to the free trips to Vienna, was some $92,000 (or around $300,000 today). When arrested, Barnett had been on the brink of becoming a whole lot more useful to his handlers, having just landed a job on the US President's Intelligence Advisory Board. He was, of course, excluded from it and went on to serve ten years in federal prison instead.[9]

In a *New York Times* article from 1982 Barnett's family revealed the impact his treachery had had on them.[10] The spy's eight-year-old son, John, had recently written a letter to his imprisoned father in which he asked, 'Why did you do it? Why did you go to the Russians? Why don't we live in a big house anymore?' His wife Sarah was in the process of divorcing David and said, 'I hope to God there is no one else out there living in the same situation I was for the past six years . . . I don't think I am gullible, but I am angry at myself that I didn't see through a lot of things.' With hindsight she could distinguish many 'lies and evasions'. Her husband had begun 'to drink much more heavily' and 'his laugh became different, more forced'. Somewhat curiously, she said he had become 'rougher' too, 'not in a physical sense of hitting anyone, but in the way he would eat'. He was in debt and had always had an 'extraordinary fascination with making a lot of money', Sarah recalled, but she also wondered if false friendship wasn't the main reason for his betrayal: 'I think some of his happiest moments were with the Russian guy.' For Moscow, it had all been textbook agent-running stuff, carried out to perfection.

Ronald William Pelton was not quite Barnett's double but he was not far off. A former National Security Agency intelligence analyst, he sold his services to the USSR in 1980 after going bankrupt. The Soviets regularly brought him to Vienna between 1980 and 1983 and held long interview sessions with him at the ambassador's residence. Pelton would be paid only $37,000 ($100,000 today), despite his revelations being much more sensitive than Barnett's. They included information on Operation Ivy Bells, a wire tap that American frogmen had fitted to a top secret undersea Soviet communications cable in the Sea of Okhotsk. When finally caught in 1985 – thanks to the intelligence of a Soviet defector – Pelton was sentenced to three life sentences and a further ten years. He was only freed in 2015. I totted it up and this meant he had spent a year behind bars for every $1,200 he had earned.[11]

Vienna was used for many other kinds of covert activity. One of the most intriguing was its role as a hub for secret book distribution programmes, some funded by the CIA and others carried out by charities and philanthropists. A key figure in these efforts was Peter Straka, whose main job was managing some of the city's ordinary bookshops. As the historian Alfred Reisch has established, 'Starting in 1966, Straka began to distribute thousands of books . . . to Czechs, Slovaks, Hungarians, Romanians, and Bulgarians, as well as to Poles . . . arriving individually or on organized tours by bus or Danube steamer in Vienna . . . At the Jungbrunnen bookstore and later at the Frick bookshops, visitors could choose books and periodicals worth up to $10 or 250 Schillings each.'[12] Straka also posted copies of banned books to people and libraries in the Eastern Bloc. His feedback indicated that around half the packages got through. But even when intercepted Peter felt the parcels were a reminder to the regimes in question that there were people in the West who were determined to breach their ideological defences.[13]

Over twenty years Straka distributed around 50,000 books. One of his most popular titles was Aleksandr Solzhenitsyn's *Gulag Archipelago*, of which he gave away 1,000 copies.[14] How many people had their horizons expanded by these gifts from neutral Vienna, gifts which often passed through scores of hands once inside the Eastern Bloc? And how many people were punished for owning them? We will never know. But a few recipients did take the brave step of writing back. A Hungarian in the mid-1960s wrote, 'You perhaps do not know what this means to us . . . It is these books which keep our faith and courage, because this is the only way for us to keep abreast of the culture in which we were brought up and to which we feel we belong.'[15]

16

Sopron, Hungary

The commuter trains that shuttle between Vienna and western Hungary take thousands of blue- and white-collar workers into Austria each morning and back to places like Sopron each night. As I discovered when I boarded one sometime after 5 p.m. to make the short journey to the town, these services also throw passengers from one sort of European milieu into another. Despite Vienna and Sopron being members of the same empire for half a century, despite the Iron Curtain between Austria and Hungary being not nearly so impassable as in many other places, and despite the present day realities of the EU and Schengen, this felt like the biggest single jump of my entire trip.

Sopron is only 65 kilometres from central Vienna, but the cultural distance is vast. It is not just that Vienna is a big capital and Sopron a small town. In fact, in some respects it feels like the reverse. Vienna is a place of decorum and reserve, and at times stifling. The city often has a silent quality and people mostly seem to get by without much public display of emotion. As the curator of one museum put it to me, 'The Viennese are quiet ones. You won't see any arguments breaking out in the streets here. A big majority just go through life thinking their own things and in most cases you never really get to know what those things are.' Sopron, on the other hand, wore its heart on its sleeve.

Sopron station and the town beyond were like a well-lit stage when I disembarked just before 7 p.m. that hot summer evening. Children were out playing on every patch of grass. Women in light cotton dresses were chatting to one another, some rocking prams with one hand as they smoked with the other. The stationmaster personally greeted at least half a dozen of the arriving passengers. One man came up to show him something on his phone and they both guffawed, apparently continuing a conversation begun on a previous occasion. No one waited for the traffic lights but jay-walked across the roads up into town. The dogs also ran free, seeming to belong to everyone and nobody at the same time.

After Vienna it was an assault on the senses. Cars honked delinquently. Smells of roasting meat wafted in the air. Big clouds of dust, puffed up by boys on mopeds, glinted gold in the late sun. As I paused to gather my bearings and work out the way to my flat, a car screeched to a halt beside me and a topless male driver jumped out and ran into a shop. He emerged moments later with three different brandy bottles, allowing his three female passengers to peruse them and decide which they preferred. He dived back in to buy it, returning with a ten-pack carton of Marlboro Red for good measure. It was Monday.

I retired early and was up shortly after dawn on the Tuesday morning to cycle to a nearby field before the sun got too high in the sky. My host had lent me his bicycle and I covered the 6 or 7 kilometres quickly because it was mostly downhill. I was well aware my return journey would be harder and hotter. The countryside was full of smells of growth. Tradesmen's vans and the occasional tractor were the only other vehicles on the road.

I was heading to the site of the Pan-European Picnic of 19 August 1989. Despite an extravagant title, this was originally conceived as a small affair. The organizers had intended to celebrate recent improvements in relations between Hungary and Austria, which were of a piece with, and to some extent inspired by, the era of *glasnost* that Gorbachev had initiated from Moscow a few years before. They also wanted to see greater change in and around Sopron itself. The picnic's location was chosen as the point where the road crossed the border between Sopron and the nearest Austrian settlement, Sankt Margarethen im Burgenland. Other crossings had just reopened but this one remained closed, necessitating a 40-kilometre round trip for people going between the two places. The picnic was to include a symbolic cutting of the barbed-wire fence and a breaking of bread between residents of each place. It was hoped this might persuade the authorities to establish a permanent checkpoint.

A German-language invitation to the Pan-European Picnic,
a flower amid the barbed wire.

The day surprised everyone, turning into a real mass escape whose ripples reverberated across the continent. What transformed the local gesture into international drama was the unavoidable wider reality of 1989. The Iron Curtain was disappearing in Hungary but, further north, in the GDR, it remained as impenetrable as ever. Hungary had long been a popular destination for East German tourists, and in the summer of 1989 they came in greater numbers still. Many of them harboured a secret wish to end their vacations by fleeing to the West.

Up to 19 August only 290 East Germans had succeeded in making it out of Hungary to Austria that summer. Hungarian border guards were still under orders to block East Germans leaving and even to shoot and kill any who resisted arrest. (This was by agreement with the East Berlin government, which continued to put massive pressure on other communist states to respect the restrictions it imposed on its own citizens.) Tensions were growing. Many GDR tourists felt disconsolate at the prospect of returning to their homeland, with its shortages and hardships, and a regime that refused to reform.

This was the context in which the German-language flyers for the Pan-European Picnic began to circulate among East Germans in Hungary. With other avenues blocked to them, thousands of the tourists separately had the idea of attending the picnic. Early on the morning of 19 August at hotels and holiday camps across Hungary they skipped breakfast and sneaked into their Trabants and Wartburgs to drive to Sopron. Most had been staying around Lake Balaton, then, as now, Hungary's premier tourist destination, some 200 kilometres to the south. They travelled in the clothes they stood up in so they would look less suspicious if stopped. Mostly, they parked several kilometres from the picnic site, covering the final stretch on foot.

The picnic's planned start time was 3 p.m. This was the moment when the old border gate was to be unlocked so residents on both sides could pass through to eat and drink with each other. Later, at around 4.30 p.m., people were supposed to claim their mementoes of the day, little pieces cut from the barbed-wire fence. The whole spectacle was to take place in the presence of border troops, who would check people's passports as they crossed back and forth.

One organizer, László Nagy, later recalled, 'We expected one and a half thousand [people]; we weren't aware that 25,000 . . . would come.'[1] But by early afternoon it was already becoming clear that attendance would exceed their wildest hopes. 'Half of Sopron city was there,' Nagy recalls, and 'at least a minimum of five thousand people came from Austria.' This initially made the two or three thousand East Germans hard to spot. But a little before 3 p.m. a group of about fifty revealed themselves by moving *en masse* towards the border gate.

László Vass, a deputy minister of state in Hungary, was on the scene. He was standing right beside the gate with the chief Hungarian border guard for the day, a man called Árpád Bella. Both were readying themselves for the opening ceremony when the surprise rush of people passed them, forced open the gate, and began running through. Seconds later, other East Germans began to appear, running out of the fields on either side, headed for the barbed-wire fence, and climbing or crawling into Austria. 'People started to make way for them,' Vass recalled afterwards, 'and pushed us a bit to the side.' The border guards still had their orders. 'Bella became very angry and he shouted to me that it was not good, and we should do something about it. He was very nervous and said it was not fair on him and his men.'[2]

This was the critical moment when a happy local event could easily have become a bloodbath. There were many such moments across the Eastern Bloc in the late 1980s and early 1990s, when representatives of law and order faced split-second decisions about whether to hold the line they had been trained to hold for years or let history take its course.

'I tried to persuade him to relax,' Vass remembered. 'I said that

I was the highest ranking government official in the area now and so I took responsibility for what had happened. He was very angry though, and answered me that I was not his supervisor. I think I said, "Don't worry, come have a beer". But he didn't come.'

While Bella wrestled with what to do next, his men cried out for direction. László Nagy was nearby. He saw the border guards shouting at Bella, 'Commander, what shall we do?' From Bella's point of view, all options were bad. He risked losing his job and possible criminal proceedings if he did nothing. But his own personal safety and that of his men might be in jeopardy if they enforced an unpopular law on a crowd of 25,000 hostile people. In the end Bella reached the same conclusion as Vass. His answer to his men was a benevolent anticlimax: 'Count them and give me a rough number!' There would be no attempt to stop the fugitives, but he would keep a tally. He probably reckoned he would need it for the long report he would be filing that evening.

By the border troops' quick estimate, 150 East Germans had already escaped in the first few minutes. Oddly enough, there then came a lull. Many GDR citizens, whose actions for the most part were not co-ordinated, hung back in the crowd. We know from later recollections that some were discouraged by the sight of so many border guards, while others feared that, after the initial burst of escapes, an official backlash would follow.

According to the day's strange logic, Bella and his Austrian counterpart used the breathing space to press on with the original plan. The border gate, closed since 1948, and reopened by force a few minutes earlier, was now sealed again so the symbolic 3 p.m. opening could occur.

For the rest of the afternoon two very different events proceeded in parallel in a crazy, carnival atmosphere. Austrian and Hungarian picnickers crossed through the open gate in orderly fashion, submitting to passports checks and receiving stamps from the border guards. They greeted one another like old friends, though most had never met before. They clinked glasses and raised toasts in their respective languages. Meanwhile, every so often from left and right small groups of East Germans would make bold breaks for freedom, peeling away from the crowds or emerging from bushes and hedges and dashing towards the Iron Curtain. The East Germans could not know that Bella had already decided to leave them unhindered. None of them could be sure how long this tolerance would last. For each GDR citizen, there was the fear of being caught, of imprisonment, and even of death.

In fact, many East Germans who came to Sopron that day did not cross. They remained too scared and returned to their cars and to what was left of their holidays, no doubt kicking themselves for their lack of courage and – as they might well still have thought then – for missing the opportunity of their lives. But at least 600 did get through, the biggest single escape since the Berlin Wall's creation twenty-eight years earlier. In the end the Pan-European Picnic punched a far bigger hole in the Iron Curtain than anyone expected.

Over the next few weeks the Hungarian authorities, after facing fierce criticism from the GDR, stepped up patrols on the frontier, specifically targeting would-be East German escapees. Inspired by stories from the picnic, however, dozens more East Germans did succeed in getting through. Many Hungarian border guards were no longer prepared to use violence to prevent escapes. Finally, on 11 September 1989, Hungary abandoned its efforts to keep the border sealed altogether – a key moment in the end of the Cold War.

Sadly, there had been time for just one more border fatality. Kurt-Werner Schulz was a thirty-six-year-old architect from East Germany's Vogtland who decided to go to Sopron the day after the Pan-European Picnic and attempt to escape with his partner and son. Their attempt failed when they were intercepted by border police who sent them away. Fixed on his goal, however,

Schulz returned the next day. Just as the trio were about to cross into Austria they were spotted once more. Schulz wrestled with a border guard to give his wife and son time to get over. In the struggle the guard's gun went off, killing Schulz.[3] Kurt-Werner Schulz thus became by some measures the Iron Curtain's final victim.

There were workmen at the picnic site during my visit, building a new visitors' centre. But the only other traveller I encountered was a man in his twenties called Kevin, who had also come by bicycle. We got talking beside one of the many monuments. Kevin was on a short break from Vienna where he worked in a five-star hotel. He was half-German and half-Hungarian and had grown up in the Black Forest. He said he liked taking trips to different parts of Hungary, to practise his Hungarian and learn more about the culture of his father's side of the family, and he also took any chance he could to get free from claustrophobic Vienna.

Kevin told me he could understand why Hungarians had been content just to pop into Austria and pop back again on the day of the picnic. His Hungarian aunt, who lives near the southern city of Pécs, was still a big defender of the Hungarian communist system. Her husband had been the mayor of the local village before 1989 and Kevin's father had always warned his children against speaking ill of communists in her presence. For Kevin, this was a forgivable eccentricity. Hungarian communism, from what he had heard, had not been nearly so unpleasant as communism in the GDR or the Soviet Union. After the failed uprising of 1956 the Hungarian government increasingly focused on trying to make the country 'the happiest barracks in the socialist camp'. Freedom was limited, considerably more so than in Czechoslovakia during the Prague Spring, but Hungary made a success of consumerism to an extent unmatched anywhere in socialist Eastern Europe except Yugoslavia. Some people actually lost a lot when the regime finally collapsed, Kevin said.

He could, of course, understand the desperation felt by many East Germans at the picnic. What surprised him most were the pictures displayed at the site of Austrians welcoming East Germans over the border. One photograph showed a placard stuck in the ground just inside Austrian territory. 'You are in Austria. No more danger! We will help!' it read. Kevin asked me, 'Can you imagine that sign nowadays when refugees are trying to cross?'

A placard just inside Austria tells East Germans on the day of the Pan-European Picnic, 'You are in Austria. No more danger! We will help!'

Where I had been thinking about the mindset of the people escaping, Kevin was contemplating the people who had received escapees, overseen and even supported by the Austrian state. Many in Austria – and Hungary too – would now like to live in a kind of fortress to which refugees have no access. In place of welcome placards, on the day of our visit there were two Austrian border guards monitoring every transiting car. (For over a decade after Hungary's EU accession in 2004 the checkpoint was unmanned, but since the 2015 refugee crisis it has been guarded once more.) The traffic was seldom stopped while we were there – it all looked local – but the guards would doubtless have acted quickly if they had suspected a vehicle of containing Middle Eastern or African migrants.

Kevin has thought about refugees a lot. He explained that the German side of his family, his mother's, had had its own experience of forced migration. Until the Second World War they lived in Yugoslavia, as members of a community called the

Danube Swabians. These were German speakers whose ancestors had left south-west Germany centuries before. After the war they were collectively punished: dispossessed and expelled because of their perceived, and in some cases real, support for the Nazis. Kevin's mother's family ended up having to retrace the steps of their forefathers all the way back to the Black Forest.

This legacy felt newly significant in 2015. As Kevin's mother watched the unfolding refugee crisis and heard Angela Merkel say, 'We can do this!' ('*Wir schaffen das!*'), she was moved to offer an empty property she owned as a home for some Afghan asylum seekers. 'She called a family meeting,' Kevin said, 'and told us her idea. We all agreed.' The plan has worked out well. 'It's been like gaining a second family. The Afghans are still there now and we visit them regularly to share meals. They call me their son. And they have even refused to remove a picture of Jesus from the wall in the living room – out of respect, they say, for the people who gave them a home.'

Not everyone was so welcoming. 'Our next door neighbours at the farm live a bit of a distance from the house but they still felt threatened by the Afghans. We could hardly believe it but in the end they actually built a high wall between the two properties.' A wall. A *Mauer*. Given where we are standing, we both can't help laughing. For Kevin, the Pan-European Picnic is mainly a lesson in how people should respond when life asks difficult questions of them. The split-second choices made by the restrained police chief Bella and the compassionate Austrian villagers back in 1989 show what humans can do when they view those in need as fully human too.

Kevin also reminded me of how little the ideological content of the Cold War means to most people born after its conclusion. The battle between left and right in the second half of the twentieth century is no longer the prism through which they view the present; it is not even the prism through which they view the Cold War. When considering the period, Kevin and other young people are more likely to focus on the enduring and universal lessons to be drawn from it. For them, the battle between East and West is evidence of the wider truth that any powerful group oppresses weaker groups unless it is kept in check. And I have found that they are perennially puzzled by the compassion people in Western Europe and America extended to oppressed peoples in Eastern Europe, given that similar compassion is so often lacking in responses to oppressed people today.

In the balmy early evening, after cycling back up the hill into town, Kevin and I drank a couple of beers and ate some snacks at an outdoor café near Sopron station. He joked that it was our picnic after the picnic. Then we both went to catch trains – he back across the border to Vienna; me onward to Budapest.

PART V

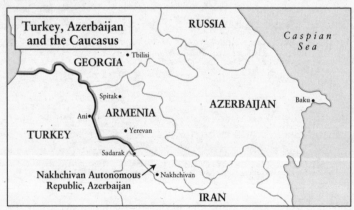

17

Nova Gorica, Slovenia, and Gorizia, Italy (I)

I leave Budapest just before midnight and travel overnight by bus to Ljubljana, the capital of Slovenia. I have made it to the former Yugoslavia. After a brief stop I board a train destined for Slovenia's border with Italy. At journey's end I will find a place that was once known as the Berlin of the South, the twin towns of Gorizia and Nova Gorica, which for decades were separated by the Iron Curtain. I had been told this would be one of the most spectacular railway trips of my life. Now I have done it, I can agree. It is hard to imagine having more pleasure for nine Euros.

The first leg took me over the Ljubljana plain into the Julian Alps. The few other passengers were either children just finished school or shoppers returning from the capital with purchases. One couple sat balancing an enormous flatscreen TV on their laps. I found myself thinking of the unsuspecting passengers on the 14:12 from Cheb to Aš back in September 1951.

At the small town of Jesenice I transferred from modern rolling stock onto a set of carriages that clearly dated back to Yugoslav times. Suddenly the train was packed with holidaymakers going to Lake Bled, a world centre for water sports, but this only lasted a few minutes. After the Lake Bled stop, just four of us remained for a two-hour ride to the edge of Italy.

The day was hot, the sun blinding. Peaks reared up to the left and right as the train rattled through a succession of passes and manmade cuttings that seemed constantly to double back on one another. For a while it felt as if we only climbed, the train's old engine audibly under strain. At the highest point we freewheeled through alpine meadows, their grass so green it looked almost fake, until the train found a turquoise river, a channel for glacial meltwater. This was the Soča (or Isonzo in Italian). Its appearance marked the beginning of our descent into Nova Gorica and we stuck with it the rest of the way. Each link in this chain had been more beautiful than the last, and the effect was a little exhausting; an overload of beauty that I hardly dared break eye contact with. The only respite was the cold, dank tunnels whose walls the train almost touched. They marked a complete change of sound, smell and temperature: the shutter on my panoramic slide show, snapping closed, open, closed.

I was in a kind of reverie much of the time. What are sometimes called the big questions circulated in my mind: questions about

the meaning of life and the nature of beauty; the kind of questions sublime landscapes often suggest to travellers. What was the Iron Curtain compared with this majestic nature? How had people ever had the hubris to impose borders in places like this?

At best, I thought, we are only ever the temporary custodians of any territory or property we control. Shutting others out ought to feel far less natural to

The Soča or Isonzo River was bright turquoise as I rode alongside it for kilometres on the Transalpina railway from Jesenice to Nova Gorica.

us than it does. From the fences around my father's farm to the spindly border of Northern Ireland, the death strip at the Brandenburg Gate, the 38th parallel between North and South Korea, or the walls between the USA and Mexico and Israel and the Occupied Territories – it all suddenly seemed like a massive confidence trick. People who make and control borders want to convince others they have power. With our nation states and flags and visas, we are all conning ourselves that we control the forces that regulate the Earth, conning ourselves that we are not actually mortal. It is all only lent to us.

The railway line I was on was a *grand projet* of the Austro-Hungarian Empire that used to rule both Slovenia and what is now the adjacent part of Italy. The first rail connection between Vienna and Trieste was completed in 1857. This line, the Bohinj or Transalpina, was the second and had been added at the start of the twentieth century. It really was an engineering feat, involving twenty-eight new tunnels and sixty-five new bridges through the Alps. They included the longest single-arch stone railway bridge in the world, the Solkan, which rattled under us just before we reached Gorizia/Nova Gorica.

The stupendously palatial Transalpina station that was my terminus was straight out of *The Grand Budapest Hotel*. At the time it was constructed Gorizia was a town of just 35,000 people, but it had become a favourite winter holiday spot for the final generation of Austro-Hungarian nobility. In the years before the First World War it was marketed as the 'Austrian Nice', and for a time trains carried passengers from as far away as Prague. Then the Habsburg Empire collapsed, the borders changed – then changed again – and the railway faded in importance. Finally, with the coming of the Cold War, Transalpina station turned into an international absurdity.

At the end of the Second World War Transalpina station entered the Republic of Yugoslavia, along with the train line, but most of the rest of Gorizia stayed in Italy, including exactly half the station square. The main entrance was boarded up, not to reopen until the 1990s, and barbed-wire fencing was rolled through the square so that walking from one side to the other became impossible. The Iron Curtain came to town.

Going through the station's ornate ticket hall today and into the square – which is still shared by Slovenia and Italy and known respectively as Trg Evrope and Piazzale della Transalpina in each language – one gets a good sense of the ridiculousness of the postwar situation. Just 20 metres from the front door the international frontier still slices through. All security installations have gone but the border is still easily discerned. Plaques in the pavement, marker blocks and various sculptures and information boards indicate where it runs, as do the different number plates of cars parked on either side. I walked back and forward for a bit, transferring myself from one country to the other, and then stood astride the boundary – two feet in one square and two nations at the same time.

My rented house was just 500 metres away and it too was on the border. In the late afternoon heat I carried my luggage by the side of the railway tracks (the tracks in Slovenia, the pavement in Italy) and noted the pervasive smell of jasmine and the little white border stones everywhere. On the street where the house

A commemorative border marker in Piazzale della Transalpina / Trg Evrope. The author's feet in one square and two nations at the same time.

was, every property but one – the one beside mine – was Italian. The owner of the adjacent property was watering his flowers as I unlocked my door. He waved a hello to me from Slovenia and I waved back. It was a perplexing start to a perplexing few days.

In 1945 it was immediately clear that there would need to be a new border between Italy and Yugoslavia. It was also generally accepted that Italy would become smaller and Yugoslavia bigger as a result of the former's culpability for the conflict. But the question of where to put the new frontier was hotly contested. Initially a temporary divide, known as the Morgan Line, was laid down. It kept Gorizia well inside Italy. But when the permanent frontier was agreed in far-off Paris in 1947, Yugoslavia and its then-backer the USSR successfully argued for more land and Gorizia was severed.

The line on the map from Paris was utterly nonsensical. As elsewhere, ordinary people on the ground mostly just had to live with this. But what was unusual in Gorizia was that a handful of local citizens successfully lobbied for their own private interests and got small changes as a result. Overall, the border runs north–south through the town, just as the negotiators intended, but the small deviations are visible to all to see: little doglegs and kinks in the otherwise straight line.

I reckoned that my next door neighbour's property must have been an example of this, though I never saw him again to ask him. But when I had read Anne McWilliams's excellent study of the archaeology of the Iron Curtain, another instance of such horse-trading had lodged in my mind. Countess Liduška of Gorizia's mansion was to be right up against the new frontier. The Paris settlement put it in Yugoslavia but Liduška, who was no socialist, thought this spelled catastrophe. According to McWilliams she set about throwing 'many lavish parties at her estate which many soldiers attended' and 'used her influences within the American army to make sure [that] the border here was redirected around her property'.[1] Sure enough, the border got rerouted so that today it still looks like a slip of the cartographer's pen. I wanted to know more about this woman who had taken on the Cold War and won. Before the trip, I had got in touch with the present day housekeeper at Villa de Nordis. She agreed I could visit when I was in town and perhaps even meet the current owners.

Villa de Nordis is about 2 kilometres north of Piazzale della Transalpina on the edge of Gorizia, where the town gives way to hilly vineyards. A high stone wall encases it on all sides which, along with the solid wooden gates, means the premises cannot be seen from street level in either country: the Liduškas clearly valued privacy as well as property. The wooden gates swung open automatically and I gave a little gasp at what I saw ahead: a driveway through a large garden, with a pillared, porticoed country house at the end. It is what past elites would have called a modest summer residence, but by today's standards it is grand.

Before I met the owners, I had imagined them to be the Countess's offspring or grandchildren. Perhaps they would be tight-lipped about family secrets, I thought, including the secret of how the border got moved. But the current lady of the house, Enrica, came out to greet me pursued by her dogs, and was immediately friendly. Without English she managed to communicate in a mixture of Italian and German that her husband, Romano, would be with us in a moment. He then emerged from a side garden dressed in shorts and T-shirt, wiping his hands on a cloth and welcoming me warmly.

We began to walk around. We were smiling a lot but couldn't really understand one another and I started to doubt if the full details of Countess Liduška's postwar diplomacy could be conveyed using only Google Translate and hand gestures. Suddenly another car appeared on the driveway. It was Enrica and Romano's friend, Paolo, an Italian who used to live in Canada and whom they had asked to join us as a translator. Relieved and touched, I followed them all inside across a beautiful floor

Villa de Nordis, the family home of Countess Liduška. It was supposed to be in Yugoslavia but the Countess used contacts to keep it in Italy.

mosaic that said 'SALVE' and sat down at a large table where elderflower cordial and snacks were laid out. The big windows were all wide open. The linen drapes billowed.

'Lia moved a border and not many individuals can say that,' Romano began.

The family's wealth and status dated back to Habsburg times, when an ancestor had been a notary at the imperial court. By the start of the Second World War the Liduškas, including the teenage Lia, were dividing their time between Gorizia and Kenya's Happy Valley, where they enjoyed horse riding and hunting, and lived near Karen Blixen.

'Because of Kenya she knew a lot of powerful British people,' Romano says, including Sarah Churchill, daughter of the British Prime Minister, who visited Villa de Nordis. It was she, Lia told Romano, who petitioned her father to get the border moved. 'Churchill personally?' I ask. Romano confirms this is what Lia said but admits he has heard other theories too. Some say Liduška met with General Eisenhower on his 1946 visit to Gorizia and secured certain undertakings from him. There were any number of other influential guests who might have come into her orbit at one of the villa's many postwar parties.

Romano guesses the threat of her home disappearing into Tito's Yugoslavia probably meant the Countess pulled hard on every lever she could.

'The tension in those years was massive,' Romano says. 'Of course, the local people on both sides knew one another. They had lived in a single country before and had had normal relations. But the Yugoslavians were aware of this and feared it, so they made sure their border troops came from far away, from Serbia. Yugoslavians could be killed for just putting a foot over the border – not killed by Italians, but by their own side.'

I wondered if Countess Liduška had ended up spending much time at this flashpoint after successfully moving the frontier. Romano says that in the late 1940s and early 1950s she and her husband re-committed themselves to the property, making substantial repairs to remove war damage. They then moved back in, and in some ways their comfortable prewar life resumed.

But of course, he adds, there had to be changes now the garden wall was an international border. The original entrance gates now opened onto Yugoslavia, so they had to be bricked up and new ones made on the other side of the property (the ones I had driven through). Two of the estate's four high walls had become the Iron Curtain. The Countess and her staff regularly found evidence of escapees. At night Yugoslav citizens would throw bags containing their smartest clothes over the walls and climb in after them. Once in the grounds they would change into these smart clothes and head for the bus or railway station, discarding their old clothes. Romano says the practice continued right up to the 1980s, despite the much lighter border regime that was in force by that point. By then people living in the immediate vicinity of Gorizia–Nova Gorica could travel freely over the frontier using a special local visa called a *propustnica* (similar to the system now in operation between Kirkenes and neighbouring places in Russia), but the Villa de Nordis was still an entry point for migrants from Hungary or Czechoslovakia.

Liduška, who had had her own lucky escape from the socialist camp, never attempted to stop them.

I realized at this point that I still didn't know what Romano and Enrica's relationship to the Countess was. Romano smiles broadly when I raise this and prepares to rehearse an explanation he has given many times before.

'I was the Countess's groundsman,' he says. 'When Lia headed to Africa each year, she needed someone to take care of the property. At some point the position fell vacant and a friend suggested me. I was still quite young but there was a spark between us. Maybe it was because, on my first visit, I managed to fix a lawnmower that hadn't worked for fifty years. Anyway, whatever the reason, she saw something in me.' Romano started living on the estate, the only person who was there all year round. He had his own house off to the side of the main mansion and combined work for the Countess with his other job as an athletics coach, something he still does.

When Lia was in Italy she would seek him out for 'teatime' at about 5.30 p.m. each day. They would sit at a table out on the lawn. Sometimes they drank tea but sometimes she would say, 'Tea is so sad. Let's make it whisky-time instead.' Whether over whisky or tea, she told him stories about her past and that of the house: about how she had kept Villa de Nordis in Italy; about how her husband had originally been the family chauffeur; about the hedonism and scandals of Happy Valley.

Lia never had children. When Romano puzzles over why she decided to leave Villa de Nordis in its entirety to him, he thinks his daughter played the key role. 'Chiara was just a baby in Lia's last years. I would bring her with me to the big house and she would play while I worked. I think seeing Chiara reminded Lia of her own childhood. I am very proud and honoured to be entrusted with this property,' Romano adds, rising to complete the tour we had begun earlier. 'I could never have imagined she would leave it to me. She was a noble and I am not.'

We leave the room and I am brought face to face with the Countess for the first time, on a table of photographs in the hallway. As I expected, she looked glamorous and monied. There was also defiance in her gaze. In one photo she was standing beside a British army general. In several others she was on horseback. Riding and swimming were her passions, Romano says; she found walking painful after an infection in youth.

Together we approach the original estate entrance, the one bricked up in 1947. Romano leads me through a side gate. In the space of ten steps we are in Slovenia, in an ordinary street of ordinary two-storey houses. About the same distance in the other direction, back inside Italy, we stand above a high ravine looking into the turquoise Isonzo. The Countess used to pick a path down this steep bank to swim in the river, right up against the border. In recent years someone – Romano does not know who – has put a simple wooden bench here. On it is carved a quotation from Konrad Adenauer, West Germany's first chancellor: '*Viviamo tutti sotto lo stesso cielo, ma non tutti abbiamo lo stesso orizzonte*' (We all live under the same sky, but not all of us have the same horizon).'

Back within the villa's walls, Romano and Enrica tell me that they now plan to turn part of the grand residence into holiday

Lia and Romano.

accommodation. A property of this size and age requires constant investment, they say. They already use the land to make organic olive oil, which they let me sample. I thank both them and our translator for their time and drive slowly out of this enchanted compound. I stop to look behind me as the gates slowly hide the villa from view.

The border had been imposed in a way that seemed blind to how humans lived in and around Gorizia. I was to discover that the blindness extended even to the dead. If you had been trying to illustrate the callousness of Cold War decision-making you could not have done better than to show people the frontier at Miren, where a 120-year-old cemetery was cut in two. The Iron Curtain literally bisected the limbs, torsos and skulls of corpses in their graves. Bricks in the ground still show where the fence once ran and bear the poignant legend 'Remember Me'. The border ploughed through the middle of, among others, the Faganeli family plots. Michael (died 1913) and Alojzija (died 1931) were left in Italy but Karlo (died 1904), Jozefa (died 1905) and Romano (died 1941) moved to Yugoslavia. Burial services for Milena and Vilja Faganeli, in 1972 and 1973, occurred with the Iron Curtain as a graveside attendee.

Meanwhile, round the back of Mount Sabotin, just north of Villa de Nordis, a different anomaly arose. Inhabitants of the village of Podsabotin had traditionally sold all their produce in Gorizia, and many had jobs there. But the village moved to Yugoslavia in 1947 and ended up stranded. Its residents could no longer visit Italian Gorizia, yet all the roads to the rest of Yugoslavia were left partly or completely in Italian territory. For almost a decade the villagers' only routes out lay either right over the top of Mount Sabotin or via an impossibly long detour which added several hours to the journey.

These revelations confused me. Romano's description of shootings at the border and people hurling their belongings and

*The Faganeli family plots at Miren cemetery. The former
border line is now marked in bricks.*

bodies into Countess Liduška's estate, the cruelty of the divided
cemetery, and the problems in Podsabotin did not really tally
with my long-held image of Yugoslavia as a friendly tourist destination for Western bargain-hunters, a happy-go-lucky purveyor
of communism-lite. What had the reality been?

To start with, in 1947 and the first part of 1948, Yugoslavia
was obediently Stalinist. Then Josip Broz Tito asserted himself,
making clear that he was not just a Kremlin pawn. He had risen
to power in his own right, having led Yugoslavians to liber-
ate their territory largely without Red Army assistance. He
enjoyed considerable domestic popularity and did not fear being
overthrown in a coup. Stalin and Tito soon clashed because of
the Yugoslav leader's lack of deference and Yugoslavia was ejected
from Cominform, then the main international body through
which the USSR controlled its satellites.

By the end of the 1940s the country was alone, allowing Tito
to pursue different policies from the ones Moscow permitted.
Quite quickly, he decided to allow certain aspects of the market

economy. Private entrepreneurs were able to run businesses with up to five employees. And Yugoslavia's relationship with the West also improved. Tito found ways to extract large amounts of money from Western countries despite having few raw materials to sell and without resorting to using his own citizens as bait for ransom demands. The West liked the fact that his country was an enemy of the Soviet Union and favoured it accordingly. Over time, tourists from richer nations would be lured by Yugoslavia's Adriatic resorts. And more than a million Yugoslavians (out of a population of twenty million) were allowed to leave and work in West Germany and elsewhere from where they sent money home (the complete opposite of East Germany's policy).[2]

The border with Italy stayed very tense at first after the break with Stalin, but this had more to do with the rawness of memories of the war than anything else. The first tentative sign of liberalization came in August 1950, when Italy and Yugoslavia opened a single crossing for a single day near Piazzale della Transalpina, a goodwill gesture to facilitate family reunions. Crowds far in excess of what had been expected made use of the concession. The Italian press reported that, despite it being a Sunday, Gorizia's shopkeepers opened for business, keen to capitalize on the trade they had been missing. 'They invaded Gorizia in search of bread and brooms,' a headline declared.

A more permanent relaxation took longer. Neither Italy nor Yugoslavia had formally ratified the border imposed in Paris in 1947 and this made progress difficult. Between 1952 and 1955 a series of small bilateral agreements addressed some of the new frontier's worst excesses. Most significantly, the *propustnica* system was introduced, allowing people living within 10 kilometres of the line to move freely across it. In effect, the local population could once again buy as much bread and as many brooms as they liked, so long as they persuaded customs officials these were for personal use.[3] (The commonest exports into Italy were fuel and meat, both hugely cheaper in Yugoslavia.)

Gradually the heat left the borderland, but a full resolution of all outstanding issues only came with the Treaty of Osimo in 1975. It was at this point that the people of Miren regained full use of their cemetery, which all moved into Yugoslavia. Simultaneously, the border moved a few metres in Italy's favour alongside the Transalpina railway line, allowing Italians to widen a key street in central Gorizia so that modern fire engines and lorries could use it.[4]

The treaty's biggest innovation was at Podsabotin. The *propustnica* system had made villagers' lives easier, because they could transit Italian territory to reach Nova Gorica, but this was still far from perfect. They had effectively spent the best part of three decades marooned on the wrong side of a mountain. In full and final resolution of the irregularity, Italy now gave Yugoslavia a narrow strip of mountainside so it could build a road to connect Podsabotin to the rest of the country.

The fix was both elegant and strange. It remains in use today, a little corridor of Slovenia threaded through Italy. On the ground it resembles a roofless tunnel bending round the mountain for a kilometre. The border markers at road level are counterintuitive because they do not mention that the territory on all sides is Italian. Literally only the road surface and concrete barriers belong to Slovenia, with even the bushes on the high verges belonging to Italy – as does the air above the tarmac. The two bridges built across the carriageway were exclusively for use by Italian border guards, preserving their access to the rest of the Italian side of the mountain. When complete these bridges and the slip roads leading to them were encased in mesh fencing and sealed with gates. But the fences are now rust-covered and the gates no longer locked. On the day I visited they were swaying back and forth in the breeze uncertain of what their purpose now was.

18

Nova Gorica, Slovenia, and Gorizia, Italy (II)

Nova Gorica, the town the Yugoslavians built around the railway station, monastery, cemetery and residential districts they gained from Italy in 1947, has its centre about a kilometre from Transalpina station and the Italian border. You sense the shift in cultures almost immediately as you walk from Gorizia. The architecture becomes modernist and functional; blocks of flats constructed at oblique angles to the road surrounded by communal lawns. The pavements on both sides are lined with busts of Slovenian and Yugoslavian heroes. Among them are two politicians who represented Slovene communities in the Italian parliament in the 1920s, when all this land belonged to Italy. The men had tried to protect Italian Slovenes from fascist persecution. But, by 1929, both of them – Engelbert Besednjak and Josip Vilfan – had had to go into self-imposed exile in Vienna. It was (and remains) a subtle reminder to Italian shoppers of the intolerance of their forebears.

Nova Gorica turns out to have had outsized importance in Tito's postwar plans. The Slovenian architect Edvard Ravnikar was employed to create an impressive new town from the oddments that Yugoslavia had been given. He applied the principles of Le Corbusier, under whom he had briefly studied. The explicit aim was to fashion a place that would 'shine across the border'.[1] Between 1947 and 1951 youth brigades were drafted in from across Yugoslavia and, even if Ravnikar's plan was never fully realized for lack of funds, they managed to build a number of

Two partisans sculpted by local artist Boris Kalin on the facade of Nova Gorica's municipal palace. They look directly into Italy with confrontational poses.

important buildings and to fix a street plan that remains to this day.

Nova Gorica's centrepiece is the municipal palace, completed in 1950. On its otherwise plain facade are four striking statues of male partisans, which, like the busts, deliver a provocative message. The two closest to the border look down the road to Italy, one freeing himself from manacles, presumably fascist Italian ones, and the other raising a fist at the old enemy. I imagine Tito personally signing off the design.

While in Nova Gorica I was meeting up with Mitja Primosig, an acquaintance of a British friend.[2] Mitja had suggested a lunch of *ćevapčići*, a dish popular throughout the former Yugoslavia and similar to kebab or kofta. We seat ourselves at a pavement restaurant and Mitja begins by lighting up a cigarette and ordering what, even without knowledge of Slovenian, I can tell is a lot of food. Mitja comes from Italy's Slovenian minority (*manjšina* in Slovenian; *minoranza* in Italian) and is a prominent lawyer over in Gorizia. Like others in the community, he has spent his life, both during and after the Cold War, travelling back and forth along the road linking Gorizia and Nova Gorica. Now in his early forties and with a passion for local history, he is also, like the men in the busts, an activist determined to preserve what remains of Slovene culture inside Italy.

The early years at the Cold War frontier were especially hard, Mitja says, and arguably hardest of all for Italian Slovenes. They had been cut off from the rest of their language group and lived in a place that both distrusted and resented them. By the time Mitja was a boy, the *propustnica* system was well established. It brought significant respite, allowing divided Slovenian families to keep in touch. 'We would come to Nova Gorica all the time with my mum. We came for parties and celebrations and shopping. Italians with no Slovene connections came to shop too but the link meant most to families like ours.' Mitja adds that one of the biggest draws today was completely illegal in Yugoslav times: 'Nova Gorica was once famous for its cheap meat and petrol but now it's famous for casinos. They cater to the Italian market because there are pretty much no casinos inside Italy.'

So, is the border now as domesticated and depoliticized as it seems? I ask, as Mitja lifts an intimidating helping of *ćevapčići* onto my plate.

'Fifteen years ago, when Slovenia first joined the European Union, the remaining physical border pretty much disappeared. That was a bright period. That was, "Wow!" Everything looked optimistic. The mayors of the two towns came to Piazzale della Transalpina and supervised the pulling up of the fence. [The then Italian Prime Minister Romano] Prodi came too, from Rome. And they put the signs there that say "Together in Europe" in the two langauges. But then in 2006 Gorizia got a new mayor and the local Italian authorities scaled back cross-border co-operation pretty radically. A lot of Gorizians now vote for right-wing parties, and one reason is that they don't want us Italian Slovenes to get anything.'

This comes as a surprise. The landscape and the sunshine

had deceived me with their beauty. Northerners often jump to conclusions about the happy, uncomplicated lives lived by people in the warm south. I realized I had just made that mistake. Mitja says that Slovenians and Italians are still carrying a lot of contested historical baggage. Slovenes remember persecution they suffered at the hands of Italians and perennially fear its return. Italians remember atrocities committed by Tito's wartime partisans and also, in some families, forced migration in the late 1940s and early 1950s out of former Italian communities on the Istrian and Dalmatian coasts. 'It is not going to explode into civil war at any moment,' Mitja says. But it does make for difficult local politics and wider cultural interactions. Anything that pleases Italians must of necessity be detrimental for Slovenes, and vice versa. 'There isn't enough trust.'

Naturally enough, Mitja knows best how this looks from the perspective of Italy's Slovenian minority. They still enjoy certain constitutional protections in Italy. Slovene is one of four official languages in the region of Friuli Venezia Giulia (the others being Italian, German and Friulian), meaning children in the *manjšina* may study at Slovenian language schools. There is state funding for cultural activities and, since Slovenia itself gained independence, there has been additional support from over the frontier. (Mitja says Slovenia was always the richest part of the old Yugoslavia, a legacy of Austro-Hungarian days when it fell under Vienna's wing. The average Slovenian is now 93 per cent as well off as the average Italian, and World Bank data shows that Slovenia's GDP per person in 2019 was the highest of any former socialist territory except Czechia.)[3]

But today's *manjšina* faces two big threats. The first is structural: the danger of creeping cultural assimilation. Mitja says over half of Gorizia's surnames are Slovene in origin but that the self-identifying community is much smaller. People marry Italians and raise their children as Italian speakers, or they leave to work elsewhere in Italy or Slovenia. Over time, the community erodes.

It is still useful for a shop worker or waiter or waitress in Gorizia to speak Slovene, to meet the needs of both locals and visitors from over the border, but keeping the language and culture alive is a constant struggle.

The second threat is newer: Italians reasserting their majority rights for the first time in decades. Before the end of the Second World War, Italy's policy in the area was openly nationalistic and discriminatory. Despite the time that has since elapsed, some Italians continue to see their manifest destiny as being the spread of Italian culture in these borderlands. As has become increasingly apparent, some have never stopped thinking of Slavs as lesser people, and a few would even like the frontier redrawn in Italy's favour. The wider populist shift in Italian politics has brought such voices to the fore and emboldened Italian chauvinists to speak their mind. 'It has slowly been getting worse,' Mitja says. 'And now the rise of nationalistic propaganda can be said to be a big problem.'

He brings up one of the *manjšina*'s major recent grievances, the erection of a statue to Gabriele d'Annunzio in the centre of nearby Trieste. 'That's a provocation plain and simple,' Mitja says. 'There is no other way of describing it.' D'Annunzio, a poet sometimes called 'Italy's Bard', has been a hero to Italian nationalists since 1919 when he led a citizen army into the disputed former Austro-Hungarian port of Rijeka (Fiume in Italian) and claimed it for Italy. After this conquest Rijeka remained Italian until the Second World War but it now forms part of Croatia. The poet pioneered a brand of muscular nationalism that soon became mainstream: to d'Annunzio is attributed the fascist salute, as well as prototypes of many other fascist policies and practices. His writings include deeply xenophobic descriptions of Slavic people. For instance, he once said of Italian Rijeka that it was to be a bulwark against a 'flood of Slav barbarians'.[4]

Mitja and other Slovenes, and Croats too, see the new statue as deeply insensitive. Its defenders argue that it mainly celebrates d'Annunzio's literary achievements; but the timing and location, on the centenary of the Rijeka invasion and in the Italian city closest to Rijeka today, suggest otherwise. Some Italians like to remember when Italy was more powerful than it is now, even if that time was associated with persecutions of minorities and ultimately crimes against humanity.

The frontier is not imminently at risk. Mitja admits that most local politicians continue to pay lip service to the need for some cross-community initiatives because it allows them to claim generous EU funding. (The EU has recently given them every incentive to continue in this mode by naming Nova Gorica and Gorizia the combined European City of Culture for 2025.) The Slovenian population of Gorizia has even received a boost recently as some young families have relocated from Nova Gorica, attracted by cheaper property prices. But Slovenes must be ever vigilant, Mitja continues. This echoed what I had heard from Miha Kovač, an academic and journalist, during a brief coffee I had with him when I passed through Ljubljana. He informed me that far-right populists in no fewer than three countries now laid claim to parts of Slovenia's territory (Italy, Austria and Hungary). 'The precedent President Putin has set is dangerous when you are a little place with a history like Slovenia's,' Miha had said.

Rival groups living in close proximity tend not to engage in open conflict all the time. Tensions ebb and flow and what causes the wind to change varies. It may take deliberate instigation to kick off a new bout of unrest, or it may be the accidental actions of a third party or a major global shock. From growing up in Northern Ireland I know it can often be pointless to try to find the original cause of fighting breaking out once more. Sometimes it is lost to history: the mythical butterfly flapping its wings.

The friction that has long existed between Slovenians and Italians is only one of many rivalries that fester on the territory of the old Yugoslavia and in its borderlands. The term 'balkanization', dating back to the early nineteenth century, was coined to describe how this part of the Ottoman Empire originally fragmented into myriad tiny, mutually hostile states. The state of Yugoslavia really did seem to solve all that, and at the end of the 1980s few would have predicted that it would go the same way, and so quickly – and no one foresaw that the process would be as deadly as it was. Yet the patchwork of Yugoslavia, which had been stitched together in Versailles and held together first by the Karađorđević monarchy and then by Tito, unravelled quickly into five, then six, and currently seven separate countries.

Why had it proved impossible to keep it united when there seemed to be so many advantages to togetherness? Why did the break-up cause 150,000 deaths and the displacement of four million people? The crucial turning point was Tito's death in 1980. Tito's great personal authority had been hugely important to Yugoslavia's continuing existence. He could balance the country's competing sectional interests and command respect and loyalty across different ethnic groups like no one else. Serbs had always dominated politics in Yugoslavia, while Slovenes had thrived in business. Meanwhile, Croats were consistently the most disadvantaged group relative to their size, but, Miha Kovač had told me, gradually even they won more autonomy and status. There were many years when life seemed good and unhappiness about the lot of one's own group did not rise above the level of kitchen and bar-room grumbling.

But Tito's successors stopped even trying to keep Serbian nationalism in check. As soon as the man was in his grave, the Serbs began to assert themselves more forcefully than ever. 'It can be said that the civil war really started much earlier than the 1990s, perhaps even in 1981,' Miha told me. He was referring to a set of spontaneous protests by ethnic Albanians in Serbia's Kosovo region. These had been violently suppressed by the Yugoslavian state, denying Kosovans' desire for cultural and political recognition and the alleviation of their poverty. Year by year, every other Yugoslav ethnicity discovered that Serbs wanted to dominate them too.

'It is important for Slovenes to remember, though many choose to forget,' Miha said, 'that our independence was not the realization of some thousand-year-old dream of Slovene nationhood. It was much more about doing what was necessary at the time. Yugoslavia was an accepted reality in Slovenia up to the mid-1980s. It was Milošević and Serb nationalism that made Slovenes determined to escape. Milošević fucked the whole thing. If anyone deserves a statue in Ljubljana or Zagreb, it's him. At what turned out to be the very final session of the federal Yugoslav parliament, which my father attended as an MP, Serb nationalists protested outside, shouting at their own MPs to throw away their headphones so everyone else would have to speak Serbian. That sort of thing was always destined to lead to collapse.'

Slovenia escaped lightly compared to other parts of the doomed federation. Miha told me how, in 1991, Slovenes simply voted in a referendum to activate a pre-existing clause in the Yugoslav constitution that allowed for secession. The Serb-dominated regime in Belgrade let them go without a major fight because it was already focused on bigger places it wanted to absorb into a new Greater Serbia – first Croatia and then Bosnia–Herzegovina.

Slovenes were largely spared the death camps and ethnic cleansing that other ethnic groups suffered, but they did see the war's effects at close hand. Intermarriage had been common in Yugoslavia. Many families now split, as their members returned to their own ethnic homelands to fight and sometimes die. One hundred thousand refugees came to the fledgling state. And Gorizia too was affected. Thousands of Croats and Bosnians fled to Italy, including across Piazzale della Transalpina and over Countess Liduška's walls.

*

The time had come for me to leave Gorizia–Nova Gorica and drive to Trieste. I had two brief stops to make as I headed for the coast.

In the hills just outside Gorizia I called at the hamlet of Piuma. From almost a kilometre away I could tell I had found the right place. Cars were parked on every spare bit of verge and loud pop music was blasting out over a wide distance. At the back of what looked like a community centre, the event Mitja had invited me to – the annual basketball competition he runs for Italian Slovenes – was in full swing. Teams of unbelievably tall young men were playing basketball while a DJ provided a running commentary over music. The crowd was mostly in their teens and twenties. There were picnics on the grass and, while some people were paying close attention to the sport, others were clearly there mainly for the drink, the chat, the flirting, and the *ćevapčići*.

The beer tent was doing a roaring trade, with Mitja himself manning the pumps. He was delighted I had come. 'We've broken our record for beer sales already,' he shouted over the din, pressing a glass into my hand. 'Thirty-three kegs emptied so far. This is the fifth year we've run the tournament and each year we break the record. The money raised will support our culture club for the rest of the season. But what is most important is it shows our young people how Slovenian culture can be cool and isn't just something for their

Mitja addresses spectators at the annual basketball tournament for members of the Slovenian minority in Gorizia.

grandparents. That's the only way we'll keep this community alive.'

My second stop, the Foiba di Basovizza, right back on the border, was much more sombre. *Foibe* are holes that riddle the limestone landscape in this part of Italy and Slovenia. They can be hugely wide and deep, and most are the result of thousands of years of erosion. Basovizza's *foiba* – a disused mineshaft – has, in the last century, become known as a mass grave. In recent years it has been ringed with monuments, as the most infamous of dozens of similar death pits. The dead in the holes, perhaps as many as 5,000 in all, are mostly Italians, all killed in the period between 1943 and the end of the Second World War.[5] Many are thought to have been thrown in alive. Their killers were sometimes members of Yugoslavia's partisan forces but sometimes just ordinary Slovenes from the immediate vicinity.

Foibe are the rawest and most gaping wounds that the local Italian community bears. To many, what happened here was nothing less than ethnic cleansing. Protestations to the contrary, from the old Yugoslav government and now from some local community groups, fall on deaf ears. Yes, there were fascists or Nazis among the dead, but many were just ordinary men murdered in an orgy of victor's revenge and score-settling.

I find an old man running a combined ticket kiosk and gift shop, but otherwise the site is empty. A macabre heaviness hangs in the air. It seems as if every police and military organization in the country has felt the need to erect a monument here. Almost all date from the last twenty years, their recentness a demonstration of the changing nature of Italian patriotism, and also a sign of one of the distorting effects of the Cold War. The uneasy relationship between Italy and Yugoslavia was the main reason why this and other *foibe* stayed in the shadows for so long. For decades Italy's national politicians neither mentioned nor

*The main monument at the site of the Foiba di Basovizza,
showing how the dead bodies were underpinned and overlaid
by the detritus of successive wars.*

visited Basovizza, fearing to offend Yugoslavia or destabilize the
Iron Curtain frontier.

Nowadays Italy's right-wing politicians are regular pilgrims
here. Visiting and venerating Basovizza are shortcuts to other
populist rallying cries: generalized patriotism, the raw deal
Italians have received from other nations, and also anti-elitism
because of the long period of silence mainstream politicians
maintained about the place. Not long before my own visit, the
right-wing politician Antonio Tajani had come on the National
Memorial Day of the Exiles and Foibe (a new annual public
holiday inaugurated in 2004). In a speech to an assembled
crowd, he used phrases including 'Long live Italian Istria!' and
'Long live Italian Dalmatia!'[6] This raised eyebrows across the
continent because neither place has been Italian since 1947 and

Tajani was president of the European Parliament at the time. He ended up having to deny that there was any inflammatory intent in what he had said, accusing his enemies of misinterpreting him and, implausibly, arguing that he had actually wanted to send a 'message of peace'.[7]

The message I was taking on to Trieste was a different one. Even in this most beautiful part of the world there was still hurt enough and hatred to last another hundred years. The Iron Curtain was only a visitor to this part of the world, the temporary nameplate on a much more enduring set of divisions.

19

Trieste, Italy

From Stettin to Trieste. That's how many of us were taught the Iron Curtain ran, but it was not the case and not how I had structured the trip. And yet here I finally was at Churchill's rhetorical conclusion to the Iron Curtain.

Much of Trieste still looks like a Habsburg city. It was the Austro-Hungarian Empire's greatest port. One local Cold War expert I spoke to, Giorgio Venturini, told me that for him the city was at heart still 'a museum of the Austro-Hungarian Empire'. Visitors sometimes complain of a certain stolidness, and it is true that Trieste's architecture can seem heavy and Mitteleuropean by comparison with other Italian cities. Its welcome is somewhat reserved too, as if the whole place has limited interest in outsiders. The cold wind, the Bora, arrives periodically without notice and makes the climate feel more northerly than Mediterranean.

On the evening I arrived, however, the air was balmy, and I sat in the soft dusk eating ice cream at Trieste's famous Caffè degli Specchi, the 'Café of Mirrors'. The square on which it stands, Piazza Unità d'Italia, would have made a momentous conclusion to the Iron Curtain. Its buildings – truly majestic – rear up on three sides, while the fourth side is the Adriatic Sea. It is easy to imagine the piazza becoming another great symbol of continental division, carrying barbed wire and chain-link fencing right to the water's edge and beyond.

In the event, however, the border was erected a few kilometres south of here. And just as postwar Trieste narrowly missed being physically marked by the Curtain, so the modern city seems to

Caffè degli Specchi on Piazza Unità d'Italia in Trieste. The three-sided square still feels like the Austro-Hungarian Empire's front door to the sea.

take little interest in what might have been. There is no Cold War museum here or at Lazaretto-Lazaret, the nearby coastal point where the border actually ended up. Instead, when the city looks back, it is to other parts of its history, and especially to its rich literary tradition: the talk is all of James Joyce, who wrote *A Portrait of the Artist as a Young Man* here and parts of *Dubliners* (and to whom a local shopkeeper compared me – my face not my writing, I hasten to add), of Italo Svevo, and latterly of Gabriele d'Annunzio. There is also a renewed focus on the Nazi occupation; the city's Risiera di San Sabba was the only Nazi death camp on Italian soil.

But in Cold War terms Trieste is more than just a memorable word on a former British prime minister's lips. Whether it likes it or not, it earned its place in the annals of that conflict the hard way. East and West did meet here, and they clashed. The Iron Curtain may never have ended in Trieste but it was one of the places where it began; a site of experimentation which for a number of years stood out as a daring anomaly in international politics.

In the 1947 postwar settlement that put a frontier through Gorizia, Trieste, which then contained 350,000 people, was also plucked from the jurisdiction of defeated Italy. Tito and Yugoslavia were waiting for it with open arms. But, instead, the four principal wartime victors decided to grant its people their own sovereignty (something they had never sought). The Free Territory of Trieste was born. It was a compromise – a rotten one, many said at the time – and it came about, like many rotten compromises, after months of bitter negotiating. It was to give the world a new chance to see in action one of the most eye-catching, star-crossed concepts of the last two centuries.

Free cities have their roots in the ancient independent and semi-independent city-states of the Greek and Roman Empires. They were revived in the Middle Ages at places like Augsburg, Bremen, Florence, Hamburg, Lübeck, Milan and Venice. Arrangements always differed slightly, but a defining feature was what might be termed the condition of privilege: privilege in trade and taxation, or in how a city's views were represented at an empire's centre; privilege in relation to service in the armed forces, and privilege before the law. In the benign conditions free cities often fostered, some great advances in world politics, culture and economics were made.

The Free City of Danzig, now Gdańsk, was Trieste's nearest and most notorious antecedent. 'They should beware of creating another danger spot in Europe,' the Polish delegate warned at the Paris conference.[1] He and others remembered how Danzig, a majority German city, had ended up marooned in Polish territory after the First World War. It was its own tiny statelet, obliged to pursue an independence that most of its population did not want. The rationale for this was understandable, giving Poland fair access to a major port. But the Danzig settlement left inhabitants especially vulnerable to Nazi ideology and the city's status became one of the big grievances on the road to the Second World War. The Free City of Danzig was only eighteen when it collapsed and was annexed by the Wehrmacht.

Trieste's free territory came into being in September 1947. Similar thinking led negotiators to agree to the idea. Trieste, a city with a majority Italian population, would in future have an almost entirely Yugoslavian hinterland, and both communities would need fair access to the port facilities. The terrain makes it easy for modern-day visitors to imagine a city-state. Ringed by mountains, the city descends steeply to two sweeping hemispheric bays. It could be the perfect miniature polity, and squinting at it through the sun I even saw echoes of the most celebrated city-state of all, Monaco.

Channeling Monaco, Trieste seen from the mountains can sometimes look like a natural city state. The reality was quite different.

But actually the Free Territory of Trieste was a much bigger, messier expanse of land, stretching 75 kilometres around the top of the Adriatic, from close to the Italian town of Monfalcone to the town of Novigrad, now in Croatia. It was the kind of thing only a committee could have designed, and problems were not long in revealing themselves. Trieste's 'freedom' turned out to be a textbook case of a solution that solved nothing. As I sat by the city's impressive Grand Canal with a double espresso, I acquainted myself with the violence that had accompanied the FTT's first days. People in every major political and ethnic camp were convinced it could not last, and many came onto the streets to show their dedication to its demise. Here, in the very centre, there had been rioting and a general strike, as residents feared lost connections to family, business and political affiliates in Italy and Yugoslavia. An eleven-year-old girl had been among the dead.[2]

The plan was to run Free Trieste as a single state. A governor would be appointed by the new United Nations Security Council with agreement from both Italy and Yugoslavia. A locally elected assembly was to add democratic credibility. Yet no governor was ever appointed – one side or other vetoed all twelve proposed candidates – and no assembly was ever elected, and in their absence the statelet became further divided in two.

The Free Territory was in fact only ever Zone A and Zone B. A temporary frontier, in effect the Iron Curtain, ran between them. Zone A, under American and British rule, was less than half the size of Zone B, which was controlled by Yugoslavia. But Zone A contained the entire city of Trieste and thus 80 per cent of the FTT's population. With borders everywhere you looked, including the natural border of the sea, the Free Territory felt anything but free.

Each zone developed in isolation, heavily influenced by its guarantors. The Yugoslav zone copied adjacent Yugoslavia. A one-party system emerged, with the Tito-backed Slovene-Italian Popular Front trouncing other parties at stage-managed local elections.[3] Customs controls with Yugoslavia quickly disappeared, while the supposedly meaningless internal division with Zone A got harder. A bespoke currency, the B lira (colloquially known as the *Jugolira* or Tito's lira) had been replaced by 1950 with Yugoslavia's own dinar.

In Zone A a British commander presided. Local police had an ex-Scotland Yard detective as their head, and their uniforms made them look like bobbies on the Adriatic beat. The A currency was the Italian lira throughout, and postage stamps were just Italian ones overprinted with the letters AMG–FTT (Allied Military Government – Free Territory of Trieste).[4] As early as 1948, after attempts to find a unifying governor ceased, Britain and the USA made clear that they saw Zone A's only viable future as reunification with Italy. Zone A's local politics were vibrant and plural in ways that Zone B's were not. Although the local councils had little real power, competition in Zone A elections was fierce. A bewildering array of parties and fronts blossomed. Reading about them reminded me of the alphabet soup of politics in civil war-era Barcelona, described in George Orwell's *Homage to Catalonia*. But, factionalism aside, there was no doubt that a large majority of the zone's citizens wanted it to stop existing so they could rejoin Italy.

Accounts by British and American servicemen mostly recall Trieste as an easy posting, except for occasional flare-ups of violence. The lifestyle was attractive and the workload usually light. With the seaside nearby, excellent coffee and wine, and numerous brothels, there was plenty to distract. A fair number of soldiers also describe meeting their future wives in the territory. Surviving photographs show light-hearted attempts to improve community relations: displays by army horsemen and dog handlers, even a troupe of US GIs who travelled round with a slapstick comedy act under the monicker 'Val-POLICE-lla'.

I got talking to a young Italian woman called Magenta. She told me that her grandfather Giovanni had been a teenager in Free Trieste's Zone A and had shared with her many stories from that time. He vividly remembered American servicemen handing out Coca-Cola to him and other children. 'The first time he saw it, he thought they were teasing him,' she told me. 'He thought it was petrol.' The British, as ever, offered tea to anyone who would have it. In the zone's early days, when food was in short supply, they prepared 'big, big vats' of the stuff, 'very milky and very sweet'.

As would later be the case at Gorizia–Nova Gorica, the frontier separating Zone A from Zone B was a speculator's dream. Here too, it was meat and cigarettes that people wanted from the Yugoslav side, while clothing and shoes were often smuggled the other way. Giovanni had told Magenta of being sent on trips for supplies. 'It was an intense process,' he'd recalled, not at all like moving round inside the boundaries of a single territory. 'You'd be stopped and searched by armed guards. They made a point of even searching the women's handbags, which at the time was very unusual.' Giovanni's sister used to hide extra meat in her bra, assuming – correctly – that guards would not breach this taboo. 'In the summer the long checks to get back into Zone A meant that by the time she reached home the meat was almost a bit cooked.' It was a time of adventure but even as a youngster Giovanni had been aware of a sense of real menace in the air.

The fate of the Free Territory of Trieste does not seem especially shocking now. Today's Italian-Slovenian border at Lazaretto-Lazaret is exactly the same as the old line that divided Zone A from Zone B. The *de facto* situation eventually turned into the permanent settlement. But the road to get there was perilous.

Tito had quickly arranged Zone B to his liking but continued to lay claim to all of Zone A. The British and the Americans had been open about wanting an Italian future for Zone A, but Italians in the zone and in Italy itself still wanted Zone B back. Wherever a new border was drawn, it was clear that some sizeable communities of Slavs and Italians would end up on what they felt was the wrong side of it.

Magenta surprised me by saying that Giovanni's uncle moved his entire family to Zone B soon after Free Trieste's establishment. He was an Italian but also a communist and 'thought it was the promised land'. While this was unusual, it was not unheard of. What was more typical, sadly, was the family's experience while in Yugoslav-controlled territory. He 'sold his house and packed everything up to move across . . . but after a year they came back like exiles because they were treated so badly. The Italian government had to put them up in temporary housing in Monfalcone.' Persecution of Slovene minorities inside Zone A occurred in these years too, even if the British and the Americans seem to have made greater attempts than Tito's forces to prevent it.

In the early 1950s Trieste city in Zone A saw increasingly frequent outbreaks of violence. These reached a crescendo in 1953 when two spells of unrest, in the spring and autumn, caused Britain and America to re-evaluate their involvement with the territory. 'The city resembled a battlefield,' the *Manchester Guardian* wrote in November 1953, 'with bands of demonstrators roaming the streets, wading through broken glass and wreckage, while British and American troops were drawn up at all trouble points. Grenades and rifle bursts rang out as the skirmishing ebbed and flowed.'[5] The main protagonists were Italian nationalists and neo-fascists demanding a faster path to reunification.

Piazza Unità d'Italia was actually where the Free Territory's death sentence was signed. In the November 1953 disturbances rioters invaded the square and started smashing up and burning the pavement furniture of Caffè degli Specchi and other restaurants. 'All over the square smouldered little bonfires of the remnants of café furniture,' according to the *Manchester Guardian* journalist. 'Demonstrators set fire to a police jeep and a grenade was thrown at another jeep, setting it on fire and injuring a policeman. The police then stormed out of the Government building and opened fire. One youth fell with a bullet in the head, and several others crumpled up wounded by bullets.'[6]

Some blamed the Western guarantors for their excessive response, but they in turn felt angry about the chaos. In short, they had had enough. Speaking to the House of Commons three days later, the British Foreign Secretary Anthony Eden warned Trieste's Italian community and its backers inside Italy that British public opinion resented 'being made the whipping boy' for problems that were not of its making. Britain, he said, was only 'trying to discharge an international responsibility at its own expense and without the slightest personal advantage to us at all'.[7]

Fresh talks were hastily arranged in London and, in 1954, Italy was obliged to trade away all claim to Zone B. This went against the prevailing orthodoxy. Neutral land, like Zone B, should not be allowed to become communist without a fight. The change would probably have been unthinkable had the Soviet Union been the occupying power. So this was the strongest sign yet that the West intended to treat Tito's regime differently. Within weeks the British and Americans had packed up and left for good.

This 1954 resolution, formalized in the Treaty of Osimo in 1975, still holds. As Jan Morris, who was stationed in Trieste after the war, described it in her book about the city, 'For a few years Trieste . . . entered the world's consciousness, as the Powers argued about what to do with it . . . Finally in 1954 the disconsolate and bewildered seaport was given its solution, and Trieste became what it has been ever since . . . Italian by sovereignty but in temperament more or less alone.'[8] The Free Territory experiment had lasted even less time than Gdańsk's – just seven years in all.

My conversation with Magenta confirmed to me that Free Trieste was not to be mourned: the violence, the chaos, the shortages, the gimcrack nature of it, and the sense of claustrophobia in what was effectively a partitioned corridor. It had had precious few supporters in its day, having been effectively stillborn. It was with some shock, therefore, that I rounded a corner on my second day in Trieste to see a series of windows at second-floor level hung with large posters saying 'Welcome to the Free Territory of Trieste' and 'USA & UK Come Back!' The old flag of the Free Territory was displayed as well, alongside the Union Jack and the Stars and Stripes.

I rang the bell of the offices where the posters were hanging but got no answer. After some more digging I discovered that a small band of vocal activists was indeed campaigning for a return of the structures of those difficult postwar years. More than that, they believed that Trieste's Free Territory status had never really ended. Because the 1947 agreement was not implemented in full, they argue that under international law the 1954 settlement and the 1975 treaty are null and void. In the logic of this movement, Triestinos have had their sovereignty stolen. The English language section of the TRIEST NGO website compares the territory's plight with that of other unrecognized national groupings, like Kurds and Uighurs. It speaks of 'a sovereign country right in the heart of Europe you've probably never heard about' (that bit is certainly true) and praises Trieste's diversity, food and 'solid work ethic'.[9]

Today's Free Trieste movement is a true oddity. Its policies are a mix of liberalism, populism and fantasy. It seeks to appeal to both the local Italian-speaking majority and the Slovene minority, and objects, understandably enough, to paying any tax to Rome. It wants a return of Trieste's free port privileges and ultimately the re-engagement of the United Nations, which would, as originally proposed, appoint the Free Territory's governor. The British and Americans might come back as peacekeepers if such a day came. In one of the few detailed examinations of the movement in English, the writer Tara Isabella Burton discovered in 2016 that a prominent leader was also a numerologist who has hinted that Trieste may be the location of the Holy Grail.[10]

Free Territory irredentists are yet to achieve a breakthrough at the polls. In city elections in 2016 two separate candidates mustered just 2,000 votes between them, or 2 per cent of the ballot. Nevertheless, the movement has featured in the thinking of some important people far from Trieste's unacknowledged borders. In particular, one Rishi Sunak, before becoming British Prime Minister, advocated for a fairer deal for Trieste in a report on post-Brexit Britain. 'The Free Port of Trieste occupies a unique position in the EU,' Sunak wrote, but 'due to its position in the single market, [it] still remains bound by many EU regulations.'[11] For him, this was a perfect example of

Brussels overreach, though many legal experts dispute whether the Trieste free port can really be said to exist in any meaningful sense today. The Free Triesters were delighted at the attention and have continued to feature the Sunak report prominently on their website.

Another interested party, perhaps more likely to make a difference in the future, is the Chinese government. In 2019 the Port of Trieste signed memoranda of understanding with Beijing under the auspices of the latter's controversial Belt and Road initiative.[12] Western diplomats worried aloud that Trieste might at some point fall under the sway of the world's greatest remaining communist power – where Josip Tito had failed, Xi Jinping might succeed. In reality, however, any Chinese annexation, economic or otherwise, remains a distant prospect, almost as unlikely as recreating the Free Territory.

And yet Trieste is already a place apart. As I sat in one of its high suburbs one lunchtime looking down on the centre, I felt the separateness almost palpably. This is a commonplace in writing about the city, and before my visit I had wanted to disprove it, but like many before me I was forced to acknowledge its truth. Just as with people, it can be quite powerful to be in the presence of a place that is making no effort to impress you or win you over. Sometimes, such aloofness can itself capture the heart.

20

Tirana and Sarandë, Albania

'My parents grew up watching Italian television but they could never hear what was being said,' Ervin told me as we sat side by side looking out onto the street in his front garden in central Sarandë, a seaside resort in southern Albania. 'Albanians knew exactly how to doctor television sets to receive the RAI signal from across the Adriatic. But they also knew that they had to watch with the sound absolutely off to avoid denunciation and prison.'

This was, he told me, quite normal back then, but only because of the extraordinary context in which people were living: the weird world of communist Albania.

'This part of Albania's coast, especially Butrint, is famous for mussels.' Ervin jumped to a new anecdote while I was still wondering how much sense a person could make of a muted television broadcasting in a foreign language. 'By law the mussels had to be exported to earn foreign currency for the government, so it was completely illegal for Albanians to eat them. Only once was my grandfather lucky enough to get hold of some. But the family had to enjoy them in absolute secrecy or else all of them could have gone to prison. That's right, Mum, isn't it?' he said, turning round for confirmation.

Ervin had struck up this conversation almost as soon as I arrived off the coach after a long journey from the capital, Tirana. Just twenty-two, he was a son in the family I was renting from. Unlike most young people, Albania's communist past intrigued him.

His mother sat above us, halfway up an outdoor staircase that led to the family's first-floor veranda. She rested some needle-work on her lap and lifted her eyes. To look at her she was a typical middle-aged Mediterranean woman in a loose-fitting black dress and with her hair cropped short. She nodded gravely. 'That's how it was,' she said, adding, 'Have you told him about the petrol scientists?'

Ervin smiled as he began his next story. At some point over the regime's five decades, the government decided to improve the productivity of Albania's oil wells. The country suffered constant fuel shortages and electricity blackouts, and the existing infrastructure, which had long been inadequate, was by this point collapsing. Engineers were despatched to Romania to discover the latest advances in oil extraction. They fulfilled their mission but when they returned and shared what they had learned they found themselves imprisoned. Another group went, and then another, each subsequently sent to jail. It was only after the authorities compared what all three groups said and confirmed that the messages were the same that the scientists were released and permitted to make the necessary changes. They had been treated as saboteurs until proven otherwise.

In winning their freedom back, Ervin said, 'they were really quite lucky'. I was learning that luck was a strange concept in communist Albania. People, whatever their position, took any crumbs of good fortune they could get and did not expect it to last.

The three-storey townhouse we are sitting outside is where Ervin grew up. Set just a couple of metres back from Sarandë's main street, it had been built by the Italian government in the 1930s. Sarandë lies close to Albania's land border with Greece and within sight of Corfu, which is less than 4 kilometres over the sea. It had been just a fishing village until the Italians occupied it and upgraded it to a port, renaming it Porto Edda after Mussolini's eldest daughter. The house was originally a distinguished residence for a fascist official.

Sarandë in southern Albania, within sight of Corfu, was a fishing village until Mussolini developed it into a port in the 1930s. Today it is a resort.

Ervin's grandfather was able to take up residence in it in later decades because he was a senior academic. It was very large by the standards of Albanian communism and allowed his entire extended family to live together in relative comfort under one roof, as they continue to today. Yet even they were never foolish enough to think they could get away with watching Italian television with the sound on, or openly eating black-market mussels. The complacency and stability that came to define elites in other European socialist countries never made it as far as Albania. From top to bottom the population lived in constant, existential uncertainty.

Ervin's great-uncle was one of thousands who were imprisoned on trumped-up charges. He was sent to Spaç, a gulag where inmates mined copper and pyrites on starvation rations. During her husband's decade-long incarceration, Ervin's great-aunt never visited him; she didn't dare, fearing guilt by association. Only his grandfather summoned the courage for a single trip. Ervin adds, after a pause, 'This wasn't the 1930s, you know. It was the 1980s. People in your country were watching *Back to the Future* and *The Terminator*.'

*

Communist Albania's creator and organizing intelligence was a man called Enver Hoxha. He had many accomplices in his forty years in power but trusted none of them, and ultimately no one was safe from his all-pervasive persecution complex. Albania's governing ideology looked fairly typical on paper. The priorities of self-sufficiency, obedience to the state, and constant readiness for attack were ones that many communist leaders pursued. But Hoxha's paranoia was unique in its fierceness and, during his unusually long time in power, it became the only thing that really mattered. *L'état, c'est moi!* Those words are at least as true of Hoxha as they ever were of Louis XIV.

Biographers think Hoxha first encountered Stalinism in the late 1930s. Having been ambivalent about left-wing politics, he seems to have had something of an epiphany and realized that the ideology was a perfect fit for his own personality and ambitions. He stuck with it to his final breath, long after the rest of the Eastern Bloc had lost interest in permanent upheaval and wasteful self-destruction.

Hoxha's youth was spent in Albania, France and Belgium. A feature seems to be that he was constantly underestimated by the people around him. A man who 'slept till noon, stayed up late at night and had no particular interests' was all that one Albanian friend of his from Paris could think to say about him. People in general thought him bland and mild-mannered. Even when in power, he was skilled at hiding his innumerable grudges, and thousands of comrades wrongly thought of him as a friend. That Paris acquaintance? He later served twenty-five years in jail.[1]

Prison and exile were norms of Albanian life to an extent unmatched anywhere else in Europe after the mid-1950s. Anyone might be locked up at a moment's notice, and the higher you went, the greater the risk. Just like Stalin, Hoxha delighted in knowing every detail of his associates' lives. He often took the lead in piecing together the improbable conspiracies that brought them down. In this way he got through six interior ministers, executing five, while the sixth only survived because Hoxha himself predeceased him. To wish the job of minister of interior on someone became a curse in everyday conversation. The most sensational fall of all was Mehmet Shehu's in 1981. Shehu, Albania's prime minister, met the same dark end as some of Stalin's close comrades in the 1930s, a death passed off as 'shameful suicide' when it was actually a Hoxha-ordered murder.[2]

I spent a large part of my week in Tirana getting to know Hoxha. He seems to be everywhere and nowhere in the Albanian capital today. The gigantic statue of him that once stood in Skanderbeg Square (a statue of North Korean proportions that dwarfed all structures round about) was toppled in 1991. His image more generally, which used to be ubiquitous on murals and posters, is now quite hard to find. Yet, the pyramid-shaped mausoleum built for him still rots slowly on the city's main boulevard, and his many publications are still on sale at every secondhand bookstall. The national gallery mainly consists of socialist realist works created under his rule. And when you engage Albanians in conversation, you soon realize that the memory of his domination lingers in many minds.

In the very centre of Tirana, the House of Leaves offers a frightening insight into the man's paranoia and the structures to which it gave rise. The building is a pretty terracotta mansion that once was a maternity hospital. Throughout Hoxha's time it was the headquarters of the surveillance department of the Sigurimi, Albania's secret police. It might legitimately be thought of as the museum of what Hoxha cared most about.

In tiny print on the walls of one room is a list of thousands of names of convicted political prisoners. In another, hundreds of tape recorders, cameras, and bugs lie abandoned, just a fraction of the communist state's secret eyes and ears. I learned that by the time the regime fell in the early 1990s, the Sigurimi had files on one million of the country's 2.8 million citizens, the majority of the adult population – a rate that even exceeded East Germany's Stasi.[3] Much of the material was collated here. In a third room a laboratory is preserved where every item of overseas correspondence was tested as it entered Albania, in case it included biological or chemical weapons. An insane apparatus of suspicion, decoupled from any real assessment of risk, blanketed the country for all Hoxha's time in charge.

The bunkers are an outworking of this too. One of the few facts to become quite well known about communist Albania is that it was the country with the most bunkers per head of population. There were perhaps as many as 750,000 in the end, more than one for every four inhabitants. These were another Hoxha insurance policy, conceived in the late 1960s and pursued rabidly for the next fifteen years.

Bunkers of every known variety were built in every kind of location: bunkers for Hoxha himself and his government, bunkers for the armed forces and the secret police, but also bunkers for the ordinary folk. Not all bunkers were created equal, however. There are significant doubts about whether the standard-issue mushroom-shaped bunkers that are still littered across the countryside would have provided any protection at all, even in the event of conventional attack.[4] (In this respect at least, I suppose, Albania was no outlier – plenty of countries provided pointless shelters for their citizens in the Cold War, if not in such quantities.)

An example of the typical mushroom-shaped bunkers that still litter the Albanian landscape.

During my stay I

visited a bunker right at the other end of the spectrum. The government's main underground headquarters, quarried deep in a hillside in suburban Tirana, is a masterpiece of the genre. Now known as Bunk'Art and open to the public, it was built between 1972 and 1978 with significant Chinese assistance. (All the oxygen purifying machines, for instance, bear instructions in Mandarin.) The complex is spread over five levels and has 106 offices. Compared to any other bunker I have visited, the dimensions are palatial.

Bunk'Art has two focal points: a double-height assembly hall which was intended as a temporary home for Hoxha's rubber-stamp parliament, and Enver and Nexhmije Hoxha's own living quarters. The Hoxha apartment exerts a magnetic draw for visitors, even if the leader himself only endured two drills down there and never stayed the night. If it would be wrong to judge him based on arrangements made for him in a bunker he scarcely used, somehow the sober wood-panelling and light-absorbing crimson fabric do fit with what we know more generally. There was precious little joy in Enver Hoxha's Albania, even at the very top.

Hoxha's time as a leader saw him and his country retreat ever deeper into solitude, like moles burrowing frantically from enemies they sensed but could not see. Albania began the postwar period with a coastline that abutted the new Iron Curtain. Corfu was almost a stone's throw away and Italy just across the Adriatic. There was also a land border with mainland Greece. But quite quickly the Albanian version of the Iron Curtain spread to encompass the entire frontier. From the late 1940s Albania was on a war footing with its principal neighbour, socialist Yugoslavia. Then, just over a decade later, it ended up with no European allies at all as Hoxha fell out with the Soviet Union and the rest of the Warsaw Pact. For decades Albania was the most isolated nation on Earth. It is still the only country to have boycotted four Olympic Games.[5] And Hoxha himself never left his territory after 1960. For years Tirana's international airport had just one flight in and out each week; there was no need for more.[6]

Hoxha's estrangement from other countries conformed to a pattern. Basically, when a regime abandoned Stalinism, Albania abandoned that regime. From Hoxha's perspective the USSR betrayed its greatest leader when Khrushchev gave his famous Secret Speech, admitting the excesses of his predecessor, in 1956. China similarly betrayed Mao in the late 1970s. Each ended up dropped. The break with China was particularly hard to stomach as it came after Hoxha had spent the previous decade running his own version of the Cultural Revolution, including fresh purges and bans on religion and beards.

As the nation's most celebrated author, Ismail Kadare, wrote in his 1985 novella *Agamemnon's Daughter*: 'We'd been friends with the Yugoslavs when they were ultra-orthodox, but we'd turned on them as soon as signs of a thaw came from Belgrade. We'd been allies of the Soviets during the worst period of Stalinist terror, but had turned our backs on them the moment they began to show a modicum of civilization. And it was the same old story with the Chinese. All other countries had ended up turning away from evil and obscurantism. But Albania remained their last bastion! We'd become the high priests of calamity and the shame of the universe. Was there any other country like ours?'[7]

Tirana contained the Hoxha regime's holy of holies, Blloku, which, although above ground, can be thought of as another bunker. The neighbourhood, whose name is short for *Blloku i Udhëheqësve* ('the Leaders' Block'), is a grid of streets about half a kilometre square, right in the heart of the capital. Today, people head there for a nice meal or to buy the latest shoes or clothes, and I stayed there myself during my time in the city. But under Hoxha it was a sealed compound inaccessible to all but a handful of Albanians; the paranoid heart of a paranoid country.

When he first came to power Hoxha might have preferred a Kremlin to live in. But since Tirana lacked one, he zoned off an entire district of the city centre and created his own Forbidden City. Daily life in Blloku was privileged by Albanian standards, but also dreadful. The only way to live there was to get promoted into the Politburo or a handful of other top positions. The standard way to leave was in a police van after being purged. Distrust flowed from the head of the regime to every corner of the land but it was at its most acute here, where Hoxha was most present.

Of an evening, the leader expected fellow Blloku residents to join him at a clubhouse where they had to watch him beat all-comers at billiards (apparently he was genuinely good so most people did not have to pretend to lose). Intermarriage within the community was the norm. As the murdered Mehmet Shehu would prove, it was dangerous to allow one's children to marry anyone from outside.[8] Shehu's fate was finally sealed when he allowed his son to marry a girlfriend from a non-Blloku family without first asking Enver's permission.[9] If it had not been for the constant witch-hunts, which led to new blood entering the Block, inbreeding might have been a problem.

Amid the modern-day bustle and advertising, it is a struggle now to imagine the old atmosphere, but I did notice a lot of coffee shops and private flats keeping caged birds, apparently an Albanian tradition.[10] Confined to their enclosed spaces, the birds seemed to divide their time between ignoring one another and fighting. Alliances formed as groups of birds launched attacks on individuals. The cages' fixtures and fittings, and the scenes that are often pinned up behind them, hinted at beautiful landscapes and exotic locations, but the reality was a kind of unending grim carnage. That, I think, was the essence of Hoxha's Blloku.

By communism's last years, the population was brutalized. Ismail Kadare said that 'it got to the point where you couldn't find Valium at the chemist'.[11] Another novelist, Fatos Kongoli, described citizens unable even to muster the energy to end their lives: '[She] was just as incapable of killing herself as I was,' the narrator of one of his novels says of a lover. 'But now she was going through a living death.'[12]

In 1990 the British photographer Martin Parr gained access to the country and created a collection of arresting images. They were among the first to show the world something of the truth. Communism was on its last legs but there was little sign of the hope that accompanied its decline elsewhere. A hair salon still had its picture of Stalin on the wall. The people look haunted, resigned to the endless continuation of their current conditions whether they were snapped working in an empty bread shop or drinking in a dilapidated communal dining room.[13] And there were no photographs of protesters because, even at that late date, there had been no protests of any kind. Hoxha had died in 1985 but he seemed still to be conducting his broken orchestra of a country from beyond the grave.

If there was one place where nostalgia for the communist past ought to be absent, I thought, surely it was Albania. A country where the 1980s felt more like the 1930s – where, as late as 1982, politicians banned the private ownership of chickens – what did any of its people have to thank their former overseers for?[14] But of course there is nostalgia for Hoxha. It is hard to explain rationally but in every other sense it is what I had come to expect. As humans, we seem hardwired both to miss and mis-remember the past.

At Bunk'Art, a room guide called Bledi was at first tight-lipped when I asked him for his views on the regime. But once he opened up a little, he insisted that 'Hoxha did some good' and said I should not believe everything I read in history books. Bledi name-checked literacy and the relative equality that the leader imposed across society as benefits of his rule. He also noted that there had been much less crime during Hoxha's reign. 'The clans were less powerful than ever before,' he said. 'Women could leave their husbands without being killed, which is an Albanian tradition that we now sadly have back again.'

I could understand the specific point Bledi was making. Hoxha's rule borrowed heavily from the tactics and ethics of Albania's clan culture, which he had grown up surrounded by. His endless settling of scores with both rivals and friends – even the hunting down of former primary school classmates in old age – was a form of vendetta.[15] But Hoxha was so powerful that no other clan could ever thrive with him in charge. Meanwhile, violence against women, whether absent or hidden under communism, is indeed a prominent part of contemporary Albania. In fact, it is entirely normalized. Around 50 per cent of Albanian women report having been physically attacked by men during their lives – and, just as worryingly, 50 per cent of women say that violence between a husband and wife is a private matter.[16]

Down in Sarandë twenty-two-year-old Ervin has no personal memories of the regime and no illusions about it either. 'People worked very hard under socialism,' he says, 'and they were basically unpaid. Maybe at some points they told themselves they were happy because they didn't see how people lived elsewhere.' But nostalgia today is at least as much about the fact that ordinary Albanians have not prospered as they hoped under capitalism, and also because of the scarring effect of the post-communist 1990s.

That first decade after communism was a truly terrible introduction to what Albanians had been missing out on. The nadir came in 1997, when a series of Ponzi schemes collapsed. These had lured perhaps as many as half the adult population into baseless investments. People did not just put their cash savings in. They mortgaged houses, shops, farms and livestock to get more money to 'invest'. When the schemes fell apart, the money disappeared, stolen by a lucky few whose names remain the subject of debate to this day. There followed a short period of chaotic violence that is sometimes called 'Albania's civil war' but was really more a spontaneous outpouring of anger and desperation.

I tentatively ask Ervin if his own family had been caught out by the pyramid schemes. 'My mother worked in a bank so she understood a bit more about money than most people. She was cautious to begin with, but in the end I think she too made a bet of about €3,000 in one scheme. She lost it all. Even now we don't know who got the money, but we know somebody did. A lot of people will never forget that disaster. They gambled and lost. You couldn't even gamble under communism, so probably they think somehow that was better.'

Lately the lot of the average Albanian has improved, but it is still far from good. After making itself a pariah for the best part of half a century, Albania has struggled to reconnect with the world. It has joined NATO and, in 2020, commenced official EU accession talks. But internationally reservations abound about its political culture and the character of Albanians themselves. These are partly rooted in reality and partly in prejudice. Across the continent, there is a widespread refusal to view Albanians as fully European, and this combines with internal corruption to hold the country back.

In Tirana and Sarandë I was often reminded of visits I had made to post-communist countries in the 1990s. In places like Prague, Warsaw and Kyiv I used to meet people, especially young people, who felt their efforts at self-advancement were doomed from the start. They saw themselves and those around them as backward compared to the rest of the continent, unskilled and unfashionable. They felt hemmed in by the poverty and old-fashioned thinking all around them, and by the deliberately restrictive visa requirements that other countries imposed on them. Of course, there are disaffected young people in every society but, on this trip, the first place I encountered them *en masse* was Albania. Even in Russia there seemed to be more variation in young people's levels of purpose and optimism.

One day, while I was having lunch in an absurd revolving restaurant on a mountain peak above Tirana, a young waiter told me of his dream to live in the UK. 'But it is hopeless,' he eventually sighed in fluent English (the result of four years' study at the University of Tirana). 'It will cost me more than £1,250 just to get a working visa for your country and I then will need to prove I have savings as well. My monthly pay here is €200 and most waiters down in the city earn €100–€150. This country is broken and we have to pay for everything – healthcare, education – even when it is supposed to be free. So, how will I ever get the money to leave? I can't. I am completely trapped.' As he talked to me he was standing on the restaurant's fixed stem. I was sitting on its revolving outer rim, and he had to keep slowly walking backwards to stay level with me. Our lives were on completely different tracks.

Smartphones and social media have made the world smaller, we are told. Certainly they have brought immediacy and accuracy to young Albanians' impressions of other cultures, particularly of what many still call 'the West'. In that sense at least Albanians are part of the global mainstream. But here, as in many other places, this brand of look-without-touching engagement with the wider world has toxic side-effects. The lifestyle these people seek can be viewed twenty-four hours a day but still remains out of reach – a recipe for envy and depression.

On my second evening in Sarandë Ervin offered to take me onto the roof and show me the sunset over the Adriatic. Sun spilled across the far horizon and from up there Corfu looked closer than ever. As the light changed, new parts of its landscape came into focus. It felt as if 'the West' was beckoning us.

Ervin told me that he was only back in Albania for a funeral, having emigrated a few years back to work in Italy. 'As an Albanian, it was very hard to get residency and a work permit for Italy,' Ervin said. 'I have to be honest: only the best-connected can do it. It isn't just that they fear poor people over there. It's hostility towards Albanians generally. The cannabis farms. The gangsters. We are Muslim so maybe we are terrorists too.' So far, that hostility has meant Ervin's brother has not been able to join him, though he would like to. He continues to juggle a job as a doctor with letting out rooms in the family home and working as an olive farmer.

'We are fast learners in Albania,' Ervin says. 'But the system is so corrupt and so broken. In the end we will have to help ourselves because you can't build a new system from the outside. Albanians will have to build it. But the change comes slowly and maybe it doesn't come at all. I know I should want to be here, making a difference for my people. But I am not sure I have the energy.' Ervin is describing what one expert has called 'the Albanian reality' and what the current prime minister, Edi Rama, once labelled Albania's 'contaminated life'.[17]

I saw no bunkers from Ervin's roof, but another Albanian phenomenon was in abundance. More than half the buildings between his house and the sea had twisted bits of metal sticking out of their roofs. These were the ragged iron ends of reinforced concrete slabs. It looked as if they would be there only temporarily until further storeys were added, so I asked Ervin if his family might soon lose their beautiful sea view and end up behind a wall of modern hotels and timeshare blocks.

'Sarandë has had a crazy few years,' he said. 'Even after communism ended we were very cut off down here, but then suddenly, in the 2000s, foreigners started coming in bigger and bigger numbers. We are very popular with people from Sweden, for some reason.' I had already noticed that most of the non-Albanians on the beach were Scandinavians broiling themselves in the 40-degree heat. In a harbour restaurant, I had seen an older Swedish woman arrive for lunch with a small dog zipped up in her handbag. In a mixture of Swedish and English, she had loudly demanded a table that the waiter could guarantee would be in shade for at least an hour.

'We do worry about losing our view,' Ervin said. 'One day it will happen because you can't own a view, at least not in Albania. But actually, you know, these bits of metal aren't what you think.'

Ervin described how owners habitually left metal sticking from their roofs in order to claim that their buildings were still under construction. In this way they could avoid property taxes. 'If anyone asks, they will point up and say they are in the process of making improvements.'

This explained why I had seen so many 'building sites' right across Albania. I think every petrol station I passed between Tirana and Sarandë had these metal ends, as had many apartment blocks and private houses. The symbolism was unavoidable. What appeared to be an economic boom was really tax evasion.

After the sun sank below the level of the sea, it left a red burn on the surface of the water. 'Enough about politics,' Ervin said. 'Tell me your favourite Premiership football team, please.' He opened another bottle of wine and turned up the music on his smartphone. The next song was by Queen. 'I Want to Break Free'.

21

Corfu, Greece

By nine o'clock the following morning I was out in the Corfu Channel on a small high-speed ferry racing towards Corfu Town. Along with half the other passengers, I was standing on deck to take in the breathtaking scenery. This narrow stretch of water, with mountainous terrain on each side, has beauty everywhere you look. People were taking pictures like their lives depended on it.

When halfway between Albania and Corfu, one can readily see how a homemade craft, or even a moderately strong swimmer, might get between the two countries in calm weather without much physical risk (certainly less than was incurred by Poles or East Germans who struck out for Bornholm). Some Albanians did make this journey during the communist era, but the Albanian authorities patrolled the coastal waters intensively and shut off much of the coastline from public access, which meant that numbers never rose above a tiny trickle. The escape route was actually more utilized in the terrible 1990s. A Scottish friend remembered being at a Corfu resort in about 1995 when a group of Albanian migrants clambered from the sea, fully clothed, and walked past her and her friends up the beach.

The Corfu Channel's midpoint was also the actual line of the Iron Curtain. As such, it played an important role in the early years of the East–West conflict. Somewhere under my ferry was the final resting place of parts of two British Royal Navy ships and some of their crew, who were targeted in one of the Cold War's first military altercations. The Corfu Channel Incident of

October 1946 caused international outrage before being largely forgotten. I had been surprised to discover the details of it just before starting my trip, and my surprise was now increased as I experienced the beauty of the place where the disaster unfolded.

Hoxha had been Britain's ally in the Second World War, but, like Stalin and Tito, then distanced himself from his Western friends. Aside from ideology, Albania was at odds with the UK over Greece. The Balkan neighbours disputed their land border, and the Albanians were supporting Greek communists in their insurgency against Athens. Britain was Greece's main backer, and the Corfu Channel frequently played host to Royal Navy patrol vessels.

The channel's ownership is still divided between Albania and Greece, without any international waters in between. For large vessels, like navy ships, the only safe navigable route lies through the middle, making it inevitable that they will cross in and out of both jurisdictions. Long-established maritime law deals with such scenarios, giving innocent ships the right of unhindered passage through this kind of shipping lane as much as any other. But in the first half of 1946 Albania began asserting greater control over the Corfu Channel and attempted to establish a rule that all non-Albanian ships should only use it with prior authorization.

In May 1946 two Royal Navy cruisers, HMS *Orion* and HMS *Superb*, sailed through without prior notification, and Albanian gun batteries on the coast fired at them. They escaped without harm but Britain protested about the attack. Tirana appeared to apologize, calling the incident 'regrettable'.[1] But only five months later, on the afternoon of 22 October, four more British warships were moving through, when one of them, HMS *Saumarez*, hit a mine. The explosion caused immediate damage to the ship's hull and started a fire in her fuel tank. Another vessel, HMS *Volage*, quickly closed in, hoping to offer assistance to the *Saumarez*, but she too struck a mine, blowing her bow off. In the space of just a few minutes thirty-nine British sailors were killed and a further five later died from their injuries.

Mines had been laid widely in the Second World War and postwar accidents were not uncommon. But Royal Navy mine-sweepers had swept the Corfu Channel twice in the preceding two years. The Admiralty in London felt confident that these deaths could only have been caused by newly laid Albanian mines. When they swept the channel a third time a few days after the attack they found twenty-two more mines, seeming to prove them right. Brandishing this evidence, London now pulled one of the newest levers in the postwar international system, referring Albania to the newly created International Court of Justice in The Hague. Britain claimed its ships had fallen victim to an unprovoked act of war. It wanted substantial damages from Hoxha's regime and compensation for the families of the dead sailors.

This time Hoxha responded with open defiance. He denied all involvement in mine-laying. Albania, he said, lacked the capability. In a telegram to the Secretary-General of the United Nations his government added that 'British warships entered our territorial waters in the vicinity of Sarandë . . . with the intention of attempting to provoke incidents and of violating the sovereignty of our country'. Albania wanted it both ways, saying the Royal Navy had got what it deserved but also that the Albanian state had had nothing to do with mines.

My first act in Corfu Town was to climb through the streets from the harbour to the British Cemetery. It lies in a secluded spot under dense tree cover. Even on a sweltering day, it looked and felt a little like England. Corfu was a British protectorate from 1815 until 1864, and most of the cemetery's older graves are in the High Victorian style. But right at the back there is an area for the dead of the Corfu Channel Incident: thirteen graves in all. The other victims, who were either lost at sea or buried elsewhere, are named on an adjacent memorial tablet. The ages, where known, range from eighteen to thirty-nine; young men blown up in their prime.

Three poppy wreaths were present. One had been laid just days before by Britain's ambassador to Greece. Almost hidden beneath them was a tender handwritten note with an original mid-century photograph pinned to it. The photo showed a handsome sailor in dress uniform. The note explained that he had been on one of the two ships not hit that day: 'Have long wanted to visit and pay our respects to those who died in the 1946 Corfu Incident. My father was onboard HMS *Mauritius*, locked in the magazine at action stations. He said it was the most terrifying experience of his naval career. He was lucky. He survived. Thank God. Otherwise myself and his granddaughter wouldn't be visiting today. WE WILL REMEMBER THEM.'

Later, when the temperature finally dropped, I sat on the beach looking towards the lights of Sarandë. I called up records of the Hague court case online. In the final ruling the judges decided that Albania had placed the mines in the channel. The

A note at the memorial to the Corfu Channel Incident, written by a survivor's child. Just visible are photographs of the sailor and his ship, HMS Mauritius.

country was ordered to pay damages and compensation totalling £840,000 (around £30 million today).

A key element in Britain's successful case had been the testimony of a Yugoslav defector, Lieutenant-Colonel Karel Kovacic. He said that, just days before the attack, his superiors had ordered him to load three Yugoslav naval vessels with mines. Kovacic further testified that an officer on board one vessel later told him they had laid the mines at the exact spot where the Royal Navy got hit. Albania and Yugoslavia were still close allies in 1946 and so the defector's story was credible. (Declassified Albanian files finally confirmed it decades later: a telegram from the Albanian Interior Minister to his Yugoslav counterpart on 24 October 1946, two days after the explosions, said Britain's ships had been hit by 'a mine within the zone mined by us'.[2])

Britain and Albania briefly set about negotiating a payment schedule for the damages, but since Albania was only prepared to pay a tiny fraction of the total the talks broke down. As retaliation London confiscated around two tonnes of Albanian gold, which it had rescued from Italian fascists.[3] The gold remained in the vaults of the Bank of England until 1996, when it was finally returned.[4]

The pro-Albanian version of the Corfu Channel Incident was taught to every Albanian schoolchild under Hoxha, and the denouement was always that Britain had stolen the nation's gold. But most impartial observers understood that the United Kingdom and specifically the forty-four dead sailors had been victims of a reckless and aggressive regime. For the West the incident was seen, along with the Berlin Blockade and the suppression of democracy across Central Europe, as evidence of the East's lawlessness and willingness to employ dirty tactics.

The truth was actually murkier. For three months in late 1948 and early 1949 correspondence ricocheted around Whitehall on the subject of whether or not to disclose the orders under which the four navy ships set sail that day. These orders were requested by the court in The Hague after a demand from Albania's legal counsel. He had hoped to prove that the UK was actually sailing with provocative intent. And, in fact, that was true.

When the Admiralty revealed its orders document, known as XCU, to the government's own lawyers, they instantly spotted that the UK's case was in jeopardy. According to Attorney General Sir Hartley Shawcross, document XCU showed 'a deliberate intention of trailing our coats' with the operation, meaning the navy had sailed with the explicit aim of eliciting a military response from Albania.[5] The purpose had been to see 'whether the Albanians had been "taught their lesson"' after the events in May. Shawcross wrote to the Foreign Secretary, Ernest Bevin, warning that because of the document the court 'may be compelled to reach the conclusion that we were deliberately committing an infringement of Albanian sovereignty in circumstances constituting an act of war'. Even if the moral high ground would remain on Britain's side – it was surely right to try to keep the Corfu Channel open, and the Albanian mines were weapons of the most indiscriminate kind – the assertion that the Royal Navy had sailed innocently would be disproved.

What happened next placed Britain squarely in the wrong. Rather than take its chances at The Hague, the government withheld XCU and pretended it didn't exist. Some senior people had expressed concern. The Solicitor General noted that the failure to disclose was 'a fraud' against the court and also that, if the truth were subsequently to come to light, it would 'profoundly shock public opinion'. But Prime Minister Clement Attlee decided concealment was the only option. As one of those involved put it, it was a case of 'my country right or wrong, my country'.

At the same time that UK lawyers were lying by omission to the International Court of Justice, British Intelligence was readying itself for a fresh operation against the Hoxha regime, one that would constitute a much more direct infringement of its sovereignty. Again Corfu was implicated. In the forests in the island's north there is an abandoned mansion, Castello Mimpeli. It was originally built for an Italian nobleman but went on to have many lives. Visited by kings and emperors in its early years, it became first a hospital and then a residence for a German commander in the Second World War. By the early 1950s it was the theatre for Corfu's first Club Mediterranean resort and later became a hotel in its own right.[6] But briefly, at the end of the 1940s, Castello Mimpeli was the headquarters for a top secret MI6–CIA plot to topple Enver Hoxha.

London and Washington's plan was to land trained guerrillas on the Albanian coast and guide them to pockets of domestic resistance, with the idea of ultimately launching an attack on Tirana. There were sound strategic and humanitarian reasons to attempt this. It was already becoming clear that Hoxha's regime was gruesome. Meanwhile, Greece's long-term safety seemed to be at risk. But it is hard to avoid the thought that, for Britain at least, revenge for the Corfu Channel Incident also played a big part in calculations.

The operation, called Operation Valuable, began in early 1949 when MI6 agents toured Albanian émigré communities in the Mediterranean.[7] They selected a group of hopefuls, who went to Malta for training. The men received instruction in weapons-handling, bomb-making and how to use radio transmitters, and then twenty were selected for the first wave of infiltration. They sailed across to Albania in two consignments, a week apart in October 1949, and ex-Royal Marines rowed them ashore.[8]

Castello Mimpeli now took over. Stuffed full of MI6 operatives and Albanian translators, Mimpeli was chosen for proximity to Albania. Concealed from view at ground level, it had upper storeys and a roof that were higher than the tree canopy. From up there Albania was clearly visible and radio transmitters could be used to send and receive messages across the strait. The man in charge at Mimpeli was Major the Honourable Alan Hare, who was just thirty years of age. He was a typical British spy of the day, the son of an earl, Eton and Oxford educated; he later became chairman of the *Financial Times*.[9]

Hare and his men listened for signals at prearranged times as soon as they knew the guerrillas had landed. The early detachments were supposed to survey the territory and make initial contact with internal resistance movements then radio back for instructions. Days passed in silence. Some men at Mimpeli were driven 'crazy by the anxiety and the waiting', particularly the translators, who feared for their brave fellow countrymen.[10] But Hare remained buoyant, at least to begin with, leading his men on day trips to the coast in between the designated radio slots. Together they swam and boated, and also went drinking in Corfu Town, all crammed into Hare's large Humber station wagon.

When the radio finally crackled to life it brought terrible news. Three of the first nine men had been killed by Albanian security forces within forty-eight hours. A fourth man absconded never to be seen again, while the surviving five met with no success. It appeared there was no organized resistance. People hated Hoxha's regime but they were already terrified of the Sigurimi and pessimistic about the prospects for change.

By the end of October another man had been killed, and Hare sent an order for the remainder to escape over the mountains to mainland Greece. All somehow managed it, but they were then detained by Greek border guards who, of course, treated them as enemies. Only with the greatest of difficulty did MI6 secure the men's release.[11] 'The Palace', which was MI6's nickname for Castello Mimpeli, was vacated, and officials in London and Washington retreated to lick their wounds while considering what to do next.

I found Mimpeli after an hour stumbling round Corfu's winding, potholed road network. Even the narrowest thoroughfares seemed endlessly to split into still narrower lanes and alleyways. The castle, which has lain empty for at least a decade, is not signposted, and most locals seem to have forgotten about it. Wire-mesh fencing and a padlocked modern gate secured the site, and, as in the 1940s, the mansion itself was invisible from outside. I was about to abandon the visit when I suddenly decided, for the first and only time on the trip, to trespass. I located a tear in the fencing and prised it open just enough to let me climb through. My heart beat faster and faster as I did this and I was reminded of something I have realized a few times through the years: that I would have made a terrible spy.

The Cold War is famous for its failed coup and assassination attempts, and Castello Mimpeli is a great place to contemplate them. The front garden has been defaced by illegal fly-tipping, while the rest of the grounds are returning to a state of wilder-ness. Despite my nerves, I made myself sit on the castle's front step and imagine those far-off days: Hare and his men coming over the brow of the hill in their Humber, refreshed by an

Castello Mimpeli, from whose crenellated roof MI6 operatives waited for news from their men in Albania. Later, it became a site for Club Med. holidays.

afternoon swim and newly hopeful of contact from over the water. Later, the sinking mood as the MI6 operatives realized they had despatched the guerrillas to their doom. As some have said, Operation Valuable may rightly be considered Britain's Bay of Pigs.[12]

The 1949 disaster was followed by further missteps each year between 1950 and 1953. The CIA took the lead in the subsequent operations but its efforts met with equally little success. It organized huge propaganda drops over Albania, but reports on the ground said the leaflets fell largely in deserted rural areas. It sent in scores more exiled Albanians, many of whom rapidly succumbed to arrest and death while the remainder continued to fail to find the anti-Hoxha underground that was supposedly hiding somewhere. In 1952 a promising internal resistance was finally located and America lavished more resources on the project, hoping that now it could foment a coup. It took more than a year for Washington to realize that it was being played by the Sigurimi. Every single member of the putative internal resistance was actually a government agent, and all the latest Albanians sent in from outside had already been executed, with perhaps as many as 300 being killed in total.

In spy organizations unsuccessful operations like this invariably give rise to talk of moles and double agents. From an early stage in the anti-Hoxha operations, some in MI6 and the CIA believed they had been compromised from inside. These worries crystallized and achieved legendary status when the former MI6 officer Kim Philby was unmasked as a Soviet double agent in the 1960s. The fact Philby had been in overall charge of MI6's Albanian efforts during the first ill-fated landings seemed conclusive proof. Philby himself even confirmed it in an interview he gave in East Germany.[13] It seemed that the Sigurimi had always been ready and waiting when guerrillas put ashore because Philby had tipped off Moscow and it had passed the message to Tirana.

The Philby conspiracy fits well with decaying Castello Mimpeli. The closed cast of characters there had been valiantly battling an evil foe. Their efforts had come to nought due to a traitor in their own ranks. Except that Philby managed to escape to his chosen country, it was *Tinker, Tailor, Soldier, Spy* in a warm climate.

But historians have recently challenged this neat explanation. Declassified archives have revealed that British and American plans constantly underestimated the strength of Hoxha's regime. Indeed, the two powers' entire strategy can be depicted as woefully simplistic. The Albanian guerrillas were always injected in tiny numbers, weeks and months apart. They had no clarity about who they were supposed to meet with or what they were supposed to do. During Operation Valuable, the radio equipment was so heavy and noisy to use that it was itself a threat to safety. The codes, meanwhile, were facile and left unchanged even after the first men were caught.

Philby may have tipped off the Eastern Bloc, but he was probably only one among many moles, and not even the most useful. In the refugee camps and other locations where Albanians were selected for training, the Sigurimi, the KGB and other communist intelligence agencies ran numerous agents. Whenever men departed a refugee camp without explanation it was simply assumed they were going to train to re-enter their homeland. Full details of their biographies, their families and home villages were sent to Tirana and barbaric countermeasures were taken. British intelligence officers who failed at Castello Mimpeli would have been wrong in later life if they believed they had been betrayed by just one bad apple. Arguably, the most significant factor in their betrayal was their own naïvety.

My Corfu host was Aristides, a short stocky architect in his fifties with thick wavy hair and a moustache. One evening I got talking to him about the early Cold War stories I had been pursuing on the island. He was particularly interested when I mentioned the evidence I had found of British ineffectiveness and duplicity. He revealed that he was a lifelong Communist Party member with a deep interest in Greece's twentieth-century history.

'The British were very bad here back in the 1940s,' he told me. 'You cannot trust them because they say only good things but then do bad things. That was what we found out. You tell me they were responsible for deaths in Albania. They were responsible for many deaths here too.'

Of all Europe's capitalist nations, Greece came closest to turning communist in the Cold War. In a civil war that killed well over 150,000, Greek communists battled with the state for three years during the late 1940s. At times it looked as if they might win but ultimately the Western-backed government prevailed. I knew the conflict had left the country deeply divided, but I had never talked to a Greek about it. From my subsequent conversations with Aristides I realized that, just as in my own homeland, many invisible wounds still fester close to the surface here.

'Tomorrow I will show you one very special place, if you would like,' Aristides said. 'My wife tells me I do too much for my guests but that is how I like it. Can you be ready at 8.30 a.m. and we will leave before it gets too hot?'

I asked where he wanted to take me. 'To another island,' he answered. Suppressing my curiosity, I said simply that I would be ready.

Aristides rapped on my bedroom door shortly after 7 a.m. the next day. He had made toasted cheese sandwiches and told me to hurry downstairs and eat them before they got cold. It seemed a strange breakfast when temperatures were set to soar over 40 degrees, but the toasties were delicious. As I munched them Aristides revealed a little more of his plan: 'I am going to take you to a place that is very holy to communists in Corfu, but first we need to hire a boat. I know a man and if we get to him before the tourists it will not be a problem.'

We were in my hire car before 8 o'clock. At the last minute, Aristides asked if he could bring his dog, Maya. Before I knew it, she had leaped through the passenger door and onto the back seat, where she sat in an alert position, panting with excitement, her tail thumping against the upholstery.

The resort Aristides took us to looked luxurious. We went round the side of the hotel straight onto the beach and walked along the shoreline between the sun-loungers and the sea. A few sunbathers were already in position and Maya ran among them, sniffing their novels, water bottles and towels.

At the beach's edge was a small jetty with boats moored at it and a man and woman sitting at an incongruous office desk. The man greeted Aristides and they immediately commenced theatrical negotiations in Greek. After a few minutes of backslapping, head-shaking and pursed lips, Aristides turned and asked me if I could afford €60 to hire a boat for two hours. I said I could and paid the money to the waiting woman, as the man fired up the boat's engine. We jumped aboard and he demonstrated how it operated. This took less than ninety seconds and no lifejackets were offered. By 8.25 a.m. we were at sea, with Aristides insisting that I gained experience of controlling the vessel while he navigated. Maya stood with her forepaws on the boat's edge and looked back towards home. Middle aged as I am, I suddenly saw the three of us as Tintin, Captain Haddock and Snowy in *The Black Island*.

Navigation was easy until we got close to our destination. It lay directly opposite the resort, perhaps a kilometre and a half away. Tiny and wooded and with a panoramic backdrop of Albanian mountains, it was picture-postcard perfect. Aristides shouted above the engine noise and introduced Lazaretto Island. Neither of us knew how to bring the boat alongside the tiny jetty but, after some violent zigzagging, we somehow managed to tie up and drop the anchor.

Trees cover the island except for a cleared avenue leading away from the jetty. Maya bounded ahead of us and dived into the undergrowth. 'She will now hunt for rabbits,' Aristides grinned. 'She will be happy for hours.' We walked behind and he explained to me that, as the name suggested, Lazaretto had once been Corfu's quarantine station. The Venetians built the first monastery and leprosarium here in the sixteenth century and the British later upgraded it. But during the Second World War the facilities were co-opted for a different purpose as occupying Italians turned Lazaretto into a concentration camp.

What Aristides wanted to show me dated from just after the war. Abruptly, we found ourselves in front of row upon row of white stone crosses, more than one hundred in total. Aristides came to a standstill and shook his head, overcome with emotion.

'These are comrades, mostly very young,' he said, echoing my own thoughts of a few days earlier at the British cemetery. 'They treated them so badly – no trial, no fairness – and they brought them here and shot them.'

We walked up and down the rows and Aristides told me the version of the executions that he knew. I have since been able to corroborate most of it from other sources. Islands like Corfu had long been favoured places for the Greek government to

Beautiful Lazaretto Island is a site of extrajudicial murder, evidence of how Greece was willing to do anything to rid itself of communism.

exile political enemies.[14] Exiles were easily monitored on an island and, if they escaped, there was more chance of catching them before they could get back to the mainland to rejoin their organizations. The practice was common during the civil war, and the prison in Corfu Town filled up with hundreds of communists and other fighters from across Greece. The regime was harsh. Torture, strict solitary confinement and summary execution were routinely used to control and punish inmates – if discipline broke down, if a prisoner refused to sign a forced confession, or even if the government suffered a bad defeat elsewhere in the country, or the number of prisoners grew too high, prisoners might be shot. Those executions took place on Lazaretto Island.

No prisoner who came to Lazaretto ever returned from it. A surviving letter I found from one who was killed there in May 1948, twenty-seven-year-old Giorgios Katsimichas, describes his last seconds before leaving the town prison: 'This moment that I'm writing to you they are taking me and other comrades for execution. Father and mother, I promise that I'll walk to the firing squad with my head high and a song on my lips. You should know that I will honour our family, our Immortal National Resistance, Greece, our People.'[15]

As Aristides and I stood there, imagining the men's final moments, I felt a chill despite the heat. 'So, did the British have a role in this?' I asked.

'Of course,' he replied. 'They had a very big, very bad role in the whole Greek civil war, and here too.'

Aristides said British generals in Athens sometimes ordered executions and more generally supported the Greek authorities in secretly disposing of opponents. In the case of Greek communists this was particularly treacherous because the communists had fought with Britain to defeat fascism. I have been unable to confirm the direct line connecting UK military officials to deaths on Lazaretto Island, but there is plentiful evidence of

Britain's broad support for state violence in Greece. As the first murmurs of civil war had rumbled back in 1944 and 1945, British troops had fought left-wing civilians in the streets of Athens, and knowingly oversaw the release of thousands of Nazi and fascist prisoners, who were armed and encouraged to go to work, by any means necessary, on supporters of the left. As the historian David Close has written, the 'terror [in Greece] was made possible only by British backing'.[16]

I followed Aristides as he walked beyond the gravestones to the remains of the Venetian monastery. It is a picturesque little ruin, especially when contrasted with the adjacent fascist-era barracks that more readily suggests a prison camp. But Aristides told me, 'This is where the firing squads stood to commit their murders, and this is where the men fell.' He pointed first at his feet and then up at the Venetian wall. 'It is exactly here that Corfu's communists gather each year to remember our dead.'

The memorial ceremonies are a relatively recent development. No members of the public were allowed on the island until 1978. 'Since then,' he explained, 'we come often and it is we who keep the land clear of weeds and who put the graves here, because they buried the men secretly all over the island without markings: 112 graves in total for all the men we know about, but many believe there were more than 200 people executed on Lazaretto overall.'

Aristides had been keeping one eye on his watch. He said we needed to make a move so as not to miss our return time, especially if I wanted to swim off the boat somewhere on the way. I told him I did not feel like swimming, so instead, as we departed, with Maya already fast asleep on the boat's floor, Aristides directed me to circle the island. Now I was able to confirm for myself how the execution site had been hidden from view. From the sea, the island still looked breathtakingly beautiful, but I now knew that it had a cursed heart.

*

Aristides, a lifelong communist, visits Lazaretto Island at least annually to remember his fallen comrades.

There was one more place I wanted to visit while on Corfu, though the mood of it now felt discordant. Perched on a rocky outcrop, with stunning views over the Corfu Channel and southern Albania, the Achilleion Palace was built in the nineteenth century as a summer residence for Austro-Hungary's Empress Sisi and was subsequently owned by Kaiser Wilhelm II. Unlike Castello Mimpeli or Lazaretto Island, it is firmly on today's tourist trail, at least partly thanks to the starring role it played in one of the East–West conflict's most famous byproducts: the Bond movies.

The Bond circus rolled into Corfu in September 1980 to make *For Your Eyes Only*, Roger Moore's fifth outing as 007. Large parts of the on-location scenes were shot on the island, with many places featuring as themselves while others served as bits of Spain and, ironically, Albania. The Achilleion Palace made two prominent appearances. First, on one of the palace's outdoor balconies Moore's oleaginous spy comforts a woman who may be an ally but equally may be a femme fatale. The mountains of Albania are just visible in this scene as a brushstroke on the horizon.

Secondly, in an evening scene, Bond attends the palace casino.

The Achilleion really was a casino at that point, and Bond wins big at cards while displaying a connoisseur's knowledge of local wine. He also meets a key contact. The Greek businessman Aris Kristatos appears to want to help Bond but subsequently turns out to be a double agent, working for the KGB and running a secret opium cartel out of Albania.

The plot twists and turns in trademark Bond ways. Major narrative developments are signposted quite poorly because viewers are not really meant to pay much attention to them. It is intentionally light, escapist fare. But when I rewatched *For Your Eyes Only* in preparation for the trip I found an unexpected, quite literal, hidden depth. The film begins with a British spy ship, the *St Georges*, being sunk by a mine off the Albanian coast. The ship had been pretending to trawl for fish, but inside Royal Navy sailors were hard at work spying on Albania. We see them and other crew members drowning, most of them unaware of what has caused the disaster. The mine that explodes looks old, the sinking nothing more than a freak accident, but eventually, in a scene set in Albania, Bond comes face to face with a stash of identical mines. The implication is clear. This was a deliberate, premeditated attack organized from Albania. In a surprisingly subtle way *For Your Eyes Only* was revisiting a forgotten part of the Western narrative of the early Cold War.

You can still live as luxuriously as Bond or one of his villains on Corfu today. There were plenty of monied travellers around during my visit and I was struck by the number of upmarket fur and leather shops that were doing a roaring trade despite the heat. But Corfu has not entirely escaped the effects of the global financial crisis of 2007 and 2008 which have so crushed the Greek mainland. A country laden with foreign debt, Greece has been forced by its European Union partners to pay back what it owes according to a savage payment schedule that stretches on for decades.

Aristides told me that the Communist Party of Greece (KKE) had grown in popularity since the crash, as one of a number of parties on the extremes of the left and right that have argued for a complete remaking of Greece's political and economic system, and a revolt against the supposedly immutable rules of global capitalism and Brussels. I myself saw more pro-communist graffiti and posters on Corfu than anywhere else on the trip, and, a few days after I left, the KKE consolidated its position by holding onto fifteen seats in the latest round of national parliamentary elections.

What particularly interested me was how Greeks had sometimes reached for Cold War analogies to explain their current situation. One of the most famous Greek commentators, who was also briefly finance minister in a government that tried to fight the EU and lost, is Yanis Varoufakis. In his 2017 memoir, *Adults in the Room*, he wrote that 'just as the Prague Spring had been smashed by Soviet tanks, in Athens hope would be crushed by the banks'.[17] Another Yanis, a shipyard worker in his fifties, told the Polish writer Witold Szabłowski at the start of the debt crisis that one of his heroes was Lech Wałęsa. 'He's a role model for us, for all Greeks fighting against dictatorship,' he said. 'He fought against a communist dictatorship, while we're fighting a capitalist one.'[18] Szabłowski thinks, but does not tell the man, that such analogies are problematic. I agree. Despite the cleverness of Varoufakis's rhyme, there is a world of difference between a tank and a bank.

The bigger point, however, is that any system of government can become discredited in the eyes of its citizens. The EU and Europe's large northern powers – France, Germany and the Netherlands – have no legitimacy for many Greeks because they imposed such harsh financial penalties on the country without considering the damage it would do. They had arguably acted as sherpas helping Greece up its mountain of debt in the first place but, once the country was at the summit, they abandoned it to get down by itself.

22

Gevgelija, North Macedonia

I left Corfu with the longest journey of the entire trip looming. By boat, two coaches and a plane I was headed to distant Azerbaijan, more than 2,500 kilometres away. I had stocked up on fresh spanakopita and other pastries at a bakery near the bus station in Corfu Town. I also made sure to enjoy all the fresh air I could while crossing back over the Corfu Channel.

In mainland Greece our coach then sped through semi-desert along the Egnatia motorway, a mega-project funded by a mixture of EU and Greek investment at a cost of more than €7 billion. It had been constructed to create better west–east links across Greece, as well as to complete an international route, the E90, that notionally runs from Lisbon to Turkey's border with Iraq (there are a few seas in the way). Sadly, the introduction of tolls in 2010 instantly rendered Egnatia a white elephant, shunned by locals and unable to pay for its own upkeep.[1] On the day I traversed it Egnatia was almost empty.

The coach was already nearing Thessaloniki when I noticed an email from a contact. He had been silent for months, but now he told me that it would be possible after all to visit a refugee camp 50 or so kilometres to the north, in Gevgelija, a frontier town in North Macedonia. I did not think for long before tearing up my itinerary and deciding to break my journey in Thessaloniki to make the detour to Gevgelija. I dashed off a hasty reply telling him I wanted to visit the camp the very next day.

*

It is no exaggeration to say that Greece and North Macedonia hate one another, both at the governmental level and, dispiritingly often, person to person. Greeks have long objected to what they see as their Slavic neighbours' appropriation of their national hero, Alexander the Great. They have even challenged Macedonians' right to use the terms 'Macedonia' and 'Macedonian'. For its part, North Macedonia has accused Greece of occupying large areas of its ancestral territory and attempting to eradicate its culture and frustrate its legitimate ambitions for statehood. These longstanding tensions colour all other dealings between the two and found a new volatile outlet during the migrant crisis of 2015, when the border town of Gevgelija ended up at the epicentre.

For much of the year, around 15,000 people a day were coming to the town from Greece, people who had already had to flee war, persecution and economic hardship in Africa, the Middle East and Afghanistan. As immigration policies hardened further north, more and more of them got stuck there. The government in Skopje's first response was to create refugee camps but it then decided to cordon off the frontier entirely. In late 2015 construction of a fence commenced. The express aim was to impede migrants' movement and effectively trap them inside Greece, with the exception of a fortunate few who would continue to be allowed north after official border checks.

The new high fence was comprehensible in narrow national policy terms but attracted shock around the world. It was far bigger than anything that had separated Greece and North Macedonia when the latter was part of Yugoslavia in the Cold War. At 3 metres high it was almost as tall as the Berlin Wall. And with its razor-wire top it became one of the main interventions that humanitarians pointed to as evidence of Europe's hardheartedness and internal division in the face of global suffering. Born out of circumstances that were of neither country's making, it seemed to suit all too well the general tenor of their fractious relationship.

I discovered that there was a dearth of public transport between Greece and North Macedonia. Consequently, I spent several hours in Thessaloniki, carting my bags through the muggy overcast streets, trying to work out how to get to Gevgelija. I eventually found a North Macedonian bus company's booking desk at the railway station just before its only evening bus departed, but the woman behind the desk immediately told me I had no chance of getting to Gevgelija that night. According to the regulations, she said, I would first need to purchase an 'intention to travel' at least a day before the day I wanted to leave. The only way to get a return ticket, she further advised, was to call a number in Skopje and reserve a seat on a specific future service. She could not help with the return leg at all and, she said, the Skopje office had most likely closed for the day.

I was reminded of the procedures in USSR shops, where shoppers first obtained a chit for the goods they wanted to buy, then carried the chit to a cashier and paid their bill, receiving a verification stamp in return, and only then went back to the original seller to get their goods. As I purchased my 'intention to travel', which generated paperwork in triplicate, I imagined my name landing in several civil servants' inboxes at once, on both sides of the border. However, the convoluted system worked and early next morning I found myself with just seven other passengers lurching out of the city.

We reached the border in under an hour. The driver announced through his microphone that we should ready our passports. He then gathered them in and took them over to a window. Everything outside seemed calm, with just a handful of cars queuing. But North Macedonia is in neither the EU nor Schengen, and there is little trust between it and Greece, so we all knew that the checkpoint was real, that the border measures were more than just formalities.

I subsequently discovered that seven of the eight of us onboard, and the driver, had mostly been thinking about the eighth passenger. He was a black man, in his early thirties, well dressed in smart trousers and a business shirt. In London or Berlin or dozens of other places he would just have been a regular commuter. But here, in a famous corridor for migrants and a place famously hostile towards them, we had all been wondering how he would fare.

A few moments later the driver returned and beckoned matter-of-factly for the man to leave the bus. He got up equally matter-of-factly and went. For ten minutes or so we were all silent, still separate from one another but now clearly focused on the same unfolding event. The man initially leaned in to the border guard's window to answer questions, but then he was left to just pace up and down, a couple of paces in one direction, a couple of paces in the other, while someone invisible decided his fate.

After ten minutes our driver made a loud sigh and got out to stand beside his bus and smoke. Somehow it served as the signal for us passengers to start speaking to one another, standing up in the aisle and hanging over the back of the seats, talking in a combination of English, Greek and Macedonian. Our sympathies were with our fellow passenger. We could not be sure who he was, of course, but we all felt he was probably just an ordinary traveller suffering for the colour of his skin.

It turned out that we were playing a very old drama. In some form or other it is as old as borders themselves. We were the privileged bystanders, watching safe but powerless as another human being experienced the full might of a frontier. As the scene unfolded we would be tempted to allow our attitude towards the man to harden. The bus driver had been here many times before and defaulted to suspicion and impatience, but we would take longer to recognize the role written for us. As ten minutes turned to thirty and then an hour some gradually lost interest in the man's plight. Our bus could not advance until the guards decided what to do with him. If he was cleared, he could rejoin us; if he was detained, his luggage would be removed. As we approached the ninety-minute mark, a few people's plans for the day – mostly appointments in Skopje – were falling apart. The poor man continued standing at the window, utterly alone. The mood on the bus had tipped towards a swift solution of any kind.

We had been delayed for just short of two hours, and the sun was now high overhead, when the man was led through a door into the checkpoint building. A guard jogged over to our driver and spoke briefly. The driver hit both hands on the steering wheel, which seemed to signal a combination of 'I knew it' and 'Let's get out of here', and leaped down to pull the man's baggage from the hold. The guard took the bags and we drove off with a mighty roar. The driver then switched on his intercom and shared the denouement with us – or as much of it as any of us would ever learn. 'Fake passport,' he said in English after some words in Greek. 'He is now arrested.'

The difficulties of the world's oppressed are often experienced out of sight of the world's privileged. We are asked to help by charities, by churches, occasionally by governments. Sometimes we can help, sometimes we can't; and sometimes we do help, but sometimes we don't. The sheer number of causes and individuals has been said to give rise to 'compassion fatigue'. What the bus journey to Gevgelija reminded me of was that even when a person is visibly suffering very nearby, people's thoughts often spring back quickly to their own, lesser concerns.

Gevgelija is just a kilometre from the border, a dusty place that currently lives on the risks some people in Greece are willing to take there. One set of risk-takers came after the collapse of

Yugoslavia to stake money at the town's casinos – the Flamingo and the Princess – which are located, just as in Nova Gorica, within sight of the checkpoints. The other set has staked every-thing to get across the border in the hope of a better, safer life elsewhere, often in Germany, Sweden or the UK. Gevgelija serves both and, whatever it thinks of them, has become reliant on the money and work they bring.

My contact had again gone strangely silent but I walked up to the entrance of the refugee camp without difficulty. It lay halfway between the town and the border, beside a dry riverbed. The huge wire fence shimmered in the glare not far off and an armed security guard at the camp entrance politely confirmed what I already suspected: I had no chance of getting inside with-out official permission and a person to meet me. I showed him my contact's name but he just shrugged.

I slunk back to the room I had rented, wondering if I should just give up. My host once again came to the rescue. The kind, well-connected stranger is a cliché of travel writing, but, as you have seen, it was frequently my experience on this journey. Of course, on that day it was not me but the man I had left behind at the checkpoint who really deserved the kindness of strangers. Baki, a healthcare lawyer, rented out his spare room as a second source of income. He was drinking white wine in his yard at the end of the working day when we got into conversation. He said he thought a cousin still worked at the camp and then texted him to ask if we could speak about his job. The cousin, Boban, replied immediately and together they thrashed out a plan for the following day.

Next morning, I cleared some admittedly irksome bureaucratic hoops with the consummate ease of a white man with a Western European passport. In a scuffed local police station I learned that I would first need permission to visit the camp from the Ministry of Internal Affairs in Skopje. The officer wrote down an email address. I imagined how long it might take to get equivalent clearance from the Home Office to visit asylum accommodation in the UK, but my North Macedonian permission came through in just forty minutes. I then returned to the station, and the police officer signed and handed me a letter with my name on it. I took a taxi to the refugee administration office, which was in a repurposed shop in the centre of Gevgelija. Here a man balancing a cigarette between his lips automatically banged my letter with an official stamp. On the wall behind him I noticed a map showing the line of the border and the camp marked in thick red felt-tip pen.

Boban and I finally met just inside the refugee-camp gate and he gripped my hand vigorously with both of his. He was athletic, in his mid-twenties, and, as I soon understood, had been willing to show me round his unusual workplace not just as a favour to his cousin but because he was genuinely proud of it. Boban had worked at the camp for four years at this point and had risen to be head of facilities management and logistics.

He told me that for months back in 2015 the number of migrants only ever seemed to rise, briefly reaching 20,000 a day. The North Macedonian government had its reasons (some questionable and some not) for locating the camp so close to Greece, but Boban said he and his colleagues always understood that their duty was to do the best they could by the people who came under their care.

The place looks spotless and orderly in the unforgiving desert light. Tents and prefabricated huts line 'streets' paved with shiny aluminium duckboards. The governments and NGOs that paid for various amenities all have their contributions prominently recognized with flags or logos on stickers: the UN, the EU, NATO, the North Macedonian, Danish, French and German governments, and the UK's Department for International Development, has each done something, a fact they want to be visible to the refugees.

'How many people are here in the camp today?' I asked.

'Just twenty-four,' Boban said. 'They are all waiting for asylum decisions. They are families with young children, or invalids, or very old people. The authorities send everyone else back to Greece these days. But if the people here succeed, they will next move to a camp in Skopje, and they will then have the right to work more or less as a normal citizen.'

I asked if many people still made it across the border without going through the official crossing. Or had the fence stopped that?

'It is nowhere near as many people as before but we still get sixty or seventy people coming through each day. But recently it has become easier for the border guards to catch them because the EU paid for some heat-seeking vans.'

I went to a tent where one group of the day's new arrivals was being processed. There were maybe forty in all. Most were young or middle-aged men, sat in little groups around white plastic garden tables. I spoke briefly to one young man who said he had come from Afghanistan but had already been living in a camp on a Greek island for three years. What did he think would happen next? 'They will send me back to Greece,' he said without malice. 'It will be my third time.'

Boban confirmed that the camp saw a lot of familiar faces these days: 'The flow used to be north, north, north, so it was always new people. Often it was hard to persuade the sick to stay long enough to get treated. They were all in a rush. But now this is the end of the road unless they get through without the authorities finding them or they qualify for asylum because they have children or are old. Maybe later today, maybe tomorrow, our police will put all these men back through the holes in the border fence, back into Greece. The police will try to mend the holes while they are there, but new holes will be made soon.'

This apparent calm predictability cannot be relied upon of course, because the people involved are desperate. In the past there have been spontaneous battles along the railway line at Gevgelija when large numbers of refugees tried to get into North Macedonia and ended up clashing with riot police determined to keep them out. The camps in Greece are still full of people; they still want to reach other parts of Europe.[2]

Boban next showed me the camp's nursery, school and football pitch. We ended up in a large parking lot that I estimated was about half as big as the camp itself. 'This is the graveyard for the cars and vans we seize from Macedonian people-smugglers,' he told me. 'Often people who cut their way through the fence have paid money to North Macedonians to meet them and drive them at high speed up to Serbia. When police catch a smuggler they take away his car and maybe fine him, but it doesn't stop the problem.'

I told Boban about the man on my bus from Thessaloniki. If, as our driver had said, he was an asylum seeker with fake documents, what would happen to him? Boban said that, unless the man was wanted in connection with some crime, he would be taken back to Thessaloniki or somewhere else in Greece and would probably immediately begin trying to escape again. Of course any false papers he had would be confiscated. He might have lost hundreds or even thousands of Euros that morning. But he would most likely gamble with anything he had left and

The entrance to Gevgelija refugee camp.

try to keep moving forward because he would not see moving back as an option.

Later that day, at the border by the North Macedonian barriers, I caught a coach that took me all the way to Istanbul: a twelve-hour journey. As I travelled I reflected on my time at the camp. I was newly aware of my enormous privilege and freedom, and of how they had assisted me each step of the way on this trip: my race, my passport, my contacts all helped, as did having enough money to change my plans at short notice.

Gaining legal refugee status mostly means breaking laws, paying middlemen, and evading capture on numerous occasions – and that refugee status in itself does not necessarily bring the hoped-for dividends. Only the luckiest are able to insert themselves into Europe's story in the way that tens of millions of people dream of doing. Many poor souls never reach a safe country of their choosing, a country where they already have relatives or a community that speaks their language and shares their culture. It was a hard, hard life, and each person living it also carried with them their own grave memories of why they risked everything in the first place and what they had lost in the process.

It is impossible to weight the relative hardships of recent escapees from Afghanistan, Syria and sub-Saharan Africa and those experienced by people escaping from the Eastern Bloc before 1990. But two observations strike me as true.

The first is that mercy has not had the same geopolitical value for recent arrivals in Europe as it did in the past. While there are strong ethical arguments for showing mercy to today's non-European migrants – of course – it does not contribute to any European government's wider strategic aims. In the Cold War, escapees to the West were a powerful proof of the East's authoritarianism and democratic illegitimacy. In that sense they were useful to the countries receiving them, but not now.

My second observation is that Europe's frontiers developed a false sense of permanence in the years after the Yugoslav wars, leading many Europeans to the conclusion that their continent would never again generate its own refugees. But we must be honest with ourselves and admit that the groundwork for new persecution inside Europe was laid under our noses in the 2010s, even as many of us chose to ignore or downplay it. Should migrant numbers surge once more, whether or not those migrants are internally displaced within our continent, we will need to be ready to respond with more compassion and at greater scale than many countries did after 2015.

At dusk I saw the mountains of Bulgaria from the coach. Then it grew dark and I fell asleep. In the middle of the night our concierge moved through and gently woke each of us with a touch to the shoulder. He told us to get ready to queue at the frontier between Greece and Turkey. We left the bus and carried our luggage through the border checkpoints, still half asleep. The coach then moved on and we closed our eyes again. A few hours later I was woken by the same gentle nudge. We were approaching Hagia Sophia in central Istanbul, the point where I disembarked.

After a listless day of carting my luggage and myself from café to café, I boarded a flight to Azerbaijan. I was now headed to my southernmost destination, Nakhchivan province, the last point where the Soviet Union or any other Warsaw Pact nation had a land border with NATO. Very little is known about Nakhchivan and very few travellers go there. It is not even connected by land to the rest of Azerbaijan, and Iran forms its southern border. It would turn out to be the most unsettling place I visited.

23

Nakhchivan, Azerbaijan

At Nakhchivan Airport I took a taxi to the city centre. Once again I was arriving in a place much too early to check into my hotel, but the night porter agreed to keep my bags so I could take a dawn walk.

I strolled up a big wide avenue and down another, uncertain of my bearings. Both streets were empty, with just the occasional car and a solitary empty bus passing through. The road surface and pavements were absolutely spotless. I watched an old woman bend over the steps of a nearby office building and sweep up every last bit of a pile of sandy dust.

There was a tall tower on a hill by the roadside. When I got to it, it turned out to be Noah's Tomb, one of several reputed burial sites for the patriarch and the one closest to Mount Ararat where his Ark came to rest. Some think the word 'Nakhchivan' originally means 'first resting place', in reference to the flood story. Up close it became clear, however, that most of this tomb dated from long after the deluge and was either brand new or had been the recipient of vicious restoration. But the view was breathtaking. Laid out before me, starting about two kilometres away and stretching as far as I could see, was Iran, vast and seemingly full of potential in the morning light.

I headed back to the hotel for a nap. It was still very quiet all around, almost eerily so since it was now 7.30 a.m. When was rush hour? Where were the traders readying their kiosks and shops for the day ahead? Where was everyone?

*

Noah's Tomb has eighth-century foundations but they are hard to see beneath recent additions. Iran is nearby and Mount Ararat in Turkey is also visible.

Nakhchivan has been an autonomous republic in various forms for the best part of a century, but its autonomy has almost always been strictly limited. After the 1917 revolution, the Russian Empire's old Nakhichevan County passed between Armenian, Azerbaijani, Ottoman and British control before being permanently subsumed into the USSR in 1920. It was the Soviets who first gave Nakhchivan autonomy, the titular form of autonomy they specialized in, which in this case meant subordination first to Baku and then to the Kremlin.

In post-Soviet times Nakhchivan's autonomous status was preserved in the newly independent state of Azerbaijan. In one sense, this was recognition of reality. Nakhchivan is geographically separate from the main landmass of Azerbaijan. A finger of Armenian territory runs down to the Iranian border and severs all land routes between the two parts of the country, making Nakhchivan the world's largest landlocked exclave. Peripheral, semi-independent and small – Nakhchivan is about the same size as the English county of Norfolk, with a population of just under 500,000 – the republic is nevertheless disproportionately important to Azeri national identity and especially to the current ruling regime in Baku.

I woke around midday feeling groggy, and ventured back into the city centre, looking for strong coffee. No sooner was I on the street again than I began to feel genuinely unnerved. Before me was a city that was still mostly empty. Yes, there was a little more traffic on the roads but the pavements were still deserted. And there were almost no shops. When I finally located an outdoor tearoom in a pretty park, it was catering to just a handful of men in business attire sitting in huddles and talking in hushed voices.

The waiters in the tearoom were as polite as could be, and the Turkish coffee they brought me was delicious. But the plot of John Wyndham's novel *The Midwich Cuckoos* popped into my head as I sipped the bittersweet liquid, and it kept returning to me in the days ahead as I encountered more of Nakhchivan's subdued inhabitants and desolate streetscapes: no graffiti, no stray dogs; no washing hung out to dry; a surfeit of unused amenities – from public chess sets to dainty boating lakes. I have since read that travel agencies specializing in out-of-the-way destinations sometimes call Nakhchivan 'the Caucasian Switzerland' because of its unexpected neatness and order (and the mountains, of course).[1] In the baking heat, and with so many new buildings, it actually reminded me more of high-end places in California, like Pasadena. But it is a very long way from either Pasadena or Zürich, and in a part of the world that is more famous for its hustle and bustle, for bazaars and vibrant street life. Why was Nakhchivan so different?

Nakhchivan is the birthplace of today's Azerbaijan. I only realized this after spending a couple of hours in the city's main square. Here, amid sprinkler-fed gardens, is a massive pink granite statue

*A pristine and empty chess pavilion and a pristine and empty
street sum up Nakhchivan's strange public realm.*

of Azerbaijan's leader after 1993, Heydar Aliyev. Aliyev was
born in Nakhchivan in 1923 and rose to become First Deputy
Premier of the Soviet Union, an important post previously held
by Vyacheslav Molotov and Lavrentii Beria among others. He
was easily the most prominent Azerbaijani in USSR history,
and in 1990 returned to his homeland to take control of the
Nakhchivan Autonomous Republic. Three years later, Aliyev

moved his power base to newly independent Baku, and he and his family and what is colloquially known as the Nakhchivan Clan have been running Azerbaijan ever since. The whole territory of Nakhchivan has been painstakingly manicured as a tribute to this leadership.

Before visiting Nakhchivan I had never witnessed a functioning personality cult at first hand. On the trip so far I had seen many vestiges of past cults, from the little girl's essay about Stalin in Vyborg to the empty, collapsed mausoleum of Enver Hoxha. But it is one thing to see remnants of a defunct personality cult and quite another to be at the heart of one that is strong, vibrant and still emerging in the present.

Behind the Aliyev statue is a huge museum and library building dedicated to the man's life, work and memory. When Heydar died in 2003, his son Ilham assumed the presidency, a role he continues to perform at the time of writing. Ilham started to invest heavily in 'Heydarism' as a new way of cementing his family's hold on power. They are a dictatorial bunch, allergic to criticism and determined to dominate every aspect of public life.

The maker of modern Azerbaijan, Heydar Aliyev, presides over an orderly, empty city that plays a central role in his country-wide personality cult.

Nakhchivan's main square shows their intention to dominate all culture and history as well.

I stepped into the Museum of Heydar Aliyev in the middle of the afternoon. I was glad to escape from the oppressive heat, and the air-conditioning system delivered an instant Alpine chill while a smiling young woman stepped forward to welcome me, saying entry was free. She was one of six who were working at the museum that day, like vestal virgins tending a shrine. They followed me round on a rota system, exchanging an invisible baton as I moved from section to section. They were silent until I paused at an exhibit for longer than about a minute, at which point one would enter my line of sight and ask gently if I needed further information.

The thing about personality cults is that they are usually equal parts ridiculous and frightening. Heydarism ticks both boxes. To an outsider, especially one from a democratic country, it is the ridiculousness that strikes you first. In Heydar's museum no piece of ephemera was too insignificant to display. There were countless outfits he had worn, mostly just banal suits and military-style uniforms made from cheap synthetic fabric. There was a carpet with his image on it. The certificates of his KGB graduation were proudly shown. His involvement with the last great folly of Soviet construction, the Baikal–Amur Mainline railroad, was documented exhaustively despite being the kind of project most politicians would pretend never to have touched. A Heydarist gloss has been applied at every other museum in town too: whatever its official focus, Heydar always has his section, as though local people and visitors need these regular side-chapels just to get by.

Heydarism also makes itself felt in street names and the names of local halls and community centres and, of course, Nakhchivan's airport. It is what inspired probably the most ridiculous of all Nakhchivan's landmarks, the Azeri flag park, which covers an entire hillside near the bus station. Topped with an unbelievably large national flag, this hill has been coated in AstroTurf and then planted with hundreds of real young trees. Because of the desert heat these saplings are constantly watered by a team of workmen. The visitor proceeds upwards via ancillary monuments before arriving at the base of the gigantic flagpole.

The frightening aspects of a personality cult eventually become impossible to ignore. To commandeer so much of a territory's resources just to glorify your own family clearly indicates an immense level of control. Heydarism is a fig leaf that is supposed to make terror and repression look like reverence and respect, and as a result it is difficult to find anyone in Nakhchivan willing to talk about the cult, the family, or even wider social life. The potential consequences of doing so are grave.

I did track down one person who was willing to speak about the situation on condition of anonymity, a local human rights activist – though he was really a former human rights activist by the time we met because, as he was to tell me, all meaningful internal resistance to the Aliyevs ended years ago. At his request, I met Yusif (not his real name) in Nakhchivan's main hammam. We entered separately, as per his instructions, and pretended to meet by chance. He had said in advance we would find a quiet corner where we could talk but, in the event, there was no need because, like most places in this weird city, the hammam was deserted. Apart from Yusif and me, the only other person was the man running it, who seemed to spend his many fallow hours watching Russian MTV and smoking. After introductions and reconfirming the ground rules for our conversation, I started with the most obvious question. Why was Nakhchivan so empty?

'You have to understand that Nakhchivan is like a supermodel,' Yusif says. 'She looks beautiful on the outside but inside she is full of pain and sadness. The people here are constantly hungry for something they cannot have because they have to look and behave in certain ways.'

Yusif goes on to describe the economic corruption and clan dominance that have been constants of the Azerbaijani experience both before and after the collapse of the USSR. Some people in Nakhchivan were direct beneficiaries of the Aliyevs in the years after independence, but many ordinary citizens were not. For them, life had been pretty normal until the late 2000s – a case of 'keep your head down and hope nobody bothers you'. But after that, this 'megastructure of Heydar and Heydarism hit us'.

To make Nakhchivan look as it does requires a lot of work, and a lot of oppression. As we sit in the empty, not-very-steamy steam room, Yusif runs through some of the big steps the local regime took to get to where it is today. Many new commercial and office buildings have gone up around town. These were typically erected on land that already contained people's houses. The residents were often evicted illegally and their houses demolished before they could mount any legal challenge. 'If you are a known critic of the regime, your home is much more likely to be put in a destruction zone,' he adds.

'Only three *khrushchyovki* remain in the whole city now,' Yusif says, referring to the distinctive Khrushchev-era five-storey houses built across the former Soviet Union. 'Everyone here is now waiting to see when they will be emptied "for repair". No one living there can be certain they will be allowed back, whatever is built in their place.'

When it comes to general cleanliness and order, Yusif says this is maintained with menaces. There is a ban on hanging wet washing out in public. Many homeowners were forced to accept new high walls around their properties so they would be invisible from outside. Street-cleaning is a duty of all state employees, which they must carry out in their spare time under threat of dismissal. Why this obsession with cleanliness? I ask. Yusif explains that the local leader, Vasif Talibov, who is related to the Aliyevs by marriage, 'wants the place to look better than anywhere else in Azerbaijan, so he can impress his big relatives when they visit for conferences and meetings. So he can impress his in-laws, basically. What you see here is his idea of what good looks like. He runs Nakhchivan like an emperor's viceroy.' The many over-restored historical monuments are Talibov's doing too. A historian by training, he has lavished money on his own selection of ancient monuments, all of which bolster the regime's idea of itself.

'You will have noticed that we do not have many shops or other businesses,' Yusif continues. 'That's because you can't run a business in Nakhchivan unless you are close to the clan. If a clan member wants a mini-market, they open it. And then they work day and night to close down all the competition. They use threats, court actions, tax inspections, and violence. It is the same with tea shops, bars, cafés, hotels. We have basically returned to state socialism here, but now the state is just one family.'

What Yusif says is backed up by the small number of inter-national human rights organizations that have carried out work in Nakhchivan. A report by the Norwegian Helsinki Com-mittee in 2009 documented these phenomena at an earlier stage, concluding back then that Nakhchivan was 'the most repressive and authoritarian region of Azerbaijan' where 'authoritarian rule and the destruction of civil society [had] been reinforced by strict censorship and grave human rights abuses'.[2] Either because they cannot make a living or out of fear for their lives, tens of thousands of Nakhchivanis have found ways to leave, mostly to live in other parts of the country or across the border in Turkey.

Yusif says he would very much like to have shown me trad-itional Azeri hospitality during my stay, to take me to his home and introduce me to his family, but he regrets that it would not be safe for either him or me. When someone else enters the hammam, we stop talking almost immediately, as agreed. I watch Yusif tense up and then we part silently some seconds later with just a nod to one another. He leaves first while I hang back for a few minutes. All subsequent texts to his Turkish mobile phone go unanswered.

Nakhchivan was of almost no interest to Moscow in the Soviet period except as one of the distant limits of its domain. The region's short border with Turkey and its long border with Iran always had to be strongly defended. Broadly the same techniques were used as on the far-off frontier with Norway. But beyond this control zone and the barracks to support it, the autonomous republic was neglected as just another backwater of the USSR's long southern underbelly. It was a genuine surprise, therefore, when Nakhchivan became one of the terminal conditions from which the USSR perished. Peripheral and ignored, the republic suddenly entered the limelight in 1988 when ethnic tensions turned violent and led to an assault on the mighty border.

The problems began because enmities between Azeris and neighbouring Armenians reawakened. The immediate cause was the fate of Nagorno-Karabakh, a territory located entirely within the main part of Azerbaijan but inhabited almost exclusively by Armenians. To recognize its distinctiveness the Soviet government had long ago granted Nagorno-Karabakh semi-autonomous status, though it was overseen from Baku. Suddenly mass protests erupted, both in Nagorno-Karabakh and in Armenia, calling for the two to be formally united because of the close cultural ties between them.

The issue had deep historical roots and there had been limited flare-ups under Soviet rule. But until the late 1980s the tried and tested Moscow approach of crushing unrest mercilessly worked every time. Now, however, the Armenian protesters were making use of Gorbachev's own reforms, raising their voices (the literal meaning of *glasnost*) to argue for restructuring (the literal meaning of *perestroika*). The Baku authorities naturally rejected the Armenians' demands, and ordinary Azeris came out onto the streets to counter-protest. Some demonstrations took on the character of pogroms, with several instances of Armenians being murdered and Armenian homes and property being destroyed. Thousands of Armenians fled to Armenia, and soon ethnic Azeris were fleeing in the opposite direction out of Nagorno-Karabakh and Armenia.[3]

Nakhchivan was drawn into this quagmire at an early stage. Although the Armenian protesters did not lay claim to the exclave, many Azeris felt it would only be a matter of time before they did. Nakhchivan was cut off from the rest of Azerbaijan by Armenian territory and there had once been a large Armenian community there, making up around 40 per cent of the population before a previous bout of ethnic cleansing in 1917. Even if only around 3,000 Armenians remained in Nakhchivan in 1988 (less than 1 per cent of the population), their small numbers did not stop them becoming targets. Five hundred were made to leave the republic in a matter of hours one day in November 1988. The resident Soviet border forces had to help them into Armenia with 'helicopters, trucks and anything else they could find' because the local Azeris were threatening violence if they stayed.[4] In retaliation the Armenian Soviet administration in Yerevan sealed all the railway and road links into and out of Nakhchivan.

The downward spiral was interrupted briefly on 7 December 1988, when another of the calamities to befall the teetering Soviet Union struck: the devastating earthquake, centred on Spitak in Armenia's north, claimed around 40,000 lives. It also stilled the squabbling Armenians and Azeris for a time, but within months the mutual loathing had resurfaced. Eventually it caused a protracted conflict over Nagorno-Karabakh and, during the course of the 1990s, it too killed 40,000 people. (It then lay dormant for two decades before exploding in flames again during the pandemic summer of 2020, leading to a further 8,000 deaths.)

Nakhchivanis played their part in the Nagorno-Karabakh

wars, but before that Nakhchivan took centre stage in a different way. The Soviet Union's most south-westerly point effectively became subject to a blockade thanks to the Armenian Soviet Republic's actions in shutting the roads and railways. The local population faced the Iron Curtain in the west and an Iron Curtain-like frontier with Iran to the south. And now they were hemmed in too by an internal frontier with hostile Armenia to the north and east. This left them literally cut off and also feeling abandoned by Moscow.

Nakhchivanis began to question why they could not have contact with their own ethnic brothers and sisters in northern Iran, a place with its own large Azeri population. A movement developed to open the Soviet–Iranian frontier. It was clearly intended partly to provoke the Kremlin, a clever tit-for-tat demand that mirrored what the Nagorno-Karabakh Armenians demanded for their community. But it was also the result of a genuine longing for old connections and growing interest in Islam after decades of state atheism.

They heard the Berlin Wall fall in Nakhchivan, and it suddenly seemed like this might be a moment when once impossible things could be accomplished. Less than a month after the shock in Berlin, on 4 December 1989, thousands of Nakhchivanis gathered at the Iranian frontier not far from Nakhchivan city and demanded the right to cross to the other side. The border is the Aras River. Protesters stayed for a month camped out on its north bank, waving and shouting to their perplexed cousins on the other side (most of whom did not think life was so great in Iran either) and demanding that the Soviet authorities dismantle the electric fence keeping them in.

From the Kremlin's perspective this looked like a dangerous precedent. Now the Soviets' outer cordon had been permanently breached in central Europe, its own sacred inner boundary became even more important. Hawks in the military and the KGB still thought the country's superpower status could be saved, but believed this was directly connected to their ability to keep the whole USSR together. Early in January 1990 Mikhail Gorbachev replaced Nakhchivan's local communist leaders to try to regain control of the situation, but protests continued and on the second weekend of January the demonstrators made their first physical attack on the border. They set fire to the fence, short-circuiting its electrics, and later pulled down its charred stumps. At least fifteen then dived into the freezing waters of the Aras and swam over to Iran.[5]

It only took a few more days for the situation to deteriorate irreparably. Partly because of the border breach and partly in response to a brutal Soviet crackdown in Baku, the Nakhchivan Supreme Soviet met in emergency session on the night of 19 January 1989 and declared that the exclave would now free itself permanently from the USSR and become an independent country. This made little Nakhchivan the first part of the Soviet Union to secede, beating Lithuania by almost two months.

Nakhchivan did not stay independent for long; it had wanted out of the USSR but did not see itself as a nation in its own right. It rejoined Azerbaijan at the earliest opportunity, paving the way for the Aliyevs' personal rise to power and guaranteeing the territory its central position in Azerbaijan's origin legend. Today's rulers want to keep this vanguard reputation, which, I think, explains a lot about the look and feel of the place. It also explains something else that can be harder to spot: the territory's uniquely vigorous pursuit of Armenophobia.

There was nothing to indicate it, but I later discovered that the very first place I visited in Nakhchivan, Noah's Tomb, was one such cleansed site. For centuries it had been holy for both Armenians and Azeris, but now it is thoroughly Islamicized. At least the tomb survived, though. It is thought that as many as eighty-nine Armenian churches in Nakhchivan, some dating from the twelfth century, have been blown up over the past thirty

years, sometimes replaced with identikit mosques but sometimes just left as flat ground. One of the most important ancient
Armenian sites in the world, the necropolis at Djulfa, about
35 kilometres south of Nakhchivan city, has also disappeared,
along with its 2,000 gravestones, many of them masterpieces of
medieval carving and calligraphy.

And it is not just Armenian architecture that has been crushed
and overlaid, but vital aspects of Armenian history. The state
museum presented an alarmingly one-sided treatment of the
interethnic violence between the two groups, with an official
narrative that deployed both manipulated facts and fake facts to
deny there had ever been Azeri violence against Armenians, or
that the 1915 Armenian genocide had taken place. It was clear
that the state-sanctioned discourse in Nakhchivan was intended
to perpetuate and exacerbate this long-running hatred. The
irresponsibility and immorality of the approach are astonishing,
and, more generally, the consolations of bigotry and chauvinism
seem paltry in this arid, airbrushed place where normal human
activity is so rationed and restricted.

Epilogue

Sadarak, Azerbaijan, and Ani, Turkey

'Between a high, solid wall and an egg that breaks against it, I will always stand on the side of the egg.'

Haruki Murakami, 'The Novelist in Wartime', speech on accepting the Jerusalem Prize, 2009.

I had just one more bus journey to make to complete the trip. As I sat at Nakhchivan bus station looking over at the supersized flag park, I began what has been a long process of reflecting on all the places I had visited and all I had seen and heard. In just over four months on the road, I had touched the extremities of a continent, covered huge distances, and experienced widely different cultures, histories and climates. Grense Jakobselv in the Arctic Circle was now some 4,500 kilometres to the north.

What linked all the places I had been was the Iron Curtain. For decades it was a daily reality for hundreds of millions of people in ways both small and great. Now it constituted a shared inheritance for them and those who came after them, whether they liked it or not, and whether they acknowledged it or not. Of course the Iron Curtain sliced through other parts of the world, but Europe was its birthplace and was always its heart, if that is an appropriate word for something that was often typified by such heartlessness. I had kept a note each time I crossed the old impossible line. Today would be my eighty-second and final crossing, for now.

*

Approaching the end of this journey, I was more convinced than ever that the Iron Curtain had been unique in important ways. The duration, severity, geographical extent, and symbolic significance of the divide outstripped anything that had come before. Initially a victory line where Allies met at the end of the Second World War, it quickly became the frontline in a new kind of conflict, and remained so for a staggering forty-five years. For all of that time, to cross it in either direction was always a political act; and in many cases even to talk about doing so was a crime.

Many have spoken of the Iron Curtain as an aberration, the product of epic misunderstandings and breakdowns in communication. But in broad terms it accurately embodied the wider relationship between the world's two great postwar systems. The nuclear weapons and other materiel that pointed across this frontier were proof of how much each camp hated the other and felt threatened by it. For half a century Europe and the world were never more than minutes from all-out war and total destruction.

Within that global context I had discovered an Iron Curtain that could sometimes respond to local needs. In particular, the baroque Inner German Border and Berlin Wall of the 1960s, 1970s and 1980s were created solely to stop East Germans fleeing, not to protect the Eastern Bloc as a whole. In Albania the fortress-like arrangements, the most extreme of any Iron Curtain frontier, were the physical incarnation of the leader Enver Hoxha's bottomless personal paranoia.

But instances of leniency had turned out to be commoner than I expected, too. This was especially so where the flow of hard currency was concerned – the GDR's covert ransom system was the most eye-catching example but almost all communist countries found ways to let in dollars and Deutschmarks. The Iron Curtain was also locally permeable in special ways between Norway and Finland and the USSR, and between Austria and

Hungary, while Yugoslavia chose a third way at an early stage which meant that for most of the Cold War it was not really closed to the West. The possibility of trust and the reality of human contact survived even the very worst of circumstances.

Nevertheless, the speed with which the Iron Curtain acquired an air of permanence still shocks. In many places the ultimate frontier quickly became like an evil god. People revered and feared it, and recognized that the safest thing to do was to steer clear of it. Even many who lived alongside the Iron Curtain deliberately chose to ignore it. What else could you do when almost everyone agreed it was permanent?

As our bus pulled out of hot, dusty Nakhchivan city I looked around at my fellow passengers. There were twenty-two of us on board. Five wore uniforms – border guards headed to the checkpoint for their day's work. Two of them chatted quietly to one another but the rest of us were silent. This, I had learned, was the Nakhchivan way. It also felt like a throwback to Iron Curtain norms. I remembered Bettina Akinro telling me how everyone on the trains she used to take through the transit corridor to West Berlin would stop talking as GDR checkpoints neared. They then remained silent until the train left the checkpoint, not wishing to draw attention to themselves, not knowing who was listening. They followed the rules; they *more than* followed the rules. In important ways they became the system.

Our speed-loving driver pushed his little bus to the limit. Nakhchivan narrows like a funnel to the west. At first you don't notice, but then the border fence with Iran appears on your left and, a little later, the border fence with Armenia on your right, and eventually Turkey looms ahead. Mobile phones started pinging across the bus, picking up and dropping the networks of the four different countries.

We reached the Sadarak checkpoint in double-quick time. The men in uniform left the bus some way short of it. Then the rest of us were told to reclaim our luggage and walk with it through the two sets of controls. I was the only person among seventeen who was not travelling on an Azeri or Turkish passport. Twice Azeri officials sent me to special queues. A third official typed the ID number of my visa into his computer and shook his head before taking my passport away to talk to his superior. I could see through the grille that they were debating whether there was anything to pursue. After three or four minutes he came back and nodded me through. On the Turkish side I was again singled out. This time the question was whether I could re-enter the country on the same tourist visa I had purchased when leaving Greece or if I needed a new one. It took a while to establish that the first visa was good enough.

When I eventually emerged at the bus everyone was standing and waiting. Of course they had noticed I was taking a long time to clear the border. My delay was a delay for them too, just as the black traveller's had been on the way into North Macedonia, just as the students' had been the time I crossed Finland's border with Russia. I looked for the telltale signs of frustration and resentment. But, in a way that made me tearful, a group of three women in headscarves actually applauded my reappearance. Then a man handed me some dried apricots from a box he had just successfully imported to Turkey. They knew what it was like to be constantly at the mercy of a great aggressive state. Like Haruki Murakami, when presented with the high solid wall and the egg, they had instinctively sided with the egg. Back on the bus, the atmosphere lightened considerably and there was far more chatter than before the frontier – more, in fact, than I had heard anywhere in Nakhchivan.

From Norway to Azerbaijan I had been surprised by many things but probably most of all by the depth and breadth of *Ostalgie*. Everyone now knows that 1991 was not 'the end of history', whatever exactly Francis Fukuyama intended by that phrase. But the collapse of most communist regimes at the end of the 1980s and the start of the 1990s did lead many experts to think that the surviving and arguably winning system – liberal capitalist democracy – was permanently entrenched. Civil wars and ethnic conflicts, personal experiences of economic collapse and other traumas, state corruption, false memories and the rose tint of old age have latterly made the 'bad' regimes of the Eastern Bloc seem attractive to millions. Some have developed detailed theories to accompany their *Ostalgie* and to connect it with their wider political aspirations. Clearly the single most significant person in that regard is Vladimir Putin. Meanwhile for others it is just something they feel in their bones, like the Russian woman in Vyborg who was sure that Soviet times had been 'kinder times'.

Of course, no country is immune from the potency of the remembered and misremembered past. There are a surprisingly large number of people in the United Kingdom, the USA, France and other long-term democracies who would also prefer to return to the past. Even the biggest lesson of the Iron Curtain, the cruelty and futility of absolute borders, is at risk of being forgotten right across Europe as large numbers on the continent fall for the false certainties of restricted movement. Flows of non-European migrants into and across the continent have contributed much to the resurgence of this powerful illusion and have even led to the actual return of impassable boundaries in certain places. Elsewhere, boundaries are challenged, and may yet be changed, because dictators have rediscovered their countries' 'manifest destiny' to rule over certain lands, irrespective of the will of the people living there. History is being wilfully misread. Totally unacceptable claims are dressed up as 'legitimate security demands'. Desperate times of persecution, many within living memory, are repackaged as happy periods of unity with the apparent purpose of creating grounds for yet more persecution.

I want you to know that I am not nostalgic for the Iron Curtain, or for any of the disappeared regimes that lay to the east of it. I am a passionate believer in the individual freedoms that the Eastern Bloc so systematically deprioritized. And I see no justification for closing our societies off from one another because of refugees or to protect ourselves from ideologies we dislike.

The regimes in Russia and Belarus seem to want to separate themselves from the rest of Europe more and more at present. They have unacceptable desires to repress their own peoples and to snatch other countries or territories and lock them into a new sphere of influence. In the short term we may sadly be faced with ostracizing them even more than they are ostracizing themselves.

But ultimately we must aim for a continent that is fully open once more. Openness brings optimism. In conversations with young people during my trip I heard a huge respect for people's individual life choices and, often, a burning passion for global fairness. Nothing is certain – was that ever so clear as now? – but these instincts may take the world in good directions in future.

If I have nostalgia, it is for the moments of liberation that I remember from the television news of my childhood, and that I had cause to dwell on so often on this journey: 9 November 1989 in Berlin and other instances of seemingly pure release and idealism. But beautiful and precious as they are, I have been forced to admit that these were just fleeting episodes and not roadmaps or manifestos to live by. Most of the problems of 8 November were still present on 10 November. The West German novelist Wolfgang Koeppen wrote in 1951, thinking about a divided Germany, that 'no one can escape their world'.[1] My interviewee Martina Schmidt had told me, reflecting on her own experience and that of others who had fled the GDR, 'You take yourself everywhere you go.'

My final glimpse of the old Iron Curtain was fittingly in a place with many potential meanings.

Today Ani is an enormous archaeological site strewn with

impressive ruined churches and mosques, a mammoth medieval wall and a collapsed bridge that once formed part of the Silk Road between China and Europe. The bridge currently marks the border between Turkey and Armenia, meaning that even if it was intact it would be closed because Turkey, like Azerbaijan, has no official relations with Armenia and is committed to denigrating and erasing Armenian culture. Yet, confusingly, Ani was once the capital of Armenia, and the site's greatest treasures date from that time.

I had come because in the Cold War Ani was completely out of bounds to all but Turkish military and border personnel. It was right on the Iron Curtain – the broken bridge *was* the Iron Curtain – and the country across the gorge was the USSR. For half a century nobody saw these majestic ruins of one of the world's great historic cities.

Ani's broken ninth-century bridge once marked the Iron Curtain and the border here remains closed due to poor relations between Turkey and Armenia.

I sat for a long time on the clifftop at Ani, looking down on the bridge and over to Armenia. A bird of prey, possibly a kite, swooped in and out of my field of vision as the sun blazed overhead. How good it was to be here where the land not long ago had been off limits. How inspiring this bridge, which called to mind the instinct of humans more than a millennium ago to interact with one another. Yet, how tragic the relations between Turkey and Armenia today, and the Iron Curtain-style fencing that still blocks the approach to this impassable bridge on both sides.

Whatever the system, it is our duty to care about its attitude towards individuals and to respond accordingly. We should trust every instinct to side with the weak. And we must be ready to learn these lessons anew each day and to share them with others. Dear readers, thank you for coming on this journey with me. To connect with others, to feel our shared humanity, is truly the greatest gift life gives.

Acknowledgements

A book of this kind would be impossible without scores of individuals freely sharing their time and memories. I was amazed during my journey, and have continued to be since, by the generosity with which people greeted my many and sometimes repeated requests for help. Foremost among them I want to thank Dirk Kummer, whose generous reply to an out-of-the-blue email in 2018 first gave me hope that this endeavour could work. I am indebted, too, to curators and archivists in local and national museums across Europe for pursuing accurate, exact knowledge about the places where they live. Some are named below but many are unknown to me personally; almost all must carry out their work under constant threat of funding cuts and distracting reorganizations – they deserve better.

For supporting my trip from Oslo to Ani and my subsequent writing I thank the following people: Bettina Akinro, Christine Ascherl, Blaze Atanasov, Annie Auerbach, Rebecca Beasley, Ingo Bötig, Ida Brink, Camilla Carlsen, Geoff Chester, Peter Chrenka of Authentic Slovakia, Amy Chuahom, Mikhail Efimov, Markman Ellis, Romano Facca, Michael Fealy, Helen Ferguson, Mernie Gilmore, Berndt Gottberg, Ian Grainger, Udo Grashoff, Betsy Greiner, Misha Griffith, Juris Gulbis, Eva Johanna Holmberg, Kevin Horvath, George Jerger, Alexander Karakabakov, Elliot Kendall, Catriona Kelly, Yasmin Khan, Ravel Kodrič, Sebastian Köpf, Miha Kovač, Ffiona Kyte, Reinis Lazda, Bryce Lease, Klaus Linnert, Katja Lucke, Ben Lyttleton, Paolo Mestroni, James Morgan, Yuliya Moshnik, John Nilsen, Thomas

Nilsen, Lars Kristian Øverland, Aristides Pappas, Martin Parr, Lena Pasternak, Boban Pesic, Sabrina Pellizon, Michael Philipp, Michael Platzer, Alise Podniece, Mitja Primosig, Paul Rachler, Minna Rauhansalo, Nini Rodgers, Philippa Ronald, Christian Schmidt, Martina Schmidt, Rüdiger Schmidt, Martin Schnabl, Barbara Schwartz, Joes Segal, Jakob Seerup, Ernst Sneve, Claire Squires, Hilde Swart, Rolf Swart, Alex von Tunzelmann, Marion Turner, Bengt Ull, Giorgio Venturini, Daina Vitola, Andreas Wagner, Rosie Waites, Ian Willoughby, Magenta Zampieri and those who have asked to remain anonymous.

The desk research and writing of the book were carried out partly at the Huntington Library in San Marino, California, and partly at the London Library. I am grateful to their staff for supporting my work and creating such peaceful havens.

For valuable detailed comments on early drafts I thank Annie Crombie, Barbara Davidson and Simon Dunton. My agent Veronique Baxter helped me shape the project from an early stage and always gives good advice. I feel particularly fortunate to have worked for a second time with my editor at Granta Books, Laura Barber; she is excellent and inspirational. In a book of this breadth I fear it is inevitable that some historical episodes will not have been explored from all angles or with full nuance and that some errors of fact will have crept in. Any such inadequacies are my own.

Finally, I thank my partner Anthony Bale, to whom I have dedicated the book, along with our cat Benny. I thank him for his unfailing love and companionship during the long pandemic lockdowns. Anthony has listened to me read from the manuscript on more occasions than I can count and, as with everything I have written before, has helped me every step of the way.

Notes

Preface: Mullafarry, Republic of Ireland

1. In March 1945 Joseph Goebbels wrote in his diary, 'as soon as the Soviets have occupied a country, they let fall an iron curtain so that they can carry on their fearful bloody work behind it', and he later used the metaphor in a published newspaper article. This and much other fascinating information about the phrase's history can be found in Patrick Wright, *Iron Curtain: From Stage to Cold War*, 2007.
2. Churchill's Iron Curtain speech remains so influential that books and museums sometimes display maps showing the Iron Curtain running through Stettin. The most notable example I have seen was at the UK's National Cold War Exhibition at RAF Cosford where, in March 2019, a map correctly showed the German Democratic Republic as being within the Soviet sphere of influence but incorrectly labelled the border city of Lübeck as Stettin.

PART I

1 Oslo, Norway

1. Quoted in Christopher Barnes, *Boris Pasternak: A Literary Biography*, 2 vols., vol.2, 1928–1960, 1998, p.342.
2. 'The Nobel Peace Prize 1990', https://www.nobelprize.org/prizes/peace/1990/press-release/. Last accessed 3 March 2022.
3. Mikhail Gorbachev, Nobel Lecture, 5 June 1991, https://www.nobelprize.org/prizes/peace/1990/gorbachev/26100-mikhail-gorbachev-nobel-lecture-1990-2/. Last accessed 3 March 2022.
4. 'Norway Finds "Russian Spy Whale" off Arctic Coast', BBC News, 29 April 2019, https://www.bbc.co.uk/news/world-europe-48090616. Last accessed 3 March 2022.

2 Kirkenes and Grense Jakobselv, Norway

1. This quotation and other information about the June 1968 Soviet show of force are taken from 'Tårnvakten', NRK, https://www.nrk.no/dokumentar/xl/hemmelige-rom-ii_-episode-5-1.12945607. Last accessed 18 April 2022.

2. I am grateful to Tor Gisle Lorentzen for sharing this information with me.

3. Interestingly, it was the Norwegian government which demanded free access be brought to an end after the fifty-nine days, perhaps fearing that the open border made smuggling too easy and also that it was a gift for Soviet intelligence officers who wanted to recruit and communicate with their Norwegian agents. See 'The Water Without Borders', http://www.pasvikelva.no/en/vannkraft. Last accessed 3 March 2022.

4. 'Murmanskii kalendar', *Komsomol'skaya pravda*, 24 September 2013, https://www.alt.kp.ru/daily/26138.2/3027336/. Last accessed 3 March 2022.

5. Marianne Hofman, 'From Suicide Attempts to Happiness and Sámi Pride', *Independent Barents Observer*, 10 January 2019, https://thebarentsobserver.com/en/life-and-public/2019/01/suicide-attempts-happiness-and-pride. Last accessed 3 March 2022.

6. Before his recruitment, Frode Berg had volunteered at charity soup kitchens just across the border inside Russia and had also helped to organize bilateral festivals and sporting events. These facts may have made him attractive to Norwegian intelligence, as someone whom the Russians would not pay too much attention to. See Reid Standish, 'How a Norwegian Retiree Got Caught Up in a Spy Scandal', *The Atlantic*, 19 May 2019, https://www.theatlantic.com/international/archive/2018/05/how-a-norwegian-retiree-got-caught-up-in-a-spy-scandal/560657/. Last accessed 3 March 2022.

7. 'Spy Swap: Five Freed in Russia–Lithuania–Norway Exchange', BBC News, 15 November 2019, https://www.bbc.co.uk/news/world-europe-50431713. Last accessed 3 March 2022.

3 Porkkala, Finland

1. Poul Grooss, *The Naval War in the Baltic*, 1939–1945, 2017, p.15.

2. The Soviets began making military use of Porkkala immediately. On 11 January 1945 Captain Aleksandr Marinesko sailed submarine S-13 out of Porkkala Naval Base into the Baltic. Nineteen days later it attacked the *Wilhelm Gustloff*, a German cruise ship that had been repurposed as a refugee vessel. *The*

Wilhelm Gustloff sank with the loss of some 9,000 lives, most of them refugees. It was and remains the largest ever loss of life in a single ship sinking. For more on this, see chapter 9.

3. The Finns were diligent in respecting Soviet demands for privacy. Research by Raija Ylönen-Peltonen, a senior archivist at the National Archives of Finland, has revealed numerous arrests on the Finnish side of the border in the early 1950s. Most of those detained were tourists or curious journalists, but in a few cases people were caught trying to enter Porkkala as a means of getting to the USSR proper. See Raija Ylönen-Peltonen, 'Amerikkalainen unelma neuvostolitosta' in Kauko I. Rumpunen ed., *Veitsen terällä: Suomen tie läpi vaaran vuosien 1944–1962*, 2014, pp.109–12.

4. Risto E. J. Penttilä, 'The Soviet Withdrawal from the Porkkala Naval Base, 1956', in Risto E. J. Penttilä ed., *Finland's Search for Security Through Defence, 1944–89*, 1991, pp.61–76, p.62.

5. Jussi M. Hanhimäki, *Containing Coexistence: America, Russia and the 'Finnish Solution' 1945–1956*, 1997, p.184.

6. Penttilä, 'The Soviet Withdrawal from the Porkkala Naval Base, 1956', in Risto E. J. Penttilä ed., *Finland's Search for Security through Defence, 1944–89*, 1991, pp.61–76, p.65.

7. The founder members of the Warsaw Pact were the USSR, Albania, Bulgaria, Czechoslovakia, East Germany, Hungary, Poland, and Romania.

8. Mika Aaltola, 'Inhorealistisia ulkopolitiikan eläintarinoita', verkkouutiset.fi, 28 April 2017, https://www.verkkouutiset.fi/inhorealistisia-ulkopolitiikan-elaintarinoita/#2cda91eb. Last accessed 3 March 2022.

9. Lotta Lounasmeri and Jukka Kortti, 'Campaigning Between East and West: Finland and the Cold War in the Presidential Campaign Films of Urho Kekkonen', *Cold War History*, 2018, https://doi.org/10.1080/14682745.2018.1532996. Last accessed 3 March 2022.

10. Stephen Castle, 'Cold War list is focus of scandal in Finland', *New York Times*, 3 February 2008, https://www.nytimes.com/2008/01/23/world/europe/23iht-spy.4.9448617.html. Last accessed 3 March 2022.

11. Sofi Oksanen, 'A Lion in a Cage: On the Finlandization of Europe', Eurozine, 19 June 2015, https://www.eurozine.com/a-lion-in-a-cage/. Last accessed 3 March 2022.

4 Vyborg, Russia

1. Mark Kramer, 'Introduction' to Alfred A. Reisch, *Hot Books in the Cold War: The CIA-Funded Secret Western Book Distribution Program Behind the Iron Curtain*, 2013, p.xxiii.

2. 'Chislo rossiyan, nostal'giruyushchikh po SSSR, dostiglo maksimuma za poslednie 10 let', BBC Russian Service, 19 December 2018, https://www.bbc.com/russian/news-46616462. Last accessed 4 March 2022.

3. Christopher Bowlby, 'Vladimir Putin's Formative German Years', BBC News, 27 March 2015, https://www.bbc.co.uk/news/magazine-32066222. Last accessed 4 March 2022.

4. 'Anti-Communists Detained at Stalin Commemoration in Moscow', *Moscow Times*, 5 March 2019, https://www.themoscowtimes.com/2019/03/05/anti-communists-detained-stalin-commemoration-moscow-a64710. Last accessed 4 March 2022.

5. 'Second Historian of Stalin's Crimes Arrested on Morals Charges in Karelia', RFE/RL, 3 October 2018, https://www.rferl.org/a/second-historian-of-stalin-s-crimes-arrested-on-morals-charges-in-karelia/29523402.html. Last accessed 4 March 2022.

6. Yana Shturma, 'Khoteli vtpustit': chem obernulas' syd'ba istorika-pedofila', gazeta.ru, 2 April 2020, https://www.gazeta.ru/social/2020/04/02/13033411.shtml. Last accessed 4 March 2022.

7. Peter Rutland and Neil Shimmield, 'Putin's Dangerous Campaign to Rehabilitate Stalin', *Washington Post*, 13 June 2019, https://www.washingtonpost.com/outlook/2019/06/13/putins-dangerous-campaign-rehabilitate-stalin/. Last accessed 4 March 2022.

8. 'Stalin-Tsentr in pamyatnik Stalinu', Levada-Tsentr, 4 April 2021, https://www.levada.ru/2021/08/04/stalin-tsentr-i-pamyatnik-stalinu/. Last accessed 4 March 2022.

9. Aleksei Naval'nyi, 'Sekretnaya dacha Putina', YouTube, 30 August 2017, https://www.youtube.com/watch?v=MrIsXKdjZdo&t=525s. Last accessed 4 March 2022. 'Novaya "dacha prezidenta"?', *Znak*, 24 August 2017, https://www.znak.com/2017-08-24/druzya_putina_okazalis_vladelcami_starinnoy_villy_iz_sherloka_holmsa. Last accessed 25 October 2021.

10. 'Putin's Palace. History of World's Largest Bribe', YouTube, January 2021, https://www.youtube.com/watch?v=ipAnwilMncI. Last accessed 4 March 2022.

11. My understanding of Aalto's library in Vyborg has benefited greatly from the work of Michael Spens. See Michael Spens, *Viipuri Library, 1927–1935: Alvar Aalto*, 1994.

5 Riga, Latvia

1. 'Income Declaration of Ex-Chairman of SIA TET Details Considerable Income From the Company', BNN, 17 February 2021, https://bnn-news.com/income-declaration-of-ex-chairman-of-sia-tet-details-considerable-income-from-the-company-222024. Last accessed 4 March 2022.

2. Chris Dziadul, 'Tet Sacks Juris Gulbis', Broadband TV News, 7 December 2020, https://www.broadbandtvnews.com/2020/12/07/tet-sacks-juris-gulbis/. Last accessed 4 March 2022.

3. 'Review of Criminal Case Involving Notorious Latvian Politicians Moves Forward as Court Prepares to Interview Witnesses', BNN, 1 October 2021, https://bnn-news.com/review-of-criminal-case-involving-notorious-latvian-politicians-moves-forward-as-court-prepares-to-interview-witnesses-228658. Last accessed 4 March 2022. 'BIJUŠAIS "TET" VALDES PRIEKŠSĒDĒTĀJS GULBIS IECELTS DIVU CEĻU BŪVES UZŅĒMUMU VALDĒS', *Puaro: Interneta Žurnāls*, 6 September 2021, https://puaro.lv/ietekme-un-nauda/bijusais-tet-valdes-priekssedetajs-gulbis-iecelts-divu-celu-buves-uznemumu-valdes/. Last accessed 4 March 2022.

4. *Vai viegli būt...? Pēc 20 gadiem*, director: Antra Cilinska, 2010.

6 Liepāja, Latvia

1. I am grateful to Reinis Lazda for this information.

PART II

7 Gotland, Sweden

1. I am grateful to Thomas Roth, Senior Curator at the Armémuseum in Stockholm, for sharing his knowledge about Gotland's Cold War defences.

2. My account of this episode is based on Marijona Venslauskaitė Boyle, *Search for Freedom: The Man From Red October*, 2005.

3. Marijona Venslauskaitė Boyle, *Search for Freedom: The Man From Red October*, 2005, p.18.

4. Bor_odin, 'U nego poluchilos'! Pobeg iz SSSR v Shvetsiyu na

kolkhoznom samolete', *Livejournal*, 28 May 2020, https://borodin.livejournal.com/6938993.html. Last accessed 4 March 2022.

5. 'Torsdag 28 april i P3 Dokumentär: Flyktingbåtarna till Gotland på 1990-talet', Sveriges Radio, 13 April 2016, https://sverigesradio.se/sida/artikel.aspx?programid=2938&artikel=6410349. Last accessed 4 March 2022.

6. Ewen MacAskill, 'Swedish Armed Forces Widen Hunt for Suspected Submarine', *Guardian*, 20 October 2014.

7. An English language version of the brochure is available here: https://www.dinsakerhet.se/siteassets/dinsakerhet.se/broschyren-om-krisen-eller-kriget-kommer/om-krisen-eller-kriget-kommer---engelska.pdf. Last accessed 4 March 2022.

8 Bornholm, Denmark

1. 'Minute from Sir O. Sargent to Mr Churchill, 9 May 1945' in Tony Insall and Patrick Salmon eds., *The Nordic Countries in the Early Cold War, 1944–51: Documents on British Policy Overseas*, Series I, pp.16–17.

2. The collection can be viewed at the following website by searching for 'Kjøller' and 'russisk': https://bornholmskebilleder.brk.dk/welcome.jspx. Last accessed 4 March 2022.

3. 'Bornholm Island (Occupation)', *Hansard*, vol.414, 24 October 1945, https://hansard.parliament.uk/Commons/1945-10-24/debates/6779bc2b-ba0a-44af-9514-ff9f242b74a8/BornholmIsland(Occupation). Last accessed 4 March 2022.

4. George Kennan's 'Long Telegram', 22 February 1946, Wilson Center Digital Archive, https://digitalarchive.wilsoncenter.org/document/116178.pdf, p.9. Last accessed 4 March 2022.

5. Patrick Wright, *Iron Curtain: From Stage to Cold War*, 2007, p.7.

6. Philip Oltermann, 'Surfboards and Submarines: the Secret Escape of East Germans to Copenhagen', *Guardian*, 17 October 2014, https://www.theguardian.com/cities/2014/oct/17/surfboards-and-submarines-the-secret-escape-of-east-germans-to-copenhagen. Last accessed 4 March 2022.

7. Jacob Svendsen, 'Truslen fra Rusland er øget: Bornholm skal igen aflytte russernes radioer', *Politiken*, 18 November 2017, https://politiken.dk/indland/art6212511/Bornholm-skal-igen-aflytte-russernes-radioer. Last accessed 4 March 2022.

9 Rügen and Priwall, Germany

1. Dieter Bub, '"Wir sind der letzte Dreck": Wehrdienstverweigerer berichten über ihren Alltag bei den "Bausoldaten" auf Rügen', *Stern*, no.22, 1983, pp.202–206.

2. Josie McLellan, *Love in the Time of Communism: Intimacy and Sexuality in the GDR*, 2011, p.7. Why was nudism more widespread in East Germany? Explanations vary. It may be that there were different habits to begin with in this more Protestant part of Germany as compared with more Catholic places in the south. But it also seems likely that the abolition of any club not affiliated to the East German regime had something to do with it. The regime would never have agreed to run nudist clubs itself, so there were no nudist clubs, unlike in West Germany. But without the clubs, there was no infrastructure of private nudist beaches where nudists could be made to bathe. Instead, when people wanted to bathe naked in the GDR they ended up doing it anywhere they pleased.

3. 'Die Nackten und die Roten', *Der Spiegel*, 11 August 1975, http://www.spiegel.de/spiegel/print/d-41471250.html. Last accessed, 4 March 2022.

4. The story is recounted on an information board on Priwall beach and also in Steffan Könau, 'Flucht aus der DDR über die Ostsee: Mario Wächtler schwamm in den Westen', *Mitteldeutsche Zeitung*, 6 September 2014, https://www.mz.de/mitteldeutschland/flucht-aus-der-ddr-uber-die-ostsee-mario-wachtler-schwamm-in-den-westen-2020654. Last accessed 4 March 2022.

PART III

10 Schlagsdorf and Helmstedt, Germany

1. 'Schnell das Ding vom Zaun', *Der Spiegel*, 12 April 1976, https://www.spiegel.de/spiegel/print/d-41238170.html. Last accessed 4 March 2022.

2. Excerpt from a letter of 27 April 1976 written by Michael Gartenschläger, in the Wall Museum, Checkpoint Charlie, Berlin.

3. Biographies of Michael Gartenschläger that I have used here can be found, in German, at the websites of the Bundesstiftung Aufarbeitung, https://dissidenten.eu/laender/deutschland-ddr/biografien/michael-gartenschlaeger/, Deutschlandfunk, https://

www.deutschlandfunk.de/lothar-lienicke-franz-bludau-todesautomatik-die.730.de.html?dram:article_id=101626, and the Freie Universität Berlin, https://www.fu-berlin.de/sites/fsed/Das-DDR-Grenzregime/01_Biografien-von-Todesopfern/Gartenschlaeger_Michael/index.html. All links last accessed 4 March 2022.

4. Anne Applebaum, *Iron Curtain: The Crushing of Eastern Europe 1944–56*, 2012, p.457.

5. John Bainbridge, 'Die Mauer', *New Yorker*, 27 October 1962.

6. A wonderful footnote is that the Schmidts' civil wedding ceremony took place to the sound of Verdi's 'Chorus of the Hebrew Slaves' from *Nabucco*. The song, about life in captivity, was one of the odd choices on the GDR's approved list of wedding music. The second verse reads '*Greet the banks of Jordan / And Zion's toppled towers / Oh, my homeland, so lovely and so lost! / Oh memory, so dear and so dead!*'

7. For a fuller description of the ransom system see Anthony Bailey, *Along the Edge of the Forest: An Iron Curtain Journey*, 1983, pp.218–219.

8. For the full story of the Schmidts' life in the GDR and subsequent escape see their memoirs, Martina Schmidt and Rüdiger Schmidt, *Mauerbruch: Eine Heimatgeschichte*, 2012 and Martina Schmidt and Rüdiger Schmidt, *Mauerbruch: Eine Zeitreise*, 2021.

9. The best sources on Lutz Eigendorf are the In Bed With Maradona website maintained by Alessandro Mastroluca (http://inbedwithmaradona.com/journal/2011/8/3/the-tragedy-of-lutz-eigendorf.html, last accessed 4 March 2022) and a German documentary film, *Tod dem Verräter. Der lange Arm der Stasi und der Fall Lutz Eigendorf*, broadcast in 2000 (https://www.heribert-schwan.de/werke/tod-dem-verraeter-der-lange-arm-der-stasi-und-der-fall-lutz-eigendorf/, last accessed 4 March 2022).

10. Martina Schmidt and Rüdiger Schmidt, *Mauerbruch: Eine Zeitreise*, 2021, pp.132–134.

11. I was to learn of a similar slow-burning atrocity at Hohenschönhausen, the Stasi prison in East Berlin. When they were photographed on arrival inmates were made to sit in a designated chair. Some reported being left in the chair for hours, and many of these prisoners subsequently died of cancer. After the regime's collapse, a compartment was found in the wall behind the chair, at head height, which may have been used to conceal radioactive substances. See also Martina Schmidt and Rüdiger Schmidt, *Mauerbruch: Eine Zeitreise*, 2021, pp.251–255 for the

story of Walter Gerber's suspected irradiation and subsequent early death.

12. Maxim Leo, *Red Love: The Story of an East German Family*, 2013, p.221.

11 Berlin, Germany

1. See, for instance, Julie Fedor, 'Chekists Look Back on the Cold War: The Polemical Literature', *Intelligence and National Security*, 26:6, December 2011, pp.842–863; Leonid Shebarshin, 'Reflections on the KGB in Russia', *Economic and Political Weekly*, December 18, 1993, 28:51, pp.2829, 2831–2832; Katherine Verdery, *My Life as a Spy: Investigations in a Secret Police File*, 2018; Elisabeth Braw, *God's Spies: The Stasi's Cold War Espionage Campaign Inside the Church*, 2019.

2. Stephen Spender, Foreword to Jörn Donner, *Report from Berlin*, 1961, p.xiii.

3. As late as 1987 direct budgetary aid to the city amounted to $7.5 billion: T. H. Elkins with B. Hofmeister, *Berlin: The Spatial Structure of a Divided City*, 1988, p.48.

4. T. H. Elkins with B. Hofmeister, *Berlin: The Spatial Structure of a Divided City*, 1988, p.250.

5. Will Lynch, 'Berlin in the '90s: An Interview With Tobias Rapp', Resident Advisor, 7 September 2011, https://www.residentadvisor.net/features/1434. Last accessed 4 March 2022.

6. Anthony Bailey, *Along the Edge of the Forest: An Iron Curtain Journey*, 1983, p.92.

7. For the full story of the cycle of paintings read Michael Philipp, *Are Communists Allowed to Dream?: The Gallery of the Palace of the Republic*, 2017.

8. Clare Copley, 'Curating Tempelhof: Negotiating the Multiple Histories of Berlin's "Symbol of Freedom"', *Urban History*, 44:4, 2017, pp.698–717, p.700.

9. Owning the novel was the crime for which Baldur Haase received three years and three months in prison in 1959. He subsequently wrote a book about it: Baldur Haase, *Orwells DDR*, 1997.

10. Frederick Kempe, *Berlin 1961: Kennedy, Khrushchev, and the Most Dangerous Place on Earth*, 2011, p.368.

12 Potsdam, Germany

1. John le Carré, *The Secret Pilgrim*, 1991, p.12.

2. Anthony Bailey, *Along the Edge of the Forest: An Iron Curtain Journey*, 1983, p.139.

3. Cited in Derek Scally, 'Artists Join Debate Before Berlin Wall Anniversary', *Irish Times*, 13 April 2019.

4. Josie McLellan, *Love in the Time of Communism: Intimacy and Sexuality in the GDR*, 2011, pp.70, 77.

5. Josie McLellan, *Love in the Time of Communism: Intimacy and Sexuality in the GDR*, 2011, p.118.

6. Josie McLellan, *Love in the Time of Communism: Intimacy and Sexuality in the GDR*, 2011, pp.132–134, 136.

7. Christa Wolf, *City of Angels: or, the Overcoat of Dr Freud, a Novel*, trans. Damion Searls, (2010), p.52.

8. Jenny Erpenbeck, 'Homesick for Sadness', trans. Susan Bernofsky, *The Paris Review*, 8 November 2014.

9. The only way to get hold of gay or lesbian erotica in East Germany was through smuggling. See Josie McLellan, *Love in the Time of Communism: Intimacy and Sexuality in the GDR*, 2011, p.132–134.

PART IV

13 Selb, Germany, and Aš, Czechia

1. Anne Applebaum, *Iron Curtain: The Crushing of Eastern Europe 1944–56*, 2012, p.233.

2. Anne Applebaum, *Iron Curtain: The Crushing of Eastern Europe 1944–56*, 2012, p.296 and Roger F. Robison, *Mining and Selling Radium and Uranium*, 2014, p.236.

3. I am very grateful to the Bavarian journalist Christine Ascherl for putting me in touch with Rolf and Hilde following her own interview with them. See Christine Ascherl, 'Der Zug in die Freiheit', *Onetz*, 11 January 2019, https://www.onetz.de/deutschland-welt/zug-freiheit-id2602458.html. Last accessed 5 March 2022.

4. National Czech & Slovak Museum & Library, 'Karel Ruml', NCSML Digital Library, https://ncsml.omeka.net/items/show/4110. Last accessed 5 March 2022.

5. 'Czech Engineer Flees With Train and 111 Passengers to Germany', *New York Times*, 12 September 1951, p.1, https://www.nytimes.com/1951/09/12/archives/czech-engineer-flees-with-train-and-111-passengers-to-germany-czech.html?searchResultPosition=9. Last accessed 5 March 2022.

6. *Radio Times*, 11–17 January 1953, p.27.

14 Bratislava, Slovakia

1. Donald P. Steury, 'Strategic Warning: The CIA and the Soviet Invasion of Czechoslovakia' in Günter Bischof, Peter Ruggenthaler and Stefan Karner eds., *The Prague Spring and the Warsaw Pact Invasion of Czechoslovakia in 1968*, 2010, pp.237–248, p.237.

2. Quoted in Mark Kramer, 'The Prague Spring and the Soviet Invasion in Historical Perspective' in Günter Bischof, Peter Ruggenthaler and Stefan Karner eds., *The Prague Spring and the Warsaw Pact Invasion of Czechoslovakia in 1968*, 2010, pp.35–58, p.53.

3. Translation taken from the website Socialism Realised: Life in Communist Czechoslovakia 1948–1989, https://www.socialismrealised.eu/catalogue/politician-in-a-swimsuit/. Last accessed 5 March 2022.

4. Milan Kundera, *The Unbearable Lightness of Being*, trans. Michael Henry Heim, 1995, p.25.

5. Milan Kundera, *The Unbearable Lightness of Being*, trans. Michael Henry Heim, 1995, pp.159–160.

6. Prokop Tomek, 'Life With Soviet Troops in Czechoslovakia and After Their Withdrawal', *Electronic Journal of Folklore*, vol.70, 2017, www.folklore.ee/folklore/vol70/tomek.pdf, pp.97–120, p.103. Last accessed 5 March 2022.

7. Miro Kern, 'Pred tridsiatimi rokmi na hranici l'udí trhali psy, teraz zverejniki zodpovedných', *Denník N*, 8 August 2016, https://dennikn.sk/531223/pred-tridsiatimi-rokmi-na-hranici-ludi-trhali-psy-zverejnili-zoznam-tych-co-za-to-zodpovedaju/. Last accessed 5 March 2022.

8. Just a few weeks later, at the start of November 1983, there was a further injection of tension when NATO ran the Able Archer training exercise. This played out a scenario in which the USSR started proxy wars in Iran, Syria and Yemen before invading Yugoslavia, Norway and Finland, and finally launching a chemical attack on West Germany. The exercise's purpose was to determine how effectively NATO would be able to respond. Some historians have argued that the exercise was interpreted in Moscow as a possible subterfuge for a real invasion and thus almost led to a pre-emptive Soviet strike, but others disagree. For an excellent discussion of the episode, see Simon Miles, 'The War Scare That Wasn't: Able Archer 83 and the Myths of the Second Cold War', *Journal of Cold War Studies*, 22:3, Summer 2020, pp.86–118.

9. Milan Kundera, *The Unbearable Lightness of Being*, trans. Michael Henry Heim, 1995, p.247.

15 Vienna, Austria

1. Graham Greene, *The Third Man and The Fallen Idol*, 2010, p.13.
2. Quoted in Frederick Kempe, *Berlin 1961: Kennedy, Khrushchev, and the Most Dangerous Place on Earth*, 2012, p.257.
3. See Edgar L. Erickson, 'The Zoning of Austria', *American Academy of Political and Social Science*, vol.267, January 1950, pp.106–113.
4. See also Dávid Maróti, 'Comparison of the International Administration in Berlin and Vienna After World War II', *Central European Papers*, 2017,V, 2, pp.65–77, p.68. http://cejsh.icm.edu.pl/cejsh/element/bwmeta1.element.desklight-7926dbfc-9e72-4a9b-97d3-b762a543c3d0/c/CEP_20170502_Maroti.pdf. Last accessed 5 March 2022.
5. Frederick Kempe, *Berlin 1961: Kennedy, Khrushchev, and the Most Dangerous Place on Earth*, 2012, p.251.
6. Quoted in Thomas Riegler, 'The Spy Story Behind *The Third Man*', *Journal of Austrian-American History*, 4, 2020, pp.1–37, p.29, https://doi.org/10.5325/jaustamerhist.4.0001. Last accessed 5 March 2022.
7. Quoted in Thomas Riegler, 'The Spy Story Behind *The Third Man*', *Journal of Austrian-American History*, 4, 2020, pp.1–37, p.29, https://doi.org/10.5325/jaustamerhist.4.0001. Last accessed 5 March 2022.
8. 'Security and Safety Service', United Nations Office at Vienna website, https://www.unov.org/unov/management_sss.html. Last accessed 5 March 2022.
9. 'Barnett, David Henry' in Defense Personnel Security Research Center, Monterey, California, *Espionage Cases 1975–2004: Summary and Sources*, p.3, https://irp-cdn.multiscreensite.com/cadac795/files/uploaded/482512.pdf. Last accessed 5 March 2022.
10. Barbara Gamarekian, 'Jailed Agent's Family Learns to Cope', *New York Times*, 16 June 1982, p.28, https://www.nytimes.com/1982/06/16/us/jailed-agent-s-family-learns-to-cope.html. Last accessed 5 March 2022.
11. 'Pelton, Roland William' in Defense Personnel Security Research Center, Monterey, California, *Espionage Cases 1975–2004: Summary and Sources*, p.36, https://irp-cdn.multiscreensite.com/cadac795/files/uploaded/482512.pdf. Last accessed 5 March 2022.

12. Alfred A. Reisch, *Hot Books in the Cold War: The CIA-Funded Secret Western Book Distribution Program Behind the Iron Curtain*, 2013, p.298.

13. Alfred A. Reisch, *Hot Books in the Cold War: The CIA-Funded Secret Western Book Distribution Program Behind the Iron Curtain*, 2013, p.299.

14. Alfred A. Reisch, *Hot Books in the Cold War: The CIA-Funded Secret Western Book Distribution Program Behind the Iron Curtain*, 2013, p.303.

15. Alfred A. Reisch, *Hot Books in the Cold War: The CIA-Funded Secret Western Book Distribution Program Behind the Iron Curtain*, 2013, p.401.

16 Sopron, Hungary

1. 'László Nagy', Paměť národa, https://www.pametnaroda.cz/en/nagy-laszlo-1957. Last accessed 5 March 2022.

2. Terry Cox, 'The Picnic on the Border: An Interview with László Vass', in *Reflections on 1989 in Eastern Europe*, ed. Terry Cox, 2013, pp.99–110, p.108.

3. 'East German Killed in Struggle With Hungarian Border Guard', *Associated Press*, 22 August 1989. https://apnews.com/article/b27458775e7a94feb2e37812f79a02ee. Last accessed 5 March 2022.

PART V

17 Nova Gorica, Slovenia, and Gorizia, Italy (I)

1. Anna McWilliams, *An Archaeology of the Iron Curtain: Material and Metaphor*, 2013, p.106.

2. See Ulf Brunnbauer, 'Yugoslav *Gastarbeiter* and the Ambivalence of Socialism: Framing Out-Migration as a Social Critique', *Journal of Migration History*, 5:13, November 2019, pp.413–437.

3. Anna McWilliams, *An Archaeology of the Iron Curtain: Material and Metaphor*, 2013, p.99.

4. Anna McWilliams, *An Archaeology of the Iron Curtain: Material and Metaphor*, 2013, p.79.

18 Nova Gorica, Slovenia, and Gorizia, Italy (II)

1. Quoted in 'In Places, Slovenia: Nova Gorica', TuDa website, https://tuda.xyz/nova-gorica/. Last accessed 5 March 2022.

2. I am very grateful to Ian Grainger for this introduction and also

for sharing his own extensive knowledge of Gorizia/Nova Gorica and the Isonzo Valley.

3. 'GDP per capita, PPP (current international $)', The World Bank, https://data.worldbank.org/indicator/NY.GDP.PCAP. PP.CD?most_recent_value_desc=false. Last accessed 7 April 2021.

4. Cited in F. L. Carsten, *The Rise of Fascism*, 1982, p.51.

5. The question of who the dead are in the *foibe* is highly controversial. Some historians and local people argue that Slovenians are among the bodies in some of the *foibe*, killed at an earlier stage for their anti-fascist activities. The *foibe* must also be seen in the context of extermination activities organized in and around Trieste by the occupying Nazis in the last years of the Second World War.

6. Jacopo Barigazzi, 'Slovenian, Croatian Leaders Accuse Tajani of "Historical Revisionism"', Politico website, 11 February 2019, https://www.politico.eu/article/slovenian-croatian-leaders-accuse-tajani-of-historical-revisionism/. Last accessed 5 March 2022.

7. 'Statement by President Tajani on his participation at the Day of Remembrance of the Victims of the *Foibe* Massacres', Le Président Parliament européen website, 11 February 2019, https://www.europarl.europa.eu/former_ep_presidents/president-tajani/fr/newsroom/statement-by-president-tajani-on-his-participation-at-the-day-of-remembrance-of-the-victims-of-the-foibe-massacres.html. Last accessed 5 March 2022.

19 Trieste, Italy

1. 'Arguments About Frontiers: Free Territory of Trieste Another Free City of Danzig?', *Manchester Guardian*, 7 September 1946, p.6.

2. 'Yugoslavs Prevented From Entering Trieste: British C.-in-C. Saves Awkward Situation', *Manchester Guardian*, 17 September 1947, p.8.

3. Nevenka Troha, 'Volitve v Okraju Koper cone B Svobodnega tržaškega ozemlja', *Prispevki za novejšo zgodovino*, 3:2002, pp.61–75, https://ojs.inz.si/pnz/article/view/2367/2696. Last accessed 5 March 2022.

4. I am grateful to Julian Barker for drawing my attention to Zone A's unusual stamps.

5. 'Rioters' Hostility to British', *Manchester Guardian*, 7 November 1953, p.1.

6. 'Rioters' Hostility to British', *Manchester Guardian*, 7 November 1953, p.1.
7. 'Trieste (Disturbances)', *Hansard*, vol. 520, 9 November 1953.
8. Jan Morris, *Trieste and the Meaning of Nowhere*, 2001, p.115.
9. TRIEST NGO website, http://www.triest-ngo.org/the-free-territory-of-trieste/. Last accessed 5 March 2022.
10. Tara Isabella Burton, 'The Free State of Trieste', Roads & Kingdoms website, 30 July 2016, https://roadsandkingdoms.com/2016/the-free-state-of-trieste/. Last accessed 5 March 2022.
11. Rishi Sunak MP, 'The Free Ports Opportunity: How Brexit Could Boost Trade, Manufacturing and the North', *Centre for Policy Studies*, November 2016, https://cps.org.uk/wp-content/uploads/2021/07/161114094336-TheFreePortsOpportunity.pdf. Last accessed 5 March 2022.
12. Jason Horowitz, 'A Forgotten Italian Port Could Become a Chinese Gateway to Europe', *New York Times*, 18 March 2019, https://www.nytimes.com/2019/03/18/world/europe/italy-trieste-china-belt-road.html. Last accessed 5 March 2022.

20 Tirana and Sarandë, Albania

1. Blendi Fevziu, *Enver Hoxha: The Iron Fist of Albania*, trans. Majlinda Nishku, 2017, p.21.
2. Patrick F. R. Artisien, 'Albania in the Post-Hoxha Era', *The World Today*, 41:6, June 1985, pp.107–111, p.108.
3. Blendi Fevziu, *Enver Hoxha: The Iron Fist of Albania*, trans. Majlinda Nishku, 2017, p.109.
4. According to Witold Szabłowski, the mushroom bunkers would have offered little if any protection. I wonder if the same would have been true of Bunk'Art as well: '[In] 1999, when the Serbs started to bombard Kosovo . . . In the process Albania was hit too, and so were the bunkers. And suddenly it turned out that these structures, which were supposed to survive an atom bomb, had just fallen apart as if they were made of clay! For lots of people it was a shock. Suddenly, they could see that the power of Communism was a matrix, a delusion, not the truth.' (Witold Szabłowski, *Dancing Bears: True Stories About Longing for the Old Days*, 2018, p.146.)
5. Sean Williams, 'A Soccer Comeback for a Long-Struggling Country', *New Yorker*, 5 September 2015.
6. Jon Halliday, 'Fear and Loathing in Tirana', *LRB*, 2 September 1982, www.lrb.co.uk/the-paper/v04/n16/jon-halliday/

fear-and-loathing-in-tirana. Last accessed 5 March 2022. Blendi Fevziu, *Enver Hoxha: The Iron Fist of Albania*, trans. Majlinda Nishku, 2017, p.243.

7. Ismail Kadare, *Agamemnon's Daughter, a Novella and Stories*, trans. David Bellos, 2007, p.45.

8. Blendi Fevziu, *Enver Hoxha: The Iron Fist of Albania*, trans. Majlinda Nishku, 2017, p.163–4.

9. Blendi Fevziu, *Enver Hoxha: The Iron Fist of Albania*, trans. Majlinda Nishku, 2017, p.218.

10. Theresa Lappe-Osthege, 'Caged Birds and Cigarettes – Exploring the Illegal Bird Trade in Albania', Biosec website, 13 September 2018, https://biosec.group.shef.ac.uk/2018/09/13/caged-birds-and-cigarettes-exploring-the-illegal-bird-trade-in-albania/. Last accessed 5 March 2022.

11. Ismail Kadare, *Agamemnon's Daughter, a Novella and Stories*, trans. David Bellos, 2007, p.96.

12. Fatos Kongoli, *The Loser*, 2007, p.126.

13. I am grateful to Martin Parr for corresponding with me about his experiences on the trip.

14. Blendi Fevziu, *Enver Hoxha: The Iron Fist of Albania*, trans. Majlinda Nishku, 2017, p.248.

15. Bledi was accurate when he described the resurgence of violence against women and old patterns of clan rivalry in post-communist Albania. See, for instance, Amanda Petrusich, 'In the Land of Vendettas that Go on Forever', *Virginia Quarterly Review*, Fall 2017.

16. 'New survey reveals violence against women occurs widely in Albania', UN Women website, 29 May 2019, https://eca.unwomen.org/en/news/stories/2019/05/new-survey-reveals-violence-against-women-occurs-widely-in-albania. Last accessed 5 March 2022.

17. Ledio Cakaj and Maria Burnett-Gaudiani, 'Albania in August', *Index on Censorship*, 3, 2004, pp.211–217, p.217.

21 Corfu, Greece

1. Here and elsewhere I have taken many details of the 1946 incidents in the Corfu Channel from Owen Pearson, *Albania in the Twentieth Century: A History*, 3 vols., vol. 3, *Albania as Dictatorship and Democracy: From Isolation to the Kosovo War, 1946–1998*, 2006.

2. Ana Lalaj, 'Burning Secrets of the Corfu Channel Incident', *Cold War International History Project*, Working Paper 70, September 2014, https://www.wilsoncenter.org/sites/default/files/media/

documents/publication/cwihp_wp_70_burning_secrets_of_
the_corfu_channel_incident.pdf, p.21. Last accessed 5 March
2022.

3. Patrick F. R. Artisien, 'Albania in the Post-Hoxha Era', *The World
Today*, 41:6, June 1985, pp.107–111, p.110.

4. Ana Lalaj, 'Burning Secrets of the Corfu Channel Incident',
Cold War International History Project, Working Paper 70,
September 2014, https://www.wilsoncenter.org/sites/default/
files/cwihp_wp_70_burning_secrets_of_the_corfu_channel_
incident.pdf, p.18. Last accessed 5 March 2022.

5. This and subsequent quotations about the XCU document come
from Anthony Carty, 'The Corfu Channel Case – and the
Missing Admiralty Orders', *The Law and Practice of International
Courts and Tribunals*, 2004, pp.1–35.

6. 'Βίλλα Μπιμπέλη – Πύργος Πολυλάδων – Καστέλλο – Castello',
http://www.corfuland.gr/el/istorika-kerkyra/corfu-history/
kastello-castello-billa-mpimpeli-pyrgos-polyladon.html.   Last
accessed 5 March 2022.

7. Owen Pearson, *Albania in the Twentieth Century: A History*, 3
vols., vol. 3, *Albania as Dictatorship and Democracy: From Isolation
to the Kosovo War, 1946–1998*, 2006, entry for 5 March 1949.

8. Owen Pearson, *Albania in the Twentieth Century: A History*, 3
vols., vol. 3, *Albania as Dictatorship and Democracy: From Isolation
to the Kosovo War, 1946–1998*, 2006, entries for 2 October 1949,
3 October 1949 and 10 October 1949.

9. 'Major Hon. Alan Hare', *The Peerage*, http://www.thepeerage.
com/p3818.htm. Last accessed 5 March 2022.

10. Nicholas Bethell, *The Great Betrayal: The Untold Story of Kim
Philby's Biggest Coup*, 1984, p.89.

11. Nicholas Bethell, *The Great Betrayal: The Untold Story of Kim
Philby's Biggest Coup*, 1984, p.135.

12. Malcolm Gladwell, 'Trust No One', *New Yorker*, 20 July 2014.

13. 'The Albania Operation', *Document* programme, BBC Radio 4, 5
July 2016, http://www.bbc.co.uk/programmes/b07j4ppw. Last
accessed 5 March 2022.

14. Polymeris Voglis, *Becoming a Subject: Political Prisoners During the
Greek Civil War*, 2002, p.41.

15. Polymeris Voglis, 'Political Prisoners in the Greek Civil War,
1945–50: Greece in Comparative Perspective', *Journal of
Contemporary History*, October 2002, 37:4, pp.523–540, p.533.

16. Cited in Ian Sinclair, 'Retrieved From the Memory Hole:
British Intervention in Greece in the 1940s', Open Democracy,

19 June 2017, https://www.opendemocracy.net/en/opendemocracyuk/retrieved-from-memory-hole-british-intervention-in-greece-in-1940s/. Last accessed 5 March 2022.

17. Yanis Varoufakis, *Adults in the Room: My Battle with Europe's Deep Establishment*, 2017, p.305.

18. Witold Szabłowski, *Dancing Bears: True Stories About Longing for the Old Days*, 2014 (English translation 2018), p.226.

22 Gevgelija, North Macedonia

1. Centre for Industrial Studies, Milan, *The Egnatia Motorway: Ex Post Evaluation of Investment Projects Co-financed by the European Regional Development Fund (ERDF) or Cohesion Fund (CF) in the Period 1994–1999*, 2012, https://ec.europa.eu/regional_policy/sources/docgener/evaluation/pdf/projects/egnatia_motorway.pdf. Last accessed 6 March 2022.

2. See, for instance, Niki Kitsantonis, 'Rumors of Open Border Prompt Migrant Protests in Greece', *New York Times*, 5 April 2019, https://www.nytimes.com/2019/04/05/world/europe/greece-migrant-protest.html. Last accessed 6 March 2022.

23 Nakhchivan, Azerbaijan

1. Heiki Maria Johenning, 'Nakhchivan Azerbaijan – Visiting the Caucasian Switzerland', Wild East website, 22 April 2021, https://wildeast.blog/en/nakhchivan-azerbaijan/. Last visited 6 March 2022.

2. Norwegian Helsinki Committee, *Azerbaijan's Dark Island: Human Rights Violations in Nakhchivan*, 2009, https://www.nhc.no/content/uploads/2018/10/Azerbaijan_final_version.pdf. Last accessed 6 March 2022.

3. 'Soviet Ethnic Crisis Forces 88,000 to Flee', *The Times*, 2 December 1988, p.24.

4. '"Revenge Killings" of Armenians', *The Times*, 25 November 1988, p.1.

5. 'A Soviet Frontier is Put to the Torch', *The Times*, 9 January 1990, p.20.

Epilogue: Sadarak, Azerbaijan, and Ani, Turkey

1. Wolfgang Koeppen, *Pigeons on the Grass*, trans. Michael Hofmann, 2020, pp.216.

Select Bibliography

In alphabetical order by author, article – when no author – and film title.

Ahonen, Pertti, 'Defending Socialism? Benito Corghi and the Inter-German Border', *History In Focus*, volume 11, 2006, https://archives.history.ac.uk/history-in-focus/Migration/articles/ahonen.html.

'Albanians Topple Hoxha's Statue', *Washington Post*, 21 February 1991.

Angelos, James, 'Whatever the Cost: "The Greek Spring"', *London Review Of Books*, 27 September 2018.

'Another Look at East German Art', *Economist*, 17 November 2017.

'Anti-Communists Detained at Stalin Commemoration in Moscow', *Moscow Times*, 5 March 2019.

Antonenko, Oksana, 'Latviya otkryla arkhivy KGB. Tam okazalis' glava tserkvi, byvshii prem'er i krupnyi biznesmen', *BBC Russian Service*, 21 December 2018, https://www.bbc.com/russian/features-46653022.

Applebaum, Anne, 'A Warning From Europe: The Worst Is Yet to Come', *Atlantic*, 28 November 2018.

Applebaum, Anne, *Iron Curtain: The Crushing of Eastern Europe 1944–56*, 2012.

Artisien, Patrick F. R., 'Albania in the Post-Hoxha Era', *The World Today*, volume 41, 1985, pp.107–111.

Ascherl, Christine, 'Der Zug in die Freiheit', Onetz, 11 January 2019, https://www.onetz.de/deutschland-welt/zug-freiheit-id2602458.html.

Ascherson, Neal, 'In High Stalinist Times', *London Review of Books*, 20 December 2012.

Ash, Timothy Garton, 'Jesus Rex Poloniae', *New York Review of Books*, 16 August 2018.

Ash, Timothy Garton, 'Time for a New Liberation?', *New York Review of Books*, 24 October 2019.

Astrasheuskaya, Nastassia, 'Polar Powers: Russia's Bid for Supremacy in the Arctic Ocean', *Financial Times*, 28 April 2019.

Bailey, Anthony, *Along the Edge of the Forest: An Iron Curtain Journey*, 1983.

Bainbridge, John, 'Die Mauer', *New Yorker*, 27 October 1962.

Bangel, Christian and others, 'East–West Exodus: The Millions Who Left', *Die Zeit*, 30 May 2019.

Barber, John, 'Can Gorbachev Succeed?', *London Review of Books*, 4 December 1986.

Barker, Alex, 'UK Foreign Secretary Rouses EU Ire Over Soviet Jibe', *Financial Times*, 1 October 2018.

Bethell, Nicholas, *The Great Betrayal: The Untold Story of Kim Philby's Biggest Coup*, 1984.

Bobrovich, Alena, 'Kak Lenin skryvalsya v Vyborge pered nachalom revolyutsii: reportazh Metro', Metro, 6 November 2017, https://m.metronews.ru/novosti/peterbourg/reviews/kak-lenin-skryvalsya-v-vyborge-pered-nachalom-revolyucii-reportazh-metro-1331863/.

Boffey, Daniel, 'EU Border "Lie Detector" System Criticised as Pseudoscience', *Guardian*, 2 November 2018.

Boyle, Marijona Venslauskaitė, *Search for Freedom: The Man From Red October*, 2005.

Braw, Elisabeth, *God's Spies: The Stasi's Cold War Espionage Campaign Inside the Church*, 2019.

'Bring Russia in From the Cold, Says Council of Europe Chief', *Financial Times*, 7 April 2019.

Brusden, Jim, 'Tusk Hits Back at Hunt Over Comparisons of EU With Soviet Union', *Financial Times*, 4 October 2018.

Buck, Tobias, 'East and West Germans Drifting Apart Politically, Berlin Warns', *Financial Times*, 26 September 2018.

Cakaj, Ledio and Maria Burnett-Gaudiani, 'Albania in August', *Index On Censorship*, volume 3, 2004, pp.211–217.

Camus, Albert, *The Plague*, translated by Tony Judt, 2001 (first published 1947).

Chazan, Guy, 'Germany's Racial Tensions Spill on to the Streets of Chemnitz', *Financial Times*, 31 August 2018.

'Chislo rossiyan, nostal'giruyushchikh po SSSR, dostiglo maksimuma za poslednie 10 let', BBC Russian Service, 19 December 2018, https://www.bbc.com/russian/news-46616462.

Coming Out, directed by Heiner Carow, DEFA, 1989.

Copley, Clare, 'Curating Tempelhof: Negotiating the Multiple Histories of Berlin's "Symbol of Freedom"', *Urban History*, volume 44, 2017, pp.698–717.

Cox, Terry, 'The Picnic on the Border: An Interview With László Vass' in *Reflections on 1989 in Eastern Europe*, ed. Terry Cox, 2013, pp.99–110.

Crouch, David, 'Sweden Bathes in Echoes of Cold War Drama as Submarine Hunt Continues', *Guardian*, 21 October 2014.

Cummings, Richard H., *Radio Free Europe's 'Crusade For Freedom': Rallying Americans Behind Cold War Broadcasting, 1950–1960*, 2010.

'Czech Deer Still Wary of Iron Curtain Boundary', *Guardian*, 23 April 2014.

'Czech President Stirs Ire With Silence Over 1968 Soviet Invasion', *Moscow Times*, 21 August 2018.

De Monchaux, Thomas, 'The Walls Before Trump's Walls', *New Yorker*, 11 December 2016.

Dickey, Colin, 'The Cold Rim of the World', Long Reads, 18 March 2015, https://longreads.com/2015/03/18/the-cold-rim-of-the -world/.

Die Legende von Paul und Paula, directed by Heiner Carow, DEFA, 1973.

'Die Nackten und die Roten', *Der Spiegel*, 11 August 1975, http://www.spiegel.de/spiegel/print/d-41471250.html.

Dowling, Siobhán, 'Cold War Espionage: 10,000 East Germans Spied for the West', *Spiegel International* online, 28 September 2007, https://www.spiegel.de/international/germany/cold-war-espionage-10-000-east-germans-spied-for-the-west-a-508518.html.

Elkins, T. H. with B. Hofmeister, *Berlin: The Spatial Structure of a Divided City*, 1988.

Ellis-Petersen, Hannah, 'Whale With Harness Could Be Russian Weapon, Say Norwegian Experts', *Guardian*, 29 April 2019.

Ellman, Michael and Vladimir Kontorovich, 'The Collapse of the Soviet System and the Memoir Literature', *Europe–Asia Studies*, volume 49, 1997, pp.259–279.

Erpenbeck, Jenny, 'Homesick for Sadness', translated by Susan Bernofsky, *The Paris Review*, 8 November 2014.

Fedor, Julie, 'Chekists Look Back on the Cold War: The Polemical Literature', *Intelligence and National Security*, volume 26, 2011, pp.842–863.

Feinberg, Melissa, *Curtain of Lies: The Battle Over Truth in Stalinist Eastern Europe*, 2017.

Ferguson, Alexander, 'Germany's Divide Exposed in Underpants War', *Independent*, 25 August 1992.

Fevziu, Blendi, *Enver Hoxha: Iron Fist of Albania*, translated by Majlinda Nishku, 2017.

Fisher, Mark, *Capitalist Realism: Is There No Alternative?*, 2009.

For Your Eyes Only, directed by John Glen, Eon Productions, 1981.

Foy, Henry, 'Five Men Freed in Russia–Lithuania–Norway Spy Swap', *Financial Times*, 15 November 2019.

Frye, David, *Walls: A History of Civilization in Blood and Brick*, 2018.

Fürstenau, Marcel, 'Understanding East Germany: A Never-ending Look At The Past', *Deutsche Welle*, 15 October 2018, https://www.dw.com/en/understanding-east-germany-a-never-ending-look-at-the-past/a-45900891.

Geißler, Denis, 'Video Games in East Germany: The Stasi Played Along', *Zeit Online*, 21 November 2018, https://www.zeit.de/digital/games/2018-11/computer-games-gdr-stasi-surveillance-gamer-crowd?utm_referrer=https%3A%2F%2Fwww.google.com%2F.

Gladwell, Malcolm, 'Trust No One', *New Yorker*, 20 July 2014.

Görlach, Manfred, 'Trapped: Memories of Three Years in East German Prisons, Potsdam and Brandenburg, 1961–64' (Abridged English Version), 1997.

Grashoff, Udo, 'Driven into Suicide By the Communist Regime of the German Democratic Republic? On the Persistence of a Distorted Perspective', University College London website, http://discovery.ucl.ac.uk/10024703/1/Grashoff-U_driven%20into%20suicide%20by%20the%20Communist%20regime_German%20Democratic%20Republic_.pdf.

Grashoff, Udo, '"The Death of Others": The Myth and Reality of Suicide in the GDR', UCL SSEES Research Blog, 27 November 2014, https://blogs.ucl.ac.uk/ssees/2014/11/27/the-death-of-others-the-myth-and-reality-of-suicide-in-the-german-democratic-republic/.

Grossman, Vasilii, *Everything Flows*, translated by Robert Chandler, 2011 (written 1955–1963, first published 1989).

Habšudova, Zuzana, 'Infamous Journey of Famous Photo', *Slovak Spectator*, 16 August 2004.

Halliday, John, 'Fear and Loathing in Tirana', *London Review of Books*, 2 September 1982.

Halliday, John, 'The Strange Death of Mehmet Shehu', *London Review of Books*, 9 October 1986.

Hansa Studios: By the Wall 1976–1990, documentary film directed by Mike Christie, 2018.

Hauswald, Harald and Stefan Wolle, *Totally East: Life in East Germany*, 2018.

Hickley, Catherine, 'Software Billionaire Plans to Turn Decaying Potsdam Restaurant into Museum for East German Art', *Art Newspaper*, 2 April 2019.

Higgins, Andrew, '4,141 Latvians Were Just Outed as KGB Informants', *New York Times*, 18 January 2019.

Hilbig, Wolfgang, *The Sleep of the Righteous*, translated by Isabel Fargo Cole, 2015 (first published 2002).

Hofmann, Michael, 'In the Doghouse', *London Review of Books*, 27 May 1993.

Hopkins, Valerie, 'Borders Have Become a Barrier to a Reborn Balkans', *Financial Times*, 22 November 2018.

Horowitz, Jason, 'A Forgotten Italian Port Could Become a Chinese Gateway to Europe', *New York Times*, 18 March 2019.

Hunter, Jefferson, 'Roadside Albania', *Massachusetts Review*, volume 53, 2012, pp.163–173.

Ikstena, Nora, *Soviet Milk*, translated by Margita Gailitis, 2018 (first published 2015).

'Jailed Spy's Relief at Going Home for Christmas', BBC News, 2 December 2019, https://www.youtube.com/watch?v=12suuAtSWV8.

Jay, Mike, 'I Don't Understand it at All: Chernobyl', *London Review of Books*, 6 December 2018.

Kadare, Ismail, *Agamemnon's Daughter, A Novella and Stories*, translated by David Bellos, 2007 (written 1985, first published 2003).

Kalashnikov, Antony, 'Soviet War Memorials in Eastern Europe Continue to Strain Relations With Russia', The Conversation, 20 August 2018, https://theconversation.com/soviet-war-memorials-in-eastern-europe-continue-to-strain-relations-with-russia-101687.

Kempe, Frederick, *Berlin 1961: Kennedy, Khrushchev, and the Most Dangerous Place on Earth*, 2011.

Kennan, George, 'The Long Telegram', 22 February 1946. Available at 'George Kennan's "Long Telegram"', US Department of State (ed.), *Foreign Relations of the United States, 1946, Volume VI, Eastern Europe; The Soviet Union*, 1969, pp.696–709.

Kitsantonis, Niki, 'Rumors of Open Border Prompt Migrant Protests in Greece', *New York Times*, 5 April 2019.

Knabe, Hubertus, 'Die DDR lebt', Hubertus Knabe website, 17 January 2019, https://hubertus-knabe.de/die-ddr-lebt/.

Kokobobo, Ani, 'Bureaucracy of Dreams: Surrealist Socialism and Surrealist Awakening in Ismail Kadare's *The Palace of Dreams*', *Slavic Review*, volume 70, 2011, pp.524–544.

Kongoli, Fatos, *The Loser*, translated by Robert Elsie, 2007 (first published 1992).

Krauthammer, Charles, 'The Pardon is for Tyrants', *Washington Post*, 9 January 1987.

Kristensen, Hans M. and Robert S. Norris, 'Worldwide Deployments of Nuclear Weapons, 2017', *Bulletin of the Atomic Scientists*, volume 73, 2017, pp.288–297.

Kundera, Milan, *The Unbearable Lightness of Being*, translated by Michael Henry Heim, 1984.

Kur'er, directed by Karen Shakhnazarov, Mosfilm, 1986.

Lalaj, Ana, 'Burning Secrets of the Corfu Channel Incident', *Cold War International History Project*, Working Paper 70, 2014.

'László Nagy', Paměť Národa, https://www.pametnaroda.cz/en/nagy-laszlo-1957.

Lears, Jackson, 'Aquarius Rising', *New York Review of Books*, 27 September 2018.

Leary, Peter, *Unapproved Routes: Histories of the Irish Border, 1922–1972*, 2016.

Le Carré, John, *The Secret Pilgrim*, 1991.

Legko li? 20 let spustya, directed by Antra Cilinska, 2010.

Legko li byt'?… 10 let spustya, directed by Antra Cilinska, 1997.

Legko li byt' molodym?, directed by Juris Podnieks, 1986.

Leo, Maxim, *Red Love: The Story of an East German Family*, translated by Shaun Whiteside, 2013.

Lodge, David, 'A Polish Notebook – On the Eve of Martial Law', *London Review of Books*, 4 February 1982.

Lomasko, Victoria, 'A Trip to Tbilisi', translated by Thomas Campbell, Drawing the Times, 27 October 2016, https://drawingthetimes.com/2016/victoria-lomasko-trip-tbilisi/.

Lounasmeri, Lotta and Jukka Kortti, 'Campaigning Between East and West: Finland and the Cold War in the Presidential Campaign Films of Urho Kekkonen', *Cold War History*, volume 20, 2020, pp.329–348.

Lounasmeri, Lotta Inari, 'Through Rose or Blue and White Glasses? Decades of News About the Soviet Union in the Finnish Press', *NORDICOM Review*, volume 34, 2013, pp.105–123.

Lubonja, Fatos, 'Privacy in a Totalitarian Regime', *Social Research*, volume 68, 2001, pp.237–254.

Lustig, Josh, 'Tereza Červeňová on Photographing Europe After the Brexit Vote', *Financial Times*, 3 August 2018.

Lynch, Will, 'Berlin in the '90s: An Interview With Tobias Rapp', Resident Advisor, 7 September 2011, https://ra.co/features/1434.

McGrane, Sally, 'Remembering Christa Wolf', *New Yorker*, 13 December 2011.

McKenna, Phil, 'The Boy Who Loved Birds', Medium, 18 February 2015, https://medium.com/thebigroundtable/ the-boys-who-loved-birds-cd6e117a608.

McLellan, Josie, *Love in the Time of Communism: Intimacy and Sexuality in the GDR*, 2011.

McWilliams, Anna, *An Archaeology of the Iron Curtain: Material and Metaphor*, 2013.

Magris, Claudio, 'La statua del Vate che divide Trieste. Perche mi schiero con D'Annunzio', *Corriere della Sera*, 12 June 2019.

Mariager, Rasmus, 'Danish Cold War Historiography', *Journal of Cold War Studies*, volume 20, issue 4, 2018, pp.180–211.

Maróti, Dávid, 'Comparison of the International Administration in Berlin and Vienna After World War II', *Central European Papers*, volume 2, 2017, pp.65–77.

Marshall, Colin, 'The East German Secret Police's Illustrated Guide for Identifying Youth Subcultures: Punks, Goths, Teds and More (1985)', Open Culture, 7 February 2019, https://www. openculture.com/2019/02/east-german-secret-polices- illustrated-guide-for-identifying-youth-subcultures.html.

Mastroluca, Alessandro, 'The Tragedy of Lutz Eigendorf', In Bed With Maradona, 2011, http://inbedwithmaradona.com/ journal/2011/8/3/the-tragedy-of-lutz-eigendorf.html.

Matthies, Bernd, 'Berlins älteste Schwulenbar muss schließen', *Tages Spiegel*, 15 March 2013.

Mazower, Mark, 'The Nazis Were Less Harsh: Mischka Danos', *London Review of Books*, 7 February 2019.

Meaney, Thomas, 'A Celebrity Philosopher Explains the Populist Insurgency', *New Yorker*, 26 February 2018.

Meaney, Thomas, 'In Whose Interest? Truman's Plan', *London Review of Books*, 6 December 2018.

Menand, Louis, 'Bloc Heads', *New Yorker*, 12 November 2012.

Menand, Louis, 'George F. Kennan's Cold War', *New Yorker*, 14 November 2011.

Menand, Louis, 'Francis Fukuyama Postpones the End Of History', *New Yorker*, 3 September 2018.

Milanovic, Branko, 'How I Lost My Past', globalinequality, 16 September 2017, http://glineq.blogspot.com/2017/09/how-i- lost-my-past.html.

Milne, Richard, 'Swedes Told How to Prepare for War as Russia Fears Grow', *Financial Times*, 17 January 2018.

Moldoveanu, Ioana, 'What it Was Like to Be Gay in Communist Romania', Vice, 28 October 2014, https://www.vice.com/en/article/ppmvx9/what-it-was-like-to-be-gay-in-communist-romania-876.

Morris, Jan, *Trieste and the Meaning of Nowhere*, 2001.

Mounk, Yascha, 'How A Teen's Death Has Become A Political Weapon', *New Yorker*, 21 January 2019.

Müller, Jan-Werner, 'Populism and the People', *London Review of Books*, 23 May 2019.

Nagibin, Yurii, *Dnevnik*, 1995.

Nairn, Tom, 'Where's the Omelette?: Patrick Wright', *London Review of Books*, 23 October 2008.

Neumann, Joachim speaking to Nick Thompson, 'Experience: I Tunnelled Under the Berlin Wall', *Guardian*, 12 July 2019.

Nikitin, Vadim, 'I Was Warmer in Prison', *London Review of Books*, 11 October 2018.

Nilsen, Thomas, 'Russians Cross Border to Norway for Pride Parade', *The Barents Observer*, 23 September 2017, https://thebarentsobserver.com/en/2017/09/pride-parade-near-border-russia.

Nolan, Daniel, 'Billy Elliot Musical Axes Dates in Hungary Amid Claims it Could "Turn Children Gay"', *Guardian*, 22 June 2018.

Odnokolenko, Oleg, 'General-leitenant Vycheslav Kondrashov: "Istoriya voennoi razvedki napolnena primerami muzhestva, otvagi i vysokogo professionalizma', *Ezhenedel'nik Zvezda*, 5 November 2018, https://zvezdaweekly.ru/news/201810261116-rKlIu.html.

Oksanen, Sofi, 'A Lion in a Cage: On the Finlandization of Europe', Eurozine, 19 June 2015, https://www.eurozine.com/a-lion-in-a-cage/.

Oltermann, Philip, 'Surfboards and Submarines: The Secret Escape of East Germans to Copenhagen', *Guardian*, 17 October 2014.

Over the East Sea to Freedom, online exhibition, 2013, http://www.ostseefluchten.de.

Parker, Richard, 'Inside the Collapsing Soviet Economy', *Atlantic*, June 1990.

'Party Chiefs Sacked After Soviet Riots', *The Times*, 28 November 1988, p.12.

Pearson, Owen, *Albania in the Twentieth Century: A History*, 3 volumes, volume 3, *Albania as Dictatorship and Democracy: From Isolation to the Kosovo War, 1946–1998*, 2006.

Penttilä, Risto E. J., 'The Soviet Withdrawal From the Porkkala Naval Base, 1956' in Risto E. J. Penttilä, *Finland's Search for Security*

Through Defence, 1944–89, 1991, pp.61–76.

Petrusich, Amanda, 'In the Land of Vendettas That Go on Forever', *Virginia Quarterly Review*, Fall, 2017.

Petterson, Per, *I Curse the River of Time*, translated by Charlotte Barslund, 2010 (first published 2008).

'Pochemu rekordnoe chislo rossiyan simpatiziruet Stalinu. Tri prichiny', BBC Russian Service, 16 April 2019, https://www.bbc.com/russian/news-47947555.

'Politician in a Swimsuit', Socialism Realised, https://www.socialismrealised.eu/catalogue/politician-in-a-swimsuit/.

Preston, Andrew, 'Heresy From Lesser Voices: The Helsinki Conference', *London Review of Books*, 20 June 2019.

Radio Times, 1923–2009, BBC Genome Project, https://genome.ch.bbc.co.uk/issues.

Ramet, Pedro, 'Disaffection and Dissent in East Germany', *World Politics*, volume 37, 1984, pp.85–111.

Ramsden, John, *Man of the Century: Winston Churchill and His Legend Since 1945*, 2002.

Reisch, Alfred A., *Hot Books in the Cold War: The CIA-funded Secret Western Book Distribution Program Behind The Iron Curtain*, 2013.

Reynolds, David, 'Enjoying Every Moment: Ole Man Churchill', *London Review of Books*, 7 August 2003.

Riding, Alan, 'A Hamlet's Wall: Hoping for Fall of Less Known Barrier', *New York Times*, 14 November 1989.

Risso, Linda, 'Radio Wars: Broadcasting in the Cold War', *Cold War History*, volume 13, 2013, pp.145–152.

Romero, Federico, 'Cold War Historiography at the Crossroads', *Cold War History*, volume 14, 2014, pp.685–703.

Rose, Steven, 'Pissing in the Snow: Dissidents and Scientists', *London Review of Books*, 18 July 2019.

Roth, Andrew, 'Putin's East German Identity Card Found in Stasi Archives', *Guardian*, 11 December 2018.

Roth, Andrew, 'Russian Artists Invite Visitors to Donate Blood to Exhibition', *Guardian*, 8 February 2019.

Ruge, Eugen, *In Times of Fading Light*, translated by Anthea Bell, 2014 (first published 2011).

Ruotsila, Markku, 'Globalising the US Christian Right: Transnational Interchange During the Cold War', *International History Review*, volume 40, 2018, pp.133–154.

Rybakov, Anatolii, *Children of the Arbat*, translated by Harold Shukman, 1988 (written 1966–1983, first published 1987).

Sawa, Dale Berning, 'Monumental Loss: Azerbaijan and "The Worst

Cultural Genocide of the 21st Century'", *Guardian*, 1 March 2019.

Scally, Derek, 'Artists Join Historical Debate Before Berlin Wall Anniversary', *Irish Times*, 13 April 2019.

Schwirtz, Michael, 'Russia Ordered a Killing That Made No Sense. Then the Assassin Started Talking', *New York Times*, 31 March 2019.

'Second Historian of Stalin's Crimes Arrested on Morals Charges in Karelia', RFERL, 3 October 2018, https://www.rferl.org/a/second-historian-of-stalin-s-crimes-arrested-on-morals-charges-in-karelia/29523402.html.

Self, Will, 'Walk the Line: Will Self Retraces the Berlin Wall, 25 Years After its Fall', *Guardian*, 10 October 2014.

Selimi, Bardhyl, 'Enver Hoxha's Personality Cult Lives on in Today's Albania', New Eastern Europe, 5 October 2018, https://neweasterneurope.eu/2018/10/05/enver-hoxhas-personality-cult-lives-todays-albania/.

Shebarshin, Leonid, 'Reflections on the KGB in Russia', *Economic and Political Weekly*, volume 28, 1993, pp.2829, 2831–2832.

Shotter, James, 'Three Seas to Turn Tide on East–West Divide', *Financial Times*, 22 November 2018.

'Slovak Tank Man', Socialism Realised, https://www.socialismrealised.eu/catalogue/slovak-tank-man/.

Smith, Tom, 'The Archive and the Closet: Same-Sex Desire and GDR Military Service in Stefan Wolter's Autobiographical Writing', *Oxford German Studies*, volume 45, 2016, pp.198–211.

Soldak, Katya, 'This is How Propaganda Works: A Look Inside a Soviet Childhood', *Forbes*, 20 December 2017.

Staalesen, Atle, 'Sámi Footballers Go to Disputed Conflict Area to Play Ball With Ukrainian Separatists', *The Barents Observer*, 25 April 2019, https://thebarentsobserver.com/en/life-and-public/2019/04/sami-footballers-go-disputed-conflict-area-play-ball-ukrainian-separatists.

Standish, Reid, 'How a Norwegian Retiree Got Caught Up in a Spy Scandal', *Atlantic*, 19 May 2018.

'Stasi plünderte Hunderttausende Westpakete', NTV, 3 December 2018, https://www.n-tv.de/politik/Stasi-pluenderte-Hunderttausende-Westpakete-article20752658.html.

Stippekohl, Siv, 'Der Flugzeugabsturz von 1986 und die Stasi', *Nordmagazin NDR*, 14 December 2018.

Svendsen, Jacob, 'Truslen fra Rusland er øget: Bornholm skal igen aflytte russernes radioer', *Politiken*, 18 November 2017.

'Sweden's 65,000 Nuclear Bunkers aren't Enough: Civil Contingencies Agency', thelocal.se, 30 October 2017, https://www.thelocal.se/20171030/swedens-65000-nuclear-bunkers-arent-enough-civil-contingencies-agency.

Szabłowski, Witold, *Dancing Bears: True Stories About Longing for the Old Days*, translated by Antonia Lloyd-Jones, 2018.

'The European Green Belt That Follows the Corridor of the Former Iron Curtain', Brilliant Maps, 4 May 2016, https://brilliantmaps.com/european-green-belt/.

The Man Who Saved the World, directed by Peter Anthony, 2013.

'The Writing on the Wall – Soviet Inscriptions on Vienna City Walls', Vienna Muses, 3 June 2015, https://www.kcblau.com/this-quarter-checked/.

Tomek, Prokop, 'Life With Soviet Troops in Czechoslovakia and After Their Withdrawal', *Folklore: Electronic Journal Of Folklore*, volume 70, 2017, pp.97–120, www.folklore.ee/folklore/vol70/tomek.pdf.

Tooze, Adam, 'Which is Worse?: Germany Divided', *London Review of Books*, 18 July 2019.

'Torsdag 28 april i P3 Dokumentär: Flyktingbåtarna till Gotland på 1990-talet', Sverige Radio, 13 April 2016, https://sverigesradio.se/sida/artikel.aspx?programid=2938&artikel=6410349,.

Varoufakis, Yanis, *Adults in the Room: My Battle With Europe's Deep Establishment*, 2017.

Vendik, Yuri and Tim Whewell, 'Zemletryasenie v Armenii: 30 let spustya britanskie spasateli vernulis' v Spitak', BBC Russian Service, 7 December 2018, https://www.bbc.com/russian/features-46440649?SThisFB&fbclid=IwAR1z-M64j_18QTfWAh9WLf_7Y6jXrld9uwWgzLAIkarmqLq3xRx4VCFJXD4.

Verdery, Katherine, *My Life as a Spy: Investigations in a Secret Police File*, 2018.

Volkov, Evgeny V., 'German Democratic Republic of the 1970s–1980s Through the Eyes of Soviet Officers (Oral Stories)', *Folklore: Electronic Journal Of Folklore*, volume 70, 2017, pp.51–70, www.folklore.ee/folklore/vol70/volkov.pdf.

'What the Fuzz Intervju 1 – Ondt Blod/John Nilsen', Eviglyttar, 17 January 2017, https://eviglyttar.no/blogg/2017/1/17/what-the-fuzz-intervju-1-ondt-blodjohn-nilsen.

Williams, Kieran, 'Inching into and out of "the Prague Spring"', Sources and Methods, Wilson Center, 20 August 2018, https://www.wilsoncenter.org/blog-post/inching-and-out-the-prague-spring.

Williams, Sean, 'A Soccer Comeback for a Long-Struggling Country', *New Yorker*, 5 September 2015.

Witt, Emily, 'The Life and Art of Wolfgang Tillmans', *New Yorker*, 10 September 2018.

Wolf, Christa, *City Of Angels: Or, the Overcoat of Doctor Freud*, a Novel, translated by Damion Searls, 2010.

Wolf, Christa, *They Divided the Sky*, translated by Luise von Flotow, 2013 (first published 1963).

Wolf, Christa, *What Remains and Other Stories*, translated by Heike Schwarzbauer and Rick Takvorian, 1993 (*What Remains* written 1979, first published 1990).

Wright, Patrick, *Iron Curtain: From Stage to Cold War*, 2007.

Zerofsky, Elisabeth, 'Viktor Orbán's Far-Right Vision for Europe', *New Yorker*, 7 January 2019.

Illustration Credits

All photographs were taken or are owned by the author except the following.

p. 39   Thomas Nilsen, editor of the *Independent Barents Observer*, pictured beside a border post on the Russian side of the frontier. Image by Atle Staalsen.

p. 101   The villagers of Ziemupe in the late 1930s posing on one of their fishing boats. In 1961 a Soviet border guard burned all the boats. Image reproduced courtesy of Diana Vitola.

p. 135   Portraits of Soviet soldiers from Alfred Kjøller's studio in Allinge. Images reproduced with the kind permission of Bornholms Museum.

p. 155   *Bausoldaten* unloading concrete slabs from a goods train at Mukran in 1983. In heatwave conditions, they had been allowed to shed their uniforms. Copyright: Archiv PRORA-ZENTRUM e.V.

p. 171   Michael Gartenschläger on one of his visits to the Inner German Border. Photo: Kai Greiser, Germany.

p. 208   Wolfgang Mattheuer's *Guten Tag* ('Good Day'), one of sixteen surprisingly ambivalent paintings commissioned for the opening of the Palace of the Republic. Painting by Wolfgang Mattheuer. ©DACS 2022.

p. 250   Alexander Dubček shows his freedom of spirit on a visit to a swimming pool in Czechoslovakia in July 1968. Copyright: TASR/Ľudovít Füle.

p. 278   Leopold Figl's copy of the draft Austrian State Treaty, showing the crossed out paragraph referring to Austrian guilt for the Second World War. The image has been reproduced with the kind permission of Renata Maria Matscher and the Haus der Geschichte Österreich.

Index

BESLAN

The Tragedy of School No. 1

'A valuable historical document, as well as a compelling, if harrowing, read' *Irish Independent*

On the morning of 1 September 2004 the children of Beslan were excited about the start of a new school year. At School No. 1 in the southern Russian town, proud parents had also turned out to enjoy the traditional celebrations. Suddenly, heavily armed terrorists stormed the playground and these ordinary lives were changed for ever. More than 1,200 hostages – mostly women and children – were herded into the school gymnasium, beginning three days of unimaginable terror and suffering.

'[A]n important work for any reader who wishes to understand what is happening in the North Caucasus . . . a many-layered but accessible tapestry of life in one of the most complex and explosive regions of the world' *Guardian*

'Skilful and sensitive . . . In this impressive book, Phillips manages simultaneously to offer a detailed account of the historical context of the atrocity, as well as the personal details of individuals caught up in the events . . . excellent' *Independent*

'Timothy Phillips has done a heroic and, one might have thought for a foreigner, impossible job: he has reconstructed from the testimony of many hundreds of witnesses the hellish events of that September . . . His work is a fitting memorial to the dead' *Literary Review*

'The claims, counter-claims and rumours which have surrounded the tragedy mean there is a need for a book which describes the events themselves, their chronology, and the facts and figures. This book does more, giving insights into possible divisions among the terrorists and highlighting the still unanswered questions . . . [it] lays bare the dysfunctional state of modern Russia, and the Caucasus in particular' *Scotland on Sunday*

THE SECRET TWENTIES

British Intelligence, the Russians and the Jazz Age

'A roaring success'
Scotsman

'Rewarding . . . spirited and nuanced . . . a major scoop'
Guardian

'Absorbing [and] engaging . . . A valuable addition to spy literature'
BBC World Histories

**A true story of deceit and double agents in London's
roaring twenties.**

At the height of the hedonistic Jazz Age, many in British society, shaken by the Russian revolution of 1917, became convinced that they were under attack from the new Soviet state. The British government launched the biggest spying operation in its peacetime history. On the strength of the evidence uncovered, Britain deported hundreds of Russians and broke off diplomatic links with Moscow. The investigation sent shockwaves through the British establishment, bringing down a government and ending careers.

Drawing on a wealth of recently declassified and previously unseen material, Timothy Phillips uncovers a world of suspicion and extremism, bureaucracy and betrayal set against the sparkling backdrop of cocktail-era London.

'Intoxicating . . . a fascinating study'
Martin Pearce, author of *Spymaster*